THE GUINNESS DICTIONARY OF
MORE
Poisonous
QUOTES

COMPILED BY COLIN JARMAN

GUINNESS PUBLISHING

Editor: Paola Simoneschi
Design: Cathy Shilling

First published in 1992 by Guinness Publishing Ltd
Publishing copyright © Guinness Publishing Ltd 1992
Published in Great Britain by Guinness Publishing Ltd,
33 London Road, Enfield, Middlesex

Typeset in Plantin Light by
Ace Filmsetting Ltd, Frome, Somerset
Printed and bound in Great Britain by
The Bath Press, Bath

A catalogue record for this book is available from the
British Library

ISBN 0–85112–700–2

CONTENTS

HOW TO USE THIS BOOK

All quotes are alphabetically listed within their individual sections.

The contents pages list the sub-sections within major groups.

More Poisonous Quotes has been compiled to be used as either reading or reference material.

1. Reading

Reading sections, as a whole, will give an insight into each subject, in both an entertaining and educational way.

2. Reference

By using the extensive index certain subjects or reviewers can be traced through the book.

There are two indexes – one is a general subject index, the other lists all the names of those quoters and quotees.

For example, the following quote found in 'CINEMA: Films' –

Chris Peachment
Emmanuelle (1974) starring Sylvia Kristel – It looks like a softcore version of *The Story of O* commissioned by *Vogue* magazine.

Time Out

can be found indexed under –

Chris PEACHMENT, *EMMANUELLE*, Sylvia KRISTEL, *THE STORY OF O* and *VOGUE*

EDITORIAL NOTES

Sections containing specific reviews are alphabetically listed in two fashions either by subject, or (as in 'Dramatic') by reviewer.

INTRODUCTION

More Poisonous Quotes is a reservoir of insult – free-flowing at the source and damned at the end.

Since so much good (or bad, depending upon your standpoint) material was collected for the first *Guinness Book of Poisonous Quotes*, a second volume of vitriol was never going to be far behind.

    The first book contained many of the classic put-downs and insults from the beginning of time. This sequel shifts the speiss spotlight onto more current subjects, with a greater proportion of its content culled from the last 15 years. This means that more of the new targets are household names, rather than some of the obscurer literary, dramatic and political figures featured in the original.

    But, whatever the period in time, no one is safe from the poison. Pillars of society are pilloried, authors written off, sportsmen run down, celebrities defamed, financiers discredited, and actors hamstrung.

COLIN M. JARMAN

CRITICISM

DEFINITIONS

Critics are professional yawners. *Anon*

A critic is a man who pans for gold. *Anon*

The most important critic is Time. *Anon*

Critics are the stupid who discuss the wise.
Anon

If your efforts are criticised, you must have done something worthwhile. *Anon*

Criticism is the disapproval of people, not for having faults, but for having faults different from ours. *Anon*

Praise and criticism are both frauds. *Anon*

A sermon is always better if you listen like a Christian rather than a critic. *Anon*

Criticism may be useful when mixed with other talents, but those whose only activity is to criticise the workers might as well be buried, talent and all. *Anon*

American critics are like American universities. They both have dull and half-dead faculties. *Edward Albee (1969)*

The exercise of criticism always destroys for a time our sensibility to beauty by leading us to regard the work in relation to certain laws of construction. The eye turns from the charms of nature to fix itself upon the servile dexterity of art. *Sir Archibald Alison*

To feel himself freer than his neighbour is the reward of the critic. *Henri Amiel*

Criticism is above all a gift, an intuition, a matter of tact and flair, it cannot be taught or demonstrated – it is an art. *Henri Amiel*

Analysis kills spontaneity. The grain once ground into flour springs and germinates no more. *Henri Amiel*

Criticism is a disinterested endeavour to learn and propagate the best that is known and thought in the world.
Matthew Arnold – 'Essays and Criticisms'

Pleasure is by no means an infallible critical guide, but it is the least fallible.
*W. H. Auden –
'The Dyer's Hand' (1962)*

A critic is a bundle of biases loosely held together by a sense of taste.
*Whitney Balliett – 'Dinosaurs in the Morning'
(1962)*

The test of a good critic is whether he knows when and how to believe insufficient evidence. *Whitney Balliett*

Never answer a critic, unless he's right.
Bernard Baruch

To be just, that is to say, to justify its existence, criticism should be partial, passionate, and political, that is to say, written from an exclusive point of view, but a point of view that opens up the widest horizons. *Charles Baudelaire (1846)*

I sincerely believe that the best kind of criticism is that which is amusing and poetic; not that cold and algebraic kind which, under the pretext of explaining everything, displays neither love nor hate. *Charles Baudelaire*

Because a critic is never criticised he passes through the world without knowing what the world thinks of him.
Clifford Bax – 'John O'London's Weekly'

I have the worst ear for criticism: even when I have created a stage set I like, I always hear the woman in the back of the dress circle who says she doesn't like blue. *Cecil Beaton (1962)*

Criticism of the arts in London, taken by and large, ends in a display of suburban omniscience which sees no further than the next door garden. *Sir Thomas Beecham*

Some critics are emotionally desiccated, personally about as attractive as a year-old peach in a single girl's refrigerator.
Mel Brooks – 'Playboy' (1974)

To ruminate upon evils, to make critical notes upon injuries and to be too acute in their apprehension, is to add unto our own tortures, to feather the arrows of enemies, and to resolve to sleep no more.
Sir Thomas Browne – 'Christian Morals'

The pleasure of criticism takes from us that of beings moved by the very beautiful things.
Jean de la Bruyère

One often hears it said that one should ignore criticism. I do not agree that it is always wise to ignore criticism of oneself and one's endeavours, even when the criticism is ill-natured, exhibitionistic, and predictable. For even when that is the character of the criticism, there is sometimes something to be learned from it not only about oneself and one's critics, but about the world we live in.
William F. Buckley Jr – 'New Republic' (1956)

As the arts advance towards their perfection, the science of criticism advances with equal pace. *Edmund Burke – 'On the Sublime and Beautiful'*

Critics are eunuchs at a gang-bang.
George Burns

To an anonymous critic – Thou eunuch of language; thou pimp of gender, murderous accoucheur of infant learning, thou pickle-herring in the puppet show of nonsense.
Robert Burns

Critics! Appalled, I venture on the name, Those cut-throat bandits in the paths of fame. *Robert Burns – 'Third Epistle to Robert Graves'*

He was in Logic, a great critic,
Profoundly skill'd in Analytic;
He could distinguish, and divide
A hair 'twixt south and south-west side.
Samuel Butler – 'Hudibras'

As small tyrants are always found to be the most severe, so are all little critics the most unmerciful, and never give quarter for the least mistake.
Samuel Butler – 'Prose Observations'

The test of a good critic is whether he knows when and how to believe on insufficient evidence. *Samuel Butler*

The rule in carving holds good as to criticism. Never cut with a knife what you can cut with a spoon. *Charles Buxton*

A man must serve his time to every trade
Save censure – critics are all ready made.
Lord Byron – 'English Bards and Scottish Reviewers'

As soon
Seek roses in December – ice in June,
Hope constancy in wind, or chaff in corn;
Believe a woman or an epitaph
You trust in critics, who themselves are sore.
Lord Byron – Ibid.

When my enemies stop hissing, I shall know I'm slipping. *Maria Callas*

In art, rebellion is consummated and perpetuated in the art of real creation, not in criticism or commentary.
Albert Camus – 'The Rebel' (1951)

That gang of spiteful rascals that are always baiting us as if we had committed murder.
Annibale Carracci (1580)

In judging others, folks will work overtime for no pay. *Charles Carruthers*

Great critics, of whom there are piteously few, build a home for the truth.
Raymond Chandler (1948)

Criticism is powerless to reach art. Art proceeds itself in a region quite beyond the reach of other expression save itself.
John Jay Chapman

A great deal of contemporary criticism reads to me like a man saying, 'Of course, I do not like green cheese: I am very fond of brown sherry.'   *G. K. Chesterton – 'All I Survey'*

Critics are like bouncers. In order to break up a fight, they have to start one.
Tommy Chong (1982)

Though by whim, envy, or resentment led, They damn those authors whom they never read.   *Charles Churchill*

Criticism may not be agreeable, but it is necessary. It fulfils the same function as pain in the body. It calls attention to an unhealthy state of things.   *Sir Winston Churchill*

I do not resent criticism, even when, for the sake of emphasis, it parts, for the time, with reality.   *Sir Winston Churchill (1941)*

What the public criticises in you, cultivate it. It is you.   *Jean Cocteau – 'Le Potomak'*

I don't care what you say about me, as long as you say something about me, and as long as you spell my name right.
George M. Cohan

F★★★ the critics. They're like eunuchs. They can tell you how to do it, but they can't do it themselves.   *Harry Cohn*

One does not value even a dog if he wags his tail for everybody and it is the same with a critic.   *Frank Colby*

Critics – murderers!   *Samuel Taylor Coleridge*

Criticism is like champagne, nothing more execrable if bad, nothing more excellent if good; if meagre, muddy, vapid and sour, both are fit only to engender colic and wind; but if rich, generous and sparkling, they communicate a genial flow to the spirits, improve the taste, and expand the heart.
Charles Colton

If democracy is to flourish, it must have criticism.   *Henry Steele Commanger*

I love criticism just so long as it's unqualified praise.   *Noël Coward*

It would be nice if sometimes the kind of

things I say were considered worthy of quotation. It isn't difficult, you know, to be witty or amusing when one has something to say that is destructive, but damned hard to be clever and quotable when you are singing someone's praises.   *Noël Coward*

Reviewing should function like a Food and Drug administration, even if that function is largely futile.   *Arlene Croce*

Criticism is not construction, it is observation.   *George Curtis*

Critics in general are venomous serpents that delight in hissing.   *W. B. Daniel*

The critic is the duenna in the passionate affair between playwright, actors and audiences – a figure dreaded, and occasionally comic, but never welcome, never loved.   *Robertson Davies*

It's only the best fruit the birds pick at.
Bette Davis

Criticism is like many other things, it drags along after what has already been said and does not get out of its rut.
Eugene Delacroix – 'Journal' (1849)

I consider criticism absolutely useless; indeed, I should even say injurious. Criticism as a rule is the opinion some gentleman or another has of a work. How should such an opinion be of use to art?   *Vincent D'Inday*

It is much easier to be critical than to be correct.   *Benjamin Disraeli*

You know who critics are – the men who have failed at literature and art.
Benjamin Disraeli – 'Lothair' (1870)

Those who do not need criticism will rarely merit to be criticised.   *Isaac D'Israeli*

Criticism is like an airport – acceptable as long as it's not in my direction.
Geoff Donald

They who write ill and they who ne'er durst write,

CRITICISM

Turn critics out of mere revenge and spite.
John Dryden – 'Conquest of Granada'

In vain they snarl aloof; a noisy crowd
Like women's anger – impotent and loud.
John Dryden (1694)

The British critics – be it to their glory,
When they abuse us, do it 'con amore'.
Augustine Duganne – 'Parnassus in Pillory'

Criticism has little power today and it is
seldom that anyone listens. *M. H. Dumesnil*

Listening to critics is like letting Muhammad
Ali decide which astronaut goes to the moon.
Robert Duvall

Think before you speak is criticism's motto;
Speak before you think is creation's.
E. M. Forster – 'Two Cheers for Democracy'

Two cheers for Democracy; one because it
admits variety and two because it permits
criticism. *E. M. Forster – Ibid.*

A critic has no right to the narrowness which
is the frequent prerogative of the creative
artist. He has to have a wide outlook or he
has not anything at all. *E. M. Forster*

I sometimes think
His critical judgement is so exquisite
It leaves us nothing to admire except his
opinion. *Christopher Fry –*
'The Dark is Light Enough' (1954)

The critic is the historian who records the
order of creation. In vain for the maker, who
knows without learning it, but not in vain for
the mind of the race. *Margaret Fuller –*
'A Short Essay on Criticism' (1858)

A critic is a man created to praise greater
men than himself, but he is never able to find
them. *Richard le Gallienne*

Any fool can criticise, and many of them do.
C. Garbett

The Twenty-Third Century scholars
understood that where human institutions
were concerned, love without criticism brings

stagnation, and criticism without love brings
destruction. And they emphasised that the
swifter the pace of change, the more lovingly
men had to care for and criticise their
institutions to keep them intact.
John Gardner – 'Looking Back from the
Twenty-Third Century'

On critics – These gentlemen flutter about the
world like bats which flap their wings in the
twilight and whose dark mass appears to you
in every direction; animals disquieted by their
fate, their too heavy bodies preventing them
from rising. Throw them a handkerchief full
of sand and they will stupidly make a rush at
it. *Paul Gauguin – 'Notes Synthétiques' (1888)*

On criticism – Preoccupied with what
concerns it particularly, its own field,
literature, it will soon lose sight of what
concerns us, painting. *Paul Gauguin (1899)*

Censure and criticism never hurt anybody. If
false, they can't hurt you unless you are
wanting in manly character; and if true, they
show a man his weak points, and forewarn
him against failure and trouble.
William Gladstone

It is through criticism that the race has
managed to come out of the woods and lead
a civilised life. The first man who objected to
the general nakedness and advised his fellows
to put on clothes was the first critic.
Edwin L. Godwin –
'Problems of Modern Democracy'

Against criticism a man can neither protest
nor defend himself; he must act in spite of it,
and then it will gradually yield to him.
Johann Wolfgang von Goethe – 'Maxims and
Reflections'

Genuine works of art carry their own
aesthetic theory implicit within them and
suggest the standards according to which
they are to be judged.
Johann Wolfgang von Goethe (1808)

Blame where you must,
Be candid where you can,
And be each critic the good-natured man.
Oliver Goldsmith – 'The Good Natured Man'

There is an unfortunate disposition in man to attend much more to the faults of his companions that offend him, than to their perfections which please him.
Charles Greville

Rudeness is the weak man's imitation of strength. *Eric Hoffer – 'The Passionate State of Mind' (1954)*

The best critic will be the epitome of the best part of any audience, its head, heart and soul.
Philip Hope-Wallace – 'The Times: Obituary' (1979)

It has become apparent what the modern conservative critic really is: a creature moving about in worlds not realised. His trade is one which requires, that it may be practised in perfection, two qualifications only: ignorance of language and abstinence from thought.
A. E. Housman – 'Manilius'

Don't abuse your friends and expect them to consider it criticism. *Ed Howe*

The fangs of the bear, and the tusks of a wild boar, do not bite worse and make deeper gashes than a goose-quill sometimes.
James Howell

To escape criticism – do nothing, say nothing, be nothing. *Elbert Hubbard*

One gets tired of the role critics are supposed to have in this culture: It's like being the piano player in a whorehouse; you don't have any control over the action going on upstairs.
Robert Hughes – 'Publishers Weekly' (1986)

A critic is a man who expects miracles.
James Huneker – 'Iconoclasts'

The critic is often an unsuccessful author, almost always an inferior one. *Leigh Hunt*

Mediocrity is more dangerous in a critic than in a writer. *Eugene Ionesco (1966)*

The critic should describe, not prescribe.
Eugene Ionesco – 'Improvisation'

Critics are a kind of freebooter in the republic of letters – who, like deer, goats and diverse other graminivorous animals, gain subsistence by gorging upon buds and leaves of the young shrubs of the forest, thereby robbing them of their verdue, and retarding their progress to maturity.
Washington Irving

I have had more bad notices than Lipton's has tea bags. *Glenda Jackson*

The bunch of critics we have now in London couldn't write decent advertising copy let alone journalism. They're blind and deaf.
Glenda Jackson (1985)

I find the pain of a little censure, even when it is unfounded is more acute than the pleasure of much praise.
Thomas Jefferson – 'Writings'

Honest criticism is hard to take, particularly from a relative, a friend, an acquaintance, or a stranger. *Franklin P. Jones*

In judging a man's worth, you should disregard his opinions. People's opinions are the least important thing about them.
Eric Julber – 'Esquire' (1969)

Criticism is a big bite out of someone's back.
Elia Kazan

It is not expected of critics that they should help us to make sense of our lives; they are bound only to attempt the lesser feat of making sense of the ways we try to make sense of our lives. *Frank Kermode*

Critics have a right to be modest and a duty to be vain. *Karl Kraus*

I won't quit [acting] until I get run over by a truck, a producer or a critic.
Jack Lemmon (1986)

I never read bad reviews about myself because my best friends invariably tell me about them. *Oscar Levant*

I like criticism when it is constructive; then it helps me. But when someone is critical just to be mean or tear something down, I must go

away from that person. It depresses me.
Sophia Loren

Nature fits all her children with something to do,
He who would write and can't write, can surely review,
Can set up a small booth as a critic, and sell us his
Petty conceit and his pettier jealousies.
James Lowell – 'A Fable for Critics'

If an author have any least fibre of worth in him,
Abuse would but tickle the organ of mirth in him;
All the critics on earth cannot crush with their ban
One word that's in tune with the nature of man. *James Lowell – Ibid.*

Freedom to criticise is held to compensate for the freedom to err – this is the American system. *Mary McCarthy*

It is critical vision alone which can mitigate the unimpeded operation of the automatic.
*Marshall McLuhan –
'The Mechanical Bride' (1951)*

Criticism is always a kind of compliment.
John Maddox – 'The Listener' (1979)

Intellectually, I'd like to think of critics as running-dog conspirators against the institutions of art. But they're just jack-offs like the rest of us. *David Mamet*

A critic is a gent who reports his prejudices and his preferences in such English as he is equipped with. *Richard Maney*

A critic . . . essential to the theatre – as ants to a picnic, as the boll weevil to a cotton field.
Joseph L. Mankiewicz – 'All About Eve' (1950)

Criticism is asserted superiority.
Henry Manning

A critic knows much more than the author he is criticising, or just as much or at least somewhat less.
Henry Manning – 'Pastime Papers' (1892)

I do not believe the people who tell me that they do not care a row of pins for the opinion of their fellows. It is the bravado of ignorance.
W. Somerset Maugham – 'The Summing Up'

It is salutary to train oneself to be no more affected by censure than by praise.
W. Somerset Maugham

A good critic is the sorcerer who makes some hidden spring gush forth unexpectedly under our feet.
François Mauriac – 'Second Thoughts' (1961)

In Australia there is no such thing as constructive criticism.
George Mikes: 'Boomerang – Australia Rediscovered' (1968)

Honest criticism means nothing: what one wants is unrestrained passion, fire for fire.
Henry Miller – 'Sexus' (1949)

There is a particular sort of shrieking hatred which the non-creative have for the half-creative and, equally, an exorbitant admiration that the non-creative have for the very fully-fledged creative. So, therefore, what you get from critics is the exorbitant admiration of the great and the shrieking hatred of those who interpret the fully great.
Jonathan Miller – 'The Listener' (1978)

I've always felt those articles somehow reveal more about the writers than they do about me. *Marilyn Monroe*

The lot of critics is to be remembered by what they failed to understand. *George Moore*

To check young Genius' proud career,
The salves who now his throne invaded,
Made Criticism his prime Vizier,
And from that hour his glories faded.
Thomas Moore – 'Genius and Criticism'

Age needs a critic; youth only a model.
Ivan Panin

Critics are like horse-flies which prevent the horse from ploughing. *Anton Pavlovitch*

Boredom, after all, is a form of criticism
William Philips (1967)

The greater part of critics are parasites, who, if nothing had been written, would find nothing to write about.
J. B. Priestley – 'Outcries and Asides'

As for you, little envious Prigs, snarling, bastard, puny Criticks, you'll soon have railed your last: Go hang yourself.
François Rabelais

Can't a critic give his opinion of an omelette without being asked to lay an egg?
Clayton Rawson

All critics should be assassinated. *Man Ray*

It would be a great help if the word 'serious' could be eliminated from the vocabulary. It must have been invented by critics not too sure of themselves, condemning all of the most exciting and profound works that have been produced through the ages.
Man Ray – 'Self Portrait' (1963)

Any jackass can kick down a barn, but it takes a good carpenter to build one.
Sam Rayburn

A friendly approval of a colleague's findings seems preferable to harsh criticism.
Gisela Richter

Criticism often takes from the tree caterpillars and blossoms together.
Gisela Richter

A critic enjoys a tremendous advantage if he has done nothing himself; but it is one that should not be abused.
Antoine Rivarol – 'Notes, Pensées et Maximes'

The lovely thing about critics is when they have a big target, they belt 'em. Because it's more fun. *Harold Robbins*

Living in the public eye accustoms one to accept criticism. One learns gradually to take it objectively and to try and think of it as directed at somebody else and evaluate whether it is just or unjust. *Eleanor Roosevelt*

No degree of dullness can safeguard a work against the determination of critics to find it fascinating. *Harold Rosenberg – 'Discovering the Present' (1973)*

The golden rule in criticism is for the critic to be on the level with the author – that is why the eighteenth-century Dr Johnson is still the grandest critic of Shakespeare, and also why we can ignore 99 per cent of the production of the critical industry.
A. L. Rowse – 'Portraits and Views' (1979)

A bad review is like baking a cake with all the best ingredients and having someone sit on it.
Danielle Steel

Of all mortals a critic is the silliest; for, inuring himself to examine all things whether they are of consequence or not, never looks upon anything but with a design of passing sentence upon it; by which means he is never a companion, but always a censor.
Sir Richard Steele

Time is the only critic without ambition.
John Steinbeck

Of all the cants that are canted in this canting world, though the cant of hypocrisy may be the worst, the cant of criticism is the most tormenting.
Laurence Sterne – 'Tristram Shandy'

Adverse criticism of one who knows is more flattering than praise of one who is ignorant.
Alfred Stevens

New York critics – I hear when one of them watched *A Star Is Born*, he talked back to the screen. *Barbra Streisand (1977)*

A true critic, in the perusal of a book, is like a dog at a feast, where thoughts and stomach are wholly set upon what the guests fling away, and consequently is apt to snarl most when there are fewest bones.
Jonathan Swift

It must be understood that ink is the great missive weapon in all battles of the learned, which, conveyed through a sort of engine called a quill, infinite numbers of these are

darted at the enemy by the valiant on both sides, with equal skill and violence, as if it were an engagement of porcupines.
Jonathan Swift

The aim of criticism is to distinguish what is essential in the work of a writer. It is the delight of a critic to praise; but praise is scarcely a part of his duty. What we ask of him is that he should find out for us more than we can find out for ourselves.
Arthur Symons –
'Coleridge's Biographia Literaria'

The critic is the naturalist of the soul.
H. Taine

You do not get a man's most effective criticism until you provoke him. Severe truth is expressed with some bitterness.
Henry D. Thoreau – 'Journal' (1854)

The only qualities for real success in criticism are ratlike cunning, a plausible manner and a little literary ability. The capacity to steal other people's ideas and phrases is also invaluable.
Nicolas Tomalin –
'Stop the Press I Want to Get on'

The man who becomes a critic by trade ceases, in reality, to be one at all.
Henry Tuckerman

You must not pay a person a compliment, and then straightaway follow it with criticism.
Mark Twain – 'Notebooks'

I like criticism, but it must be my way.
Mark Twain

The critic's symbol should be the tumble-bug; he deposits his egg in somebody else's dung, otherwise he could not hatch it.
Mark Twain

The trade of the critic, in literature, music, and the drama, is the most degraded of all trades.
Mark Twain – 'Autobiography'

The public is the only critic whose opinion is worth anything at all.
Mark Twain – Ibid.

One mustn't criticise other people on

grounds where he can't stand perpendicular himself.
Mark Twain – 'A Connecticut Yankee at the
Court of King Arthur'

Everything is infinitely fine, and any opinion is somehow coarser than the texture of the real thing.
John Updike

Critics are like pigs at the pastry cart.
John Updike

They search for ages for the wrong word, which, to give them credit, they eventually find.
Peter Ustinov (1952)

Critics are like those of whom Demetrius declared that he took no more account of the wind that came from their mouths than that which they expelled from their lower parts.
Leonardo da Vinci

Really to stop criticism they say one must die.
Voltaire – 'Les Trois Empereurs en Sorbonne'

Don't pay attention to bad reviews. Today's newspaper is tomorrow's toilet paper.
Jack Warner

It is exactly because a man cannot do a thing that he is the proper judge of it.
Oscar Wilde (1890)

Though indignation may make a great poet, bad temper always makes a poor critic.
Oscar Wilde

Don't you loathe the critics? Their mere existence seems to me an impertinence.
P. G. Wodehouse

Hot, envious, nosy, proud, the scribbling fry
Burn, hiss and bounce, waste paper, stink, and die.
Edward Young

CRITICS

Robert Benchley
An enchanting toad of a man.
Helen Hayes

Jay Cocks

There are a lot of pear-shaped critics, like that Jay Cocks. One way or another I'll get that man. Not physically, but I'll get him.
Charles Bronson – 'Playboy' (1975)

Pauline Kael

Oh, f*** Pauline Kael, f*** her! And I don't use that language all the time. I don't care what she has to say. She's a bitch. She's spiteful, and she's wrong. Let's not talk about Pauline Kael. *George Cukor*

Pauline Kael is the Rambo of film critics . . . a demented bag-lady. *Alan Parker (1990)*

John McClain

His body went to his head. *Dorothy Parker*

Dwight MacDonald

Many people are not satisfied to be unique in the eyes of God, and spend considerable time in flight from any orthodoxy. Some make a profession of it, and end up, as for instance the critic Dwight MacDonald has, with an intellectual and political career that might have been painted by Jackson Pollock.
William F. Buckley Jr – 'Up from Liberalism' (1968)

Henry L. Mencken

He edited a magazine called *The Smart Set*, which is like calling Cape Kennedy 'Lovers' Lane'. *Ben Hecht – 'Letters from Bohemia'*

What he believed in and what his readers wanted to be told were soon indistinguishable; his work became a series of circus tricks, a perpetual search for some new object of middle-class culture to belabour and some new habit or caprice of 'Homus Americanus' to ridicule.
Alfred Kazin – 'On Native Grounds'

A writer who denounces life and makes you want to live. *Walter Lippman*

Mencken, with his filthy verbal haemorrhages, is so low down in the moral scale, so damnably dirty, so vile and degenerate that when his time comes to die it will take a special dispensation from Heaven to get him into the bottommost pit of Hell.
'Jackson News'

Mr Mencken talks about truth as if she were his mistress but he handles her like an iceman. *Stuart P. Sherman*

With a pig's eyes that never look up, with a pig's snout that loves muck, with a pig's brain that knows only the sty, and a pig's squeal that cries only when he is hurt, he sometimes opens his pig's mouth, tusked and ugly, and lets out the voice of God, railing at the whitewash that covers the manure about his habitat.
William A. White (1928)

Nina Myskow

Jawbone of ass with double helpings of tongue on a plate of tripe. *Benny Hill*

Rex Reed

Do you really want to be influenced by someone who's been in the same building as *The Gong Show* – let alone been on it.
Kevin Kline (1983)

Myra Breckenridge (1970) – Film critic Rex Reed makes his 'acting' debut as Myron. He manages to carry considerable enthusiasm into his masturbation sequence.
Michael Medved

John Ruskin

I doubt whether art needed Ruskin any more than a moving train needs one of its passengers to shove it.
Tom Stoppard – 'T.L.S.' (1977)

The deceptive lucidity of his intoxicating style displayed, or concealed, an intellect as profound, penetrating, and subtle as any that England has seen; and as fanciful, as glancing, and as wayward as the mind of a child. *G. M. Young – 'Victorian England'*

Tom Shales

Terrible Tom – the TV tiger. *'Time'*

George Bernard Shaw

Shaw, you ought to be roasted alive: though even then, you would not be to my taste.
Sir James Barrie

That old man with the beard, he knows nothing – he knows nothing, that old man with the beard! *Mrs Patrick Campbell*

Oh dear me – it's too late to do anything but accept you and love you – but when you were quite a little boy somebody ought to have said 'hush' just once.
Mrs Patrick Campbell (1912)

Shaw is a Puritan who missed the Mayflower by five minutes.
Benjamin de Casseres – 'Mencken and Shaw'

His brain is a half-inch layer of champagne poured over a bucket of Methodist near-beer.
Benjamin de Casseres – Ibid.

Mr Shaw is (I suspect) the only man on Earth who has never written any poetry.
G. K. Chesterton – 'Orthodoxy' (1908)

An Irish smut-dealer. *Anthony Comstock*

The simplest clues to life escape him, as he scales impossible pinnacles of unnecessary thought, only to slip down the other side.
Edward Gordon Craig

He believed in art for action's sake.
Michael Holroyd

Jester to the cosmos and the most serious man on the planet. *James Huneker*

Nobody can read Freud without realising he was the scientific equivalent of another nuisance, G. B. Shaw.
Robert M. Hutchins

Shaw, most poisonous of all the poisonous haters of England; despiser, distorter and denier of the plain truths whereby men live; topsy-turvy perverter of all human relationships; a menace to ordered social thought and ordered social life; irresponsible braggart, blaring self-trumpeter; idol of opaque intellects and thwarted females; calculus of contrariwise; flipperty gibbet Pope of chaos; portent and epitome of this generation's moral and spiritual disorder.
Henry A. Jones

An orthodox Scotch Presbyterian of the most cocksure and bilious sort . . . Life to him is

not a poem, but a series of police regulations.
H. L. Mencken

John Simon
You have to make important differences between critics and assassins. There are important differences between John Simon and Sirhan Sirhan. Sirhan Sirhan is in jail.
Rocco Landesman (1990)

Frank Rich and John Simon are the syphilis and gonorrhoea of the theatre.
David Mamet

G. W. Stonier
Some people write for Comic Cuts
    And some for journals tonier;
Some journals the 'phone affect,
    Others are even phonier;
Some seed must fall on stony ground,
But need that ground be Stonier?
James Agate – 'Ego 5' (1940)

Kenneth Tynan
You have the right face for a critic . . . You have the look of a blooming martyr.
Edward Gordon Craig

Arthur B. Walkley
A whipper-snapper of criticism who quoted dead languages to hide his ignorance of life.
Herbert Beerbohm Tree

Edmund Wilson
A vanishing type, the free man of letters.
Van Wyck Brooks

The man in the iron necktie.
e. e. cummings

Alexander Woollcott
Louisa May Woollcott. *Anon*

Listening to Mr Woollcott on the radio is like being hit with a cream puff; you are uninjured but rather sickened.
Robert Forsythe

Observations of his billowy amplitudes suggest that the world might be a safer globe on which to live were the abdomens of its inhabitants more convex than concave.
Percy Hammond

INSULTS

GENERAL

Sticks and stones may break my bones, but words will never hurt me.   *Anon*

Do not insult the mother alligator until after you have crossed the river.   *Haitian proverb*

Men will let you abuse them if only you will make them laugh.
Henry Ward Beecher (1887)

It is uncommon to annihilate a man with words – although it is often undertook.
Josh Billings

What is England? From Swift to Huxley our writers have been giving us private tuition courses in self-hatred.
Gerald Brenan – 'The Face of Spain' (1950)

Love, friendship, respect, do not unite people as much as common hatred for something.
Anton Chekhov

An injury is much sooner forgotten than an insult.   *Lord Chesterfield (1745)*

So long as I am acting from duty and conviction, I am indifferent to taunts and jeers. I think they will probably do me more good than harm.
Sir Winston Churchill (1945)

As long as there are readers to be delighted by calumny, there will be found reviewers to calumniate.   *Samuel T. Coleridge*

There is a place in society for nasty-minded, rude people.   *Peter Cook*

He who allows himself to be insulted, deserves to be so.   *Pierre Corneille*

It's not as if we just insult women. Our insults go across the board.
Mike D (of the Beastie Boys) (1987)

Calumny is only the noise of madmen.
Diogenes

As to abuse – I thrive on it. Abuse, hearty abuse, is a tonic to all sane men of indifferent health.
Norman Douglas – 'Some Limericks' (1928)

He that flings dirt at another dirtieth himself most.   *Thomas Fuller*

It is easier to ridicule than commend.
Thomas Fuller

If you slander a dead man, you stab him in the grave.   *Thomas Fuller*

Each of us carries within himself a collection of instant insults.   *Dr Haim Ginott (1969)*

Calumny requires no proof. The throwing out of malicious imputations against any character leaves a stain which no after-refutation can wipe our. To create an unfavourable impression, it is not necessary that certain things should be true, but that they have been said.   *William Hazlitt*

Rudeness is the weak man's imitation of strength.   *Eric Hoffer*

Abuse a man unjustly, and you will make friends for him.   *Edgar Watson Howe*

If you can't answer a man's argument, all is not lost; you can still call him vile names.
Elbert Hubbard

Abuse is not so dangerous when there is no vehicle of wit or delicacy, no subtle conveyance. The difference between coarse and refined abuse is as the difference between being bruised by a club and wounded by a poisoned arrow.
Samuel Johnson

A fly, Sir, may sting a stately horse and make him wince; but one is but an insect and the other a horse still. *Samuel Johnson*

Few attacks either of ridicule or invective make much noise, but by help of those that they provoke. *Samuel Johnson*

A hundred hisses outweigh a thousand claps. The former come more directly from the heart. *Charles Lamb (1806)*

Embroidered on her favourite cushion – If you can't say something good about someone, sit right here by me. *Alice Roosevelt Longworth [Alice, daughter of President Theodore Roosevelt, earned the nickname 'Princess Malice']*

The only gracious way to accept an insult is to ignore it; if you can't ignore it, top it; if you can't top it, laugh at it; if you can't laugh at it, it's probably deserved. *Russell Lynes – 'Reader's Digest' (1961)*

One of the basic human rights is to make fun of other people whoever they are. *Anthony Powell – 'The Strangers in the Game'*

One of the worst things about life is not how nasty the nasty people are. You know that already. It is how nasty the nice people can be. *Anthony Powell – 'A Dance to the Music of Time'*

I succeeded by saying what everyone else is thinking. *Joan Rivers*

I can't see that she could have found anything nastier to say if she'd thought it out with both hands for a fortnight. *Dorothy L. Sayers – 'Busman's Holiday'*

Rudeness is better than any argument, it totally eclipses intellect. *Arthur Schopenhauer – 'Position' (1851)*

It is often better not to see an insult than to avenge it. *Seneca*

Nobody can apologise for insults but I, who never gave any. *William Seward*

Be thou as chaste as ice, pure as snow, thou shalt not escape calumny. *William Shakespeare – 'Hamlet'*

Malice is like a game of poker or tennis; you don't play it with anyone who is manifestly inferior to you. *Hilde Spiel – 'The Darkened Room'*

He who slings mud generally loses ground. *Adlai Stevenson (1954)*

Latent in every man is a venom of amazing bitterness, a black resentment, something that curses and loathes life. *Paul Valéry*

TARGET UNKNOWN

If brains was lard, she couldn't grease a frying pan. *Anon*

She has so many chins that she uses a bookmark to find her mouth. *Anon*

He's not man enough to pull on stretch socks. *Anon*

She is so conceited that she has her dental X-rays re-touched. *Anon*

She has a face like a million dollars – green and wrinkled. *Anon*

He was born ignorant and he's been losing ground ever since. *Anon*

There are only two things I dislike about her – her face. *Anon*

What he lacks in intelligence, he more than makes up for in stupidity. *Anon*

He has more chins than the Peking telephone directory. *Anon*

At Christmas, I would rather hang her and kiss the mistletoe. *Anon*

His origins are so low, you'd have to limbo under his family tree. *Anon*

The last time I saw him he was walking down Lovers' Lane holding his own hand. *Fred Allen*

He's the kind of bore who's here today and here tomorrow. *Binnie Barnes*

His mind is so open – so open that ideas simply pass through it. *F. H. Bradley*

She's got such a narrow mind, when she walks fast her earrings bang together!
John Cantu

I piss on you all – from a considerable height.
Louis-Ferdinand Céline

He has all the virtues I dislike and none of the vices I admire. *Winston Churchill*

Pushing forty? She's clinging on for dear life.
Ivy Compton-Burnett

He's a little man, that's his trouble. Never trust a man with short legs – brains too near their bottoms. *Noël Coward*

He left his body to science – and science is contesting the will. *David Frost*

I thought men like that shot themselves.
King George V

No-one can have a higher opinion of him than I have – and I think he is a dirty little beast. *W. S. Gilbert*

He must have had a magnificent build before his stomach went in for a career of its own.
Margaret Halsey

He looked like a composite picture of five thousand orphans too late to catch a picnic steamboat.
O. Henry [William S. Porter]

She felt in italics and thought in capitals.
Henry James

Her only flair is in her nostrils. *Pauline Kael*

On an American socialite – She tries so hard to be a 'Grande Dame' and only succeeds in being damned grand. *Harry Lehr*

He is as good as his word – and his word is no good. *Seamus MacManus*

I don't wish to belong to any club that would want me as a member. *Groucho Marx*

They ought to tear you down and put up a new building! *Groucho Marx*

She looks at the world through green-coloured glasses. *Sonia Masello*

She's got what I call bobsled looks: going downhill fast.
Craig Nove – 'Incandescence' (1979)

When he talks he reminds me of Moses – every time he opens his mouth the bull rushes. *Robert Orben*

I know she's outspoken, but by whom?
Dorothy Parker

I can't believe that out of 100,000 sperm, you were the quickest. *Steven Pearl*

He's so ugly, when you walk by him, your pants start to wrinkle. *Mickey Rivers*

The trouble with her is that she lacks the power of conversation but not the power of speech. *G. B. Shaw*

I like him and his wife. He is so ladylike, and she is such a perfect gentleman. *Sydney Smith*

If only he'd wash his neck, I'd wring it.
John Sparrow

I don't like her. But don't misunderstand me: my dislike is purely platonic.
Sir Herbert Beerbohm Tree

She is the kind of woman who climbed the ladder of success – wrong by wrong.
Mae West

His mother should have thrown him away and kept the stork. *Mae West*

He had just about enough brain to make a jay-bird fly crooked. *P. G. Wodehouse (1914)*

CURSES

GENERAL

A curse sticks to no one but the curser.
German saying

INSULTS

May the head of the curser be baked in the oven, served up as food for me, dead and gone to the night.   *Maori saying*

First human being who hurled a curse instead of a weapon was the founder of civilisation.   *Sigmund Freud*

I have heard it said that a curse was like a stone flung up to the heavens, and mayest return on the head that sent it.
                    Sir Walter Scott

SPECIFIC

May you hang from the edge of a cliff, while your mother tries to remember your father's name.   *Anon*

May the curse of Mary Malone and her nine blind, illegitimate children chase you so far over the hills of Damnation that Jesus Christ himself cannot find you with a telescope.
                    Anon

NATIONAL

May the fleas [sweat] of a thousand camels infest your armpits.   *Arabian*

May your left ear wither and fall into your right pocket.   *Arabian*

May you piss vinegar all night.   *French*

May you grow like a turnip with the head down and the roots up.   *Yiddish*

SATIRE

GENERAL

Satire should, like a polished razor keen,
Wound with a touch that's scarcely felt or seen.
                    Lady Mary Wortley Montagu

GOSSIP

GENERAL

A gossip is a person with a keen sense of rumour.   *Anon*

A gossip is a person who pumps up to a conclusion.   *Anon*

A gossip is one who knows how to add to . . . and to.   *Anon*

Gossip is letting the chat out of the bag. *Anon*

Gossip is the knife of the party.   *Anon*

Gossip travels faster over sour grapevines.
                    Anon

Gossip is like grapefruit – the juicier the better.   *Anon*

Gossip goes in one ear and over the back fence.   *Anon*

Gossip needs no carriage.   *Russian proverb*

Whoever gossips to you will gossip of you.
                    Spanish proverb

Invasion of privacy
  Worries many,
But it really doesn't
Bother me any.
You see, I like people,
Gossip and laughter.
Evasion of privacy
Is what I am after.   *Richard Armour*

Some people act like blotters when it comes to gossip – they soak it all in but get it all backwards.   *Wilfred Beaver*

Gossip is a wither report.
                    Raymond J. Cvikota

Gossips seem to live by heard instinct.
                    Raymond J. Cvikota

Gossip is a sort of smoke that comes from the dirty tobacco-pipes of those who diffuse it; it proves nothing but the bad taste of the smoker.   *George Eliot*

Gossip is a dreadful curse,
A plague, a scourge, or even worse,
  A sneaky sordid nasty thing
And always oh so interesting.
                    Donna Evleth

Even doubtful accusations leave a stain
behind them. *Thomas Fuller*

There are some women who do not like
passing on gossip. They are content with
inventing it. *Juliette Greco*

A tongue is just a little thing that weighs a
tiny bit.
Then why do such a lot of folks have trouble
holding it? *Margaret Hillert*

Gossip is vice enjoyed vicariously – the
sweet, subtle satisfaction without the risk.
Kin Hubbard

Blood sport is brought to its ultimate
refinement in the gossip columns.
Bernard Ingham (1986)

Gossip is the opiate of the oppressed.
Erica Jong

The difference between news and gossip lies
in whether you raise or lower your voice.
Franklin P. Jones

Gossip, unlike river water, flows both ways.
Michael Korda

Gossip and manure are only good for one
thing – and that's spreading. Gossip don't
mean a damn unless you spread it around.
Doris Lilly

Gossip isn't scandal and it's not merely
malicious. It's chatter about the human race
by lovers of the same.
*Phyllis McGinley –
'Woman's Home Journal' (1957)*

Gossip is the tool of the poet, the shoptalk of
the scientist and the consolation of the
housewife, wit, tycoon and intellectual. It
begins in the nursery and ends when speech
is past. *Phyllis McGinley – Ibid.*

What is whispered in the ear is heard miles
away. And that tells us that we must always
guard our tongues against gossip.
'The Mickey Mouse Club'

Gossips are people who have only one

relation in common – God.
Christopher Morley

Another good thing about gossip is –
that it is within everybody's reach,
And it is much more interesting than any
other form of speech. *Ogden Nash*

If you want to get the most out of life why
the thing to do is to be a gossiper by day and
a gossipee by night. *Ogden Nash*

Some people will believe anything if you
whisper it to them. *Louis B. Nizer (1940)*

Never gossip about people you don't know.
This deprives simple artisans like Truman
Capote of work. The best subject of gossip is
someone you and your audience love dearly.
The enjoyment of gossip is thus doubled; to
the delight of disapprobation is added the
additional delight of pity.
P. J. O'Rourke (1983)

I wish I had as much in bed as I get in the
newspapers. *Linda Rondstadt*

Hating anything in the way of ill-natured
gossip ourselves, we are always grateful to
those who do it for us and do it well. *Saki*

The things most people want to know about
are usually none of their business.
G. B. Shaw

Gossip is just news running ahead of itself in
a red satin dress. *Liz Smith*

Poring over fragments of other people's lives,
peering into their bedrooms when they don't
know we're there, we thrill to the glamour
and the power of secret knowledge, partly
detoxified but also heightened by being
shared. *Patricia Meyer Spacks (1985)*

What some invent, the rest enlarge.
Jonathan Swift

Show me someone who never gossips and I'll
show you someone who isn't interested in
people. *Barbara Walters*

There is only one thing in the world worse

than being talked about, and that is not being talked about.   *Oscar Wilde*

I don't at all like knowing what people are saying behind my back. It makes one far too conceited.   *Oscar Wilde*

Gossip is when you hear something you like about somebody you don't.   *Earl Wilson*

Gossip is the art of saying nothing in a way that leaves practically nothing unsaid.
               Walter Winchell

Today's gossip is tomorrow's headlines.
               Walter Winchell

GOSSIP COLUMNS

A gossip columnist is one who writes others' wrongs.   *Anon*

The best gossip columnist is a person on top of the quote 'em poll.   *Anon*

Gossip is a newscaster without a sponsor.
               Anon

This country has gone mad for gossip – TV, newspapers, radio, movies, books, magazines, all our media are obsessed with private lives. Prying, spying, eyeing – the hounding of public figures has reached such proportions that we may have to declare open and closed hunting seasons.
               Shana Alexander – 'Talking Woman'

Rumour, the most efficient of press agents.
               Bruce Barton Jr

Gossip columnists are the spies of life.
               Doris Dolphin

Gossip columnists are diseases, like flu. Everyone is subject to them.
               James Goldsmith – 'Time' (1978)

I don't care what is written about me so long as it isn't true.   *Katharine Hepburn*

It is really difficult to get out of gossip columns once you've got in.
               Mick Jagger

A gossip columnist is a writer of both faked and friction.   *Colin M. Jarman*

It is the gossip columnist's business to write about what is none of his business.
               Louis Kronenberger –
               'The Cart And The Horse' (1964)

Enquiring minds want to know.
               Advert for 'National Enquirer'

GOSSIP COLUMNISTS

Anon
She tells enough white lies to ice a cake.
               Margot Asquith

She always tells stories in the present vindictive.
               Tom Peace – 'Reader's Digest' (1957)

Rona Barrett
I think of gossip as a word that is used to describe something that is trivial, and trivia, as opposed to its larger context, which is the dissemination of news before, perhaps, the news occurs. We were brought up to believe gossip was dirty journalism – trivia about trivial people. And you read it in your bathroom.

I function as a red light. I say, 'Stop it!' Columnists often become phantom parents to the great. They're looking for people like me to become the mother figure and slap them down.

Rona Barrett is usually accompanied at parties by tales.   *Anon*

She doesn't need a steak knife. Rona cuts her food with her tongue.   *Johnny Carson*

On her reputed threat to leave 'Tomorrow Coast-to-Coast' citing differences with co-host Tom Snyder – Snyder's already found a replacement for Rona: Charles Manson.
               Johnny Carson

Rona has without question blazed a trail. She has made Hollywood poop marketable on national TV. One may question whether this was a trail worth blazing. She has all the

warmth of a self-service station at 2 a.m.
Tom Shales – 'Washington Post' (1981)

On television, she has a curiously effective way of leaning over the nation's backyard fence (she really does seem to be leaning forward, in official confiding position) and making frivolous piffle sound urgent; and she has broken many a legitimate piece of solid entertainment-industry news. For this reason, she shrinks from that onerous appellation, 'gossip', as if it were an icky old, smelly old thing. *Tom Shales*

Nigel Dempster
It you can't take it, then don't give it.

Dempster thinks he has the might of a duke and the gravitas of a senior politician. He believes that if Britain's 200 top men were profiled, he would be among them.
Rory Knight Bruce – 'Evening Standard' (1991)

Frances Farmer
The nicest thing I can say about Frances Farmer is that she is unbearable.
William Wyler

Joyce Haber
They should give Haber open-heart surgery – and go in through the feet. *Julie Andrews*

Hedda Hopper
I wasn't allowed to speak while my husband was alive, and since he's gone no-one has been able to shut me up. *(1952)*

Nobody's interested in sweetness and light.

Being a Hollywood reporter as well as an actress I'm more or less on both sides of the fence.

She was a venomous, vicious, pathological liar, and quite stupid. *Ray Milland*

Timid? As timid as a buzzsaw!
Casey Shawhan

Peter Jenkins
I thoroughly dislike him – he is a decayed gossip columnist of the Gaitskell variety.
Tony Benn

Amanda Lear
I hate to spread rumours – but what else can one do with them?

Aileen Mehle (Suzy Knickerbocker)
What I do is kick them in the pants with a diamond-buckled shoe.
'New York Times' (1967)

Martha Mitchell – *Wife of John Mitchell (US Attorney-General)*
I tried to be a member of the Silent Majority but I felt like Martha Mitchell with a mouthful of Novocain. *Liz Carpenter*

If it hadn't been for Martha, there'd have been no Watergate. *Richard Nixon*

Men who could blow whole countries off the face of the earth were powerless if Martha Mitchell reached for the phone.
Eric Sevareid

She was called the 'mouth that roared' and the 'worst tressed woman in America'. *'Time'*

Maury Paul Cholly Knickerbocker
Even when people snub me I feel like saying to them, 'Thank you for just existing. I wouldn't be wearing solid gold garter clasps if it weren't for you!'

Louella Parsons
She never avoids phrases like 'the reason is because' unless it is impossible to not do so, and she likes her infinitives split. *Anon*

Louella Parsons is stronger than Samson. He needed two columns to bring down the house. Louella can do it with one.
Samuel Goldwyn

Hearst's Hollywood stooge. *Joel Faith*

You turn the whole nation into a swerving circle without too much needle. *Bob Hope*

Her writings stand out like an asthmatic's gasp. *Nunnally Johnson*

Not a bad old slob. *James Mason*

She was, for all her lifelong love affair with

motion pictures, a reporter first. She would skewer her best friend on the greasy spit of scandal if circumstances warranted it.
Paul O'Neil – 'Life' (1965)

Lolly . . . would sit at her telephone all night long, if necessary, interpreting the denials of those she was interrogating as the great horned owl interprets the squeaking of distant mice. *Paul O'Neil – Ibid*

Her friends stand by her. When she prematurely published the claim that a certain actress was pregnant, the actress's husband hastened to prove her correct.
'Time Magazine' (1961)

Drew Pearson

I operate by sense of smell. If something smells wrong, I go to work.

He adapted the untiring and often merciless skill of investigative political reporting to the modern idiom of the insider's gossip. *Anon*

His success and power rested in large measure in the practised impugning of others.
Jack Anderson

He will go down in history as Pearson-the-sponge, because he gathers slime, mud and slander from all parts of the earth and lets the ooze out through his radio broadcasts and through his daily contributions to a few newspapers which have not found him out yet. *Theodor Bilbo*

He can find scandal in Snow White's relations with the Seven Dwarfs.
William F. Buckley Jr – 'National Review' (1964)

The Quaker scavenger whose lies and contumely have been deplored by every American President in living memory.
William F. Buckley Jr – 'National Review' (1967)

He is not a sunnavabitch. He is only a filthy brain child, conceived in ruthlessness and dedicated to the proposition that Judas Iscariot was a piker. *William Jenner*

Drew Pearson is America's No. 1 keyhole peeper, muckraker, propaganda peddling prostitute of the nation's press and radio.
William Jenner

A man who has been able to sugar-coat his wares so well that he has been able to fool vast numbers of people with his fake piety and false loyalty. *Joe McCarthy*

Years ago, when he first came to Washington, he was nearly all one colour, having only about the normal number of spots on his escutcheon. Today, by rolling in the muck of virtually all his working hours, he has more spots than you can shake a leopard at. *Eleanor Patterson*

A miscalled newscaster specialising in falsehoods and smearing people with personal and political motivation.
Westbrook Pegler

Pearson is an infamous liar, a revolting liar, a pusillanimous liar, a lying ass, a natural born liar, a liar by profession, a liar of living, a liar in the daytime, a liar in the night-time, a dishonest, ignorant, corrupt and grovelling crook. *Kenneth McKeller*

There is one columnist in Washington who wouldn't have room on his breast if he got a ribbon for every time he's been called a liar. In Missouri we have a four-letter word for those who knowingly make false statements.
Harry S. Truman

Everyone makes mistakes but this S.O.B. makes a racket, a business, a mint of money writing fiction in the guise of news reporting.
Walter Winchell

Liz Smith

I depend a lot on innuendo. Frequently, I simply report the rumour. The words 'they say' should make it clear to everyone that even I don't know whether it's true or not.

SELF-CRITICISM

I believe that it is harder still to be just toward oneself than toward others.
André Gide – 'Journals' (1940)

Woody Allen
I'm short enough and ugly enough to succeed on my own.

Candice Bergen
It's impossible to be more flat-chested than I am.

David Bowie
I'm not an innovator, I'm really just a photostat machine. *(1975)*

Lord George Brown
Most British statesmen have either drunk too much or womanised too much. I never fell into the second category.

Truman Capote
I'm about as tall as a shotgun and just as noisy.

Baron Edward H. Carson
My only great qualification for being put in charge of the Navy is that I am at sea.

Prince Charles
(when asked by David Frost to describe himself) – Sometimes a bit of a twit.

Brian Clough OBE
My wife says it stands for 'Old Big 'Ead!'

Bette Davis
I have eyes like a bullfrog, a neck like an ostrich and long limp hair.

I was never beautiful like Miss Hayward or Miss Lamarr. I was known as the little brown wren. *(1979)*

Jason Donovan
I am just a male tart.

Kirk Douglas
I'm a sonuvabitch. Plain and simple. *(1964)*

Queen Elizabeth
(to a portrait painter, who asked her to smile) – Oh dear, have I got on what my family call my piggy face?

Harrison Ford
I'm just an ordinary 42-year-old creaky set of bones. *(1985)*

Michael J. Fox
I'm tough. Cockroach tough!

George Harrison
We're just a bunch of crummy musicians really. *(1962)*

Ernest Hemingway
(on why he left his wife) – Because I am a bastard.

David Icke
I am a snowplough.

Glenda Jackson
If anyone thinks I look sexy stripped, they must think Minnie Mouse is sexy.

Elton John
I've always looked like a bank clerk who freaked out!

Sophia Loren
I'm a giraffe. I even walk like a giraffe with a long neck and legs. It's a pretty dumb animal, too. *(1979)*

Desmond Lynam
There's a simple recipe about this sports business. If you're a sporting star, you're a sporting star. If you don't quite make it, you become a coach. If you can't coach, you become a sports journalist. If you can't spell, you introduce *Grandstand* on a Saturday afternoon.

Shirley MacLaine
I'm certain I was a prostitute in some other life. *(1984)*

Victor Mature
I'm no actor and I've got 64 pictures to prove it.

Dennis Norden
My singing voice is to melody what bubble-gum is to gourmet cuisine.

Robert Redford
As a director, I wouldn't like me as an actor. As an actor, I wouldn't like me as a director.

Burt Reynolds
Nobody is worth what they pay me.

Julia Roberts
I look like a lampshade on legs.

Steven Spielberg
When I grow up, I still want to be a film
director. *(1985)*

Sylvester Stallone
The eyes droop, the mouth is crooked, the
teeth aren't straight, the voice, I've been told,
sounds like a Mafioso pall-bearer. Between 3
pm and 8 pm, I look great. After that, it's all
downhill. Don't photograph me in the
morning or you're going to get Walter

Brennan. *(1985)*

Barbra Streisand
A large part of me is nebbish – plain, dull,
uninteresting. *(1971)*

Twiggy
(on her body) – It's not what you'd call a
figure, is it?

Frankie Vaughan
I'm not a crooner – I'm just a song salesman
(1959)

Shelley Winters
My face was always so made up it looked as
though it had the decorators in.

CREATIVE ARTS

Authors and actors and artists and such
Never know nothing, and never know much.
Sculptors and singers and those of their
    kidney
Tell their affairs from Seattle to Sydney.
Playwrights and poets and such horses' necks
Start off from anywhere, end up at sex.
Diarists, critics, and similar roe
Never say nothing and never say no.
People Who Do Things exceed my
    endurance;
God, for a man that solicits insurance.
Dorothy Parker – 'Bohemia'

PAINTING

GENERAL

Who of the gods first taught the artist's craft
Laid upon the human race the greatest curse.
Antiphanes

What is art? Prostitution. *Charles Baudelaire*

Most of those who call themselves artists are
in reality picture dealers, only they make the
pictures themselves. *Samuel Butler*

To my mind the old masters are not art; their
value is in their scarcity.
Thomas A. Edison –'Golden Book' (1931)

As my poor father used to say in 1863,
Once people start on all this art good-bye
    moralitee!
A. P. Herbert – 'Lines For A Worthy Person'

Modern art is a cliché of the enemies of
religion and not even the sanctity of marriage
is safe from the so-called intellectuals.
Sir Leslie Herpron (1966)

I must have gone on looking at pictures for
ten years before I would honestly admit to
myself that they merely bored me.
Aldous Huxley

How vain painting is – we admire the realistic
depiction of objects which in their original
state we don't admire at all.
Blaise Pascal – 'Pensées' (1670)

There are moments when art attains almost
to the dignity of manual labour.
Oscar Wilde

ART CRITICISM

This tendency to degenerate into a mere mouthing of meaningless words seems to be peculiar to so-called art criticism. There has never been, so far as I know, a critic of painting who wrote about it simply and clearly as Sainte-Beuve, say, wrote about books, or Schumann or Berlioz about music. Even the most orthodox of the brethren, when he finds himself before a canvas that genuinely moves him, takes refuge in esoteric winks and grimaces and mysterious gurgles and belches.   *Henry L. Mencken –*
'Selected Prejudices' (1927)

The true function of art is to criticise, embellish and edit nature. The artist is a sort of impassioned proof-reader, blue-pencilling the bad spelling of God.
Henry L. Mencken

I criticise by creation, not by finding faults.
Michelangelo

I despise the opinion of the press and the so-called critics. I know my worth, and am harder on myself than anybody else.
Claude Monet (1883)

The art would lie open for ever to caprice and casualty, if those who are to judge of their excellencies had no settled principles by which they are to regulate their decisions.
Sir Joshua Reynolds – 'Discourses' (1790)

The born critic, thanks to the exceptional sheepness [sic] of his wits, finds out exactly what it is not all about. He invariably sees, not the faults of the work of art, not those of the artist, but his own. To return to the sheep, critics are a special kind of human being. To be a critic, one has to be born to it. Critics are sheepborn, sheepsuckled by a schoolmarm and half- asheep [sic] when faced with a work of art. The difference between artist and critic is this; the artist creates, the critic bleates [sic].
Kurt Schwitters – 'Critics'

To analyse a work of art into its elements is as useless as throwing a violet into a crucible.
Percy B. Shelley

In judging paintings, you should consider whether the first impression pleases the eye and whether the artist has followed the rules; as for the rest, everyone makes some mistakes.   *Tintoretto*

To say that a work of art is good but incomprehensible to the majority of men, is the same as saying of some kind of food that it is very good but that most people can't eat it.   *Leo Tolstoy*

I like the kind of critics who just put people's names down.   *Andy Warhol (1972)*

You should not say it is not good. You should say you do not like it; and then, you know, you're perfectly safe.
James M. Whistler

ART MOVEMENTS

We in England don't have movements if we can help it.
Laurence Binyon – 'Saturday Review'

'The Eight'
'Exhibition' – (1908)
Is it fine art to exhibit our sores?   *Anon*

English Art
There is nothing on earth more terrible than English music, except English painting. They have no sense of sound, or eye for colour, and I sometimes wonder whether their sense of smell is not equally blunted and dulled. I should not be surprised if they cannot even distinguish between the smell of a ball of horse-dung and an orange.
Heinrich Heine

English painting is entirely derivative: it is what study and imitation of the French have made it.   *G. J. Renier*

French Art
As Northcote says, 'French painters know as little of nature as a hackney-coach horse knows of pasture.' In fact, it is worse . . . they neglect the look of nature altogether.
John Constable (1825)

Since Matisse, French painting has hardly been noted for colour (or indeed anything much beyond tricksiness and etoliated chic). The awfulness of latter-day French mannerisms, the second-hand novelties, the Swingles Singers-style tepid abstractions are paraded without qualm or shame.

William Feaver –
'The Observer' (1985)

French Romanticism

Throwing handfuls of white and blue and red at the canvas, and letting what would stick, stick. *'Literary Gazette' (1842)*

Impressionism

This school has abolished two things: line, without which it is impossible to reproduce the form of a living being or object; and colour; which gives form the appearance of reality . . . A child's scrawls have a naïveté and a sincerity that make you smile, but the excesses of the school are nauseating or revolting. *Emile Cardon – 'La Presse'*

Here we can see that it is raining, we can see the sun shining, but nowhere can we see painting. *Pablo Picasso*

Eyesight painting. *John Sloan*

Modern Art

The real meaning of this Cubist movement is nothing else than the total destruction of the art of painting.

Kenyon Cox – 'Harper's Weekly' (1913)

Modernism is dying in all the countries of the world. Let us hope it will soon be just an unhappy memory. *Giorgio de Chirico*

I can't tell what those new painters are saying,
Although to some they're the new sensation,
As on canvas they keep throwing or spraying
The pigment of their imagination.

Leonard Dittell

So-called modern or contemporary art in our modern beloved country contains all the isms of depravity, decadence and destruction. Cubism aims to destroy by designed order. Futurism aims to destroy by a machine myth.

Dadaism aims to destroy by ridicule. Expressionism aims to destroy by aping the primitive and insane. Klee, one of its three founders, went to the insane asylums for his inspiration. Abstractionism aims to destroy by the creation of brainstorms. Surrealism aims to destroy by the denial of reason. Salvador Dali (Spanish realist) is now in the United States. He is reported to carry with him at all times, a picture of Lenin. Abstractionism, or non-objectivity in so-called modern art, was spawned as a simon-pure, Russian Communist product . . . Who has brought down this curse upon us; who of us let into our homeland this horde of germ-carrying art vermin?

George A. Dondero –
'Speech to Congress' (1949)

I don't like art today, I think it has gone to hell. *Peggy Guggenhiem*

Modern art is a cliché of the enemies of religion and not even the sanctity of marriage is safe from the so-called intellectuals.

Sir Leslie Herpron (1966)

Anyone who sees and paints a sky green and pastures blue ought to be sterilised.

Adolf Hitler

One reassuring thing about modern art is that things can't be as bad as they're painted. *M. Walthall Jackson*

Three men riding on a bicycle which has only one wheel. I guess that's surrealist.

Don Kingman

Jazz music is rendered; cubist pictures are executed; the perpetrators should be both. *'Newspaper Enterprise Association'*

It looks like something to hang your towel on. *Prince Philip*

Abstract painting is abstract. It confronts you. There was a reviewer a while back who wrote that my pictures didn't have any beginning or any end. He didn't mean it as a compliment but it was. It was a fine compliment. *Jackson Pollock*

Pop art is advertising art advertising itself as art that hates advertising.　*Harold Rosenberg*

A morbid and decadent youth
Says – 'Beauty is greater than Truth' –
And by Beauty I mean
The obscure, the obscene –
The diseased, the decayed, the uncouth.
　　　　　Cecil J. Sibbert – 'The Outspan'

From all the slimy muck that is creeping into so-called art nowadays. Heaven help us!
　　　　　　　　　　　　Tom Walls

POP ART

America has been a pioneer in throwaway cups and saucers, milk containers, tablecloths. Now it is a pioneer in throwaway art.
　Brian O'Doherty – 'New York Times' (1963)

POST-IMPRESSIONISM

Works of idleness and impotent stupidity, a pornographic show . . . An extremely bad joke or a swindle.
　　　　W. S. Blunt – 'My Diaries' (1920)

PRE-RAPHAELITES

They were full up and slopping over with Art, but they hadn't troubled to master Craft.
　　　　　　　　*Robertson Davies –
　　　　　'What's Bred in the Bone' (1985)*

The puddling twaddle of Preraphaelism.
　　　　　　　　George Inness (1884)

EXHIBITIONS

The exhibition is now no more than a bazaar where mediocrity spreads itself out with impudence.　　　　*Jean A. D. Ingres*

Pissarro was not wrong – although he went a bit too far when he said that all necropolises of art should be burnt.　*Paul Cézanne (1906)*

Museums are just a lot of lies, and the people who make art their business are mostly imposters.　　　　*Pablo Picasso*

'Burn the museums!' This old revolutionary slogan can now be realised by the museums themselves. A museum set on fire would today attract the usual crowd that visits its exhibitions. 'Burn the museums!', it turns out, calls not for the end of art but for the expansion of art institutions to include the medium of combustion.
　　　　　　　　*Harold Rosenberg –
　　　　　'Discovering the Present' (1973)*

Visiting museums bastardises the personality, just as hobnobbing with priests makes you lose your faith.　　　*Maurice Vlaminck*

I never go to museums. I avoid their odour, their monotony and severity.
　　　　　　　　Maurice Vlaminck

Grafton Gallery Exhibition (1910)
Why talk of the sincerity of all this rubbish? Idleness and impotent stupidity, a pornographic show . . . the gross puerility which scrawls indecencies on the walls of a privy.　　　　　*Charles Ricketts*

The art stops where a child would begin.
　　　　　　　　　　'The Times'

GALLERIES AND ACADEMIES

National Portrait Gallery, London
If you went round the National Portrait Gallery without knowing who the portraits were of, you would be as bored as if they were so much wall-paper.　*Lord David Cecil*

Royal Academy, London
The reputation of the Academy has got to a point where election would be positively distressing to a serious painter.
　　　　　　　'Evening Standard' (1961)

As for our little bits of R.A.s calling themselves painters, it ought to be stopped directly.
　　　　　　　　John Ruskin (1843)

ARTISTS

John James Audobon
I cannot help thinking Mr Audobon a dishonest man.　　　*John Keats (1819)*

CREATIVE ARTS

Francis Bacon
The only major influence on Bacon has been his own surname. A 'slumped but aphoristical co-watcher'.

Julian Barnes (1985)

Aubrey Beardsley
His was a passing fad, a little sign of decadence and nothing more.

'New York Times' (1898)

A monstrous orchid . . . I invented Aubrey Beardsley.

Oscar Wilde

Ford Madox Brown
Do you not see that his name never occurs in my books – do you think that would be so if I could praise him, seeing that he is an entirely worthy fellow? But pictures are pictures, and things that arn't arn't.

John Ruskin (1862)

Edward Burra
Burra loved to insinuate – so much so that three-quarters of the Burras at the Hayward are sheer tittle-tattle.

William Feaver – 'The Observer' (1985)

Michelangelo Caravaggio
Gloomy Caravaggio's gloomier stain.

Lord Byron (1819)

Paul Cézanne
I began a happening in New York by announcing in front of three thousand spectators that Cézanne was a catastrophe of awkwardness – a painter of decrepit structures of the past. I was applauded, principally because nobody knew who Cézanne was.

Salvador Dali

As for M. Cézanne, his name will be forever linked with the most memorable artistic joke of the last fifteen years.

Camille Mauclair (1905)

'A Modern Olympia' – Why look for a dirty joke or a scandalous theme in the Olympia? In reality it is only one of the weird shapes generated by hashish.

Marc de Montifond – 'L'Artiste'

M. Cézanne gives the impression of being a sort of madman who paints in fits of delirium tremens.

Marc de Montifond – 'L'Artiste'

Cézanne was fated, as his passion was immense, to be immensely neglected, immensely misunderstood, and now I think, immensely overrated.

Walter Sickert (1911)

To convince Cézanne of anything is like teaching the towers of Nôtre Dame to dance.

Emile Zola

John Constable and David Cox
These two men represent in their intensity the qualities adverse to all accurate science or skill in landscape art; their work being the mere blundering of clever peasants.

John Ruskin (1897)

Salvador Dali
Faced with a virtual complete record of the old phoney's unswerving bathos, it was impossible not to burst out yawning . . . the uproar of banality numbed the mind.

Clive James – 'Flying Visits' (1984)

The naked truth about me is to the naked truth about Salvador Dali as an old ukelele in the attic is to a piano in a tree, and I mean a piano with breasts.

James Thurber – 'Merry-Go-Round' (1945)

Charles Daubigny
If landscape can be satisfactorily painted without either drawing or colour – Daubigny is the man to do it.

P. G. Hamerton

Jacques-Louis David
'Coronation of Napoleon' – As a picture it does not possess anything of the language of art . . . it is below notice as a work of execution.

John Constable (1822)

Eugene Delacroix
'Massacre of Scio' – With the best will in the world I cannot admire Delacroix and his *Massacre of Scio'*. This work always appears to me to be a picture that was originally intended to depict a plague, and whose author, after having read the newspapers, turned it into a *Massacre of Scio*.

Stendhal – 'Le Journal de Paris' (1824)

André Derain
More a poster designer than a painter.
Louis Vauxcelles – 'L'Illustration' (1905)

Raoul Dufy
Dufy is merely a childish scene-painter, a scribbler of all sorts of nursery nonsense.
Sir Lionel Lindsay –
'Addled Art' (1946)

Caspar D. Friedrich
'Monk By The Sea' – Because of its monotony and boundlessness, with nothing but the frame as foreground, one feels as if one's eyelids had been cut away.
Heinrich von Kleist

Paul Gauguin
Many of his figures are distorted, and all of them have a smutty look, as if they had been rubbed with lampblack or coal dust. When the Parisian becomes a degenerate, he is the worst degenerate of all, a refined, perfumed degenerate. *John Burroughs*

Théodore Géricault
'Raft of the Medusa' – He could have made it terrible, and he has made it merely disgusting. *'P.A.' – 'La Revue' (1819)*

Mark Gertler
In general, borrowings in painting merely turn out duller than originals, but Mr Gertler manages to make his definitely more unpleasant. *Anthony Blunt*

'Merry-Go-Round' (1916) – It is horrible and terrifying . . . a terrible and dreadful picture.
D. H. Lawrence

Gilbert and George
The Morecambe and Wise of sober-suited, straight-faced pretension.
Paul Taylor – 'Time Out' (1981)

Vincent van Gogh
Van Gogh is the typical matoid and degenerate of the modern sociologist. *Jeune Fille au Bleu* and *Cornfield with Blackbirds* are the visualised ravings of an adult maniac. If this is art it must be ostracised, as the poets were banished from Plato's republic.
Robert Ross – 'The Morning Post' (1910)

I have always disliked Van Gogh's execution most cordially. I execrate his treatment of the instrument I love, those strips of metallic paint that catch the light like so many dyed straws; and when those strips make convolutions that follow the form of ploughed furrows in a field my teeth are set on edge. *Walter Sickert –*
'The Fortnightly Review' (1911)

Benjamin Haydon
'The Judgement Of Solomon' – Why did you paint it so large? A small canvas might have concealed your faults. *William Hazlitt*

Sir Godfrey Kneller
The portraits of Kneller seem all to have been turned into a machine.
William Hazlitt – 'The Champion' (1814)

Edwin Landseer
Good furniture pieces, unworthy of praise, and undeserving of blame.
John Ruskin – 'Modern Painters'

Leonardo da Vinci
Leonardo da Vinci did everything and did nothing very well.
Marie Bashkirtseef – 'Journal' (1883)

Roy Lichtenstein
The worst artist in the US. *'Life Magazine'*

Edouard Manet
'Déjeuner sur l'Herbe' – Is this drawing? Is this painting? I see garments without feeling the anatomical structure that supports them and explains their movements. I see boneless fingers and heads without skulls. I see side-whiskers made of two strips of black cloth that could have been glued to the cheeks. What else do I see? The artist's lack of conviction and sincerity.
Jules Castaganry – 'Salons'

'The Absinthe Drinker' – There is only one absinthe drinker, and that's the man who painted this idiotic picture.
Thomas Couture (1860)

A French idiot named Manet, who certainly must be the greatest and most uncritical ass who ever lived. *Dante Gabriel Rossetti (1881)*

'*Déjeuner sur l'Herbe*' – Unfortunately the nude hasn't a decent figure and one can't think of anything uglier than the man stretched out next to her, who hasn't even thought of taking off, out of doors, his horrid padded cap.   *Théophile Thore (1863)*

André Mantegna
His paintings had no semblance of living things, but only of antique statues and suchlike things.   *Giorgio Vasari (1568)*

Henri Matisse
Before buying the 'Woman with Hat' – It was a tremendous effort on his part, a thing brilliant and powerful, but the nastiest smear of paint I had ever seen.   *Leo Stein (1947)*

Hans Memling
A single picture by Memling is delightful, but a collection of several monotonous.
                    Sir Martin Conway (1921)

Michelangelo Buonarroti
He was a good man but he did not know how to paint.   *El Greco*

Every figure of his looks as if he was insulted and preparing to return a blow. If they sleep they seem as if they would kick; if they move when they are awake, they seem as if all their muscles are cracking.
                    Benjamin Haydon –
                    'Encyclopaedia Britannica' (1838)

'*Sistine Chapel Fresco*' – It is like an immense field of battle, or charnel house, strewed with carcasses and naked bodies: or it is a shambles of art. You have huge limbs apparently torn from their bodies and stuck against the wall; anatomical dissections, backs, and diaphragms, tumbling 'with hideous ruin and combustion down', neither intelligible groups nor perspective nor colour. The whole is a scene of enormous, ghastly confusion, in which you can only make out quantity and number, and vast, uncouth masses of bone and muscle.
                    William Hazlitt –
                    'The Vatican'

Few have heard of Fra Luca Pacioli, the inventor of double-entry book-keeping; but

he has probably had more influence on human life than has Dante or Michelangelo.
                    Herbert J. Muller

'*Bacchus*' – The countenance of this figure is the most revolting mistake of the spirit and meaning of Bacchus. It looks drunken, brutal, and narrow-minded, and has an expression of dissoluteness the most revolting.   *Percy B. Shelley*

John Milais
'*Christ in the Carpenter's Shop*' – In the foreground is a hideous, wry-necked, blubbering red-haired boy in a nightgown, who appears to have received a poke in the hand from the stick of another boy . . . and to be holding it up for the contemplation of a kneeling woman so horrible in her ugliness that she would stand out from the rest of the company as a monster in the vilest cabaret in France, or the lowest gin-shop in Europe.
                    Charles Dickens – 'Household Words' (1850)

Claude Monet
It is only too easy to catch people's attention by doing something worse than anyone else has dared to do it before.   '*Charivari*'

A skilful but short-lived decorator.
                    Edgar Degas (1888)

William Morris
Of course we all know that Morris was a wonderful all-round man, but the act of walking round him has always tired me out.
                    Sir Max Beerbohm

Gregoire Muller
'*Grob*' – Is a girl in a G-string with 'USA F★★★ ME' emblazoned across her arse art? We think not.   '*Time Out' (1991)*

Edvard Munch
He might perhaps as well have been a criminal as an artist, and the hand which applied colours to the canvas in this way might have been equally capable of wielding a knife or throwing a bomb.   *F. X. Salda*

John Opie
The fellow can paint nothing but thieves and murderers, and when he paints thieves and

murderers he looks in the glass. *Henry Fuesli*

Samuel Palmer
What the Hanging Committee means by hanging these pictures without the painter to explain them is beyond conjecture.
'The European Magazine' (1825)

Pablo Picasso
Picasso kept finding new ways of avoiding maturity.
Clive James – 'Flying Visits' (1984)

His sickness has created atrocities that are repellent. Every one of his paintings deforms man, his body and his face. *V. Kemenov*

Many painters and writers have made beautiful works out of repulsive subjects. Picasso enjoys making repulsive works out of beautiful subjects. *Raymond Mortimer*

If I met Picasso in the street I would kick him in the pants. *Sir Alfred Munnings – 'Speech at The Royal Academy' (1949)*

Picasso has a whim of iron.
John Richardson – 'Picasso in Private'

'Still Life with a Bull's Head' – My little grand-daughter of six could do as well.
Norman Rockwell

'Demoiselles d'Avignon' – These figures are not gods, nor Titans, nor heroes; they are not even allegorical or symbolic figures. They are naked problems, white numerals on a black background. *André Salmon (1912)*

Nicolas Poussin
'Perseus with the Head of Medusa' – Every principle of composition is violated . . . I remember turning from it with disgust.
Sir Joshua Reynolds – 'Discourses' (1790)

Pierre A. Renoir
On his portrait – I look like a Protestant clergyman. *Richard Wagner*

Joshua Reynolds
'Portrait of the Marlborough Family' – The composition abounds with every absurdity, and as to the plagiarisms they are really

capital . . . The worst of all oil Olios that was ever exhibited.
Rev. Henry Bate – 'The Morning Post' (1778)

Such artists as Reynolds are at all times hired by the Stans for the depression of Art – a pretence of Art, to destroy Art.
William Blake (1808)

The stunted, leering little monkeys that Sir Joshua Reynolds persuaded us to accept as representatives of tall and beautiful English children. *George Moore – 'Vale' (1914)*

Dante Gabriel Rossetti
Rossetti, dear Rossetti, I love your work, But you were really a bit of a jerk.
George MacBeth

'The Wedding of St George and The Princess Sabra' – There was also a queer remnant of a dragon's head which he had brought up in a box with its long red arrow tongue lolling out so comically, and the glazed eye which somehow seemed to wink at a spectator, as much as to say, 'Do you really believe in St George and the Dragon If you do, I don't . . .' *James Smeetham (1860)*

Rossetti is not a painter, he is a ladies' maid.
James M. Whistler

Sir Peter Paul Rubens
To my eye Rubens's colouring is most contemptible. His shadows are of a filthy brown somewhat the colour of excrement.
William Blake (1808)

John Sargent
He was stinking and undistinguished as an illustrator and non-existent as an artist.
Roger Fry – 'Nation' (1929)

Walter Sickert
He has invented a formula which leaves out almost everything, and is therefore suitable to his own talent and to the talents of a large following, principally ladies.
George Moore (1890)

Graham Sutherland
'Lord Beaverbrook' – Looking very much like

a diseased toad bottled in methylated spirit.
Quentin Bell

'*Winston Churchill*' – The portrait is a complete disgrace. It is bad-mannered; it is a filthy colour. Churchill has not got all that ink on his face – not since he left Harrow at any rate. *Lord Hailsham*

Titian
Why should Titian and the Venetians be named in a discourse on art? Such idiots are not artists.
Venetian, all thy colouring is no more
Than boulster'd plasters on a crooked whore.
William Blake (1808)

Henri de Toulouse-Lautrec
He has but one idea in his head, and this is vulgarity. *'Daily Chronicle'*

He will certainly leave the trace of his curious and immoral talent, which was that of a deformed man, who saw ugliness in everything about him and exaggerated that ugliness, while recording all the blemishes, perversities and realities of life.
Edmond Lepelletier –
'L'Echo de Paris' (1899)

J. M. W. Turner
'*The Battle of Waterloo*' – Before referring to the catalogue, we really thought this was the representation of a drunken hubbub on an illumination night, and that the host, as far gone as his scuffling and scrambling guests, was with his dame and kitchen wenches looking with torches for a lodger and wondering what was the matter.
'The Annals of the Fine Arts' (1818)

'*Army of Medes*' – To save trouble the painter seems to have buried his whole army in the sand of the desert with a single flourish of the brush. *'The Star' (1801)*

Andy Warhol
Multi-images of Marilyn Monroe are now as dated as hulahoops. Where does that leave Warhol's art? On the wall, is the unfortunate answer. *Kenneth McLeish –*
'Arts in the Twentieth Century' (1985)

I haven't seen any of Warhol's films, but of course they stink of titillation. *Cliff Richard*

Benjamin West
The flattering, feeble dotard, West,
Europe's worst dauber, and poor Britain's best. *Lord Byron*

James M. Whistler
'*Etchings of Venice*' – We have seen a great many representations of Venetian skies, but never saw one before consisting of brown smoke with clots of ink in diagonal lines.
P. G. Hamerton

'*Nocturne: Battersea Reach*' – A few smears of colour, such as a painter might make in cleaning his paint brushes. *'Knowledge'*

'*Arrangement in Silver and Black*' – The artist has represented this bilious young lady as looking haughty in a dirty white dress, and a grey hat with the most unhealthy green feather . . . two dyspeptic butterflies hover wearily above her head in search of a bit of colour, evidently losing heart at the grey expanse around. *'Society'*

'*Portrait of the Painter's Mother*' – This picture has found few admirers and for this result the painter has only to thank himself.
'The Times'

SCULPTURE

SCULPTORS

Antonio Canova
The sculptor born dead, whose heart is at Frari, whose hand is at the Academy, and the rest of him – I don't know where.
Roberto Longhi

Sir Jacob Epstein
'*Consummatum Est*' – Christ spent his life curing cripples. If He had seen Himself as Epstein has seen Him, He would have realized that there was not one piece of Himself that was not crippled.
Sir Charles Allom (1937)

'*Rima*' – A bestial figure, horribly misshapen, with the face and head of a microcephalous idiot. *John Collier*

'*Genesis*' – This man who cracks bad jokes with a chisel . . . The face is the face of a moron, thick lips pout with a beastly complacence under the stone blob which I presume is the nose. Artistically, the thing is absurd. Anatomically, it is purely comical.
'Daily Express'

'*Bowater House Group*' – The whole rubbishy mess, the straining buttocks, swinging balls, flopping breasts and turd-like black surface put it high on any list of the very ugliest public statues in London, if not the world.
Richard Dorment – *'The Literary Review'*
(1987)

'*Rima*' – It's nothing but a piece of unrealized affectation. I confess it makes me feel physically a little sick. The wretched woman has two sets of breasts and a hip joint like a merry thought. No, really!
John Galsworthy (1925)

'*Rima*' – His work is what you'd expect – dull, mechanical, lifeless – making the sculpture look as though Epstein had gnawed it with his teeth. *Eric Gill*

'*Bust of Lady Gregory*' – Poor Aunt Augusta. She looks as if she could eat her own children. *Sir Hugh Lane*

If people dug up remains of this civilization a thousand years hence, and found Epstein's statues and that man Ellis, they would think we were just savages.
Doris Lessing –
'Martha Quest'

'*Consummatum Est*' – All the necessary criticism of *Consummatum Est* is contained in the title. That is to say, Mr Epstein has used many hundredweights of alabaster to say a great deal less than is contained in two words. *'The Times'*

'*Consummatum Est*' – From the pictures it only looks to me like a child's first attempt with plasticine, the sort of unfortunate child who later gets looked at by a doctor and sent home. *'Universe'*

Henri Matisse
The goitrous, torpid and squinting husks provided by Matisse in his sculpture are worthless except as tactful decorations for a mental home.
Percy Wyndham Lewis –
'The Art of Being Ruled' (1926)

Michelangelo
'*Venus of Medici*' – I have seen the *Venus of Medici*, and I think that if she were dressed in modern clothes she would be hideous, especially about the waist. *Anton Chekhov*

Henry Moore
Sculptures in Hyde Park – They look as if something's fallen off a Jumbo Jet.
Laura Milligan

The statues are hideous beyond words, they seem to be a sort of primitive caveman production, and unworthy of a good place on any public building in London.
'Morning Post' (1929)

Ben Panting
On the forecourt [of the Odette Gilbert Gallery] he showed a huge bronze of genitals entwined in full coitus. A load of bollocks.
'Time Out' (1991)

ARCHITECTURE

GENERAL

All architecture is great architecture – after sunset. *G. K. Chesterton*

How simple-minded of the Germans to imagine that we British could be cowed by the destruction of our ancient monuments! As though any havoc of the German bombs could possibly equal the things we have done ourselves! *Sir Osbert Sitwell*

ARCHITECTS

Most architects think by the inch, talk by the yard, and should be kicked by the foot.
Prince Charles

Very few architects know anything about architecture. For 500 years architecture has been a phoney.   *Frank Lloyd Wright*

BUILDINGS

Albert Memorial
It has all the earmarks of an eyesore.

Anon American tourist

All Souls, Oxford
It would make a grand Co-op.   *Anon tourist*

AT&T Building, Manhattan, New York
Blown up 50 times domestic scale, this pediment is perversely simplified to the rudimentary detail of a doll house doorway.

J. M. Dixon (1978)

East Building, National Gallery, Washington DC
A shocking fun-house atmosphere . . . deeply philistine unseriousness akin to *Airport '78*.

Richard Hennessy – 'Artforum'

Empire State Plaza, New York
Half a cantaloupe sliced on the bias, a croquet wicket with avoirdupois, an upside-down orange half from a Kraft salad, and four little towers and a high tower resembling forms of cubistic coition.

'Progressive Architecture'

Eurodisney, Paris
A horror of cardboard, plastic and appalling colours, a construction of hardened chewing gum and idiotic folk-lore taken out of comic books written for obese Americans . . . A cultural Chernobyl.   *Jean Cau (1992)*

I respect cultural expressions of a foreign origin, but this is not my cup of tea.

François Mitterand (1992)

The J. Paul Getty Museum, Malibu, California
The worst failing of the museum is as a piece of architecture and archaeology. It is a faithful reproduction of nothing that ever existed, re-created by inappropriate technologies and frequently lacking in basic design judgement.

John Pastier – 'Los Angeles Times'

D. W. Griffith and Walt Disney would turn green with envy if they were to see what J. Paul Getty hath wrought. Purist archaeologists and art historians will no doubt turn purple.

Henry Seldis – 'Los Angeles Times'

Here was Los Angeles trying to rise above its comical image as one vast breakaway movie set, where nothing was what it seemed to be and now our richest patron had built a sandcastle for his second childhood and set us back 2,000 years.   *J. Smith – 'Westways'*

Paris Opera House
A stranger would take it for a railway station and, once inside, would mistake it for a Turkish bath.   *Claude Debussy (1921)*

Portland Building, Portland, Oregon
An enlarged juke-box or the oversized beribboned Christmas package.

Pietro Belluschi

This is a dog-building, turkey.   *John Storrs*

San Francisco – building project south of the city
They're all made out of ticky-tacky, and they all look just the same.

Malvina Reynolds – 'Little Boxes'

Skyscrapers
On having the costs and technology of a newly built New York skyscraper explained to him –
Dear me, how remarkable.
Then being told that the building was designed to last for over a thousand years – Dear, dear me, what a great pity!   *Lord Balfour*

Large buildings in London and elsewhere today are too often designed in the lift going down to lunch.   *Sir William Holford (1960)*

FASHION

GENERAL

Fashion which elevates the bad to a level of good, subsequently turns its back on bad and good alike.   *Eric Bentley*

Fashion condemns us to many follies; the

greatest is to make oneself its slave.
Napoleon Bonaparte

Art produces ugly things which frequently become beautiful with time. Fashion, on the other hand, produces beautiful things which always become ugly with time. *Jean Cocteau*

Elegance does not consist in putting on a new dress. *Coco Chanel*

Fashionability is a kind of vulgarity.
George Darley

Fond pride of dress is sure a very curse;
Ere fancy you consult your purse.
Benjamin Franklin

Gone are the clothes of yesteryear
That came with vest and britches.
Gone are the custom-tailored suits
That kept us all in stitches.
Gone are the artisans of yore
Who cut the cloth beyond compare –
Gone in a culture that prefers
Blue jeans and wash-and-wear.
Robert Gordon

Fashion is gentility running away from vulgarity, and afraid of being overtaken.
William Hazlitt

Fashion is the abortive issue of vain ostentation and exclusive egotism; it is haughty, trifling, affected, servile, despotic, mean and ambitious, precise and fantastical, all in a breath – tied to no rule, and bound to conform to every whim of the minute.
William Hazlitt

Regarding styles of hair and clothes
On which the young routinely pounce,
What has become, do you suppose,
Of that old saying 'Neatness Counts'?
G. Sterling Leiby

Fashion exists for women with no taste, etiquette for people with no breeding.
Queen Marie of Romania (1938)

Fashion is an imposition, a rein on freedom.
Golda Meir

Fashion is something barbarous, for it

produces innovation without reason and imitation without benefit. *George Santayana*

Fashions, after all, are only induced epidemics. *G. B.Shaw*

To call a fashion wearable is the kiss of death. No new fashion worth its salt is ever wearable. *Eugenia Shepherd –*
'New York Herald-Tribune' (1960)

Why not be oneself? That is the whole secret of successful appearance. If one is a greyhound, why try to look like a Pekinese?
Edith Sitwell

Conformism is so hot on the heels of the mass-produced avant-garde that the 'ins' and 'outs' change places with the speed of mach 3.
Igor Stravinsky

Distrust any enterprise that requires new clothes. *Henry D. Thoreau*

On the whole, I think that it cannot be maintained that dressing has in this or any country risen to the dignity of an art.
Henry D. Thoreau (1854)

Every generation laughs at the old fashions, but follows religiously the new.
Henry D. Thoreau (1854)

Clothes are a sign of insincerity; a sign of suppressed vulgarity and vanity; a pretence that we despise gorgeous colours and the graces of harmony and form, and we put them on to propagate that lie and back it up.
Mark Twain – 'Following the Equator'

If you have to talk about fashion, then you are not in it. *Michaele Vollbracht*

Fashion is the method by which the fantastic becomes for a moment universal. *Oscar Wilde*

Fashion is a form of ugliness so intolerable that we have to alter it every six months.
Oscar Wilde

The only way to atone for being occasionally a little over-dressed is by being always absolutely over-educated. *Oscar Wilde*

CREATIVE ARTS

Fashion is what one wears oneself – what is unfashionable is what other people wear.
Oscar Wilde – 'An Ideal Husband' (1895)

FASHION DESIGNERS

A dress designer merely possesses the gift of the garb.
Marvin Alisky

Fashion designers are people who live off the fad of the land.
Frank Tyger

STYLES AND TYPES

Designer Wear
These designer nappies are embellished with a print of Cabbage Patch Kids in muted hues of pink, blue and green, done not quite in Empire style and without either a court train or redingote, but flared about the bottom in an alencon lace effect, sprinkled throughout with tiny pink dots not unlike stephanotis adorning the Plaza Hotel's Grand Ballroom.
Philip Dougherty (1984)

Furs
Chinchilla is said to be more chic than mink, though personally it reminds me of unborn burlap.
Patrick Dennis – 'Life' (1962)

A correspondent comments on the absence of feminine furs this summer. Perhaps it isn't hot enough yet.
'Pittsburgh Chronicle'

Mink is for football games. Please. Out in the fresh air, sit in it, eat hotdogs in it, anything. But not evening, not elegance, I beg of you.
Valentina – 'Ladies Home Journal' (1958)

Hair styles
A crew cut is a furry with a singe on top.
Anon

If you read the papers, you will notice that no girl with short hair has made an advantageous marriage lately. So what's the sense of looking like a shaved bulldog?
Elizabeth Arden

She was what we used to call a suicide blonde – dyed by her own hand.
Saul Bellow

A beard is that ornamental excrement which groweth beneath the chin.
Thomas Fuller (1662)

Violet will be a good colour for hair at just about the same time that brunette becomes a good colour for flowers. *Fran Lebowitz (1981)*

On Princess Anne's hair – Hay. And hay is for horses.
Tommy de Maio

Nature herself abhors to see a woman shorn or polled; a woman with cut hair is a filthy spectacle, and much like a monster.
William Prynne (1632)

I could not endure a husband with a beard on his face. I had rather sleep in the woollen.
William Shakespeare –'Much Ado About Nothing'

Elvis Presley now sports a glossy something on his summit that adds at least five inches to his altitude and looks like a swatch of hot buttered yak wool.
'Time' (1966)

Hats
Her hat is a creation that will never go out of style. It will look ridiculous year after year.
Fred Allen

Communists all seem to wear small caps, a look I consider better suited to tubes of toothpaste than to people.
Fran Lebowitz – 'Metropolitan Life' (1978)

To carry an umbrella without any headgear places a fellow in a social no man's land – in the category of one hurrying round to the corner shop for a bottle of stout on a rainy day at the behest of the nagging landlady.
John Newton – 'Time and Tide' (1964)

A hat should be taken off when you greet a lady and left off for the rest of your life. Nothing looks more stupid than a hat. When you put on a hat you are surrendering to the same urge that makes children wear mouse ears at Disneyworld or drunks wear lampshades at parties. Wearing a hat implies that you are bald if you are a man and that your hair is dirty if you are a woman. Every style of hat is identified with some form of undesirable (derby = corrupt ward heeler; fedora = Italian gangster; top hat = rich bum;

pillbox = Kennedy wife, et cetera).
P. J. O'Rourke – 'Modern Manners' (1983)

A nature magazine estimates that there are only two birds to every acre in the United States. This may be because there are more than that to every hat. *'Washington Post'*

Hats divide generally into three classes: offensive hats; defensive hats, and shrapnel. Shrapnel hats look as if they have dropped on to the wearer's head by accident.
Katherine Whitehorn – 'How To Wear a Hat' (1963)

Hot pants
Hot pants are the limit. People complain you are not with it, but certain things I will not do. *Princess Anne (1971)*

Jeans
The jean! The jean is the destructor! It is a dictator! It is destroying creativity. The jean must be stopped.
Pierre Cardin – 'People' (1976)

Keep a girl in jeans from 4 to 14, and you'll wind up with a butch on your hands.
Suzanne Godart

Blue jeans? They should be worn by farm girls milking cows! *Yves Saint Laurent*

Jewellery
Don't ever wear artistic jewellery; it wrecks a woman's reputation. *Colette*

Kilts and tartan
On Ohio's computer-designed 'State' tartan – I called it McVomit.
Micheil MacDonald (1984)

A kilt is an unrivalled garment for fornication and diarrhoea. *John Masters*

Scotsmen are sour, stingy, depressing beggars who parade around in schoolgirls' skirts with nothing on underneath.
P. J. O'Rourke – 'National Lampoon' (1976)

Lace
It is difficult to see why lace should be so

expensive; it is mostly holes.
Mary Wilson Little

Ladies' wear
The man that got off that stuff about how womankind is advancing by great strides had evidently not seen the new hobble skirt.
'Auburn Globe'

On miniskirts – Never in the history of fashion has so little material been raised so high to reveal so much that needs to be covered so badly. *Sir Cecil Beaton (1969)*

All women dress like their mothers, that is their tragedy. No man ever does. That is his.
Alan Bennett – 'Forty Years On' (1968)

By actual count, there are only six women in the country who looked well in a jumpsuit. Five of them were terminal and the other was sired by a Xerox machine. *Erma Bombeck – 'If Life is a Bowl of Cherries . . .' (1978)*

On his reasons for banning miniskirts from the Henley Regatta – You are going to have middle-aged idiot women displaying thighs that should have been kept secret years ago.
Peter Conti

A skirt is no obstacle to extemporaneous sex, but it is physically impossible to make love to a girl while she is wearing trousers.
Helen Lawrenson

If women dressed for men, the stores wouldn't sell much – just an occasional sun visor. *Groucho Marx*

Your right to wear a mint-green polyester leisure suit ends when it meets my eye.
Fran Lebowitz – 'Metropolitan Life' (1978)

I don't like anything that's exaggerated. I've often said a fashionable woman should be attractive, not an attraction. *Pearl Nipon*

If God intended for women to wear slacks, He would have constructed them differently.
Emily Post

A dress has no purpose unless it makes a man want to take it off. *Françoise Sagan*

Women who are not vain about their clothes are often vain about not being vain about their clothes. *Cyril Scott*

The trouble with most Englishwomen is that they will dress as if they had been a mouse in a previous incarnation – or hope to be one in the next – they do not want to attract attention. *Edith Sitwell*

All women's dresses are merely variations on the eternal struggle between the admitted desire to dress and the unadmitted desire to undress. *Lin Yutang (1967)*

I wonder why older women feel they should dress in beige? Beige clothes, beige hair, beige skin; they look like pale liquid toffees. *Mary Wesley*

Make-up
I am absolutely in favour of women doing anything they can to bring out their good features, but when they paint each one a different colour they bring them out so far that I for one would like to push them back in again. *Elsie Janis*

Men's wear
A fashionable gentleman who much concerns himself with the fashions of gentlemen is neither fashionable nor a gentleman. *Stewart Alsop*

Men who wear turtlenecks look like turtles. *Doris Lilly – 'New York Post' (1967)*

Every time a woman leaves off something she looks better, but every time a man leaves off something he looks worse. *Will Rogers*

There will be little change in men's pockets this year. *'Wall Street Journal' (1948)*

If anything is worse than your own Tuxedo that doesn't fit, it's a borrowed one that doesn't fit. *Wall Street Journal (1958)*

National costume
Australia already has a national dress for men: shorts with long stockings; the wrong shoes, a short-sleeved knitted shirt, a pullover and very often a tie. *Hardy Amies*

We don't bother much about dress and manners in England, because as a nation we don't dress well and we've no manners. *G. B. Shaw*

A thorough survey may prove that it is impossible to buy a plain white or decently tasteful shirt in the whole of Las Vegas. *Jann Wenner – 'Rolling Stone'*

Pyjamas
For fifty years pyjamas were manufactured almost exclusively in broad coloured stripes which reduced men's attractiveness in the bedroom to that of multi-coloured zebras. *Mary Eden*

Shoes and socks
The new Italian pointed shoes are very comfortable, if you happen to have one toe. *Anon*

One of the few lessons I have learned in life is that there is invariably something odd about women who wear ankle socks. *Alan Bennett – 'The Old Country' (1978)*

And what about Gladiator boots. Remember them? They were the polished leather boots that hit just above the knee. You could look stylish in them or sit down. You couldn't do both. *Erma Bombeck – 'If Life is a Bowl of Cherries . . . ' (1978)*

Englishwomen's shoes look as if they had been made by somebody who had often heard shoes described, but had never seen any. *Margaret Halsey (1938)*

High heels were invented by a woman who had been kissed on the forehead. *Christopher Morley*

When you see silk-clad ankles in weather like this, you wonder whether she is trying to catch a husband or pneumonia. *'Pittsburgh Dispatch'*

Shoes are the prison cells of pride. *John G. Whittier*

Silk

If I kept a seraglio, the ladies would all wear linen gowns, or cotton – I mean stuffs made of vegetable substances. I would have no silk: you cannot tell when it's clean.

Samuel Johnson (1773)

Ski-wear

The idea is to look like a cross between subway graffiti and Papua New Guinea. The skier, even at a dead stop, will snap, sizzle and smoke.

Maria Sterling (1987)

Theatrical and movie costumes

'The Running Man' (1987) – Big Arnie's (Schwarzenegger) quilted outfit makes him look like a duvet.

Brian Case – 'Time Out'

Wim Wender's 'Notebook on Cities and Clothes' (1989) – The result has all the panache of a hastily assembled jumble of out-takes from a *Clothes Show* filler.

Wally Hammond – 'Time Out'

'Pygmalion' (1992) – As for the costumes, by Jasper Conran, notably in the Ascot scene, it seemed as if the play had been suddenly abandoned in favour of a fashion display at some dress house.

Beryl Bainbridge – 'The Oldie'

The costumes looked as though they had been selected by Helen Keller.

George J. Nathan

Kay Strozzi – appearing in 'The Silent Witness' – She had the temerity to wear as truly horrible a gown as I have ever seen on the American stage. There was a flowing skirt of pale chiffon – you men don't have to listen – a bodice of rose-coloured taffeta, sleeves of which ended shortly below her shoulders. Then there was an expanse of naked arms, and then, around the wrists, taffeta frills such as are fastened about the unfortunate necks of beaten white poodle dogs in animal acts. Had she not luckily been strangled by a member of the cast while disporting this garment, I should have fought my way to the stage and done her in myself.

Dorothy Parker – 'New Yorker' (1931)

Ties

Neckties strangle clear thinking.

Lin Yutang (1954)

Trousers

Punk's major achievement was the abolition of the flared trouser – the most noble abolition since William Wilberforce outlawed this country's slave trade.

Julie Burchill – 'The Method Rhythm'

Underwear

Unmentionables are those articles of ladies' apparel that are never discussed in public, except in full-page adverts.

'Changing Times'

A corset, in economic theory, is substantially a mutilation, undergone for the purpose of lowering the subject's vitality and rendering her permanently and obviously unfit for work.

Thorstein Veblen

Bralessness – It is not a very uplifting subject. Personally, I'm a firm believer in not tipping one's hand or, in this case, other portions of one's anatomy. I've been getting by for years on what I didn't show the boys.

Mae West

WEARERS

Anon

She looked as if she'd wrinkled her clothes and ironed her face.

Anon

Paddy Ashdown, Neil Kinnock and John Major

These political leaders all look like chat-show hosts in their beige trousers and woolly jumpers.

John Richmond (1992)

'Ban-the-bomb' feminists

You don't have to signal a social conscience by looking like a frump. Lace knickers won't hasten the holocaust, you can ban the bomb in a feather boa just as well without, and a mild interest in the length of hem-lines doesn't necessarily disqualify you from reading *Das Kapital* and agreeing with every word.

Jill Tweedie

Thomas Carlyle

That anyone who dressed so very badly as

did Thomas Carlyle should have tried to construct a philosophy of clothes has always seemed to me one of the most pathetic things in literature. *Max Beerbohm – 'Works'*

Coco Chanel

Chanel never influenced fashion one bit.
Pierre Cardin

Geena Davis

At the 1992 Oscar Ceremony – The 'Oscar for the Most Audacious Frock' definitely went to Geena Davis, whose white satin Bill Hargate gown looked like a wedding dress from behind, a can-can outfit from in front, and nothing on earth from the side.
'The Sunday Times' (1992)

Princess Diana

Princess Di wears more clothes in one day than Gandhi wore in his whole life.
Joan Rivers

Sheila E

The talented, flamboyant drummer, whose exhibitionist taste in fashion makes the typical streetwalker's fare seem suitable for the corporate boardroom.
Wayne Robbins – 'Newsday' (1987)

Boy George

Boy George is all England needs – another queen who can't dress. *Joan Rivers*

John Major

No advert for a country that boasts Savile Row.
Geoffrey Aquilina-Ross – 'For Him' (1992)

John Major is appalling; no excuses – Man from Austin Reed.
Peter Howarth – 'GQ' (1992)

Norma Major

Our Norma went for a Crimplene full-frontal on the cover of the *Sunday Times Magazine*. Not only did she wear Crimplene, but it was brown Crimplene. *'Time Out' (1992)*

Imelda Marcos

On her extravagant wardrobe – Compared to Imelda Marcos, Marie Antoinette was a bag lady. *Stephen Solarz (1986)*

Jonathan Ross

He still sports the spivvy whistle [and flute] of an 80s estate agent.
Steven Smethurst – 'Punch' (1992)

Helena Rubenstein

An old Polish frog with a huge casket of jewels. *Cecil Beaton*

Vita Sackville-West

On her habit of wearing gaiters with her jewellery – She looked like Lady Chatterley above the waist and the game-keeper below.
Cyril Connolly

Yves Saint-Laurent

Saint-Laurent has excellent taste. The more he copies me, the better taste he displays.
Coco Chanel (1971)

Diana Vreeland

She had rouged her cheeks to a colour otherwise seen only on specially ordered Pontiac Firebirds, and in her ears she wore two feathered appliances resembling surfcasting jigs especially appetising to a striped bass. *George V. Higgins –*
'Wall Street Journal' (1984)

Wallis Simpson (Duchess of Windsor)

The Duchess of Windsor never tried to hide her American upbringing or her love of fashion, even though the English prefer a royal family dressed in gum boots and head scarves. *Lady Diana Mosley*

Mae West

She was dressed in a peignoir of beige lace, with a blonde wig above false eyelashes – a kind of Mount Rushmore of the cosmetician's art. *Dwight Whitney (1965)*

Orson Welles

He was clad in a black barrage balloon cleverly painted to look like a dinner jacket.
Clive James – 'The Observer' (1980)

Katarina Witt

Protesting about her 'brief' ice skating costume – We're here to skate in a dress and not a G-string. *Peter Dunfield*

Mr Blackwell (Richard Sylvan Selzer)

'Mr Blackwell', an American fashion designer, originally released his list of the 'World's Worst Dressed Women' as a publicity gimmick for his own design house. This fashion bashing is now an annual occurrence and has grown to include men and women from all walks of celebrity life. A few examples of Mr B's handiwork are:

André Agassi
Looks like he missed the last train to Woodstock. With neon-coloured spandex worn under denim-look shorts, he's tennis's flower-child gone to seed. *'Tennis' (1990)*

Bea Arthur
This night-time Golden Girl is a tunic-draped 'daymare'.

Jill Clayburgh
She dresses like an African bush waiting for a safari.

Cher
Any attempt to look more masculine and she will need the operation.

Joan Collins
A hymn to overstatement if ever there was one.

Joan Collins and Diahann Carroll
The Dynasty ladies look like a pair of burnt-out Christmas trees.

Linda Gray and Victoria Principal
The *Dallas* girls show that glamour by excess proves too much is too much.

Bo Derek
The love child of the 1980s gets a minus ten for fashion.

Chris Evert
If tailored is in, so is boring.

Margaux Hemingway
A Hanukkah bush – the day after Christmas.

Finola Hughes
On her role in 'General Hospital' – She's Batgirl dressed by Mao Tse-Tung.

Martina Navratilova
In her leather-appliqued skirts and '70s wire-rim eye-glasses, she's the 'Tootsie' of tennis.
'Tennis' (1990)

Valerie Perrine
She looks like the Bride of Frankenstein doing the Ziegfeld Follies.

Helen Reddy
She doesn't know who she is. She wears see-through clothes that show her bosoms – whatever they are.

Aranxta Sanchez-Vicario
She looks like a refugee from a Bruce Springsteen concert hitting all the wrong fashion shots. *'Tennis' (1990)*

Barbra Streisand
She looks like the masculine Bride of Frankenstein.

Elizabeth Taylor
Elizabeth Taylor looks like two small boys fighting under a mink blanket.

Vanna White – *hostess of 'Wheel of Fortune'*
Mall fashions at their worst.

LITERARY

LITERATURE

GENERAL

The reason why so few good books are
written is that so few people who write know
anything. *Walter Bagehot*

How these authors magnify their office. One
dishonest plumber does more harm than a
hundred poetasters. *Augustine Birrell*

If you were a member of Jesse James' band
and people asked you what you were you
wouldn't say 'Well, I'm a desperado.' You'd
say something like 'I work in banks' or 'I've
done some railroad work.' It took me a long
time just to say 'I'm a writer.' It's really
embarrassing. *Roy Blount Jr*

Best-sellerism is the star system of the book
world. A best-seller is a celebrity among
books. It is a book known primarily
(sometimes exclusively) for its well-
knownness. *Daniel J. Boorstin*

A best-seller was a book which somehow sold
well simply because it was selling well.
Daniel J. Boorstin

I wonder whether what we are publishing
now is worth cutting down trees to make
paper for the stuff. *Richard Brautigan*

Canadian books may occasionally have had a
mild impact outside Canada. Canadian
literature has had none. *E. K. Brown*

It is one of the paradoxes of American
literature that our writers are forever looking
back with love and nostalgia at lives they
couldn't wait to leave.
Anatole Broyard (1973)

They lard their lean books with the fat of
others' works. *Robert Burton*

Books should be tried by a judge and a jury
as if they were crimes. *Samuel Butler*

One hates an author that's all author.
Lord Byron

'Tis pleasant sure to see one's name in print
A book's a book though there's nothing in't.
Lord Byron

Novel writing has to be learned but it can't
be taught. This bunkum and stinkum of
college creative-writing courses – writers
make their decision to write in secret. The
academics don't know that. They don't know
that the only thing you can do for someone
who wants to write is to buy him a
typewriter. *James Cain*

I think you must remember that a writer is a
simple-minded person to begin with and go
on that basis. He's not a great mind, he's not
a great thinker, he's not a great philosopher:
he's a story-teller. *Erskine Caldwell*

Those who write clearly have readers; those
who write obscurely have commentators.
Albert Camus – 'Notebooks'

Bad authors are those who write with
reference to an inner context which the
reader cannot know. *Albert Camus – Ibid.*

In America only the successful writer is
important, in France all writers are
important, in England no writer is important,
and in Australia you have to explain what a
writer is. *Geoffrey Cottrell –
'New York Journal/American' (1961)*

Books are the monuments of vanished minds.
William D'Avenant – 'Gondibert'

There are times when I think that the reading
I have done in the past has had no effect
except to cloud my mind and make me
indecisive. *Robertson Davies*

A Frenchman can humiliate an Englishman
just as readily as an Englishman can
humiliate an American and an American a

Canadian. One of Canada's most serious literary needs is some lesser nation to domineer over and shame by displays of superior taste. *Robertson Davies*

There is one last thing to remember: writers are always selling somebody short.
Joan Didion (1968)

An author who speaks about her own books is almost as bad as a mother who talks about her own children. *Benjamin Disraeli*

Books are fatal: they are the curse of the human race. Nine-tenths of existing books are nonsense and the clever books are the refutation of that nonsense. The greatest misfortune that ever befell man was the invention of printing. *Benjamin Disraeli*

When I want to read a book I write one.
Benjamin Disraeli

I have the conviction that excessive literary production is a social offence. *George Eliot*

The chap who said that truth was stranger than fiction died before fiction reached its present state of development.
'Elmira Star Gazette'

Talent alone cannot make a writer. There must be a man behind the book.
R. W. Emerson

People do not deserve to have good writing, they are so pleased with bad.
R. W. Emerson

It has come to be practically a sort of rule in literature that a man having once shown himself capable of original writing is entitled to steal from the writings of others at discretion. *R. W. Emerson*

A writer is congenitally unable to tell the truth and that is why we call what he writes fiction *William Faulkner*

The first thing an unpublished author should remember is that no one asked him to write in the first place. With this firmly in mind he has no right to become discouraged just because other people are being published.
John Farrar

There's one good kind of writer – a dead one.
James Farrell

Books are made not like children but like pyramids . . . and they're just as useless! and they stay in the desert! . . . Jackals piss at their foot and the bourgeois climb up on them.
Gustave Flaubert

Paperbacks blink in and out of print like fireflies. They also, as older collectors have ruefully discovered, fade and fall apart even more rapidly than their owners.
Paul Gray – 'Time' (1982)

Novels are receipts to make a whore.
Matthew Green – 'The Spleen'

Instead of marvelling with [Samuel] Johnson how anything but profit should incite men to literary labour I am rather surprised that mere emolument should induce them to labour so well. *Thomas Green*

A diary is all penned-up emotions.
Honey Greer

The preface is the most important part of the book. Even reviewers read a preface.
Philip Guedalla

Fiction is the most uncreative form of publishing. *Paul Hamlyn (1968)*

They're fancy talkers about themselves, writers. If I had to give young writers advice I would say don't listen to writers talking about themselves. *Lillian Hellman*

Writing is the only trade I know of in which snivelling confessions of extreme incompetence are taken as credentials probative of powers to astound the multitude.
George V. Higgins – 'Harper's' (1984)

The paperback is very interesting but I find it will never replace a hardcover book – it makes a very poor doorstop.
Alfred Hitchcock

LITERARY

I never saw an author in my life, saving
perhaps one, that did not purr as audibly as a
full-grown domestic cat on having his fur
smoothed the right way by a skilful hand.
Oliver Wendell Holmes Sr

The essay is a literary device for saying
almost everything about almost anything.
Aldous Huxley

A bad book is as much of a labour to write as
a good book. It comes as sincerely from the
author's soul.
Aldous Huxley – 'Newsweek' (1956)

What a sense of superiority it gives one to
escape reading a book which everyone else is
reading. *Alice James*

As a rule reading fiction is as hard to me as
trying to hit a target by hurling feathers at it.
I need resistance to cerebrate!
William James

The novel is a prose narrative of some length
that has something wrong with it.
Randall Jarrell

The greatest deterrent to education is the
inordinate passion prevalent for novels.
When this poison infects the mind it destroys
its tone and revolts against wholesome
reading. Reason and fact plain and
unadorned are rejected. The result is a
bloated imagination, sickly judgement and
disgust towards all the real business of life.
Thomas Jefferson (1818)

The root of all bad writing is to compose
what you have not worked out for yourself.
Unless words come into the writer's mind as
fresh coinages for what the writer himself
knows that he knows to be true it is
impossible for him to give back in words that
direct quality of experience which is the
essence of literature. *Alfred Kazan*

A publisher who writes is like a cow in a
milkbar. *Arthur Koestler*

An essayist is a lucky person who has found a
way to discourse without being interrupted.
Charles Poore – 'New York Times' (1962)

Good authors too who once knew better
words
Now only use four-letter words
Writing prose
Anything goes   *Cole Porter – 'Anything Goes'*

The obscurity of a writer is generally in
proportion to his incapacity. *Quintilian*

The writer has taken unto himself the former
function of the priest or prophet. He
presumes to order and legislate the people's
life. There is no person more arrogant than
the writer. *Cornelius Register*

I hate books for they only teach people to talk
about what they do not understand.
Jean-Jacques Rousseau – 'Emile'

On accepting the Nobel Prize – The profession
of book writing makes horse racing seem like
a solid stable business.
John Steinbeck (1962)

Most American writers I find phony but it's a
phony country. *Gore Vidal*

The multitude of books is making us
ignorant. *Voltaire*

I never could understand how two men can
write a book together – to me that's like three
people getting together to have a baby.
Evelyn Waugh

Fiction is a confidence trick trying to make
people believe something is true that isn't.
Angus Wilson

A young musician plays scales in his room
and only bores his family. A beginning
writer, on the other hand, sometimes has the
misfortune of getting into print.
Marguerite Yourcenar – 'Time' (1981)

LITERARY CRITICISM

I believe that critics who presume to dictate
to writers or writers who set themselves up as
lodestones are enemies of art since if they
have any effect at all it is to deflect the aim of
true writers.
Brian Aldiss – 'The Guardian' (1971)

Attacking bad books is not only a waste of time but bad for the character.
W. H. Auden – Ibid.

Writing reviews can be fun but I don't think the practice is very good for the character.
W. H. Auden – Ibid.

The critic in *The Vicar of Wakefield* lays down that you should always say that the picture would have been better if the painter had taken more pains but in the case of the practised literary man you should often enough say that the writing would have been much better if the writer had taken less pains.
Walter Bagehot –
'Literary Studies: Shakespeare'

Of all fatiguing futile empty trades, the worst I suppose is writing about writing.
Hilaire Belloc – 'The Silence of the Sea'

Friendly attacks should begin with faint praise but be careful not to use adjectives or phrases of which the publisher can make use in advertisements.
John Betjeman

A serious reviewer should have an axe to grind. If you don't your judgements will appear ephemeral, casual, even indifferent. But when you have an axe to grind it is essential that you should not know what it is and neither should anyone else.
Anatole Broyard

It's surprising that authors should expect kindness to be shown to their books when they are not themselves known for kindness toward their characters, their culture or by implication their readers.
Anatole Broyard

One thing I learned about my first novel was what all the reviewers thought of it from Little Rock to Broken Hill, for I subscribed to a press-cutting agency, a thing I have not done since. I learned thus what I have had no occasion to unlearn: that reviewers do not read books with much care and that their profession is more given to stupidity and malice and literary ignorance even than the profession of novelist.
Anthony Burgess

Speak of the moderns without contempt and

of the ancients without idolatry.
Lord Chesterfield

Either criticism is no good at all (a very defensible position) or else criticism means saying about an author the very things that would have made him jump out of his boots.
G. K. Chesterton (1906)

A literary critic is a person who can find a meaning in literature that the author didn't know was there.
'Cleveland Times'

Reviewers are usually people who would have been poets, historians, biographers etc. if they could: they have tried their talents at one or at the other and have failed, therefore they turn critics.
Samuel Taylor Coleridge – 'Lectures on Shakespeare and Milton'

As long as there are readers to be delighted with calumny there will be found reviewers to calumniate.
Samuel Taylor Coleridge

It is wrong to read the books one reviews. It creates a prejudice.
George Croly

The most noble criticism is that in which the critic is not the antagonist so much as the rival of the author.
Israel D'Israeli – 'Curiosities of Literature'

To sit up and criticise me for saying 'vest' instead of 'waistcoat', to talk about my splitting the infinitive and using vulgar commonplaces here and there, when the tragedy of man's life is being displayed, is silly. More, it is ridiculous. It makes me feel that American Criticism is the joke that English authorities maintain it to be.
Theodore Dreiser

Essays entitled critical are epistles addressed to the public through which the mind of the recluse relieves itself of its impressions.
Margaret Fuller –
'A Short Essay on Criticism' (1858)

A man's mind is hidden in his writings, criticism brings it to light.
Solomon Ibn Gabirol –
'The Choice of Pearls' (c. 1050)

There is a type of critic whose attitude suggests that the book he is reviewing was written by his kind permission and that the author has grossly abused the privilege.

Lambert Jeffries

It is rarely that an author is hurt by his critics.

Samuel Johnson

Professional critics are incapable of distinguishing and appreciating either diamonds in the rough state or gold in bars.

They are traders and in literature know only the coins that are current. Their criticism has scales and weights but neither crucible nor touchstone.

Joseph Joubert

Confronted by an absolutely infuriating review it is sometimes helpful for the victim to do a little personal research on the critic. Is there any truth to the rumour that he had no formal education beyond the age of eleven? In any event, is he able to construct a simple English sentence? Do his participles dangle? When moved to lyricism, does he write, 'I had a fun time'? Was he ever arrested for burglary? I don't know that you will prove anything this way but it is perfectly harmless and quite soothing.

Jean Kerr

Most critics write critiques which are by the authors they write critiques about. That would not be so bad, but then most authors write works which are by the critics who write critiques about them.

Karl Kraus

It is safer to assume that every writer has read every word of every review and will never forgive you.

John Leonard

It does no harm to repeat as often as you can: 'Without me the literary industry would not exist: the publishers, the agents, the sub-agents, the sub-sub-agents, the accountants, the libel lawyers, the departments of literature, the professors, the theses, the books of criticism, the reviewers, the book pages – all this vast and proliferating edifice is because of this small, patronised, put-down and underpaid person.'

Doris Lessing

I regard reviews as a kind of infant's disease to which new-born books are subject.

G. C. Lichtenberg

One of the greatest creations of the human mind is the art of reviewing books without having read them.

G. C. Lichtenburg

Critics are sentinels in the grand army of letters stationed at the corners of newspapers and reviews to challenge every new author.

Henry W. Longfellow – 'Kavanagh'

What a sense of security in an old book which time has criticised for us! *James Lowell*

He takes the long review of things
He asks and gives no quarter.
And you can sail with him on wings
Or read the book – it's shorter.

David McCord

Book reviewers are little old ladies of both sexes.

John O'Hara

The balance sheets of our great publishing houses would not be materially affected if they ceased from tomorrow the publication of poetry and literary criticism, and most publishers would rejoice to be relieved of the unprofitable burden of vain solicitations which such publication encourages.

Herbert Read

I never read anything concerning my work. I feel that criticism is a letter to the public which the author, since it is not directed to him, does not have to open and read.

Rainer Maria Rilke

It is necessary a writing critic should understand how to write. And though every writer is not bound to show himself in the capacity of a critic every writing critic is bound to show himself capable of being a writer for if he be apparently impotent in this latter kind he is to be denied all title and character in the other. *Earl of Shaftesbury*

As a bankrupt thief turns thief-taker so an unsuccessful author turns critic.

Percy B. Shelley – 'Adonais'

The critics will say as always that literature is

decaying. From the time of the first critic up to now they have said nothing else.

Sir Osbert Sitwell

Lovers of literature will look for the remains of the golden treasure in that shipwreck on the bottom of the sea of criticism.

Josef Skovorecky

Literary criticism should arise out of a debt of love. *George Steiner –*
'An Essay in the Old Criticism' (1959)

Book critics are a weird subspecies. We may pull all-nighters but they tend to take place at home where page 648 leads inexorably to page 649. *Jean Strouse (1980)*

Answering criticism of his 'Julian' – What is in question is a kind of book reviewing which seems to be more and more popular: the loose putting down of opinions as though they were facts and the treating of facts as though they were opinions.

Gore Vidal – 'New York Times' (1964)

I have long felt that any book reviewer who expresses rage and loathing for a novel is preposterous. He or she is like a person who has just put on full armour and attacked a hot fudge sundae or banana split.

Kurt Vonnegut Jr

Professional reviewers read so many bad books in the course of duty that they get an unhealthy craving for arresting phrases.

Evelyn Waugh

Most writers accept vituperation as a healthy counterpoint to unintelligent praise.

Evelyn Waugh

Judgement in literature is impugned to the extent that it is exercised.

Reed Whittemore – 'New Republic' (1971)

WRITERS

Jane Austen
'Pride and Prejudice' – I had not seen *Pride and Prejudice* till I read that sentence of yours and then I got the book. And what did I find? An accurate daguerreotyped portrait of a commonplace face, a carefully fenced, highly cultivated garden with neat borders and delicate flowers but no glance of a bright, vivid physiognomy, no open country, no fresh air, no blue hill, no bonny beck. I should hardly like to live with her ladies and gentlemen in their elegant but confined houses.

Charlotte Brontë – 'Letter to G. H. Lewes'
(1848)

Edward Bulwer-Lytton
Intrinsically a poor creature, this Bulwer has a bustling, whisking agility and restlessness which may support him a certain degree of significance with some but which partakes much of the nature of levity. *Thomas Carlyle*

Thomas Carlyle
'Essay on Burns' –
  As I was lying on the green
A little book it chanced I seen.
Carlyle's *Essay on Burns* was the edition;
  I left it lying in the same position.
Anon

Lord Chesterfield
If he is rewarded according to his desert his name will stink to all generations.
John Wesley – 'Diary' (1775)

Dante
Few have heard of Fra Luca Pacioli, the inventor of double-entry book-keeping, but he has probably had more influence on human life than has Dante or Michelangelo
Herbert J. Muller

Charles Dickens
He is a man with a very active fancy, great powers of language, much perception of what is grotesque and a most lachrymose and melodramatic turn of mind – and this is all. He has never played any part in any movement more significant than that of a fly . . . on a wheel *'Saturday Review' (1857)*

Of Dickens's style it is impossible to speak in praise. It is jerky, ungrammatical and created by himself in defiance of rules. . . . No young novelist should ever dare to imitate the style of Dickens.
Anthony Trollope – 'Autobiography'

Edward Fitzgerald
His tranquillity is like a pirated copy of the peace of God.   *James Spedding (1835)*

Margaret Fuller
She took credit to herself for having been her own Redeemer if not her own Creator.
Nathaniel Hawthorne

Robert Graves
He wrote much that is excellent, much that is mediocre and much that is so worthless as to prejudice the value of the rest.
Lord Birkenhead

Thomas Hardy
An abortion of George Sand.   *George Moore*

Henry James
A magnificent but painful hippopotamus resolved at any cost upon picking up a pea.
H. G. Wells –
'Boon'

James Joyce
'Ulysses' – The key to reading *Ulysses* is to treat it like a comedian would as a sort of gagbook.   *Brendan Behan*

D. H. Lawrence
I ask you, is anything in life or literature past or present in earth, heaven or hell, anything more devastatingly tedious than D.H.L.'s interest in the human genitalia?
G. W. Lyttelton

Harriet Martineau
Broken into utter wearisomeness, a mind reduced to these three elements: Imbecility, Dogmatism and unlimited Hope.
Thomas Carlyle

Henry Miller
Miller is not really a writer but a non-stop talker to whom someone has given a typewriter.   *Gerald Brenan*

J. B. Priestley
The conversations in his novels may be true to life but they are at times remote from art. Mr Priestley's pages, like Prohibition beer, are often ten per cent inspired.
Lord Birkenhead

Samuel Richardson
'Pamela' – In *Pamela* Richardson produced an essay in vulgarity of sentiment and morality alike which has never been surpassed.   *W. E. Henley – 'Athenaeum'*

That fellow Richardson could not be contented to sail quietly down the stream of reputation without longing to taste the froth from every stroke of the oar.
Samuel Johnson

George Sand
A great cow-full of ink!   *Anon*

This may be an apocryphal amalgam of Baudelaire and Nietzsche.
She is above all and more than anything else of a cow-like stupidity.   *Charles Baudelaire*

George Sand or *Lactea ubertas.*
Friedrich Nietzsche
[*Lactea ubertas* = Milky abundance]

Sir Walter Scott
'The Field of Waterloo'
The corpse of many a hero slain
Pressed Waterloo's ensanguined plain
But none by salvo or by shot
Fell half so flat as Walter Scott.
Thomas, Baron Erskine (1815)

Sir Walter Scott (when all is said and done) is an inspired butler.
William Hazlitt – 'Mrs Siddons'

Lawrence Sterne
A bawdy blockhead.   *Oliver Goldsmith*

Bishop William Stubbs *and*
Professor E. A. Freeman – *historians*
Ladling the butter from adjacent tubs,
    Stubbs butters Freeman, Freeman butters
Stubbs.   *J. E. Rogers*

Leo Tolstoy
A degenerate mystic.
Max Nordau – 'Degeneration'

John Updike
'Couples' – Reading *Couples* is like studying science while watching pornographic movies put together from random scraps on the cutting-room floor.   *John Gardner*

LITERARY

P. G. Wodehouse
He had a naïve insistence on visiting Hitler's Berlin and broadcasting unpatriotic claptrap on radio during the war.   *Harold Wilson*

Emile Zola
His symbolism, his pessimism, his coprolalia and his predilection for slang sufficiently characterize M. Zola as a high-class degenerate. That he is a sexual psychopath is betrayed on every page of his novels. His consciousness is peopled with images of unnatural vice, bestiality, passivism and other aberrations. Every porter of a brothel is capable of relating of low debauch.
Max Nordau – 'Degeneration'

BIOGRAPHY

Our Grubstreet biographers watch for the death of a great man like so many undertakers on purpose to make a penny on him.   *Joseph Addison – 'Freeholder'*

Monckton Milnes
'Life of Keats' – Fricassee of dead dog.
Thomas Carlyle

LIBRARIES

Meek young men grow up in libraries.
Ralph W. Emerson

Slop-shops in literature.
Mrs Elizabeth Griffith

A library makes me sick.
Friedrich Nietzsche – 'Ecce Homo'

We call ourselves a rich nation and we are filthy and foolish enough to thumb each other's books out of circulating libraries!
John Ruskin – 'Sesame and Lilies'

A circulating library in a town is an evergreen tree of diabolical knowledge.
Richard B. Sheridan – 'The Rivals'

LITERARY MOVEMENTS

A literary movement consists of five or six people who live in the same town and hate each other cordially.   *George Moore*

The Bloomsbury Group
The Young Men's Christian Association – with Christ left out, of course. *Gertrude Stein*

POETRY

GENERAL

I have never yet known a poet who did not think himself super-excellent.   *Cicero*

A poet is a liar who always speaks the truth.
Jean Cocteau

Poetry is religion without hope. *Jean Cocteau*

Turn pimp, flatterer, quack, lawyer, parson, be chaplain to an atheist or stallion to an old woman, anything but poet, for a poet is worse, more servile, timorous and fawning than any I have named.
William Congreve – 'Love for Love' (1695)

Poets arguing over modern poetry: jackals snarling over a dried-up well.
Cyril Connolly – 'The Unquiet Grave' (1945)

Poets are a very worthless, wicked set of people.   *William Cowper (1784)*

A poet laureate is just a bard in a gilded cage.
Raymond J. Cvikota

The poet ranks far below the painter in the representation of visible things and far below the musician in that of invisible things.
Leonardo da Vinci – 'Notebooks'

Poetry is a counterfeit creation, and makes things that are not as though they were.
John Donne

True judgement in Poetry takes a view of the whole together: 'tis a sign that malice is hard driven when 'tis force to lay hold on a word or syllable.   *John Dryden – 'Sylvae' (1685)*

Correct English is the slang of prigs who write history and essays, and the strongest slang of all is the slang of poets.
George Eliot – 'Middlemarch'

Poetry is not a career but a mug's game.
T. S. Eliot

Poetry is commonly thought to be the language of emotion. On the contrary, most of what is so called proves the absence of all passionate excitement. It is a coldblooded, haggard, anxious, worrying hunt after rhymes which can be made serviceable, after images which will be effective, after phrases which are sonorous – all this under limitations which restrict the natural movements of fancy and imagination.

Oliver Wendell Holmes Jr

I could no more define poetry than a terrier can define a rat. *A. E. Housman*

I never knowed a successful man who could quote poetry. *Kin Hubbard*

As civilisation advances, poetry declines.
Thomas Macaulay – 'Edinburgh Review'
(1825)

I detest that breed of men who think that poetic purity
Must be buried in incomprehensible obscurity. *Arthur Magill*

Poetry is the language of a state of crisis.
Stéphane Mallarmé

When one hears of a poet past thirty-five he seems somehow unnatural and obscene.
H. L. Mencken – 'Prejudices' (1919)

Poets are born, not paid. *Wilson Mizner*

Poetry? I too dislike it. There are things that are important beyond all this fiddle.
Marianne Moore

There is nothing more dangerous to the formation of a prose style than the endeavour to make it poetic. *J. Middleton Murry*

I'd rather be a great bad poet than a good bad poet. *Ogden Nash*

Perhaps the saddest lot that can befall mortal man is to be the husband of a lady poet.
George J. Nathan

Blank verse is neither rhyme nor reason.
J. K. Paulding – 'The Bucktails' (1815)

Poetry is an evasion of the real job of writing prose. *Sylvia Plath*

Poets, like whores, are only hated by each other. *William Wycherley*

POETRY CRITICISM

The corruption of a poet is the generation of a critic.
John Dryden – 'Examem Poeticum: Dedication'

When poets' plots in plays are damn'd for spite
The critics turn and damn the rest that write.
John Haynes – 'Miscellany Poems'

'Tis cruel that critics should love to belabour
Our plagiarist poet with stock and stone
For if he has borrowed the thoughts of his neighbour
'Tis harsh treatment to assume the faults are his own. *Isaac ben Jacob*

God's most candid critics are those of his children whom he has made poets.
Sir Walter Raleigh

POETS

Matthew Arnold
Aberdeen granite tomb . . . with his childish mittened musings. *Edith Sitwell – 'Pope'*

W. H. Auden
The high-water mark, so to speak, of Socialist literature is W. H. Auden, a sort of gutless Kipling.
George Orwell – 'The Road to Wigan Pier'

William Blake
That William Blake
Who beat upon the wall
Till Truth obeyed his call.
W. B. Yeats – 'An Acre of Grass'

Robert Burton
'The Anatomy of Melancholy' – He composed his book with a view of relieving his own melancholy but increased it to such a degree that nothing could make him laugh.
James Granger

Lord Byron

Byron! He would be all forgotten today if he had lived to be a florid old gentleman with iron-grey whiskers writing very long, very able letters to *The Times* about the repeal of the Corn Laws.

Max Beerbohm – 'Zuleika Dobson'

Samuel Taylor Coleridge

The rogue gives you Love Powders and then a strong horse drench to bring 'em off your stomach that they mayn't hurt you.

Charles Lamb

Homer

So they told me how Mr Gladstone read Homer for fun, which I thought served him right.

Sir Winston Churchill

John Milton

'Paradise Lost' – No man wished it a minute longer.

Samuel Johnson

Lady Mary Wortley Montagu

A dilapidated macaw with a hard, piercing laugh, mirthless and joyless, with a few unimaginative phrases, with a parrot's powers of observation and a parrot's hard and poisonous bite.

Edith Sitwell

Seneca

Seneca writes as a Boar pisses, by jerks.

Dr Ralph Kettell

Lord Tennyson

He could not think up the height of his own towering style.

G. K. Chesterton

Walt Whitman

He is morally insane . . . an American driveller.

Max Nordau – 'Degeneration'

DRAMATIC

THEATRE

GENERAL

The modern theatre is a skin disease, a sinful disease of the cities. It must be swept away with a broom; it is unwholesome to love it.

Anton Chekhov

English plays,
Atrocious in content,
Absurd in form,
Objectionable in action,
Execrable English Theatre!

Johann Goethe

Theatre is what works even with an audience of a dozen pensioners, not a matter of higher aesthetics.

John Osborne –
'A Better Class of Person' (1981)

Where are the plays of today? They're either so chockful of intellect that they send you to sleep – or they reek of sentiment till you yearn for the smell of cabbage.

Alfred Sutro

DRAMA CRITICISM

The dramatic critic's meat is the ham actor.

Anon

At any London first night you'll see the critics creeping off to the pub halfway through Act III. Of course, they pretend they've got to catch the early editions.

Basil Boothroyd

The satisfied grunt of the *Daily Mail*, the abandoned gurgle of the *Sunday Times*, and the shrill enthusiastic scream of the *Daily Express*.

Noël Coward

The dramatic critic is asleep. The play does not interest him. He will give it thunder in the paper.

Eugene Field – 'The Tribune Primer'

Award-winning plays are written only for the

DRAMATIC

critics. *Lew Grade (1970)*

Dramatic criticism is venom from contented
rattlesnakes. *Percy Hammond*

Asking a working actor what he thinks of
critics is like asking a lamp-post how it feels
about dogs. *Christopher Hampton*

There is no more absolutely thrilling
experience in dramatic criticism than to be
absolutely certain that all the others are
wrong. *Harold Hobson – 'Indirect Journey'*

It is widely believed that the New York
reviewer's verdict on a play is nearly final,
and the reviewer is therefore most often
painted as a slaughterer of innocents, a man
whose principal dedication is to the task of
keeping the maximum number of people
away from the theatre and the maximum
number of plays from succeeding. The
reverse would be closer to the truth. One of
the first things a New York newspaper critic
learns is that he must all but explode with
enthusiasm, must in fact seriously outwrite
himself if he is to push people into the
theatres at all. The fact that he is willing to do
so, willing to perjure himself above and
beyond his actual respect for the play, willing
to employ all those extravagant, overworked,
and downright embarrassing adjectives in the
cause of theatrical liveliness is the real
measure of his devotion to the trade.
Walter Kerr – 'Pieces of Eight' (1952)

Coughing in the theatre is not a respiratory
ailment. It is a criticism.
Alan Jay Lerner – 'The Street Where I Live'

How can you write a play of which the ideas
are so significant that they will make the critic
of *The Times* get up in his stall and at the
same time induce the shop girl in the gallery
to forget the young man who is holding her
hand? *W. Somerset Maugham –*
'Cakes and Ale' (1930)

A dramatic critic is a person who surprises
the playwright by informing him what he
meant. *Wilson Mizner*

The worst convention of the critics of the

theatre current at the turn of the century was
that a playwright is a person whose business
is to make unwholesome confectionery out of
cheap emotion. *G. B. Shaw*

On why he never read reviews – If it is abuse –
why, one is always sure to hear of it from one
damned good-natured friend or other.
Richard B. Sheridan

THEATRELAND

The National Theatre, London
Colditz-on-Thames. *John Osborne*

PLAYWRIGHTS

Bertolt Brecht
If it hadn't been for Adolf Hitler he'd still be
behind the bacon counter in Oberammergau.
Anon

The state of alienation known as Brechtian,
but what we used to call 'bored stiff'.
John Coleman

Brecht was a great lyrical poet, but a second-
rate dramatist.
D. J. Enright – 'The Observer' (1984)

A. A. Milne
I see no future for Mr A. A. Milne, whose
plots are as thin as a filleted anchovy, and
whose construction is reminiscent of
Victorian fretwork. It seems to me that Mr
Milne is obsessed by the bogey of impossible
stage-butlers who would be sacked directly
they opened their mouths in real life. He
conceives a fragment, splits it and pads it in
cotton-wool through three acts but so far he
has not conceived one idea of value.
H. Dennis Bradley (1925)

John Osborne
On the 'Angry Young Man' – He's as f***ing
angry as Mrs Dale. *Brendan Behan*

William Shakespeare
There are moments when one asks
despairingly why our stage should ever have
been cursed with this immortal 'pilferer' of
other men's stories and ideas.
G. B. Shaw – 'Saturday Review' (1896)

It is our duty to the great and famous dead to say that Mr Shaw's capers are vulgar, fatuous and extremely wearisome.   *Alfred Noyes*

An idiot child screaming in hospital.
                                        H. G. Wells (1914)

Neil Simon

Julius J. Epstein's 'Pete 'n' Tillie' (1972) – The wisecracks stay on this side of possibility – that is, we don't feel, as we do so often with Neil Simon, that the characters have private gag writers in their homes. *Stanley Kauffmann*

Dylan Thomas

'Under Milk Wood' – It seemed to me that the man who wrote it had a mind like a sewer. . . . I therefore conclude that Dylan Thomas must have been an exceptionally unpleasant person.   *George Murray –*
                                      'Daily Mail' (1957)

Oscar Wilde

Oscar Wilde and his epigrams are shown up
as brilliant bores
Before the unpretentious penetration of the
comment that
It never rains but it pours.   *Ogden Nash –*
       'I'll Take the Bromide, Please' (1940)

He was over-dressed, pompous, snobbish, sentimental and vain.
       Evelyn Waugh – 'Harper's Bazaar' (1930)

PLAYS AND MUSICALS
(listed by reviewer)

Anon

Robert Bolt's 'Gentle Jack' – Mr Bolt was a schoolmaster; he should now bend over and take six of the best.

Henrik Ibsen's 'Ghosts' – An open drain.

Brooks Atkinson

'The Women' (1936) – Stingingly detailed pictures of some of the most odious harpies ever collected in one play.

Lady Birdwood

'Oh Calcutta' (1970) – How long is the British taxpayer through the Arts Council going to finance its own moral collapse?

Charles Brackett

Mae West's 'Diamond Lil' (1928) – Pure trash, or rather, impure trash.   *'New York Times'*

James Christopher

'An Evening with Gary Lineker' (1992) – Unfortunately, *An Evening with Gary Lineker* is about as meaningful as a night in with the Swiss Family Robinson . . . 90 spectacularly dull minutes.   *'Time Out'*

'Commercial Advertiser'

James A. Hernes' 'Sag Harbour' (1900) – It looks as if he had set about the construction of a popular drama with a certain local atmosphere, without having a story to tell, a character to present, or one strong mood to create; in short, without having anything to say.

Nick Curtis

'A Mad Dream' (1992) – Neither mad nor dreamy, but dull.   *'Time Out'*

Nicholas de Jongh

Tommy Steele's 'Some Like It Hot' (1992) – A team of top-level critics, several of them with reputations, swooped late last week on a London theatre. The crowd is believed to have come in search of the popular drug 'E' – better known as Entertainment. But supplies of the drug, which is known to induce intense feelings of pleasure, expressed in outbursts of uncontrollable laughter and the need to clap, ran out within minutes of the show's opening.   *'The Evening Standard'*

Walter P. Eaton

'Ben Hur' (1899) – A thing of bombastic rhetoric, inflated scenery, pasteboard piety, and mechanical excitement.

Jane Edwardes

'Moby Dick' (1992) – There have been many crimes committed in the name of entertainment, but no other show I have seen has been quite so willing to sacrifice plot, logic, character and coherence in favour of a fast giggle.   *'Time Out'*

'Some Singing Blood' (1992) – Thin-blooded rather than tuneful.   *'Time Out'*

Gentlewoman

Henrik Ibsen's 'Rosmersholm' (1891) – These Ibsen creatures are neither men nor women, they are ghouls.

Martin Gottfried

'Annie' (1977) – Greasepaint sentimentality . . . cheap nostalgia . . . mawkishness . . . unabashed corniness.   *'New York Post'*

Percy Hammond

Anonymous vaudeville act – They've played it so long that they can play it in their sleep, which yesterday they did.

'Getting Gertie's Garter' (1921) – There is no more interest in a garter as a naughty thing than there is in a virgin's wimple.
'New York Herald Tribune'

Arthur Hornblow

'The Gold Diggers' (1919) – A trivial hodge-podge of chorus girl slang, bedroom suggestiveness and false sentiment.   *'Theatre'*

Martin Hoyle

Robin Brown's 'Manslaughter' (1992) – The first night's proceeds went to Justice for Women. I await a benefit in aid of Anaesthetics for Critics.   *'The Times'*

Kenneth Hurren

Ronald Harwood's 'Reflected Glory' (1992) – Ronald Harwood's navel-contemplating introspection could bore a sensitive auditor into the floor.   *'Mail on Sunday'*

Henry James

Oscar Wilde's 'An Ideal Husband' – So helpless, so crude, so bad, so clumsy, feeble and vulgar.

Rick Jones

'Roadshow' (1992) – This play proves as vacuous an entertainment as its material [a radio station roadshow].   *'Time Out'*

'Ruby in the Dust' (1992) – Patrice Chaplin's play . . . like a doorway down-and-out, could do with some change.   *'Time Out'*

'Sikulu' (1992) – Interested agents might recommend a change of name. I recommend a change of play.   *'Time Out'*

'The Three Musketeers' (1992) – When the fighting stops there isn't much to the show. . . . The mind wanders during the limp love scenes and starts to muse on why musketeers don't use muskets and who might do well in the épée section at the Olympics.   *'Time Out'*

Adolph Klauber

'Today' (1913) – An indecent, vicious play.
'New York Times'

Rhoda Koenig

'The Pocket Dream' (1992) – A TV sketch of no freshness or art extended for a few hours, like a sausage that is half-cereal and half-donkey. Actually, the donkey's rear end could probably write a better show than this.
'Punch'

'Majdalany'

Alan Sillitoe's 'Saturday Night and Sunday Morning' – I still think that Mr Sillitoe, on the evidence of this film, has little to say except that a good wage, accessible sex, and a telly aren't everything. Any Sunday school teacher could have made the same point in fewer words.   *'Daily Mail' (1960)*

Ward Morehouse

'John Loves Mary' (1947) – Definitely of the manufactured variety and one for which there would be no second and third acts, if the simple truth had been told in the first.
'The Sun'

George J. Nathan

'Shanghai Gesture' (1926) – A pâté of box-office drivel.

'New Yorker'

Otto Harbach's 'The Cat and the Fiddle' (1931) – Mr Harbach has really outdone himself in banality.

'New York Sun'

G. B. Shaw's 'Mrs Warren's Profession' (1905) – A dramatized stench.

Benedict Nightingale

Dario Fo's 'The Pope and the Witch' (1992) –

Far too much jiggery-popery. *'The Times'* Heidi Thomas's 'Some Singing Blood' (1992) – We critics are used to finding bits of plays, sometimes quite large and long bits, pretty preposterous. But seldom before now have I spent an entire evening in a theatre believing nothing at all. . . . Why do Thomas and director Jules Wright ask us not so much to suspend disbelief as to hang, draw and quarter it? *'The Times'*

Dorothy Parker's 'Famous Mrs Fair' – It is almost impossible to discern just what the raving is about. *'New Yorker'*

'Pictorial World'
Henrik Ibsen's 'Hedda Gabler' (1891) – A bad escape of moral sewer-gas.

Michael Ratcliffe
Stage adaptation of Victor Hugo's 'Les Miserables' – Victor Hugo on the garbage.
'The Observer'

Frank Rich
David Merrick's 'Oh, Kay!' – If there is any serious doubt that David Merrick is one of the greatest showmen in Broadway history, it can be dispelled by the fact that his flops are as fabled as his hits. . . . This loose adaptation of the Gershwins' 1926 musical is a chintzy, innocuous slab of stock that is likely to leave more than a few theatre-goers shrugging their shoulders and asking, 'Didn't I doze through that a couple of summers ago in a barn?' *Oh, Kay!* can be labelled a Merrick enterprise only because of the size of his billing and the ubiquitousness of a shade of red that has been standard issue in all his productions since *Hello, Dolly!* Romantically or not, I would like to believe that the legendary showman, notoriously the toughest of audiences, is seeing another kind of red as he surveys the pallid entertainment to which he has unaccountably lent his name.
'New York Times' (1990)

[Rich made it clear that 'Oh, Kay!' was not just a one-man show; he also took exception to many others involved, including the leads – Angela Teek – ice-cold . . . strident of voice and mechanical of gesture – *and Brian Mitchell* – the robotic leading man.
Don Siretta – This choreographer seems to impose the same style on every show – even one as different from *Oh, Kay!* as *Pal Joey*, and one can fully expect to find tap dancers having a go at the *Ascot Gavotte* some day when *My Fair Lady* rolls off his assembly line. . . . *The critic continued his rich vein* – Don Siretta's opening and closing dance routines (and surely the word routine was coined to describe them). . . .
James Rachett (who adapted the original score) – has clumsily transported the libretto to an ersatz Jazz Age Harlem, with eye-popping gags and stereotypes that are less redolent of the Cotton Club than of *Amos 'n' Andy*.
In the same edition of the 'New York Times', Rich's fellow columnist Alex Witchel took David Merrick to task over his treatment of an actor in the show. In an attempt to hit back against the romantically linked columnists, Merrick took out an advert in the 'Times' – a large heart and relevant quotes from the critics . . . with his own by-line – At last, people are holding hands in the theatre again! To Frank and Alex – All My Love, David Merrick.
The 'Times' printed the advert, but quickly withdrew it, officially stating – The ad contained inappropriate personal references.
David Brown, another Broadway producer, agreed to a point – Absolutely. And some reviews should be pulled for inappropriate personal references.
The final word was left to David Merrick – This is war. Alex Witchel is the enemy. I feel sorry for Frank Rich.]

'Saturday Review'
Henrik Ibsen's 'The Master Builder' (1885) – Rather *The Master Bewilderer!*
Henrik Ibsen's 'Hedda Gabler' (1891) – Photographic studies of vice and morbidity.

G. B. Shaw
William Shakespeare's 'Julius Caesar' – It is impossible for even the most judicially minded critic to look without a revulsion of indignant contempt at this travestying of a great man as a silly braggart, whilst the pitiful gang of mischief-makers who destroyed him are lauded as statesmen and patriots. There is not a single sentence uttered by Shakespeare's Julius Caesar that is, I will not say worthy of him, but even worthy of an average Tammany boss. Brutus is nothing

but a familiar type of English suburban preacher; politically he would hardly impress the Thames Conservancy Board.

'Saturday Review' (1898)

Milton Shulman

Agatha Christie's 'The Mousetrap' – A tired, old-fashioned, obvious thriller. The mystery is no longer who-did-it but who still wants to see it.

Samuel Beckett's 'Waiting for Godot' (1956) – This is another of those plays that tries to lift superficiality to significance through obscurity. It should please those who prefer to have their clichés masquerading as epigrams.

Howard Taubman

'A Funny Thing Happened on the Way to the Forum' (1962) – Noisy, coarse, blue and obvious, like the putty on a burlesque comedian.

'Variety'

'Twentieth Century' (1932) – It's ominous when an audience leave a musical whistling the scenery.

Richard Watts Jnr

'Johnny Belinda' (1940) – Just trash!

'New York Herald Tribune'

Paula Webb

'My Mother Said I Never Should' (1992) – A badly paced production in need of 'more haste, less speed', as my mother used to say.

'Time Out'

Arthur Wimperis

An anonymous vaudeville show – My dear fellow, a unique evening! I wouldn't have left a turn unstoned.

Stark Young

'The Wingless Victory' (1936) – Semi-tosh from start to finish.

'New Republic'

DANCE

Dancing is in itself a very trifling, silly thing. It is one of those established follies to which people of good sense are sometimes obliged to conform.   *Lord Chesterfield*

Dancing is a very crude attempt to get into the rhythm of life.

G. B. Shaw – 'Back to Methuselah' (1921)

AEROBICS

Contrary to popular cable TV-induced opinion, aerobics have absolutely nothing to do with squeezing our body into hideous shiny Spandex, grinning like a deranged orang-utan, and doing cretinous dance steps to debauched disco music.

Cynthia Heimel – 'Sex Tips for Girls' (1983)

BALLET

My own personal reaction is that most ballets would be quite delightful if it were not for the dancing.   *Anon*

I had some ballet training. It was like a game to me.   *Fred Astaire*

I don't understand anything about the ballet. All I know is that during the intervals the ballerinas stink like horses.   *Anton Chekhov*

The regular and insatiable supporters of ballet are people too sluggish of intellect to listen to a play on the one hand, and too devoid of imagination to listen to fine music without accompanying action, on the other.

Alan Dent – 'News Chronicle' (1952)

Am I supposed to believe that a man prancing about at the Royal Ballet in a pair of tights is part of my heritage?   *Terry Dicks*

I am the enemy of ballet, which I look upon as false, absurd and outside the domain of art. I thank God that a cruel destiny did not inflict on me the career of a ballet dancer.

Isadora Duncan – 'My Life' (1928)

Although one may fail to find happiness in a theatrical life, one never wishes to give it up after having tasted its fruits. To enter the School of Imperial Ballet is to enter a convent where frivolity is banned, and where merciless discipline reigns.   *Anna Pavlova*

The ballet is simply a lewd performance.

Leo Tolstoy

The Bolshoi Ballet

In its glory days it was possible to call the Bolshoi over-the-top, even vulgar. . . . Now they are playing safe and falling flat. Most are like well-trained robots mechanically clocking their way through what should be an exhilarating evening.

Allen Robertson – 'Daily Mail' (1992)

Mikhail Baryshnikov

'Dancers' (1987) – A lot of ballet nonsense with Baryshnikov as a celebrated dancer who likes to play hide the salami with his leading ladies. *Nigel Floyd – 'Time Out'*

BALLROOM DANCING

A dreary, neuralgic cocktail of starch and Babycham set to music.

James Christopher – 'Time Out'

BREAKDANCING

'Electric Boogaloo' – In which the dancers move as if they had an electric current going through them – if only. *Julie Burchill*

'Breaking' in which athletic types perform as if they were having a molar drilled without novocaine while being simultaneously knee-capped . . . all to that disco beat.

Deborah Steels – 'Time Out' (1984)

THE TWIST

I'm not easily shocked, but the Twist shocked me – half-Negroid, half-Manhattan – and when you see it on its native heath, wholly frightening. I can't believe that London will ever go to quite these extremes – the essence of the Twist, the curiously perverted heart of it, is that you dance alone.

Beverley Nicholls (1962)

DANCERS

The Chippendales

If the girls in the audience think Chippendales mean sex, then there's a goldmine for gigolos in the heartlands of Ilford. *Lorelei Lee – 'Time Out' (1992)*

Isadora Duncan
'My Life' – She was no writer, God knows.

Her book is badly written, abominably written. There are passages of almost idiotic naïveté, and there are passages of horrendously flowery verbiage. There are veritable Hampton Court mazes of sentences. *Constant Reader [Dorothy Parker] – 'New Yorker' (1928)*

Maria Jahan

'That's Dancing' (1985) – The gymnastic gracelessness of flashdancer Maria Jahan.

Nigel Floyd

Ginger Rogers

When Ginger Rogers danced with Astaire, it was the first time in the movies when you looked at the man, not the woman. *Gene Kelly*

John Travolta

'That's Dancing' (1985) – The tight-trousered posturing of John Travolta. *Nigel Floyd*

CINEMA

GENERAL

Film business? I enjoy the film but the business is shit. *Oliver Stone (1987)*

TECHNICAL

Cinemascope

'Running Scared' (1972) – There seems to be something about the panoramic screen that seduces film-makers into filling it with irrelevant local colour and drawing the whole proceedings out to a length that matches its width. *Brenda Davies*

The wide screen will make bad films twice as bad. *Samuel Goldwyn*

It is a formula for a funeral or for snakes, but not for human beings. *Fritz Lang*

The worst shape ever devised. *Rouben Mamoulian*

Possessed by Dr DeLuxe, it made all films look like very cheap colour advertisements in magazines. *James Mason*

Cinemascope is a system that shows a Boa

Constrictor to better advantage than a man.
George Stevens

Colorisation of b/w movies

It's not colour, it's like pouring 40 tablespoons of sugary water over a roast.
John Huston (1986)

Set design

'Gone With the Wind' (1939) – The house that Rhett Butler built for Scarlett could have been in Omaha, so little does it resemble any dwelling in the Atlanta of the Reconstruction period.
Margaret Mitchell

Technicolor

I dislike Technicolor, in which all pinks resemble raspberry sauce, reds turn to sealing wax, blues shriek of the wash-tub, and yellows become suet pudding.
James Agate – 'Down Argentine Way' (1940)

How I hate Technicolor, which suffuses everything with stale mustard.
Edward Marsh (1965)

SCREENWRITERS

You can't tell a book by its movie.   *Anon*
[*The 'Los Angeles Times' had the following simile* – Never judge a book by a motion picture with the same title.]

In Hollywood, writers are considered only the first drafts of human beings. *Frank Deford*

American motion pictures are written by the half-educated for the half-witted.
Sir John Irving – 'New York Mirror' (1963)

A screenwriter is a man who is being tortured to confess and has nothing to confess.
Christopher Isherwood

We in this industry know that behind every successful screenwriter stands a woman. And behind that woman is his wife.
Groucho Marx

We used to wonder what had become of the authors of the old-fashioned dime novels till we began to read the subtitles in the movies.
'New York Tribune'

Screenwriters are a lot like little gypsies swimming in an aquarium filled with sharks, killer whales, squid, octopuses and other creatures of the deep. And plenty of squid shit.   *Joseph Wambaugh – 'Playboy' (1979)*

What is a writer but a schmuck with an Underwood?   *Jack Warner*

Anon

Listen, dear, you couldn't write f*** on a dusty venetian blind.   *Coral Brown*

Peter Baldwin, Ennio de Concini, Tonino Guerra, Julian Halevy and Cesare Zavattini

'A Place for Lovers' (1969) – The five scriptwriters who supposedly worked on this film must have spent enough time at the water-cooler to flood a camel.   *'Time'*

John O'Hara

When O'Hara is good he is very, very good; when he is bad he is writing for Hollywood – an exercise in tedium.
'New York Herald-Tribune' (1962)

Mel Tolkin

He looks like a stork that dropped a baby and broke it and is coming to explain to the parents.   *Mel Brooks*

Christopher Wood

'Rosie Dixon: Night Nurse' (1978) – Christopher Wood's screenplay is stamped with the Gold Seal of the Ancient Order of Most-Elementary British Scriptwriters.
John Pym – 'Time Out'

SOUNDTRACKS

Film music is like a small lump that you place below the screen to warm it.   *Aaron Copland*

Movie music is noise, even more painful than my sciatica.   *Sir Thomas Beecham (1958)*

A film musician is like a mortician – he can't bring the body back to life, but he's expected to make it look better.   *Alfred Deutsch*

No music has ever saved a good picture, but a lot of good pictures have saved a lot of bad music. *Jerry Goldsmith*

On leaving Twentieth Century Fox – I do not want to spend the rest of my life manufacturing music to be played while Debbie Reynolds speaks. *André Previn (1964)*

Film music should have the same relationship to the film drama that somebody's piano-playing in my living room has on the book I am reading. *Igor Stravinsky*

Larry Adler

'Genevieve' (1953) – It just isn't funny anymore; and Larry Adler's whining harmonica score only makes things worse.
Geoff Andrew – 'Time Out'

Burt Bacharach and Hal David

'Lost Horizon' (1973) – There are a dozen songs which are so pitifully pedestrian it's doubtful that they'd sound good even if the actors could sing, which they can't.
Arthur Cooper – 'Newsweek'

Neil Diamond

'Jonathan Livingstone Seagull' (1973) – Neil Diamond composed and sings an ear-splitting and stomach-turning score, its platitudes and decibels running abreast and amuck. *John Simon – 'Esquire'*

John Paul Jones

'Scream for Help' (1984) – Underscored by ex-Led Zep star John Paul Jones with a soundtrack so inappropriate as to be positively existential.
Anne Billson – 'Time Out'

Michel Legrand

'The Thomas Crown Affair' (1968) – The whole thing is as irritatingly meaningless as its Oscar-winning song, 'Windmills of My Mind', a sad product of its times.
Geoff Arnold – 'Time Out'

'The Thomas Crown Affair' (1968) – Michel Legrand's haunting but inappropriate 'Windmills of My Mind' endlessly going round and round. *Angela and Elkan Allan*

Ennio Morricone

'A Fistful of Dollars' (1964) – The music sounded like a mixture of Puccini, Roderigo and Duane Eddy recorded in a bathroom.
Christopher Frayling –
'Viva Leone' (BBC TV, 1989)

'Moment by Moment' (1978) – Ostensibly a vehicle for John Travolta . . . accompanied by some of the worst easy-listening muzak LA could dredge up. Yuk. *'Time Out'*

HOLLYWOOD

The only community in the world where the entire population is suffering from rumourtism. *Anon*

Malice in Wonderland. *Anon*

Siberia with palms. *Anon*

Paradise with a lobotomy. *Anon*

The place where girls go to look for husbands and husbands look for girls. *Anon*

Where the average actor has more lines in his face than in his script. *Anon*

There is nothing wrong with Hollywood that six first-class funerals wouldn't solve. *Anon*

Here there are two types of people – those who own their own swimming pools and those who can't keep their heads above water. *Anon*

In Hollywood you can be forgotten while you're out of the room going to the toilet.
Anon

A Hollywood actress is always talking about her last picture or her next husband. *Anon*

A Hollywood marriage is one in which the couple vow to be faithful until after the honeymoon. *Anon*

Hollywood buys a good story about a bad girl and turns it into a bad story about a good girl. *Anon*

A Hollywood aristocrat is anyone who can trace his ancestry back to his father. *Anon*

Where today's stand-outs are tomorrow's
stand-ins.   *Anon*

In Hollywood, it's not who you know, it's
who you yes!   *Anon*

Never buy anything in Hollywood that you
can't put on the Chief.   *Hollywood saying*
[The 'Chief' was the railroad cut out of L.A.]

In Hollywood the eternal triangle consists of
an actor, his wife and himself.
                              Hollywood saying

A place where people from Iowa mistake
each other for movie stars.   *Fred Allen*

You can take all the sincerity in Hollywood,
place it in the navel of a fruit fly and still have
room for three caraway seeds and a
producer's heart.   *Fred Allen*

An Associate Producer is the only guy in
Hollywood who will associate with a
Producer.   *Fred Allen*

Hollywood is like being nowhere and talking
to nobody about nothing.
  Michelangelo Antonioni – 'The Sunday Times'
                                      (1971)

The home of furs and Ferraris, glitter and
glamour, the places where movie stars can be
spotted in palm-fringed cafés, and where
limousines are as frequent as *Rocky* sequels.
  Scott Armstrong – 'Christian Science Monitor'
                                      (1986)

This is a back-stabbing, scum-sucking, small-
minded town.
  Roseanne Barr – 'Hollywood Reporter' (1990)

The people here are not so much evil as
simply children. They do not have a parent
setting values. There are no leaders.
Everyone is nervous and uncertain.
                              Rona Barrett

The people are unreal. The flowers are
unreal, they don't smell. The fruit is unreal, it
doesn't taste of anything. The whole place is
a glaring, gaudy, nightmarish set, built up in
the desert.   *Ethel Barrymore (1932)*

It looks, it feels, as though it had been
invented by a Sixth Avenue peepshow man.
                            Ethel Barrymore

A place where great-grandmothers dread to
grow old.   *Phyllis Batelli*

What I like about Hollywood is that one can
get along by knowing two words of English –
swell and lousy.   *Vicki Baum*

Of all the Christbitten places in the two
hemispheres, this is the last curly kink in the
pig's tail.   *Stephen V. Benet*

Hollywood is like Picasso's bathroom.
                            Candice Bergen

Hollywood is full of genius. And all it lacks is
talent.   *Henri Bernstein*

I came out here with one suit and everybody
said I looked like a bum. Twenty years later
Marlon Brando came out with only a sweat
shirt and the town drooled over him. That
shows how much Hollywood has progressed.
                            Humphrey Bogart

A cultural boneyard.   *Marlon Brando*

Hollywood is a chain gang and we lose the
will to escape. The links of the chain are not
forged with cruelties but with luxuries.
                          Clive Brook (1933)

To survive there, you need the ambition of a
Latin-American revolutionary, the ego of a
grand opera tenor, and the physical stamina
of a cow pony.   *Billy Burke*

There is one word which aptly describes
Hollywood – nervous.   *Frank Capra*

What Hollywood seems to want is a writer
who is ready to commit suicide in every story
conference. What it actually gets is a fellow
who screams like a stallion in heat and then
cuts his throat with a banana.
                          Raymond Chandler

A village of tasteless producers and scentless
flowers, controlled by frightened little men
armed with buckets of sand to extinguish any

fires of creative originality that might break out. *Art Cohn*

Hollywood grew to be the most flourishing factory of popular mythology since the Greeks. *Alistair Cooke – 'America' (1973)*

Living in Hollywood is like living in a lit cigar butt. *Phyllis Diller (1970)*

I'm plenty proud of Hollywood. I say if you want to grow a plant, put it where there's some good horseshit around to grow it in. *Kirk Douglas – 'Esquire' (1970)*

Hollywood is the only place where you can fail upwards. *John G. Dunne*

On being asked to describe Hollywood – Can a fish describe the murky water in which it swims? *Albert Einstein*

I can match bottoms with anyone in Hollywood. *Mia Farrow*

The only place in the world where a man can get stabbed in the back while climbing a ladder. *William Faulkner*

I've been asked if I ever get the DTs. I don't know; it's hard to tell where Hollywood ends and the DTs begin. *W. C. Fields*

You can't find true affection in Hollywood because everyone does the fake affection so well. *Carrie Fisher*

A mining-camp in lotus land. *F. Scott Fitzgerald*

Life in the big 'H' – We were like pawns in a game of chess; we were permitted to move in only one direction. Only queens could move in all directions. *Geraldine Fitzgerald*

They've got great respect for the dead in Hollywood, but none for the living. *Errol Flynn*

Hollywood's wonderful – they pay you for making love. *Jane Fonda*

Working in Hollywood does give one a

certain expertise in the field of prostitution. *Jane Fonda*

Life is not Hollywood. *Jane Fonda*

I call it Hollyweird. A fickle town, without rhyme or reason. *Frederic Forrest (1980)*

Hollywood is like a World's Fair that's been up a year too long. *Sonny Fox*

Hollywood is the only place where you can wake up in the morning and hear the birds coughing in the trees. *Joe Frisco*

People in Hollywood are not showmen, they're maintenance men, pandering to what they think their audiences want. *Terry Gilliam – 'Time' (1986)*

Hollywood is an emotional Detroit. *Lillian Gish*

Hollywood is now a place to retire. *Paulette Goddard*

Hollywood is too much publicised. There are too many people here. Some of them should go back on a slow train. *Samuel Goldwyn*

A world of dwarfs casting long shadows. *Sheila Graham*

No one has a closest friend in Hollywood. *Sheila Graham (1964)*

Hollywood directors go around with a chip on their shoulder – which is a true indication of wood a little higher up. *Texas Guinan*

Hollywood sounds like something for a Christmas decoration – but it's just Western for poison ivy. *Texas Guinan*

On the nickname 'Tinseltown' – From the German verb 'tinzelle' – literally, 'to book a turkey into 1200 theatres and make one's money before word of mouth hits'. *Charlie Haas – 'People' (1987)*

God felt sorry for actors, so he gave them a place in the sun with a swimming pool. The price they had to pay was to surrender their talent. *Cedric Hardwicke*

The most beautiful slave-quarters in the world. *Moss Hart*

The most boss-ridden town in the world. *Ben Hecht*

I am a Hollywood writer; so I put on my sports jacket and take off my brain. *Ben Hecht*

Hollywood held the lure – tremendous sums of money for work that required no more effort than a game of pinochle. *Ben Hecht*

People's sex habits are as well known in Hollywood as their political opinions, and much less criticised. *Ben Hecht – 'New York Mirror' (1959)*

Good evening, ladies and gentlemen – and welcome to darkest Hollywood. Night brings a stillness to the jungle. It is so quiet you can hear a name drop. The savage beasts have already begun gathering at the waterholes to quench their thirst. Now one should be especially alert. The vicious table-hopper is on the prowl and the spotted back-biter may lurk behind a potted palm. *Alfred Hitchcock*

There'll always be an England, even if it's in Hollywood. *Bob Hope*

In Hollywood, gratitude is Public Enemy Number One. *Hedda Hopper*

Our town worships success, the bitch goddess whose smile hides a taste for blood. *Hedda Hopper*

Hollywood is simply geared to cheat you left, right and bloody centre. *John Hurt (1986)*

Hollywood has always been a cage; a cage to catch our dreams. *John Huston*

Thought is barred in this terrible City of Dreadful Joy, and conversation is unknown. *Aldous Huxley*

Hollywood is a locality where people without reputation try to live up to it. *Tom Jenk*

The title 'Little Napoleon' in Hollywood is equivalent to the title 'Mister' in any other community. *Nunnally Johnson*

In Hollywood, I played poker with the film magnates. I played for about a minute because they regard ten thousand dollars as tissue paper. *Al Jolson*

If somewhere in the Hollywood entertainment-world someone has managed to break through with something that speaks to you, then it isn't all corruption. *Pauline Kael*

You never meet anyone in Hollywood without an appointment. *Grace Kelly*

After his novel 'Seven Days in May' had been turned into a movie – Hollywood is the place where they take an author's steak tartare and make cheeseburger out of it. *Fletcher Knebel (1963)*

Living in Hollywood is marvellous. The general sensation is like slowly sinking into a giant hopper of warm farina. *Harry Kurnitz*

If you want to be successful in Hollywood, be sure and go to New York. *Bert Lahr*

I am a Hollywood creation. Hollywood is good at doing that sort of thing. *Veronica Lake*

In Hollywood blood is thicker than talent. *Joe Laurie Jr*

Strip away the phoney tinsel of Hollywood and you find the real tinsel underneath. *Oscar Levant*

Anybody in Hollywood who has her appendix and tonsils is a doctor. *Carole Lombard*

Hollywood is where they write the alibis before they write the story. *Carole Lombard*

Cary Grant, born Archie Leach, was a poor boy who could barely spell 'posh'. That's

acting for you – or maybe Hollywood.
Melvin Maddocks –
'Christian Science Monitor' (1986)

A cultural desert. *Maurice Maeterlinck*

Hollywood is not uncivilised. It is decivilised.
Patrick Mahony

Hollywood is a town where inferior people have a way of making superior people feel inferior. *D. F. Malone*

In Hollywood, brides keep the bouquets and throw away the groom. *Groucho Marx*

Hollywood provided the sort of luxury that only exists today for the sons of Latin-American dictators. *Groucho Marx*

In Hollywood, the women are all peaches. It makes one long for an apple occasionally.
W. Somerset Maugham –
'Diners Club Magazine' (1964)

This place is the true and original arse-hole of creation. The movie dogs, compared with the rest of the population, actually seem like an ancient Italian noblesse. *H. L. Mencken*

Just outside pious Los Angeles, a colony of moving picture actors. Its morals are those of Port Said.
H. L. Mencken – 'Americana' (1925)

Over in Hollywood they almost made a great picture, but they caught it in time.
Wilson Mizner

Hollywood is a carnival with no concessions.
Wilson Mizner

Hollywood is a sewer with service from the Ritz-Carlton. *Wilson Mizner*

I've spent many years in Hollywood, and I still think the movie heroes are in the audience. *Wilson Mizner*

Hollywood is a trip through a sewer in a glass-bottomed boat. *Wilson Mizner*

A sunny place for shady people.
Ferenc Molnar

Hollywood's a place where they'll pay you a thousand dollars for a kiss and fifty cents for your soul. *Marilyn Monroe*

When you're a failure in Hollywood – that's like starving to death outside a banquet hall with the smells of filet mignon driving you crazy. *Marilyn Monroe*

A place where you spend more than you make, on things you don't want, to impress people you don't like. *Ken Murray*

Ten million dollars' worth of intricate machinery functioning elaborately to put skin on baloney. *George Jean Nathan*

Hollywood has gone from Pola to Polaroid.
Pola Negri

Writers, being human and usually broke, scented the easy money to be picked up in Hollywood. *David Niven*

Kenya – along with Hollywood Boulevard – boasts one of the main animal crossings in the world.
Carol and Neil Offen – 'Esquire' (1986)

I guess Hollywood won't consider me anything except a cold potato until I divorce my husband, give my baby away, and get my name and photograph in all the newspapers.
Maureen O'Hara

The only 'ism' Hollywood believes in is plagiarism. *Dorothy Parker*

The city of dreadful day. *S. J. Perelman*

A dreary industrial town controlled by hoodlums of enormous wealth, the ethical sense of a pack of jackals and taste so degraded that it befouled everything it touched.
S. J. Perelman – 'Paris Review' (1964)

Hollywood is one big whore. It breeds decadence. *Freddie Prinze*

In Europe an actor is an artist. In Hollywood, if he isn't acting, he's a bum.
Anthony Quinn

Hollywood is not a geographical location; it was a fate worse than *The Reader's Digest*.
Frederic Raphael (1985)

Nobody goes Hollywood – they were that way before they came here. Hollywood just exposed it. *Ronald Reagan*

I look upon going to Hollywood as a mission behind enemy lines. You parachute in, set up the explosion, then fly out before it goes off.
Robert Redford

In Hollywood, if you don't have happiness, you send out for it. *Rex Reed*

Hollywood is like an empty wastepaper basket. *Ginger Rogers*

Hollywood is a great place. I mean great like a sausage factory with lots of systems that turn out fine sausages. In Italy I have no sausages but I have freedom.
Roberto Rossellini

On the formation of United Artists – The lunatics have taken over the asylum.
Richard Rowlands (1919)

In a capital of atheism, like Hollywood, what can a man believe in? *Joseph M. Schenk*

Hollywood is an extraordinary kind of temporary place. *John Schlesinger*

Nothing in Hollywood is permanent. Once photographed, life here is ended.
David O. Selznick

Hollywood's like Egypt, full of crumbling pyramids. It'll never come back. It'll just keep on crumbling until finally the wind blows the last studio props across the sands.
David O. Selznick

They know only one word of more than one syllable here, and that's fillum.
Louis Sherwin

Too many freeways, too much sun, too much abnormality taken normally, too many pink stucco houses and pink stucco consciences. *Clancy Sigal*

The only way to be a success here is to be as obnoxious as the next guy. *Sylvester Stallone*

Hollywood stands in the way of much that a film might be. *Charles Stepman*

Hollywood is a community of lonely people searching for even the most basic kind of stimulation in their otherwise mundane lives.
Rod Steiger

The only way to avoid Hollywood is to live there. *Igor Stravinsky*

Hollywood is loneliness beside the swimming pool. *Liv Ullman*

I love Hollywood. Everybody's plastic. I want to be plastic. *Andy Warhol*

Whatever goes into the Hollywood grist mill, it comes out the same way. It is a meat-grinder that will take beef and suet, pheasant and turnips, attar of roses and limburger and turn it all into the same kind of hash that has served so many so well for so long.
Herman Weinberg

Hollywood studios are nothing but Ramada Inns; you rent space, you shoot and out you go. *Billy Wilder*

I never stayed longer than six weeks in Hollywood. Corruption begins on the morning of the seventh week.
Thornton Wilder

A combination of Heaven, Hell and a lunatic asylum. *Albert William*

Where they shoot too many pictures and not enough actors. *Walter Winchell*

Where they place you under contract instead of observation. *Walter Winchell*

A town that has to be seen to be disbelieved.
Walter Winchell

On 'A Song to Remember' (1940), a biopic of Frédéric Chopin – It is the business of Hollywood to shape the truth into box -office contours. *Richard Winnington*

In Hollywood all marriages are happy. It's trying to live together afterwards that causes problems. *Shelley Winters*

A rotten gold-plated sewer of a town. *James Woods*

Hollywood is divided into two groups. Those who do cocaine and those who don't. *Terence Young*

CANNES FILM FESTIVAL

In Cannes, a producer is what any man calls himself if he owns a suit, a tie, and hasn't recently been employed as a pimp. *Anon*

What is Cannes? It is 10,000 people looking for the 10 people who really count. The 10,000 storm around trying to see the 10. They boast if they have seen them, keep it a secret if they haven't and try to give the impression that they know where they are, even if they don't. *French publicity officer*

My idea of hell. *Dirk Bogarde (1975)*

Butlins-on-acid. *Frank Clarke (1988)*

'Another Country' – Inevitably it went down well at the Cannes Film Festival, where movies critical of their own country's shortcomings are always favoured.
Margaret Hinxman – 'The Daily Mail' (1984)

It's like a fire in a brothel during a fire. *Eldar Riazanov*

DIRECTORS AND PRODUCERS

Most studio moguls would be selling cars if it weren't for the nepotism in Hollywood – used cars that don't run.
Joseph Wambaugh (1980)

I have worked with so many English-speaking directors who didn't know what the f*** they were talking about.
Tom Conti (1983)

Movie studio chief – He's the only man I ever knew who had rubber pockets so he could steal soup. *Wilson Mizner*

Woody Allen
His Kraft is Ebing. *Margot Kernan (1984)*

I have never been a fan of Woody Allen's. I'm sorry. Somebody closed the door on me there. I've never been able to appreciate his humour. I find him neurotic. *George C. Scott*

Lindsay Anderson
He's a prime example of somebody who, once he has created something, tries to support it with a scaffolding of theory. But it's all rubbish: either it's worked or it hasn't. *Tony Richardson*

Michelangelo Antonioni
'Zabriskie Point' (1970) – Although Mr Antonioni spent months travelling the country to research his film, he probably could have obtained the same insights by watching prime-time American television for one week at St Regis Hotel and then shooting the entire film in Spain.
Vincent Canby – 'New York Times'

One of my most unfavourite directors, because he tells the same story all the time in the same style. To me he is like a fly that tries to go out of a window and doesn't realise there is glass, and keeps banging against it, and never reaches the sky. *Franco Zeffirelli*

Clive Barker
'Nightbreed' (1990) – Barker calls his shambolic, uninvolving narrative 'scattershot': put less kindly, it's as explosive and directionless as a blunderbuss.
Nigel Floyd – 'Time Out'

Bernardo Bertolucci
A mere alert dung beetle. *John Simon (1965)*

Peter Bogdanovich
Peter wanted to do *The Long Goodbye* . . . the way he does all of his films, as a photostat of other films. *Robert Altman*

'Nickelodeon' (1976) – To make a clinker out of a gift of a subject like silent movie-making is some feat, yet Bogdanovich does it with honours. *Chris Peachment – 'Time Out'*

'Saint Jack' (1979) – Hard to imagine how

anyone could make less of such a promising subject. *'Time Out'*

John Boorman

'Where the Heart Is' (1990) – It's an established law of nature that when John Boorman goes off the deep end, he really, really, goes off the deep end. This chaotic allegorical farce . . . plays like a cross between a sitcom and a brain seizure.

Owen Gleiberman –
'Entertainment Weekly' (1990)

Mel Brooks

The death of Hollywood is Mel Brooks and special effects. If Mel Brooks had come up in my time he wouldn't have qualified to be a busboy. *Joseph L. Mankiewicz*

John Cassavetes

'Big Trouble' (1986) – It looks as if Cassavetes merely wanted a) to prove he could make a blandly stylish commercial piece, and b) the cash. *Geoff Andrew – 'Time Out'*

As a director, too much of the time he is groping when he should be gripping.
Andrew Sarris (1968)

William Castle

'The Chance of a Lifetime' – Definitely one that Castle built in the air. He has sorely missed the chance of HIS lifetime. *Anon*

'The Chance of a Lifetime' – William Castle, in his directorial debut, proves he is totally unfit to handle a motion picture – any picture.
'The Hollywood Reporter'

Michael Cimino

'Heaven's Gate' (1980) – It fails so completely that you might suspect Michael Cimino sold his soul to the devil to obtain the success of *The Deer Hunter*, and the devil has just come around to collect.

Vincent Canby –
'New York Times'

'The Year of the Dragon' (1985) – A movie that is often so inept it's funny – Mike, have you thought of driving a bus or becoming a piano-tuner or otherwise doing something useful? *Ralph Novak*

Robert Clouse

'Golden Needles' (1974) – Clouse once again proves himself one of the least competent directors around.

Verina Glaessner – 'Time Out'

David Cohen

'The Pleasure Principle' (1992) – An unprincipled sex romp that plays like an amateur episode of *Confessions of a Medical Journalist*. . . . Cohen borrowed the budget from his bank, thereby setting back the cause of British film finance by a couple of decades. *Iain Johnstone – 'The Sunday Times'*

Harry Cohn

You had to stand in line just to hate him.
Hedda Hopper

He liked to be the biggest bug in the manure pile. *Elia Kazan*

Francis Ford Coppola

Coppola couldn't piss in a pot. *Bob Hoskins*

Whatever Francis does for you always ends up benefiting Francis the most.
George Lucas

He is his own worst enemy. If he directs a little romance, it has to be the biggest, most overdone little romance in movie history.
Kenneth Turan

David Cronenberg

In 1975 I started to wonder what this David Cronenberg cult could've looked like: thick glasses, runny noses, celibate since birth and probably Communists for all we knew.
Martin Scorsese (1983)

George Cukor

'The Blue Bird' (1976) – A desperately pedestrian, hideously glitzy version of Maeterlinck's delicate fantasy. . . . You'd never believe in a month of Sundays that Cukor directed it. *Tom Milne – 'Time Out'*

Michael Curtiz

Jean Negulesco always reminds me of Michael Curtiz on toast. Mr Curtiz, in turn, has always seemed like Franz Murnau under onions. *James Agee*

Boaz Davidson

'The Last American Virgin' (1982) – *Puberty Blues* and *Porky's* look positively progressive beside such sickening junk. Boaz should stick to sucking popsicles.

Sheila Johnston – *'Time Out'*

[N.B. *In 1977, Davidson directed 'Lemon Popsicle'.*]

Cecil B. de Mille

That B. could stand for many things – Barnum, Ballyhoo, Box-Office, Baloney, Billion dollars. But, prosaically enough, it stands for Blount.

Norah Alexander

An American Benito Mussolini.

Charles Bickford

'Cleopatra' (1934) – I like to see fifty horse-drawn chariots coming at me head-on with a great clatter of coconut shells. . . . Whatever else he may be, he is grandiose. What a boon he would be to the Roosevelt administration and the New Deal, if they would only make him the Secretary of Extravagance.

Don Herold – *'Life Magazine' (1934)*

He made small-minded pictures on a big scale.

Pauline Kael

Cecil B. de Mille
Much against his will
Was persuaded to leave Moses
Out of the War of the Roses.

Caroline A. Lejeune

'Samson and Delilah' (1949) – Perhaps de Mille's survival is due to the fact that he decided in his movie nonage to ally himself with God as his co-maker and get his scripts from the Bible, which he has always handled with the proprietary air of a gentleman fondling old love letters. *'New Yorker'*

Nothing in his distinguished career persuades me that the movies are any the better for it and I am quite willing to uphold the contrary.

Gilbert Seldes – *'The Seven Lively Arts'*

Vittorio de Sica

'A Place for Lovers' (1969) – Even a director who had made no movies would have a hard time making one as bad as this.

Roger Ebert – *'Chicago Sun-Times'*

Stan Dragoti

'She's Out of Control' (1989) – Dragoti's dire, dishonest, seldom humorous social comedy has all the nauseating hallmarks of a big-budget sitcom.

Wally Hammond – *'Time Out'*

Blake Edwards

'A Fine Mess' (1986) – Clever of Blake Edwards to review his frenetic comedy in the title. *Don Atyeo* – *'Time Out'*

A man of many talents – all of them minor.

Leslie Halliwell

Federico Fellini

'The Voice of the Moon' (1989) – A noisome, sprawling slab of pretentious nonsense . . . embarrassingly self-indulgent, it is virtually unwatchable. *Geoff Andrew* – *'Time Out'*

Richard Fleischer

'Mr Majestyk' (1974) – Fleischer handles a heavy script and most of the acting like no one should handle a melon.

Micheline Victor – *'Time Out'*

Bryan Forbes

'Deadfall' (1968)
Q. When is a thriller not a thriller?
A. When it's a Forbes.

Adrian Turner – *'Time Out'*

He perpetually pursues the anticliché only to arrive at anticlimax. *Andrew Sarris (1968)*

John Ford

John is half-tyrant, half-revolutionary; half-saint, half-satan; half-possible, half-impossible; half-genius, half-Irish.

Frank Capra

John Frankenheimer

'Year of the Gun' (1992) – Frankenheimer kneecaps himself.

Brian Case – *'Time Out'*

He went from boy-wonder to has-been without ever passing through the stage of maturity. *Neil Sinyard*

DRAMATIC

William Friedkin
'Cruising' (1980) – Friedkin – like Coppola – has always had difficulty with endings; this one is arbitrary – it's as if he just gave up.

David Pirie – 'Time Out'

Jean-Luc Godard
'King Lear' (1987) – Another of his essays on the impossibility of making movies in our time, this has all the dreariness of a pathologist's dictated notes.

Wally Hammond – 'Time Out'

Since Godard's films have nothing to say, we could perhaps have ninety minutes of silence instead of each of them.   *John Simon*

'Nouvelle Vague' (1990) – Stillborn stuff from a former enfant terrible, who seems to be suffering from terminal regression, it is vague rather than nouvelle.

Geoff Andrew – 'Time Out'

Samuel Goldwyn
He filled the room with a wonderful panic and beat your mind like a man in front of a slot-machine, shaking it for the jackpot.

Ben Hecht

He created a caricature of himself, and then wore it as a disguise.   *Benjamin Sonnenberg*

Lew Grade
'Saturn 3' (1980) – Just another miserable muddle from the Lew Grade empire; there's more fun to be had cleaning out your cat litter tray.   *Frances Lass – 'Time Out'*

Larry Hagman
'Son of Blob' (1971) – The Blob has now been pasteurized from a blood-streaked slime into a pinkly healthy jelly which carries about it as much threat as a weight-watcher's breakfast. It moves sluggishly, but is easily beaten at its game by Larry Hagman's laboured direction.

Tom Milne

Curtis Hanson
'The Hand that Rocks the Cradle' (1992) – Hanson treats a stalk 'n' slash night like a bring 'n' buy sale.

Anthony Lane –
'Independent on Sunday'

Dennis Hopper
'The Last Movie' (1971) – The work of a kid playing with a toy.

Joseph Gelmis – 'Newsday'

Hugh Hudson
'Revolution' (1985) – It's the first 70mm film that looks as if it was shot hand-held on 16mm and blown up for the big screen. Director? I didn't catch the credits. Was there one?   *Tony Rayns – 'Time Out'*

John Irvin
'Next of Kin' (1989) – Together with Hamburger Hill, this illustrates that Irvin probably couldn't stage an action scene if you held a gun to his head.

Nigel Floyd – 'Time Out'

Just Jaeckin
'Madame Claude' (1976) – Jaeckin, the man to blame for initiating the deadly rash of 'Emmanuelliana', has a knack for making movies in which sex appears about as much fun as a trip to the launderette.

Paul Taylor – 'Time Out'

Charles Jarrott
'Lost Horizon' (1972) – The narrative has no energy, and the pauses for pedagogic songs are so awkward you feel the director's wheelchair needs oiling.   *Pauline Kael*

Stanley Kramer
'Guess Who's Coming to Dinner?' (1967) – A wishy-washy, sanctimonious plea for tolerance, directed with Kramer's customary verbosity and stodginess.

Geoff Andrew – 'Time Out'

Stanley Kubrick
His tragedy may have been that he was hailed as a great artist before he had become a competent craftsman. However, it is more likely that he has chosen to exploit the giddiness of middlebrow audiences on the satiric level of *Mad* magazine.

Andrew Sarris (1968)

Carl Laemmle
The prototype of the slightly mad movie mogul – impulsive, quixotic, intrepid, unorthodox, unpredictable.   *Norman Zierold*

Sheldon Lettich
'Double Impact' (1992) – Sheldon Lettich
directs with the limpness you associate with
the vegetable he's nearly named after.
Jonathan Romney – 'Time Out'

Ben Levin
*'The Favour, the Watch and the Very Big Fish'
(1992)* – According to the press blurb,
Levin's humour combines 'doomed Polish
Romanticism and laconic Anglo-Australian
jokiness'. Something has been lost in the
translation.
Colette Maude – 'Time Out'

Joseph Losey
A versatile director who commands a wide
range of styles for wrecking a movie.
Dwight Macdonald

George Lucas
Like all the so-called movie brats, he bears an
unfortunate resemblance to Charles Manson.
Julie Burchill

Sidney Lumet
'Murder on the Orient Express' (1974) – Lumet
ensures a smooth ride, but as usual takes too
long to say what he means and brings the
Express in 20 minutes late.
Chris Peachment – 'Time Out'

'The Morning After' (1986) – It's as if a
talented director has made the most of what
he had, when what he had was never quite
enough. *Nigel Floyd – 'Time Out'*

Adrian Lynn
'Jacob's Ladder' (1990) – Lynn directs like a
sadistic psychiatrist under contract to MTV.
*Owen Gleiberman –
'Entertainment Weekly' (1990)*

Peter Markle
'Youngblood' (1986) – Rob Lowe's
performance is quite decent, and he cannot
be blamed for the puerile humour of a
director who considers putting false teeth
into someone's beer to be a good joke.
Tim Rivers

Louis B. Mayer
A hard-faced, badly-spoken, crass little man

. . . had the glibness of a self-taught evangelist.
Charles Bickford

So many people came to his funeral because
they wanted to make sure the S.O.B. was
dead. *Sam Goldwyn*

He has the memory of an elephant and the
hide of an elephant. The only difference is
that elephants are vegetarians and Mayer's
diet is his fellow man.
Herman J. Mankiewicz

Csar of all the rushes. *Budd Schulberg*

Paul Mazursky
'Scenes from a Mall' (1990) – Thematically,
the film comes over as a piss-take of
Mazursky by Mazursky. *Wally Hammond –
'Time Out'*

George Miller
'Les Patterson Saves the World' (1987) – The
plot is a shotgun wedding of *Carry On Follow
That Camel* with those ropey James Coburn
spy comedies from the '60s. . . . The director
is not George 'Mad Max' Miller but a
namesake who should be occluding dental
cavities in Moonnee Ponds.
Don Atyeo – 'Time Out'

Alan Parker
'Birdy' (1984) – A trifle self-indulgent – well,
it is directed by Alan Parker.
Colin Shearman – 'Time Out'

Sam Peckinpah
He is like an old dog you sometimes have to
apologise for. *Kris Kristofferson*

'Bring Me the Head of Alfredo Garcia' (1974) –
Peckinpah clearly doesn't lack talent – what
he lacks is brains. *John Simon*

Sydney Pollack
'Bobby Deerfield' (1977) – A classic example
of a Hollywood director being struck down
by a lethal 'art' attack as soon as he sets foot
in Europe . . . making the characters and
settings into something very like a prolonged
Martini ad. *David Pirie – 'Time Out'*

Otto Preminger
He's a horrible man, phew! But who ever

hears of him anymore? Is he dead?
Dyan Cannon

I'd never make another film, rather than work for Otto Preminger again. I don't think he could direct his nephew to the bathroom.
Dyan Cannon (1972)

I thank God that neither I nor any member of my family will ever be so hard up that we have to work for Otto Preminger.
Lana Turner

He's really Martin Bormann in elevator shoes, with a face-lift by a blindfolded plastic surgeon in Luxembourg. *Billy Wilder*

I hear Otto's on holiday – in Auschwitz.
Billy Wilder

David Puttnam
Whenever you work with David you have a fairly aggressive and bloody time. You could never do two films in a row with him. You have to go and bathe your wounds in between. *Michael Apted*

Satyajit Ray
'Pather Panchali' (1955) – . . . so amateurish that it would barely pass for a rough cut in Hollywood. *'New York Times'*

Carol Reed
His career demonstrates that a director who limits himself to solving technical problems quickly lapses into the decadence of the inappropriate effect. *Andrew Sarris (1968)*

Tony Richardson
'The Border' (1981) – A Tex-Mex stew that looks to have all the right spicy ingredients [Jack Nicholson, Harvey Keitel and Warren Oates], but emerges under gringo chef Richardson as not exactly indigestible, merely flavourless. *Paul Taylor – 'Time Out'*

Matthew Robbins
'Batteries Not Included' (1987) – Robbins' handling of the human element is as sickly and soggy as a dunked doughnut.
Elaine Paterson – 'Time Out'

Nicholas Roeg
Nothing in Roeg's style appears to be spontaneous, it's all artifice and technique . . . like an entertainment for bomb victims.
Pauline Kael

Robert Rossen
'Alexander the Great' (1956) – Rossen has aimed for greatness and lost honourably.
Andrew Sarris

Ken Russell
'Salome's Last Dance' (1987) – Russell's customary irreverence a matter of flatulent, leering, Carry On-style humour, the decor sub-Beardsley, the whole thing redolent of a retarded pornographer's revue.
Geoff Arnold – 'Time Out'

The film director who now specialises in vulgar travesties of the lives of dead composers. *Nicholas de Jongh*

His originality these days seems to consist of disguising the banal behind a barrage of garish, distorted, noisy and fleeting images looted from every juvenile fantasy from Rider Haggard to Superman, with nods to Dali and Bosch, and strong tincture of Kubrick.
'The Sunday Times'

Mike Sarne
'Myra Breckenridge' (1970) – As an adaptation of Gore Vidal's novel, this is a major travesty. As a Hollywood comedy, it's a major disaster. As a 20th Century-Fox movie, it's the best argument yet for employing a director who can direct.
Tony Rayns – 'Time Out'

He looks like a wolf with rabies.
Rex Reed (1970)

Dore Schary
A man whose few successes were even more distasteful than his many failures. *John Simon*

Joel Schumacher
'The Lost Boys' (1987) – Directed with a cavalier disregard for intelligibility, this has to be one of the most anaemic vampire flicks ever made. *Nigel Floyd – 'Time Out'*

George Seaton
'Airport' (1969) – George Seaton wrote and

directed *Airport*. There are times when he could have done with a following wind.
Alexander Walker

David O. Selznick
A typical Hollywood combination of oafishness and sophistication.
John Houseman

Selznick stormed through life demanding to see the manager. *Lloyd Shearer*

Spyros Skouras *(1893–1971)* – *President of 20th Century-Fox*
The only Greek tragedy I know.
Billy Wilder

Robert Sparr
'A Swingin' Summer' (1965) – Given the director's obsession with bikini bottoms, this really is the arse-end of the beach movie cycle. *Paul Taylor – 'Time Out'*

Steven Spielberg
Spielberg isn't a film-maker, he's a confectioner. *Alex Cox*

The poet of junk-food and pop-culture.
Sheila Johnston

Robert Stigwood
The Robert Stigwood Organisation is to the cinema what McDonald's is to cuisine.
David Shipman

Oliver Stone
'The Hand' (1981) – Anyone having seen *Salvador* and *Platoon* who thinks that Oliver Stone is the best thing since sliced bread would do well not only to remember his scripts for *Midnight Express* and *Year of the Dragon*, but to catch this grotesque, unimaginative fiasco.
Geoff Andrew – 'Time Out'

Oliver Stone, I don't like. But then, nobody likes Oliver Stone. *Alan Parker (1990)*

Irving Thalberg
On a clear day you could see Thalberg.
George S. Kaufman

He was like a young pope. *Budd Schulberg*

J. Lee Thompson
'The White Dawn' (1974) – Thompson's direction clings to the increasing number of action set pieces with all the relief of a drowning man clutching a life raft.
Chris Peachment – 'Time Out'

Michael Todd
He was born with an inability to look backward. *Art Cohn (1959)*

Raoul Walsh
To Raoul Walsh, a tender love scene is burning down a whorehouse.
Jack L. Warner

John Walters
'Mondo Trasho' (1969) – Everyone should try to see at least one early Walters film: whether you can take two is a matter of personal bad taste. *Jennifer Selway – 'Time Out'*

Jack L. Warner
A man who would rather tell a bad joke than make a good movie. *Jack Benny*

I can't see what J.W. can do with an Oscar – it can't say yes. *Al Jolson*

Working for Warner Brothers is like f***ing a porcupine. It's a hundred pricks against one. *Wilson Mizner*

He never bore a grudge against anyone he wronged. *Simone Signoret*

Orson Welles
Orson Welles hails a cab like God and tips like a Jesuit. *Anonymous cab driver*

He is a kind of giant with a child-like face, a tree filled with birds and shadows, a dog who has snapped his chain and lies in the flowerbeds, an active idler, a wise fool, isolation surrounded by humanity, a student who dozes in class, a strategist who pretends to be drunk when he wants to be left in peace. *Jean Cocteau*

The oldest enfant terrible in the world.
Paul Holt

By the sixties he was encased in make-up and

his own fat, like a huge operatic W. C. Fields.
Pauline Kael

The sad thing is that he has consistently put
his very real talents to the task of glorifying
his imaginary genius. *John Simon*

Herbert Wilcox

'*Nurse Edith Cavell*' *(1939)* – Mr Herbert
Wilcox proceeds on his appointed course. As
slow and ponderous and well protected as a
steamroller, he irons out the opposition. We
get from his film almost everything except
life, character and faith. *Graham Greene*

Billy Wilder

Underneath his aggressive gruff exterior is
pure Brillo. *Harry Kurnitz*

At work he is two people – Mr Hyde and Mr
Hyde. *Harry Kurnitz*

Michael Winner

The D. W. Griffith of British Schlock.
Tim Healey – '*The World's
Worst Movies*' *(1986)*

'*The Big Sleep*' *(1978)* – Winner's insistence
as a director on making everything as explicit
as possible is stultifying beyond belief.
Rod McShane – '*Time Out*'

To say that Michael Winner is his own worst
enemy is to provoke a ragged chorus from
odd corners of the film industry of 'Not while
I'm alive!' *Barry Norman*

'*The Sentinel*' *(1976)* – The only frightening
thing about *The Sentinel* is its director's mind.
David Pirie – '*Time Out*'

'*The Stone Killer*' *(1973)* – Film-making as
painting by numbers. '*Sight and Sound*'

Darryl F. Zanuck

Sam Goldwyn without the accent.
Eddie Cantor

Goodbye, Mr Zanuck; it certainly has been a
pleasure working at Sixteenth Century Fox.
Jean Renoir

Adolph Zukor

First and last in the alphabet of screen fame.
Terry Ramsaye

FILMS
(listed by reviewer)

Anon

'*Apocalypse Now*' *(1979) directed by Francis F.
Coppola* – It should have been called
Apocalypse Later.

'*A Bridge Too Far*' *(1977) directed by Richard
Attenborough* – A film too long.

Gilbert Adair

'*The Cat and the Canary*' *(1979) starring
Honor Blackman* – So mechanically are
characters shunted through the
indistinguishable rooms and corridors that
one is surprised not to see the parquet
marked off in neat little squares, as on a
Cluedo board. '*Monthly Film Bulletin*'

'*Making Love*' *(1982) starring Kate Jackson* –
This is a three handkerchief movie, but for
the nose. It stinks.

Derek Adams

'*Jaws 3-D*' *(1983) starring Dennis Quaid* – Put
in a baking tray, gas mark 7, and enjoy a
turkey. '*Time Out*'

James Agee

'*Summer Storm*' *(1944) starring George
Sanders* – Most of it had for me the sporty
spaciousness of an illustrated drugstore
classic.

'*The Green Years*' *(1946) starring Charles
Coburn* – It has been described in the ads as
'wonderful' by everyone within Louis B.
Mayer's purchasing power except his horses,
so I hesitate to ask you to take my word for it:
the picture is awful.

'*The Brothers*' *(1947)* – Heavy breathing,
heavier dialect, and any number of quaint
folk customs. The island and its actual
inhabitants are all right; the rest is Mary
Webb with hair on her chest.

'*Carnegie Hall*' *(1947)* – The thickest and
sourest mess of musical mulligatawny I have

yet had to sit down to.

'The Egg and I' (1947) starring Marjorie Main
– Marjorie Main, in an occasional fit of fine
wild comedy, picks up the show and
brandishes it as if she were wringing its neck.
I wish to God she had.

'Give My Regards to Broadway' (1948) –
Vaudeville is dead. I wish someone would
bury it.

Geoff Andrew

'Boardwalk' (1979) starring Lee Strasberg –
Death Wish meets *On Golden Pond* –
eminently missable.   *'Time Out'*

'Arthur' (1981) co-starring John Gielgud –
How can one applaud a movie which relies
heavily on the novelty value of Gielgud as a
bitter butler pronouncing profanities in a
posh accent?   *'Time Out'*

*'Chariots of Fire' (1981) starring Ben Cross and
Ian Charleson* – This is an overblown piece of
self-congratulatory emotional manipulation
perfectly suited for Thatcherite liberals. Pap.
'Time Out'

Nigel Andrews

*'Bonfire of the Vanities' (1991) adapted from
Tom Wolfe's novel* – Warner Brothers spent
$50m dressing Wolfe in sheep's clothing.
'Financial Times' (1992)

Don Atyeo

*'Les Patterson Saves the World' (1987) starring
Barrie Humphries* – Better to chew one's foot
off than spend more than ten minutes in the
bugger's company.   *'Time Out'*

Chris Auty

*'I Escaped from Devil's Island' (1973) starring
Jim Brown* – Not exactly recommended,
unless you misspent your youth reading
stories like *'How I Wrestled with a Python and
Won'*.
'Time Out'

Lew Ayres

*'Fingers at the Window' (1942) starring Basil
Rathbone* – The kind of picture actors do
when they need work.

Peter Ball

*'Blazing Saddles' (1974) directed by Mel
Brooks* – Proves there is more corn in
Hollywood than Oklahoma, and a lot is just
Hollywood jerking off.   *'Time Out'*

Peter Barnes

'Kiss Me Stupid' (1964) starring Dean Martin
– A work of ferocious tastelessness . . .
Swiftian in its relentless disgust.

Rona Barrett

'Meteor' (1979) starring Sean Connery – How
could director Ronald Neame spend almost
$17 million and then the best special effect is
Sean Connery's toupee?

'Quintet' (1979) starring Paul Newman – Did
you wonder just what in hades those dogs in
almost every other scene were chewing on?
No, not the scenery – Paul Newman did that.
Yes, it was the script! Better an avalanche
should have covered the silly thing before
they went to the trouble of filming it.

*'Airport 1979: The Concorde' (1979) starring
Alain Delon* – This trash is to movies what
airline food is to gourmet meals.

'Beyond the Poseidon Adventure' (1979) – Sally
Field and Michael Caine were so damned
wooden they could have floated the *Poseidon*
up to the surface in ten seconds flat.

'Skatetown USA' (1979) – We can imagine
only one thing worse than having to sit
through this movie one more time: a Leif
Garret concert.
[*Leif Garret had also starred in the 1978 film
'Skateboard'.*]

'Dreamer' (1979) – We wouldn't dream of
saying something so obvious about a bowling
movie as: 'It belongs in the gutter.' But we'll
go ahead anyway and say it (there, we feel
better already).

'Goldengirl' (1979) starring Susan Anton –
Susan Anton was unusually cast as an
Olympic runner – hate to steal a line from the
likes of Stanley Kramer, but the runner
stumbles.

'*The Runner Stumbles*' *(1979) directed by Stanley Kramer* – So stupefying as to give sincerity a bad name.

Welford Beaton

'*The Hunchback of Nôtre Dame*' *(1939) starring Charles Laughton* – The most horrible thing the screen has given us – a ghastly story made more ghastly by the treatment given it.

Paul Beckley

'*The Entertainer*' *(1960) starring Laurence Olivier* – Has set itself to scratching the dandruff out of the mane of life.

Sheila Benson

'*Beverly Hills Cop II*' *(1987) starring Eddie Murphy* – Fifteen minutes of *BHC II* and you begin to know how a tenderised flank steak feels.   '*Los Angeles Times*'

Philip Bergson

'*Orca: Killer Whale*' *(1977) starring Richard Harris* – The biggest load of cod imaginable.

Michael Billington

'*Tell Me that You Love Me, Junie Moon*' *(1969) starring Liza Minnelli* – Like seeing a venerated senior citizen desperately trying to show he's in love with today by donning see-through clothes.   '*Illustrated London News*'

'*The Long Goodbye*' *(1973) based on Raymond Chandler's novel* – A spit in the eye to a great writer.

'*Illustrious Corpses*' *(1974) starring Max von Sydow* – Like watching layer after layer peeled off some diseased flower until the poisoned root is reached.
'*Illustrated London News*'

'*The Great Scout and Cathouse Thursday*' *(1976) starring Lee Marvin* – It takes more than a dollop or two of sentiment and acres of dirty talk to make a movie.
'*Illustrated London News*'

'*The Man Who Fell to Earth*' *(1976) starring David Bowie* – Once you have pierced through its glittering veneer, you find only another glittering veneer underneath.

'*Murder by Death*' *(1976) starring, amongst others, Alec Guinness* – Plenty of scene-stealing actors, but not many scenes worth stealing.   '*Illustrated London News*'

'*The Seven Per Cent Solution*' *(1976) starring Nicol Williamson* – Comes into the category hit and myth. . . . A heavyweight spoof in which Sherlock Homes is placed under hypnosis of Sigmund Freud. The audience is then placed under hypnosis by director Harold Ross.   '*Illustrated London News*'

Anne Billson

'*Gabriela*' *(1983) starring Sonia Braga* – It would be unfair to call *Gabriela* smut, since it consists of so much wishy-washy soap
'*Time Out*'

'*Over the Brooklyn Bridge*' *(1983) directed by Menahem Golan* – Golan's masterstroke is to underline the essential transience of his project by naming it after a landmark well known as a high spot for the potential suicide. One can only wish the entire cast and crew had taken the plunge.   '*Time Out*'

'*Hardbodies*' *(1984) directed by Mark Griffiths* – What this needs to make it a great film is a new script, a completely different cast, a decent director, and a soundtrack devoid of any dismal disco muzak.   '*Time Out*'

'*Protocol*' *(1984) starring Goldie Hawn* – Hawnsville yawnsville.   '*Time Out*'

'*She'll Be Wearing Pink Pyjamas*' *(1984) starring Julie Walters* – The sort of film that gives women a bad name.   '*Time Out*'

'*Car Trouble*' *(1985) starring Julie Walters* – One might have said that the plot would have been improved by the introduction of an axe-wielding maniac, except that there already is an axe-wielding maniac and he doesn't improve it at all.   '*Time Out*'

'*Clue*' *(1985) based on the 'Cluedo' board-game* – The plot looks as though it had been devised by dice-throwing. All concerned should go directly to jail.   '*Time Out*'

'Rambo: First Blood Part II' (1985) starring Sylvester Stallone – Culture slips back into comic strip mode for retarded schoolboy types.   'Time Out'

'Remo Williams: The Adventure Begins' (1985) starring Joel Gray – Although the hero spends much of his time hanging off high places such as the Statue of Liberty, the film itself never gets off the ground.   'Time Out'

'Screwballs II – Loose Screws' (1985) – There is a song called 'I've Got a Rubber in My Wallet'. How strange that this film should have an '18' certificate when it is so obviously aimed at infants.   'Time Out'

'Wild Geese II' starring Scott Glenn – A right load of proper gander.   'Time Out'

'Biggles' (1986) starring Neil Dickson – Biggles! Boggles! Buggles! Bunkum!
                                'Time Out'

Ian Birch
'Xanadu' (1980) starring Olivia Newton-John – An experience so vacuous it's almost frightening.

Geoff Brown
'Bootleggers' (1974) starring Slim Pickens – Any film which actually stars Slim Pickens can't be all good, and Bootleggers isn't remotely good.   'Time Out'

'Mame' (1974) starring Lucille Ball – An elephantine budget matched with minuscule imagination.

'Mixed Company' (1974) starring Barbara Harris – On the whole this movie gives a whole new meaning to the word 'yuck'.
                                'Time Out'

'Vampira' (1974) starring David Niven – One consolation is that the movie wasn't called Fangs Ain't What They Used To Be.
                                'Time Out'

'A Star Is Born' (1976) starring Barbra Streisand – 70mm screens have been filled with some vacuous stuff in their time, but this monstrous stuff takes the biscuit. It's set in the rock world, but the kind of rock these people peddle is the softest thing next to jelly.
                                'Time Out'

'That's Entertainment Part II' (1976) directed by Gene Kelly – That's not entertainment!
                                'Time Out'

'The Bad News Bears in Breaking Training' (1977) – Bad news indeed.   'Time Out'

'Watership Down' (1978) directed by Martin Rosen – All one can say about this animated feature is thank God for myxomatosis.
                                'Time Out'

'Clash of the Titans' (1981) starring Laurence Olivier – There's a real possibility some audiences will be turned to stone before Medusa even appears.
                                'Monthly Film Bulletin'

'Hook' (1992) directed by Steven Spielberg – An over-inflated balloon of a film.   'The Times'

Mike Bygrave
'The Cannonball Run' (1980) starring Burt Reynolds – Looks like something knocked off on rest days from Smokey and the Bandit II. . . . Strictly for those willing to pay for a series of TV chat show performances
                                'Time Out'

Vincent Canby
'McKenna's Gold' (1969) starring Gregory Peck – A thriving example of the old Hollywood maxim about how to succeed by failing big.

'At Long Last Love' (1975) – Starring Cybill Shepherd and Burt Reynolds, who have, between them, four left feet and who sing with a gallantry that reminds me of small children taking their first solo swim across the deep end.   'New York Times'

'One From the Heart' (1982) directed by Francis F. Coppola – As a romantic comedy One From the Heart is about as frothy as 2001.

Brian Case
'Way Upstream' (1986) starring Barrie Rutter –

Way offbeam.   *'Time Out'*

'Hamburger Hill' *(1987) directed by John Irvin* – In its juggernaut functionalism, *Hamburger Hill* may be the McDonald's of the war movie.   *'Time Out'*

'Superman IV' *(1987) starring Christopher Reeve* – About as dreary as a summit conference in Belgium.   *'Time Out'*

'Awakenings' *(1990) starring Robert de Niro and Robin Williams* – Dramatically, it's a twin-tub, with a big slot on top to pour in the caring.   *'Time Out'*

'Hook' *(1992) directed by Steven Spielberg* – *Hook* looks like a theme park. . . . Never say Neverland again.   *'Time Out'*

Kenneth Cavander

'Throne of Blood' *(1957) directed by Akira Kurosawa* – Its final impression is of a man who storms into a room with an impassioned speech to deliver and then discovers that he has forgotten what he came to say.
         'Monthly Film Bulletin'

Charles Champlin

'Wild Rovers' *(1971) starring William Holden* – An existentialist western which will not do much for existentialism, the western, or the box office.   *'L.A. Times'*

'The Long Goodbye' *(1973) starring Elliot Gould* – The trouble is that this [Philip] Marlowe is an untidy, unshaven, semi-literate dimwit slob who could not locate a missing skyscraper and who would be refused service at a hot-dog stand.

'Barry Lyndon' *(1975) starring Ryan O'Neal* – The motion picture equivalent of one of those very large, very expensive, very elegant and very dull books that exist solely to be seen on coffee tables.

'Private Benjamin' *(1980) starring Goldie Hawn* – A movie you don't salute, you court martial; the script went AWOL.

'Raise the Titanic' *(1980) starring Jason Robards* – The mistake was keeping the

Titanic afloat long after the picture had begun to sink.

Tom Charity

'Deep Star Six' *(1988) starring Taurean Blacque* – This simply rehashes the phony trappings of countless TV shows, to boldly go where we have been before.   *'Time Out'*

James Christopher

'Return from the River Kwai' *(1988) starring Edward Fox* – A tacky lager lout view of war.

Al Clark

'The Passage' *(1978) starring Anthony Quinn* – File under 'Carry On Garrotting' and forget.

Jane Clarke

'Little Miss Marker' *(1980) starring Walter Matthau* – A film which aspires to a heart of gold, but is alloy all the way.   *'Time Out'*

Jay Cocks

'What's Up, Doc?' *(1972) starring Barbra Streisand* – Seeing it is like shaking hands with a joker holding a joy buzzer; the effect is both presumptuous and unpleasant.

Andrew Collins

'My Girl' *(1992) starring Macaulay Culkin* – *My Girl* (and one day there will be a law against films being made to fit song titles of the lucrative Motown back catalogue) is clearly the worst film ever made.
         'Melody Maker'

Richard Combs

'Autumn Leaves' *(1956) starring Joan Crawford* – Extraordinary combination of domestic Guignol and elephantized soap-opera.

'The Great Gatsby' *(1974) starring Robert Redford* – Pays its creator the regrettable tribute of erecting a mausoleum over his work.   *'Monthly Film Bulletin'*

'The Eiger Sanction' *(1975) starring Clint Eastwood* – All the villains have been constructed from prefabricated Bond models.   *'Monthly Film Bulletin'*

'Britannia Hospital' *(1982) starring Malcolm McDowell* – It has all the intensity, along with

the flailing incoherence, of a soapbox jeremiah.

'Firefox' (1982) directed by and starring Clint Eastwood – What is most curious about this farrago is that Eastwood, the actor and the director, should have walked through it all with scarcely a thought for each other.

'Hanky Panky' (1982) starring Gene Wilder – The plot, rather like Mr Wilder, rushes hither and yon at the slightest excuse without ever adding up to very much. Even McGuffins are supposed to make more sense than this.

John Conquest
'Grand Theft Auto' (1977) directed by and starring Ron Howard – Looking like something that Peckinpah might have made as a boy, this can best be described as an automotive snuff movie.   *'Time Out'*

Arthur Cooper
'Lost Horizon' (1973) directed by Charles Jarrott – The set for Shangri-La resembles the valley of the Jolly Green Giant – a fitting showcase for a film that is so much spinach.
'Newsweek'

Noël Coward
'Bitter Sweet' (1940) starring Jeanette MacDonald and Nelson Eddy – An affair between a mad rockinghorse and a rawhide suitcase.

Peter Cox
'Hook' (1992) directed by Steven Spielberg – Sitting through two hours and twenty minutes is at times like running through treacle wearing flippers.   *'The Sun'*

Eileen Creelman
'Break of Hearts' (1935) starring Katharine Hepburn – The audience's heart never breaks.
'New York Sun'

Judith Crist
'Goodbye Again' (1961) starring Ingrid Bergman – The kind of 'woman's picture' that gives women a bad name.

'The Inspector' (1961) starring Stephen Boyd – A sluggish mélange of melodrama, romance, mystery and what the inactive might call action.

'The Man Who Shot Liberty Valance' (1962) starring John Wayne – Like Queen Victoria, John Wayne has become lovable because he stayed in the saddle into a new era.

'Cleopatra' (1963) starring Elizabeth Taylor – The small screen does more than justice to this monumental mouse.

'The Birds' (1963) directed by Alfred Hitchcock – Enough to make you kick the next pigeon you come across.

'A Global Affair' (1963) starring Bob Hope – Squaresville incarnate, with a side trip into Lerrsville.

'Behold a Pale Horse' (1964) starring Gregory Peck – A fine example of a high-class failure.

'Love Has Many Faces' (1964) starring Lana Turner – For connoisseurs of perfectly awful movies.

'The Man in the Middle' (1964) starring Robert Mitchum – For once Mitchum seems to have an excuse for keeping his eyes at half mast.

'The Agony and the Ecstasy' (1965) starring Charlton Heston – All agony, no ecstasy.

'Brainstorm' (1965) directed by William Conrad – A sub-B potboiler for those who find comic books too intellectual.

'The Ambushers' (1967) starring Dean Martin – The sole distinction of this vomitous mess is that it just about reaches the nadir of witlessness, smirky sexiness and bad taste – and it's dull, dull, dull to boot.

'Not With My Wife You Don't' (1966) starring Tony Curtis – It has all the verve, subtlety and sophistication of its title.

'Five Card Stud' (1968) starring Dean Martin – So mediocre you can't get mad at it.

'John and Mary' (1969) starring Dustin Hoffman – Despite all the 'now' sets and

surfaces, it's like an old comedy of the thirties – minus the comedy.

'*Marooned*' *(1969) starring Gregory Peck* – It has all the zip, zest and zing of a moonwalk, and I suspect a computer fed with a dictionary could come up with better dialogue.

'*McKenna's Gold*' *(1968) starring Gregory Peck* – Twelve-year-olds of all ages might tolerate it.

'*Airport*' *(1970) starring Burt Lancaster* – The best film of 1944.

'*Puppet on a Chain*' *(1970) written by Alistair MacLean* – One suspects that a marionette also sat in for Alistair MacLean.

'*The Salzburg Connection*' *(1972) starring Barry Newman* – So dull you can't tell the CIA agents from the neo-Nazis or double agents – or the inept actors from the blocks and stones in the handsome Austrian locales.

'*The Return of a Man Called Horse*' *(1976) starring Richard Harris* – Maintains a tidy balance between nausea and boredom.

Bosley Crowther
'*Satan Met a Lady*' *(1936) starring Bette Davis* – One lives through it in constant expectation of seeing a group of uniformed individuals appear suddenly from behind the furniture and take the entire cast into protective custody.

'*Valley of the Dolls*' *(1967) directed by Mark Robson* – It's every bit as phony and old-fashioned as anything Lana Turner ever did.
'*New York Times*'

'Cue'
'*The Flame*' *(1947)* – A good picture to stay away from, with or without a good book.

Giovanni Dadomo
'*Let's Get Laid*' *(1977) starring Fiona Richmond* – It's like a George Formby movie with tits.
'*Time Out*'

'*Turkey Shoot*' *(1981) starring Steve Railsback* – Turkey shite, more like . . . the pic's about as lively as a snail full of downers. '*Time Out*'

'*Six Weeks*' *(1982) starring Dudley Moore* – The Moral Majority will lap up every tear-jerking minute: if you're lucky you may just be able to keep your lunch. '*Time Out*'

'*Lovesick*' *(1983) starring Dudley Moore* – A love story slightly less moving than an Interflora advert. '*Time Out*'

'*Alfredo, Alfredo*' *starring Dustin Hoffman* – Snails are both faster and funnier than this limp sex comedy. '*Time Out*'

'Daily Express'
'*The Man Between*' *(1952) starring James Mason* – A cold-hearted film about people with cold feet.

'Daily Mail'
'*The Blues Brothers*' *(1980) starring John Belushi and Dan Aykroyd* – There is not a soupçon of wit or ingenuity in this brainless exercise in overspending.

Hugo Davenport
'*Hook*' *(1992) directed by Steven Spielberg* – What Spielberg has done is to reduce Neverland to the lowest common denominator of American junk culture. . . . It has the ugliness of wilfully arrested adolescence. '*Daily Telegraph*'
[*A still from the movie was captioned* – Thoroughly panned!]

Frances Dickinson
'*Grease 2*' *(1982) starring Michelle Pfeiffer* – As gaudily tempting a soft-centre as ever graced a Woolworth counter. '*Time Out*'

Peter John Dyer
'*A Taste of Honey*' *(1961) starring Rita Tushingham* – Tart and lively around the edges and bitter at the core.

Roger Ebert
'*The Blue Lagoon*' *(1980) starring Brooke Shields* – This movie made me itch.

Fiona Ferguson
'*Love and Bullets*' *(1978) starring Charles Bronson* – Love and Bullets, my eye; embarrassment and tedium is more like it.
'*Time Out*'

'The Humanoid' (1979) starring Richard Kiel –
The sets resemble Brent Cross and the
spaceships could have come out of a
cornflakes packet.   *'Time Out'*

Otis Ferguson
'Becky Sharp' (1935) starring Miriam Hopkins
– As pleasing to the eye as a fresh fruit
sundae, but not much more.

*'Mary of Scotland' (1936) starring Katharine
Hepburn* – Events are walked through as
though they were rooms in a museum, and
closing time at three.

*'The Cowboy and the Lady' (1938) starring
Gary Cooper* – Just a lot of chestnuts pulled
out of other people's dead fires.

*'The Wizard of Oz' (1939) starring Judy
Garland* – As for the light touch of fantasy, it
weighs like a pound of fruitcake soaking wet.

*'Seven Sinners' (1940) starring Marlene
Dietrich* – Nothing to worry about, unless you
happen to be in the theatre, watching it go
from fairly good to worse than worse.

Nigel Floyd
*'The Cheap Detective' (1978) starring Peter
Falk* – Neil Simon-scripted spoof of films
based on Chandler/Hammett private eye
novels, with *Casablanca* thrown in for bad
measure. *The Cheap Idea* might have been a
better title.   *'Time Out'*

'Creepshow 2' (1987) starring George Kennedy
– The only thing terrifying about *Creepshow 2*
is the thought of *Creepshow 3*.   *'Time Out'*

*'Fatal Attraction' (1987) starring Michael
Douglas* – A predictable dog's dinner of
Pavlovian thriller clichés, this will appeal
strongly to those who think women should be
kept on a short lead.   *'Time Out'*

'Mannequin' (1987) starring Kim Cattrall – A
film about, by and for dummies. *'Time Out'*

'Kansas' (1988) starring Matt Dillon – Like
the eponymous state, this has corn as far as
the eye can see.   *'Time Out'*

'Zandalee' (1990) starring Nicolas Cage – This
flaccid effort wants to be *Last Tango in New
Orleans*, but feels like nine and a half weeks
in *Full Moon Junction*.   *'Time Out'*

'Hudson Hawk' (1991) starring Bruce Willis –
Bruce Willis and Co. may know how to
plunder *North by Northwest*, but they can't
tell a 'Hawk' from a movie that won't soar.
                                 'Time Out'

William F. Fore
'The Enforcer' (1976) starring Clint Eastwood –
A new low in mindless violence is reached in
this film, which is so bad it would be funny if
it were not for the gut-thumping killings from
beginning to end.   *'Monthly Film Bulletin'*

Philip French
*'Gator' (1976) directed by and starring Burt
Reynolds* – The relentless violence, the
sentimentality, the raucous stag party
humour, the inability to cut off a scene once
it has made its point, attest to the influence of
Robert Aldrich.   *'The Times'*

Gerald Garrett
*'The Impossible Years' (1968) starring David
Niven* – A comedy of the generation gap
which didn't bridge it but fell right into it.

W. Stephen Gilbert
*'That's Entertainment!' (1974) directed by Jack
Haley Jnr* – On with the motley, Hollywood
begins to package its feasts, and *That's
Entertainment!* has all the flavour of the Vesta
dehydrated line.

John Gill
*'Silkwood' (1983) starring Meryl Streep and
Cher* – Ultimately it's rather akin to making a
film about Joan of Arc and concentrating on
her period pains.

John Gillett
'The Heist' (1971) starring Warren Beatty – An
essay in virtuoso film construction . . . rather
as if one was watching a perfect machine in
full throttle but with nowhere to go.

Verina Glaessner
'The Towering Inferno' (1974) starring Paul

Newman, Steve McQueen, Fred Astaire and Richard Chamberlain – Several generations of blue-eyed charmers act their roles as if each were under a separate bell-jar.

'Harry and Walter Go to New York' (1976) starring Michael Caine – The film provides its own epitaph, when Caine's underworld star, asked why he keeps on cracking safes, remarks that 'every cell tingles with the possibility of failure'. Failure realised, and with precious little tingle.   *'Time Out'*

Joanne Glasbey
'Elvira, Mistress of the Dark' (1988) starring Cassandra Peterson – Vamp high camp, where Elvira is more mistress of the dork.
'Time Out'

Steven Goldman
'Dancing in the Dark' (1985) directed by Leon Marr – It makes for a rather tedious and highly non-moving use of exposed silver nitrate on plastic.   *'Time Out'*

Steve Grant
'Hamlet' (1990) starring Mel Gibson – To go or not to go, strewth, that is the question.
'Time Out'

'Lambada' (1989) starring Eddie Peck – A hideous mutation which . . . makes *Saturday Night Fever* look like class movie making. . . . It has an abysmal script, acting which makes Madame Tussaud's look like a roller disco.
'Time Out'

Benny Green
'The Odessa File' (1974) starring Jon Voight – As resistible a parcel of sedative entertainment as ever induced narcolepsy in a healthy man.   *'Punch'*

'The Incredible Sarah' (1976) starring Glenda Jackson – A job lot of obligatory Hollywood platitudes strung together with all the skill of Captain Hook trying to thread a needle.
'Punch'

'The Sailor Who Fell from Grace' (1976) starring Sarah Miles – This everyday tale of torture, scopophilia, copulation, masturbation, dismemberment and antique dealing deserves to be traded back to the Japs and made required viewing for timorous kamikaze pilots.   *'Punch'*

Graham Greene
'The Great Ziegfeld' (1936) starring William Powell – This huge inflated gas-blown object bobs into the critical view as irrelevantly as an airship advertising somebody's toothpaste at a south coast resort. It lasts three hours. That is its only claim to special attention.

'Disputed Passage' (1939) starring Dorothy Lamour – I should describe the flavour as a rather nauseating blend of iodine and glucose.

'The Guardian'
'The Best Little Whorehouse in Texas' (1982) starring Burt Reynolds – A sanitized, coyly predictable piece of brothel creeping, set to muzak by a poorly programmed computer.

Otis L. Guernsey Jnr
'The Secret Behind the Door' (1948) starring Joan Bennett – A dog-wagon *Rebecca* with a seasoning of psychiatrics.

Arsenio Hall
'Rocky IV' (1985) starring Sylvester Stallone and Dolph Lundgren – Unbelievable – two white men fighting for the World Heavyweight title!

Wally Hammond
'Arthur 2: On the Rocks' (1988) starring Dudley Moore – As funny as a cerebral haemorrhage.   *'Time Out'*

'The Bonfire of the Vanities' (1990) starring Tom Hanks – If anything, it's a Hanks 'little boy lost' movie, more in the *Big* tradition than The Big Tradition.
'Time Out'

Richard Hatch
'The Missouri Breaks' (1976) starring Marlon Brando and Jack Nicholson – A picture of which it might be said they shouldn't make 'em like that any more.   *'Nation'*

Tim Healey
'Santa Claus Conquers the Martians' (1964) –

The movie is so treacly it can make your fillings squeak.
'The World's Worst Movies' (1986)

'The Bitch' starring Joan Collins – They should have called it *The Botch*.
'The World's Worst Movies' (1986)

A. P. Herbert
'The Terror' (1928) – The characters speak as if they were dictating important letters.
'Punch'

Penelope Houston
'Storm Over the Nile' (1955) starring Laurence Harvey – The material appears not so much dated as fossilised within its period.

'Exodus' (1960) directed by Otto Preminger – After three and a half hours the approach seems more exhausting than exhaustive.

'Suspect' (1960) starring Tony Britton and Ian Bannen – A better standard of second feature film is badly needed, but the way to do it is not by making pictures which look as though they have strayed from TV.

Tom Hutchinson
'Naked Lunch' (1992) based on William Burroughs' novel – This is the movie of the book they said could never be filmed. They were right. It hasn't been. *'Mail on Sunday'*

'Once Upon a Crime' (1992) starring John Candy and Cybill Shepherd – It's the first feature film for director Eugene Levy, whose timing is as adequate as a watch with no hands. *'Mail on Sunday'*

Jo Imeson
'Mommie Dearest' (1981) starring Faye Dunaway – The only thing that is not transparent about this film is why it was ever made. *'Monthly Film Bulletin'*

Clyde Jeavons
'Bluebeard' (1972) starring Richard Burton – Somewhere between (and a long way behind) *Kind Hearts and Coronets* and *The Abominable Dr Phibes*. *'Monthly Film Bulletin'*

'Firepower' (1979) starring Sophia Loren – The nearest thing yet to film-making by numbers, with identikit characters jet-setting across a

travel brochure landscape to an orchestration of gunfire, car smashes and colourful explosions. *'Monthly Film Bulletin'*

Sheila Johnston
'D.A.R.Y.L.' (1985) featuring a Data Analysing Robot Youth Lifeform – This Dreary Android Runaway Yawn Lags way behind the Spielberg thoroughbreds it tries so hard to ape. *'Time Out'*

Iain Johnstone
'The Last Boy Scout' (1992) starring Bruce Willis – As interesting as watching stubble grow on Bruce Willis's chin.
'The Sunday Times'

Pauline Kael
'The Professionals' (1966) written and directed by Richard Brooks – It has the expertise of a cold old whore with practised hands and no thoughts of love.

'The Way West' (1967) starring Kirk Douglas – A jerk's idea of an epic.

'Paint Your Wagon' (1969) starring Lee Marvin – One of those big movies in which the themes are undersized and the elements juggled around until nothing fits together right and even the good bits of the original show you started with are shot to hell.

Stefan Kanfer
'The Thomas Crown Affair' (1968) starring Steve McQueen – A glimmering, empty film reminiscent of an haute couture model – stunning on the surface, concave and undernourished beneath.

'The Last Movie' (1971) directed by Dennis Hopper – A shotgun wedding of R. D. Laing and *The Late Show*. *'Time'*

Stanley Kauffmann
'The Roots of Heaven' (1958) directed by John Huston – The Huston who did [*The Treasure of the*] *Sierra Madre* would have lighted his cigar with this script.

'The Fugitive Kind' (1960) directed by Sidney Lumet – Lumet is usually clever at least part of the time – an acquisitive magpie who has picked up, along with the selly trash, a few

small gems. This time he brings us nothing but bits of coloured glass.

'Judgment at Nuremberg' (1961) directed by Stanley Kramer – Some believe that by tackling such themes Kramer earns at least partial remission from criticism. How much? 20 per cent off for effort?

'Cheyenne Autumn' (1964) starring Richard Widmark – The acting is bad, the dialogue trite and predictable, the pace funereal, the structure fragmented and the climaxes puny.

'The Greatest Story Ever Told' (1965) starring Max Von Sydow – What we are looking at is really a lengthy catalogue of greeting cards for 1965 – for those who care enough to send the very best.

'True Grit' (1969) starring John Wayne – Readers may remember it as a book about a girl, but it's a film about John Wayne.

'Brother Sun, Sister Moon' (1972) starring Alec Guinness as Pope Innocent III – If I were Pope, I would burn it.

'The King of Marvin Gardens' (1972) starring Jack Nicholson – Glum news from the people who made *Five Easy Pieces*, which had a lot of good work in it along with some pretentious flab. In their new picture the flab has taken over.

'The Way We Were' (1973) starring Barbra Streisand – Not one moment of the picture is anything but garbage under the gravy of false honesty.

'The Great Gatsby' (1974) starring Robert Redford – A total failure of every requisite sensibility.

Nigel Kendall
'The Doctor' (1992) starring William Hurt – Terminally awful.

Mark Kermode
'Critters 2' (1988) starring Scott Grimes – The effect is perhaps not unlike watching Sooty in a video nasty. *'Time Out'*

'Necessary Roughness' (1992) starring Scott

Bakula – Another dose of cinematic groin-strain from the sport which (sadly) wouldn't die. Not even a game of two halves, this tale of college (American) football is marginally less funny than wearing a jock-strap on your head and less original than putting Ralgex down your opponent's shorts. . . . A technical foul, off-side, and time-wasting.

Jack Kroll
'The Omen' (1976) starring Gregory Peck – The latest serving of deviled ham.
'Newsweek'

Anthony Lane
'The Bedroom Window' (1987) starring Steve Guttenberg – A real snore.
'Independent on Sunday' (1992)

Frances Lass
'Private Popsicle' (1982) directed by Boaz Davidson – The plot is as fresh as an Italian's armpit, the dubbing was seemingly done by a blind deaf mute, and the jokes are as funny as bubonic plague. *'Time Out'*

'Easy Money' (1983) starring Rodney Dangerfield – The fact that it took four writers to concoct this pile of doggy-doo riddled with sexism and racism doesn't make it any funnier than woodwork in a cripple's crutch.
'Time Out'

Caroline A. Lejeune
'Alice Adams' (1935) starring Katharine Hepburn – As trivial as a schoolgirl's diary, and just about as pathetically true.

'Aloma of the South Seas' (1941) starring Dorothy Lamour, Jon Hall and a volcano!
Extensive tour
  Of D. Lamour,
  Nearly all
Of Jon Hall.
  Sudden panic
Cause volcanic
And a torso
  Or so . . .

'Aloma of the South Seas' (1941) starring Dorothy Lamour – There are snake dances, sacrifices, private swimming baths, a Holy Mountain. The mountain, by the way, has

the privilege of belching when it is dissatisfied, something that the well-bred critic must not do.

'No Leave, No Love' (1946) – No Comment!

'Desert Fury' (1947) starring Lizabeth Scott – The only fury I could sense was in my balcony.

'Ruthless' (1948) starring Zachary Scott – Beginning pictures at the end
Is, I'm afraid, the modern trend.
But I'd find *Ruthless* much more winning
If it could end at the beginning.

'A Kiss for Corliss' (1949) starring David Niven and Shirley Temple –
I sometimes think that David Niven
Should not take all the parts he's given;
While of the art of Shirley Temple
I, for the moment, have had ample.

Raoul Levy
'La Dolce Vita' (1959) directed by Federico Fellini – *La Dolce Vita* can play havoc with one's cavities.

Pare Lorentz
'Blonde Venus' (1932) starring Marlene Dietrich – The story has all the dramatic integrity of a sashweight murderer's tabloid autobiography.

'Los Angeles Magazine'
'Can't Stop the Music' (1980) starring the Village People – Considering the low level of wit, perhaps the Village People should consider renaming themselves the Village Idiots.

Ian Lyness
'Hook' (1992) directed by Steven Spielberg – It is neither a hit nor a miss, but a mess.
'The Daily Express'
[*Headline for the review* – Boring Peter Gets A Panning.]

Loretta Lynn
'Nashville' (1975) starring Ned Beatty – I'd rather see *Bambi*.

Dwight Macdonald
'Ben Hur' (1959) directed by William Wyler – A [D. W.] Griffith can make a hundred into a crowd, while a Wyler can reduce a thousand to a confused cocktail party. . . . Watching it is like waiting at a railroad crossing while an interminable freight train lumbers by, sometimes stopping altogether.

'It's a Mad Mad Mad Mad World' (1963) directed by Stanley Kramer – To watch on a Cinerama screen in full colour a small army of actors inflict mayhem on each other with cars, planes, explosives and other devices for more than three hours with stereophonic sound effects is simply too much for the human eye and ear to respond to, let alone the funny bone.

Helen MacKintosh
'Charlie Chan and the Curse of the Dragon Queen' (1980) starring Peter Ustinov – Confucius say, 'High time comedies get act together, this one fall apart at scanty seams.'
'Time Out'

'Fame' (1980) directed by Alan Parker – It's a crack at the American Dream which carries all the exhilaration and depth of a 133-minute commercial break.   *'Time Out'*

Don MacPherson
'Zombie Flesh Eaters' (1979) starring Tisa Farrow – Subtle it ain't, but the title alone should keep art lovers away.   *'Time Out'*

'The Mirror Crack'd' (1980) starring Angela Lansbury – It's obvious after the first five minutes that this is a complete no-no, the cinema equivalent of a bellyflop . . . a Miss Marple mystery masquerading as a Royal Command Performance in which all the American stars look stoned.   *'Time Out'*

Pauline McLeod
'Hook' (1992) directed by Steven Spielberg – Peter down the pan.   *'Daily Mirror'*

Rod McShane
'Endless Love' (1981) starring Brooke Shields – Endless? It's interminable.   *'Time Out'*

Derek Malcolm
'Wombling Free' (1977) written and directed by

Lionel Jeffries – A fiasco! If you really must take your kids, it would be less of a pain to go shopping at the same time. *'The Guardian'*

'The Cheap Detective' (1978) starring Peter Falk – There is about enough talent around for a twenty-minute sketch at the Edinburgh fringe. *'The Guardian'*

'Best Defense' (1984) starring Dudley Moore – About as funny as getting hijacked by a group of kamikaze terrorists. *'The Guardian'*

Richard Mallett
'Captain Horatio Hornblower, RN' (1951) starring Gregory Peck – No point makes a strong enough impression to suggest a main line of criticism. *'Punch'*

'Manchester Guardian'
'The Wicked Lady' (1945) starring Margaret Lockwood – A mixture of hot passion and cold suet pudding.

John Marriott
'Follow Me, Boys!' (1966) – Corn badly needs cutting. *'Mail on Sunday' (1992)*

'Bogie' (1980) – Barely breathing biopic of Humphrey Bogart. . . . The man himself must be snarling in his grave.
'Mail on Sunday' (1992)

Angela Mason
'The Best Little Whorehouse in Texas' (1982) starring Burt Reynolds – The dialogue is Texas crude, the sentiment Bible Belt coy, and the songs conveyor-belt Broadway: stale air on a G-string. *'Time Out'*

Colette Maude
'Stop, or My Mom Will Shoot!' (1992) starring Sylvester Stallone – *Rocky V* offered more originality.

Michael Medved
'Santa Claus Conquers the Martians' (1964) – This film proves it's possible to insult the intelligence of a three-year-old.

'Spinout' (1966) starring Elvis Presley – Digesting this is like dining on Fruit Loops cereal soaked in Coca-Cola, with a hefty side-order of Screaming Yellow Zonkers (please hold the onions). In other words, spin out and throw up.

Scott Meek
'Ben Hur' (1959) starring Charlton Heston – A bit like a four-hour Sunday school lesson.
'Time Out'

'Come Play With Me' (1977) starring Alfie Bass – Accept an invitation to go swimming in a piranha-infested river rather than play with this lot. *'Time Out'*

'They All Laughed' (1981) directed by Peter Bogdanovich – The temptation to respond, 'No, they didn't!' is overwhelming, and unfortunately it's also accurate. . . . It plods where it should sparkle, like a celebration where the champagne's gone flat.
'Time Out'

Tom Milne
'The L-Shaped Room' (1962) starring Leslie Caron – It's all a bit like a po-faced trial run for TV's *Rising Damp*. *'Time Out'*

'Soldier Blue' (1970) starring Candice Bergen – A desert romance that's shot like an ad-man's wet-dream – all soft focus and sweet nothings. *'Time Out'*

'The Exorcist' (1973) starring Linda Blair – No more nor less than a blood and thunder horror movie, foundering heavily on the rocks of pretension. *'Monthly Film Bulletin'*

'Escape from Alcatraz' (1979) starring Clint Eastwood – An almost entirely interior film masquerading as an exterior one.
'Monthly Film Bulletin'

'Silver Dream Racer' (1980) starring David Essex – Watching this grotesque hotch-potch of implausible characters being shunted through improbable situations is uncannily akin to being assaulted by a non-stop stream of TV commercials. *'Monthly Film Bulletin'*

'When Time Ran Out' (1980) starring Paul Newman – Disaster movies don't come any more disastrous than this.
'Monthly Film Bulletin'

'Escape to Victory' (1981) starring Michael Caine – Even readers of Boy's Own Paper might have blenched . . . ludicrous beyond belief.   'Monthly Film Bulletin'

'Green Ice' (1981) starring Ryan O'Neal – Painfully miscalculated from the word go, it's a load of old cobblers coated in picture postcard scenery.   'Time Out'

'Blade Runner' (1982) written by Hampton Fancher and David People – A narrative so lame that it seems in need of a wheelchair.
                    'Monthly Film Bulletin'

'Hero' (1982) starring Derek McGuire and Caroline Kenneil – The non-professional cast, alas, are distressingly amateurish, and since the script seems half-strangled in what it is trying to say, the result looks not unlike a clumping village pageant.   'Time Out'

'Psycho III' (1986) starring Anthony Perkins – Sadly, the slashings have become distinctly déjà vu, and the plot is as full of holes as Janet Leigh's corpse.   'Time Out'

'Monthly Film Bulletin'
'The Lost World' (1960) starring Claude Rains – Resembles nothing so much as a ride on a rundown fairground Ghost Train.

'East of Sudan' (1964) starring Anthony Quayle – Nathan Juran could direct this kind of thing blindfold, and for once would appear to have done so.

'The Greatest Story Ever Told' (1965) directed by George Stevens – George Stevens was once described as a water buffalo of film art. What this film more precisely suggests is a dinosaur.

'Grand Prix' (1966) starring James Garner – Off the track the film is firmly stuck in bottom gear.

'Joanna' (1968) directed by Michael Sarne – An unnecessarily protracted punishing of a very dead quadruped.

'Lady in Cement' (1968) starring Frank Sinatra – While Tony Rome [starring Frank Sinatra (1967)] seemed to herald a return to the forties thriller, Lady in Cement marks nothing more exciting than a return to Tony Rome.

'A Lovely Way to Die' (1968) starring Kirk Douglas – The net result is rather as though Philip Marlowe had met Doris Day on his not very inspiring way to the Forum.

Joseph Morgenstern
'Valley of the Dolls' (1967) directed by Mark Robson – One of the most stupefyingly clumsy films ever made by alleged professionals, has no more sense of its own ludicrousness than a village idiot stumbling in manure.   'Newsweek'

Penelope Mortimer
'Guess Who's Coming to Dinner?' (1967) starring Spencer Tracy – A load of embarrassing rubbish.

Art Murphy
'Jonathan Livingstone Seagull' (1973) – The sort of slippery, equivocal goo found on weighing machine cards, fortune cookies and dime astrology guides.   'Variety'

'New Yorker'
'A King in New York' (1957) written and directed by and starring Charles Chaplin – The worst film ever made by a celebrated film artist.

'The Last Tycoon' (1976) starring Robert de Niro – So enervated it's like a vampire movie after the vampires have left.

'Grease' (1978) starring John Travolta – A bogus, clumsily jointed pastiche of late fifties high school musicals, studded with leftovers from West Side Story and Rebel Without a Cause.

Andrew Nickolds
'Snatched' (1975) starring Jody Ray – Guarantees a high walk-out rate even on a wet afternoon.

'The Observer'
'Author, Author!' (1982) written by Israel Horowitz – In trying to dig a little deeper than

the average Neil Simon comedy, it only prepares its own grave.

Roger Parsons
'Stunts' (1977) starring Robert Forster – Less than cunning.

Elaine Paterson
'Assassination' (1986) written by Richard Sale – The plot shambles along as predictably as a dot-to-dot quiz. *'Time Out'*

'Every Time We Say Goodbye' (1986) starring Tom Hanks – A script so sugary it goes for your fillings. . . . Strictly for addicts of 'Mills & Boon' *'Time Out'*

'Ishtar' (1987) starring Dustin Hoffman and Warren Beatty – Accept that you're watching one of the worst films ever made and you may find it hilarious. *'Time Out'*

Chris Peachment
'Glen or Glenda' (1952) starring Bela Lugosi – Without doubt a candidate for one of the worst films ever made. *'Time Out'*

'Emmanuelle' (1974) starring Sylvia Kristel – It looks like a softcore version of *The Story of O* commissioned by *Vogue* magazine. *'Time Out'*

'Permission to Kill' (1975) starring Dirk Bogarde – A goodish cast demonstrates little more than the fact that actors, too, sometimes have to take on jobs to pay the rent. . . . As one of them says towards the end: 'There are no words adequate to describe what we've just seen.' A fair demonstration of the script's lack of any awareness. *'Time Out'*

'A Piece of the Action' (1977) starring Bill Cosby – A kind of black version of Dale Carnegie's *How to Win Friends and Influence People.* *'Time Out'*

'Caravan' (1978) starring Anthony Quinn – This slice of epic schlock has all the seductive power of a syphilitic camel. . . . No great sheiks. *'Time Out'*

'Caddyshack' (1980) starring Chevy Chase – If you're still at the age when farting and nose-picking seem funny, then *Caddyshack* should knock you dead. *'Time Out'*

'The Sea Wolves' (1980) starring Roger Moore, David Niven, Gregory Peck and Trevor Howard – As a genre – the arterio-sclerotic war movie – it'll never catch on. *'Time Out'*

'The World According to Garp' (1982) starring Robin Williams – It's the kind of movie that's brave – or stupid – enough to ask the meaning of life without having enough arse in its breeches to warrant a reply. *'Time Out'*

'Xtro' (1982) starring Bernice Stegers – A British horror picture incompetent enough to be prime drive-in fodder, if we only had such a thing. *'Time Out'*

'New York Nights' (1983) starring Corrine Alphen – Warning: the Surgeon General has determined that watching this film will give you herpes. *'Time Out'*

'Blind Date' (1984) starring Kirstie Alley – It just comes out a Babycham picture in a Moët bottle. *'Time Out'*

'Body Double' (1984) directed by Brian De Palma – Unblinking tosh of this order needs to be put on the protected list. *'Time Out'*

'The River' (1984) starring Mel Gibson – This is one river that seems unlikely to run. *'Time Out'*

'Out of Africa' (1985) starring Meryl Streep and Robert Redford – For all that it may have come out of Africa, the film's final destination is not many miles from Disneyland. *'Time Out'*

'A View to a Kill' (1985) starring Roger Moore – Once 007 was licensed to kill, now he not only eats quiche, but he cooks it himself. *'Time Out'*

'Heartburn' (1986) starring Meryl Streep and Jack Nicholson – The substance of the film is the kind of *Guardian* women's page slop in which the getting and raising of babies is suddenly a unique experience. . . . A movie of colossal inconsequence. *Heartburn?* No, just a bad attack of wind. *'Time Out'*

'Once Upon a Crime' (1992) produced by Dino De Laurentiis – The Ishtar Golden Turkey Award for Horribly Unfunny Comedy goes to this multinational clunker from Dino De Laurentiis.   'The Independent on Sunday'

Chris Petit

'Alfie Darling' (1975) starring Alan Price – The film looks incredibly like an advert with no product to sell.   'Time Out'

'Adventures of a Private Eye' (1977) starring Christopher Neil – Surprising, really, that this rock-bottom British 'sex' comedy wasn't called Adventures of a Private DICK! – that's about the level of the humour.   'Time Out'

David Pirie

'The VIPs' (1965) starring Elizabeth Taylor and Richard Burton – It's the sort of film that the British cinema could well do without.
'Time Out'

'The Sailor from Gibraltar' (1966) starring Jeanne Moreau – The most meaningless movie of the '60s.   'Time Out'

'Memories with Miss Aggie' (1974) starring Deborah Ashira – Looks like some meandering American fringe theatre production in which everyone has swallowed too much Valium. Even the most diehard porno audience will be panting . . . to get out of the cinema.   'Time Out'

'Lucky Lady' (1975) starring Gene Hackman and Liza Minnelli – The story is virtually non-existent, the period detail coyly derivative, and much of the comedy would be shamed even by the most meagre Anna Neagle vehicle of the '40s.   'Time Out'

'Capricorn One' (1977) co-starring Telly Savalas – The climactic introduction of Telly Savalas in a crop-dusting plane must rank as one of the most desperate measures to save a thriller since William Castle hung luminous skeletons from the cinema roof.   'Time Out'

'Star Wars' (1977) directed by George Lucas – Hollywood began in an amusement arcade, so it's appropriate that its most profitable film should be as formally enchanting and psychologically sterile as a Gottlieb pinball machine. Star Wars is at least 40 years out of date as science fiction.   'Time Out'

'The Boys from Brazil' (1978) starring Gregory Peck – There are more phony German accents than in a prep school version of Colditz.   'Time Out'

'Raiders of the Lost Ark' (1981) directed by Steven Spielberg – George Miller's choreography [in 'Mad Max 2' (1981)] of his innumerable vehicles is so extraordinary that it makes Spielberg's Raiders of the Lost Ark look like a kid fooling with Dinky toys.
'Time Out'

'Harry & Son' (1984) directed by and starring Paul Newman – The result is a curiously indigestible phenomenon, like being forced to eat five courses of avocado by an overbearing dinner-party host.   'Time Out'

John Preston

'Yentl' (1983) starring Barbra Streisand – The end result looks like nothing so much as the raw material for every Woody Allen Jewish joke ever coined.

Richard Rayner

'The Bride' (1985) starring Sting – A monster movie with a difference . . . not so much a movie, more a monster . . . preposterous as a love story and possessing all the horror of an advert for Holsten Pils.   'Time Out'

'Water' (1985) starring Michael Caine – This movie has the conviction of a farce negligently translated from an obscure foreign language.   'Time Out'

'Highlander' (1986) starring Christopher Lambert and Sean Connery – Scotch missed.
'Time Out'

Tony Rayns

'It Conquered the World' (1956) directed by Roger Corman – It makes Dr Who look like 2001.   'Time Out'

'Savages' (1972) directed by James Ivory – No wit, no thought, no surrealist flair, just vacuous decoration. It plays like a Ken

DRAMATIC

Russell movie worked over by a taxidermist.
'Time Out'

'The Four Musketeers' (1974) starring Michael
York – The whole sleek formula has rolled
over to reveal a very soft, very flabby
underside. 'Time Out'

'Welcome to Blood City' (1977) starring Jack
Palance – An utterly spineless sci-fi Western
. . . even Jack Palance can't lend it more
credibility than a playground version of
Gunfight at the OK Corral. 'Time Out'

'Andy Warhol's Bad' (1978) starring Carroll
Baker – If ever a movie lived up to its title.
'Time Out'

Rex Reed

'The Bible' (1966) directed by John Huston –
At a time when religion needs all the help it
can get, John Huston may have set its cause
back a couple of thousand years.

'Hurry Sundown' (1967) starring Michael
Caine – Critic Wilfrid Sheed wrote recently
that no film is ever so bad that you can't find
some virtue in it. He must not have seen
Hurry Sundown.

'Blue' (1968) starring Terence Stamp – I
don't know which is worse – bad cowboy movies
or bad arty movies. Blue is both.

'The Magus' (1968) starring Michael Caine –
This may be the most misguided movie ever
made.

'Can Hieronymus Merkin Ever Forget Mercy
Humppe and Find True Happiness?' (1969)
written and directed by and starring Anthony
Newley – If I'd been Anthony Newley I
would have opened it in Siberia during
Christmas week and called it a day.

'Secret Ceremony' (1969) starring Elizabeth
Taylor – This piece of garbage is so totally
ridiculous that I can't imagine why anyone
would want to be in it, let alone see it.

'The Secret of Santa Vittoria' (1969) directed by
Stanley Kramer – A brainless farrago of flying
rolling pins and rotten vegetables, filled with

the kind of screaming, belching, eye-rolling
fictional Italians only Kramer could invent.

'Sweet Charity' (1968) starring Shirley
Maclaine – The kind of platinum clinker
designed to send audiences flying towards
the safety of their television sets.

Frank Rich

'At Long Last Love' (1975) starring Burt
Reynolds – It's like watching a musical unfold
within The Night of the Living Dead.
'New York Times'

'Echoes of a Summer' (1975) starring Jodie
Foster – The only honest thing about this
movie is its desire to make a buck.
'New York Post'

'Lucky Lady' (1975) starring Liza Minnelli – A
manic mess that tries to be all things to all
people and ends up offering nothing to
anyone.

David Robinson

'Won-Ton-Ton, the Dog Who Saved
Hollywood' (1976) – The film tries to conceal
its deficiencies in comic ideas and comic skill
by doing everything at the pace of a
clockwork toy with a too-tight spring.
'The Times'

Nick Roddick

'The Bounty' (1984) starring Mel Gibson – A
long voyage to nowhere.
'Monthly Film Bulletin'

Jonathan Romney

'The Pleasure Principle' (1992) – More pain
than pleasure. 'Time Out'

Cynthia Rose

'Supersonic Man' (1979) starring Michael Coby
– this Superman spin-off doesn't just fall flat;
it's right down there with the most incoherent
movies ever made. . . . Supersonic Man looks
like Ted Kennedy in tights. Send back the
cornflakes: this one isn't even fit for Saturday
morning.

Jonathan Rosenbaum

'Rollerball' (1975) starring James Caan – A
classic demonstration of how several million
dollars can be unenjoyably wasted.

Mark Sanderson

'*Oxford Blues*' *(1984) starring Rob Lowe* – Or
A Wank at Oxford. . . .   '*Time Out*'

'*Death Wish III*' *(1985) starring Charles
Bronson* – This is nothing more than
cinematic masturbation.   '*Time Out*'

'*Vampire at Midnight*' *(1987) starring Jason
Williams* – Scares don't come into it, and the
general corn-flakiness of the whole enterprise
just goes to show that old Terror Teeth was
one of the very first cereal killers.   '*Time Out*'

'*The Dead Can't Lie*' *(1988) starring Tommy
Lee Jones as Eddie Mallard* – Mallard's movie
is a dead duck.   '*Time Out*'

Richard Schickel

'*Boom!*' *(1968) starring Elizabeth Taylor and
Richard Burton* – The title could not be more
apt, it is precisely the sound of a bomb
exploding.   '*Life*'

'*Convoy*' *(1978) starring Kris Kristofferson* –
Roughly as much fun as a ride on the New
Jersey turnpike with the window open. It not
only numbs the brain but pollutes the senses.
                                      '*Time*'

Jennifer Selway

'*FM*' *(1978) starring Michael Brandon* – Set in
a slick little LA music station, QSKY (7.11
on your FM dial). . . . A lot of pie in the
QSKY.   '*Time Out*'

Wifrid Sheed

'*Hurry Sundown*' *(1967) starring Michael
Caine* – To criticize it would be like tripping
a dwarf.

Robert E. Sherwood

'*Robin Hood*' *(1922) starring Douglas
Fairbanks* – The high water mark of film
production. It did not grow from the
bankroll, it grew from the mind.

'Sight and Sound'

'*Lucky Lady*' *(1975) starring Liza Minnelli* – It
sports its calculation on its sleeve like
rhinestones.

John Simon

'*Nine Hours to Rama*' *(1962) starring José
Ferrer* – The only interesting line in the movie
is the thin brown one visible on the inside of
every white collar.

'*The Silence*' *(1963) directed by Ingmar
Bergman* – The pearls are there, but the
string is too weak to hold them.

'*Eight and a Half*' *(1963) written and directed
by Federico Fellini* – It merely palls on us, and
finally appals us.

'*Les Parapluies de Cherbourg*' *(1964) starring
Catherine Deneuve* – We are told that in Paris
the opening night audience wept and the
critics were ecstatic. It would have made a
little more sense the other way round.

'*Dr Zhivago*' *(1965) directed by David Lean* –
David Lean's *Dr Zhivago* does for snow what
his *Lawrence of Arabia* did for sand.

'*The Greatest Story Ever Told*' *(1965) starring
Max Von Sydow* – God is unlucky . . . his
only begotten son turns out to be a bore. The
photography is inspired by Hallmark Cards.
. . . As the 'Hallelujah Chorus' explodes
around us stereophonically and
stereotypically it becomes clear that Lazarus
was not so much raised from the tomb as
blasted out of it.

'*Those Magnificent Men in Their Flying
Machines*' *(1965)* – It could have been a good
bit funnier by being shorter: the winning time
is 25 hours 11 minutes, and by observing
some kind of neo-Aristotelian unity the film
seems to last exactly as long.

'*Bonnie and Clyde*' *(1967) starring Warren
Beatty and Faye Dunaway* – The formula is
hayseed comedy bursting sporadically into
pyrotechnical bloodshed and laced with
sentimental pop-Freudianism.

'*Camelot*' *(1967) starring Richard Harris* –
This film is the Platonic idea of boredom,
roughly comparable to reading a three-
volume novel in a language of which one
knows only the alphabet. [*The film went on to
win three Oscars.*]

'*In Cold Blood*' *(1967) directed by Richard
Brooks* – It marks a slight step up for its
director, best remembered for reducing *Lord*

Jim to Pablum and *The Brothers Karamazov* to pulp. [*Brooks was nominated for an Oscar.*]

'The Bride Wore Black' (1967) directed by François Truffaut – Truffaut has called the film a love story; others have taken it as a tribute to his master, a Hitchcockian thriller. It is neither, it is a piece of junk.

'Reflections in a Golden Eye' (1967) starring Marlon Brando – One feels trapped in a huge overheated hothouse containing nothing but common snapdragons.

'Candy' (1968) starring Marlon Brando – As an emetic liquor is dandy, but *Candy* is quicker.

'The Milky Way' (1968) directed by Luis Buñuel – A mere trifle wrapped in a triple cloak of befuddling obscurantism.

'The Arrangement' (1969) starring Kirk Douglas – As dead as the flower arrangement in an undertaker's parlour.

'Butch Cassidy and the Sundance Kid' (1969) starring Paul Newman and Robert Redford – A mere exercise in smart-alecky device-mongering, chock-full of out of place and out of period one-upmanship, a battle of wits at a freshman smoker.

'Hard Contract' (1969) starring James Coburn – Like a flat-footed James Bond story that soaked its feet in a hot bath of existentialism.

'The Prime of Miss Jean Brodie' (1969) starring Maggie Smith – The novel lost a good deal in its stage simplification, and loses still more in its movie reduction of that stage version.

'Beyond the Valley of the Dolls' (1970) written by Roger Ebert – Awful, stupid and preposterous . . . also weirdly funny and a real curio, rather like a Grandma Moses illustration for a work by the Marquis de Sade.

'Myra Breckenridge' (1970) based on Gore Vidal's novel – Whatever the novel may be like, it surely cannot be this sort of witless, lip-smacking, continuously inept cop-out.

'Jonathan Livingstone Seagull' (1973) directed by Hall Bartlett – Seagulls, as the film stresses, subsist on garbage, and, I guess, you are what you eat.

'Adventures of Sherlock Holmes' Smarter Brother' (1975) produced and directed by Gene Wilder – Wilder has bitten off more than he can chew, and I can swallow.

'The Draughtsman's Contract' (1982) directed by Peter Greenaway – So pretentious, hollow and odious that it set my teeth on edge; I had the urge to throw something equally rotten back at the screen. *'National Review' (1990)*

Rupert Smith
'Cocktail' (1988) starring Tom Cruise – If a visitor from Mars needed a crash course in sexism, this would serve. . . . A tale of cock, signifying nothing. *'Time Out'*

Robert Stebbins
'Lost Horizon' (1937) directed by Frank Capra – One is reminded of a British critic's comment on *Mary Queen of Scotland*: 'the inaccuracies must have involved tremendous research'.

'The Sunday Express'
'King Richard and the Crusaders' (1954) based on Sir Walter Scott's 'The Talisman' – Do not adjust your set – the sound you hear is Sir Walter Scott turning in his grave.

'The Sunday Times'
'One from the Heart' (1982) directed by Francis F. Coppola – If this is the essence of cinema, then Salvador Dali is the essence of painting.

'Best Friends' (1982) starring Burt Reynolds and Goldie Hawn – A print-out of a script conference at which everyone collapsed at everyone else's contributory sally.

Paul Taylor
'Zorba the Greek' (1965) starring Anthony Quinn – The dreadful movie that launched a thousand package tours. *'Time Out'*

'McKenna's Gold' (1968) starring Gregory Peck – Treasure of the Sierra Madness. *'Time Out'*

'Fun with Dick and Jane' (1976) starring Jane Fonda – It's the sort of thing that would undoubtedly amuse Norman Tebbitt.

'Time Out'

'Go Tell the Spartans' (1977) starring Burt Lancaster – It's brought up-to-date to the extent that our human/wise/rebellious hero can die with a final exclamation of 'Oh, shit!' – an apt summation of a film that parades characters and quotes to be dismissed with a self-satisfied cynical shrug. Message-mongering for morons. *'Time Out'*

'Stand Up Virgin Soldiers' (1977) starring Robin Askwith – All too easily characterized as 'Confessions of a National Serviceman'. One for old Singapore sweats and lovers of jokes about parading privates. *'Time Out'*

'The Greek Tycoon' (1978) starring Anthony Quinn – Set somewhere in Martini-land, *The Greek Tycoon* is an everyday story of a shipping magnate and an assassinated president's widow – a sort of Harold Robbins out of *TitBits* tabloid biopic. *'Time Out'*

'The Prisoner of Zenda' (1979) starring Peter Sellers – Here the intrigues of Ruritanian royalty are conveyed with all the comic panache of an overlong Christmas variety show sketch on TV. *'Time Out'*

'All Quiet on the Western Front' (1980) starring Richard Thomas – A horrible instance of international packaging that has all the excitement of a financial balance sheet.

'Time Out'

'Private Benjamin' (1980) starring Goldie Hawn – Another depressing example of the big-screen gag-string sitcom, it turns exclusively on a plot that grew from a concept that developed from an idea that somebody should never have had – Goldie Hawn joins the army. *'Time Out'*

'Venom' (1981) starring Klaus Kinski – Venom spells box-office poison. *'Time Out'*

David Thompson
'9½ Weeks' (1981) starring Mickey Rourke and

Kim Basinger – Bump and grind for the Porsche owner.

'Time'
'The Man from Colorado' (1949) starring Glenn Ford – No more humour than a lawyer's shingle.

'Valley of the Dolls' (1967) directed by Mark Robson – The story is about girls who take all sorts of pills, but *Valley of the Dolls* offers only bromides.

'The Nightcomers' (1971) directed by Michael Winner – In all of this there is hardly enough of either terror or common sense to impose on the average tufted titmouse.

'Time Out'
'Force Ten from Navarone' (1978) starring Harrison Ford – A sequel too far.

'Alien' (1979) directed by Ridley Scott – An empty bag of tricks whose production values and expensive trickery cannot disguise imaginative poverty.

'Night Games' (1979) directed by Roger Vadim – The only nice thing about it is that after 107 minutes, it ends.

'The Stunt Man' (1979) starring Peter O'Toole – Stunted, not stunning.

Barry Took
'Close Encounters of the Third Kind' (1977) – Frankly, I thought it was tripe designed and made quite brilliantly for village idiots.

'Punch'

'Pete's Dragon' (1977) starring Mickey Rooney – For a Disney film it's terribly made, in parts so clumsy that it looks like the work of the Burbank Amateur Camera Club. *'Punch'*

'The Stick Up' (1977) starring David Soul – The worst film of this or possibly any year.

'Punch'

'The Swarm' (1978) starring Michael Caine – The story is of a banality matched only by the woodenness of the acting. *'Punch'*

Christopher Tookey

'1871' (1991) – The film looks like some unperformable Brecht play mounted by the amateur dramatic wing of the Militant Tendency. *'The Sunday Telegraph'*

'All I Want for Christmas' (1991) starring Thora Birch – The film goes downhill as fast as a toboggan ride down Everest.
'The Sunday Telegraph'

'Until the End of the World' (1992) directed by Wim Wenders – It's an aimless, meaningless and seemingly endless road-air-and-rail movie. . . . *Until the End of the World* is so dreadful that it would have difficulty in winning a prize at the Berlin Film Festival.
'The Sunday Telegraph'

Adrian Turner

'Young Winston' starring Simon Ward – A frightfully Boering biopic chronicling the adventures of Winston Churchill. . . . It comes across rather like an episode of the *Antiques Roadshow* on location at Blenheim Palace.

Shaun Usher

'Harley Davidson and the Marlboro Man' (1991) starring Mickey Rourke – This is one for action fans who are immune from unintentional parody. *'The Daily Mail' (1992)*

'Variety'

'Killer Fish' (1978) starring Lee Majors – A slapdash actioner which casts its rod in water so overfished of late that it's amazing there's still anything down there biting.

'Caligula' (1979) original screenplay by Gore Vidal – Far more Gore than Vidal.

'The Shining' (1980) starring Jack Nicholson – The truly amazing question is why a director of Stanley Kubrick's stature would spend his time and effort on a novel that he changes so much it's barely recognizable, taking away whatever originality it possessed while emphasizing its banality. The answer presumably is that Kubrick was looking for a 'commercial' property he could impose his own vision on, and Warner Bros, not having learned its lesson with *Barry Lyndon*, was silly enough to let him do it.

'Death Wish II' (1981) starring Charles Bronson – Bad art is one thing, *Death Wish II* is ludicrous.

'The Aviator' (1985) starring Christopher Reeve – Doesn't fly.

Alexander Walker

'The Devils' (1970) written and directed by Ken Russell – A garish glossary of sado-masochism . . . a taste for visual sensation that makes scene after scene look like the masturbatory fantasies of a Roman Catholic boyhood.

Dominic Wells

'Black Eagle' (1988) starring Jean-Claude Van Damme – Refile under codename Black Turkey. *'Time Out'*

'Rocky V' (1990) starring Sylvester Stallone and Sage Stallone – The scenes between Sly and his real-life son Sage have a certain poignancy, but there are more perceptive insights into parent-child relationships in an Oxo ad. *'Time Out'*

'Star Trek VI' (1992) starring William Shatner – It's zimmer frames ho! *'Time Out'*

H. G. Wells

'Metropolis' (1926) directed by Fritz Lang – Quite the silliest film.

David Wilson

'The Green Berets' (1968) starring John Wayne – Propaganda as crude as this can only do damage to its cause.

Richard Winnington

'Devotion' (1944) starring Ida Lupino and Olivia de Havilland – I would like to know who was devoted to whom and why?

'Caesar and Cleopatra' (1945) starring Vivien Leigh – It cost over a million and a quarter pounds, took two and a half years to make, and well and truly bored one spectator for two and a quarter hours.

'London Town' (1946) directed by Wesley Ruggles – I can't see the point of importing an

American director and giving him all the time and money in the world to play with when we can make bad musicals on our own, and quicker.

'The Fugitive' (1947) based on Graham Greene's novel 'The Power and the Glory' – The most pretentious travesty of a literary work since *For Whom the Bell Tolls*.

'Unconquered' (1947) directed by Cecil B. De Mille – De Mille bangs the drum as loudly as ever but his sideshow has gone cold on us.

'Bonnie Prince Charlie' (1948) starring David Niven – I have a sense of wonder about this film . . . it is that London Films, having surveyed the finished thing, should not have quietly scrapped it.

William Wolff
'Jonathan Livingstone Seagull' (1973) – This film is strictly for the gullible.   *'Cue'*

Peter Young
'Cape Fear' (1992) starring Robert De Niro – De Niro has reduced all the horror scenes to comedic proportions. They should have named it *Carry On Ketchup!*
'Jazz FM' (1992)

STAR CRITICISMS

Eddie Cantor
'The Eddie Cantor Story' (1953) featuring songs by Eddie Cantor – If that's my life – I didn't live.

Goldie Hawn
'Overboard' (1987) starring Goldie Hawn – It was like having a big fish on the end of your line and bringing it up and it just kind of wiggles off the hook.

Susan Hayward
'The Lost Moment' (1947) starring Susan Hayward – Their name for it may have been *The Lost Moment*, but after I saw it, I called it *The Lost Hour and Thirty-five Minutes.*

George Maharis
'Quick, Before It Melts' (1964) starring George Maharis – You had to catch it quick, before it disappeared.

Jean Negulesco
'The Conspirators' (1944) directed by Jean Negulesco – Secretly we called the film *The Constipators*, with Headache [Hedy] Lamarr and Paul Haemorrhoid [Henreid].

Mickey Rooney
'Quicksand' (1950) starring Mickey Rooney – I sank!

MOVIE INSULTS

Why don't you bore a hole in yourself and let the sap run out?
Groucho Marx – 'Monkey Business'

Love flies out the door when money comes innuendo.
Groucho Marx – 'Monkey Business'

Marry me and I'll never look at another horse.   *Groucho Marx – 'A Day at the Races'*

Why, you're one of the most beautiful women I've ever seen, and that's not saying much for you.
Groucho Marx – 'Animal Crackers'

I could dance with you until the cows come home. On second thoughts, I'd rather dance with the cows until you come home.
Groucho Marx – 'Duck Soup'

You call this a party? The beer is warm, the women are cold, and I'm hot under the collar. In fact, a more poisonous barbecue I've never attended.
Groucho Marx – 'Monkey Business'

He was so crooked, that when he died they had to screw him into the ground.
Bob Hope – 'The Cat and the Canary'

Almira Sessions: My ancestors came over here on the *Mayflower*.
Mae West: You're lucky. Now they have immigration laws.   *'The Heat's On'*

Women should be kept illiterate and clean, like canaries.   *Roscoe Karns – 'Woman of the Year'*

'The Man Who Came to Dinner' (1941) –

Monty Woolley reduced the nurse in *The Man Who Came to Dinner* to the potency of a pound of wet Kleenex. It was probably the best thing that had happened to the art of insult since the Medicis stopped talking in the 16th century.   *Richard Severo –*
'New York Herald-Tribune' (1963)
[*Severo may have been referring to the following line in the film:* My great-aunt Elizabeth ate a box of chocolates every day of her life. She lived to be a hundred and two, and when she had been dead three days, she looked healthier than you do now.
The Kaufman/Hart screenplay also contained the immortal lines:
You have the touch of a sex-starved cobra.
Gentlemen, will you all now leave quietly, or must I ask Miss Cutler to pass among you with a baseball bat?
I can feel the hot blood pounding through your varicose veins].

I've met a lot of hard-boiled eggs in my time, but you – you're twenty minutes.
        Jan Sterling – 'Ace in the Hole' (1951)

He's just swallowed his pride. It'll take him a moment or two to digest it.
        Patricia Neal – 'The Hasty Heart'

If I smelled as bad as you, I wouldn't live near people.   *Kim Darby – 'True Grit'*

Mister, the stork that brought you must have been a vulture.
        Ann Sheridan – 'Torrid Zone'

CELEBRITIES

FAME

Fame is being insulted by Groucho Marx.
        Denis O'Brien (1968)

Fame tends to be a lot of shits thinking you're no longer a threat.   *Valerie Raworth*

Fame is the aggregate of all the misunderstanding that collects around a new name.   *Rainer Maria Rilke*

Popularity is a crime from the moment it is sought; it is only a virtue where men have it whether they will or no.   *Sir George Savile*

These days a star is anyone who can hold a microphone. A superstar is someone who has shaken hands with Lew Grade. A super-superstar is someone who has refused to shake hands with Lew Grade.
        Harry Secombe

Egotism is usually just a case of mistaken nonentity.   *Barbara Stanwyck*

ACTING

GENERAL

Why must all the actors bellow like sealions conversing with walruses on the further side of an ice flow in a blizzard?
        James Agate (1945)

An actor's success has the life expectancy of a small boy about to look into a gas tank with a lighted match.   *Fred Allen*

Actresses don't have husbands, they have attendants.   *Margaret Anglin*

Acting is the art of keeping people from coughing.   *Jean-Louis Barrault*

For an actress to be a success, she must have the face of Venus, the brains of Minerva, the grace of Terpsichore, the memory of Macaulay, the figure of Juno, and the hide of a rhinoceros.

        Ethel Barrymore

I can't think of anything grimmer than being an ageing actress – God! it's worse than being an ageing homosexual. *Candice Bergen*

An actor is a guy who, if you ain't talking about him, ain't listening. *Marlon Brando*

Acting is the expression of a neurotic impulse. It's a bum's life. Quitting acting, that's the sign of maturity. *Marlon Brando*

Acting is an empty and useless profession. *Marlon Brando*

Every actor has a natural animosity toward every other actor, present or absent, living or dead.
Louise Brooks – 'Lulu in Hollywood' (1982)

This is a monstrous saying. 'No respectable woman on the stage!' There are thousands of respectable women and only about six actresses. *Robert Buchanan*

Acting is all about honesty. If you can fake that, you've got it made. *George Burns*

On how to play a drunk – The best research is being a British actor for 20 years.
Michael Caine

A fan club is a group of people who tell an actor he's not alone in the way he feels about himself. *Jack Carson*

Remember I am an artist. And you know what that means in a court of law. Next worst to an actress.
Joyce Cary – 'The Horse's Mouth'

I don't believe in astrology. The only stars I can blame for my failures are those that walk about the stage. *Noël Coward*

The relationship between the make-up man and the film actor is that of accomplices in crime. *Marlene Dietrich*

Actors are a nuisance in the earth, the very offal of society. *Timothy Dwight*

Show me a great actor and I'll show you a lousy husband; show me a great actress and

you've seen the devil. *W. C. Fields*

You spend your whole life trying to do something they put people in asylums for.
Jane Fonda

Modesty is the artifice of actors, similar to passion in call-girls. *Jackie Gleason*

Actors and burglars work better at night.
Cecil Hardwicke

Actors are only honest hypocrites.
William Hazlitt

Acting is the most minor of gifts and not a very high-class way to earn a living. After all, Shirley Temple could do it at the age of four.
Katharine Hepburn

Life's what's important. Walking, houses, family. Birth and pain and joy. Acting's just waiting for a custard pie. That's all.
Katharine Hepburn

Actresses will happen in the best regulated families. *Oliver Herford*

The arrival of talking movies will in no way affect my favourite motion picture actors – the horses. *Don Herold*

All actors are whores – we sell our bodies to the highest bidder. *William Holden*

No actress is better than her last picture.
Hedda Hopper

Turn an actor like ham, when you can find one, loose on good material when you can find that, and lyricism will ensue. Give him rubbish to act and he will destroy himself like a Bugatti lubricated with hair-oil.
Clive James – 'The Observer' (1975)

An actor-manager is one to whom the part is greater than the whole. *Ronald Jeans*

On eager substitute actors – They're not understudies, they're overstudies.
George S. Kaufman

What a set of barren asses actors are.
John Keats (1819)

An actor can remember his briefest notice well into senescence and long after he has forgotten his phone number and where he lives.
Jean Kerr – 'Please Don't Eat the Daisies' (1957)

Don't go to piano bars where young, unemployed actors get up and sing. Definitely don't be a young, unemployed actor who gets up and sings.
Tony Lang (1985)

When actors begin to think, it is time to change. They are not fitted for it.
Stephen Leacock

I'm not sure that acting is something for a grown man to be doing. *Steve McQueen*

Some of the greatest love affairs I've known have involved one actor – unassisted.
Wilson Mizner

Acting is the lowest of the arts, if an art at all, and makes slender demands on the intelligence of the individual exercising it. You can teach a child to act, but you can teach no child to paint pictures, or model statues, or to write prose.
George Moore – 'Mummer Worship'

It is a great help for a man to be in love with himself. For an actor, however, it is absolutely essential.
Robert Morley – 'Playboy' (1979)

Do not confound an aphrodisiacal actress with a talented one. *George J. Nathan*

An actor without a playwright is like a hole without a doughnut. *George J. Nathan*

Acting is like letting your pants down: you're exposed.
Paul Newman – 'Time' (1982)

Acting is a masochistic form of exhibitionism. It is not quite the occupation of an adult. *Sir Laurence Olivier*

In the old days an actress tried to become a star. Today we have stars trying to become actresses. *Sir Laurence Olivier*

Some actors think they are elevating the stage when they're merely depressing the audience.
George A. Posner

In Europe an actor is an artist. In Hollywood, if he isn't working, he's a bum.
Anthony Quinn

The Cinema Woman is a Popcorn Venus – a delectable, but insubstantial hybrid of cultural distortions. *Marjorie Rosen*

I made the mistake early in my career, when I moved to Hollywood, of being attracted to actresses. I used to go out exclusively with actresses and other female impersonators.
Mort Sahl (1976)

A movie star is not an artist but an art object.
Richard Schickel

It is nearly impossible for a woman to remain pure who adopts the stage as a profession.
Clement Scott

The prettier an actress gets, the worse she acts. *Gene Shalit*

A character actor is one who cannot act and therefore makes an elaborate study of disguise and stage tricks by which acting can be grotesquely simulated. *G. B. Shaw*

The physical labour that actors have to do wouldn't tax an embryo.
Neil Simon – 'The Sunshine Boys' (1975)

An actress is someone with no ability who sits around waiting to go on alimony.
Jackie Stallone (1990)

I'm an actor! An actress is someone who wears boa feathers. *Sigourney Weaver (1983)*

You can pick out actors by the glazed look that comes into their eyes when the conversation wanders away from them.
Michael Wilding

In reply to Alfred Hitchcock's comment 'All actors are cattle' – Show me a cow who can earn a million dollars a film.
Michael Winner

ACTORS AND ACTRESSES

Anon
On her leading man – Fine, if you like acting
with two and a half tons of condemned veal.
Coral Browne

On an actor who shot his brains out in a suicide
– He must have been a marvellous shot.
Noël Coward

She's as tough as an ox. When she dies she'll
be turned into Bovril.   *Dorothy Parker*

Dear, she is one of Nature's gentlemen.
Oscar Wilde

Julie Andrews
'Star!' (1968) a biopic of Gertrude Lawrence –
Julie Andrews has been compared to
everything from a mechanically charming air
hostess to a knitted coverlet for a toilet roll,
but one comparison she has escaped –
especially since *'Star!'* – is to Gertrude
Lawrence.   *Geoff Brown – 'Time Out'*

'Darling Lili' (1970) – The failure of
Avalanche [starring Rock Hudson] and
'Darling Lili' – one movie had a glacier, the
other had Julie Andrews. I guess the audience
couldn't tell the difference.   *Rock Hudson*

Fred Astaire
I can sing as well as Fred Astaire can act.
Burt Reynolds

Tallulah Bankhead
'Eugenia' [1957] – Only Mae West as Snow
White could have seemed more unsuited to
the part.   *Louis Kronenberger*

Lionel Barrymore
I always said that I'd like Barrymore's acting
till the cows came home. Well, ladies and
gentlemen, last night the cows came home.
George J. Nathan

Freddie Bartholomew
'Anna Karenina' (1935) – The only real blot is
provided by Freddie Bartholomew as the
heroine's darling child, looking and sounding
the way sickly chocolate tastes.
Geoff Brown – 'Time Out'

Sarah Bernhardt
Mrs Campbell played Mélisande and Mme
Bernhardt Pelléas; they are both old enough
to know better.   *Anon*

Marlon Brando
Actors like him are good but on the whole I
do not enjoy actors who seek to commune
with their armpits, so to speak.   *Greer Garson*

Albert Brooke
He has a face like an open sandwich.
Rex Reed

Richard Burton
'The Assassination of Trotsky' (1972) –
Another miserable Richard Burton
performance – his Trotsky resembles nothing
so much as Lionel Barrymore playing Dr
Gillespie.   *Gary Arnold – 'Washington Post'*

Wooden as a board with his body, relies on
doing all his acting with his voice.
John Boorman (1984)

Mrs Patrick Campbell
I don't like her. But don't misunderstand me,
my dislike is purely platonic.
Herbert Beerbohm Tree

Dyan Cannon
'Author! Author!' (1982) – Cannon is in her
hairy, furry, woolly way, radiantly two-
dimensional.   *Jennifer Smith – 'Time Out'*

Richard Chamberlain
A man with the sex appeal of a sheep and the
comic timing of a manatee.
Chris Peachment – 'Time Out' (1985)

Carol Channing
'Gentlemen Prefer Blondes' (1949) – She goes
through the play like a dazed automaton –
husky enough to kick in the teeth of any
gentleman on the stage.   *Brooks Atkinson*

Charles Chaplin
I despise Chaplin. I think he was a faggot. So
prissy, so English – I mean that in the worst
sense. I just want to reach into the screen and
punch the little f***er.   *Tony Hendra (1984)*

If people don't sit at Chaplin's feet, he goes out and stands where they are sitting.

Herman J. Mankiewicz

Maurice Chevalier
He was sour, scowling, and ill-humoured, as well as a notorious tight-wad. *James M. Cain*

Montgomery Clift
'*A Place in the Sun*' *(1951)* – Mr Montgomery Clift gives the performance of his career in *A Place in the Sun*; which is not saying a great deal, since he had already demonstrated in *The Heiress* that he didn't belong on the same screen with first-class actors.

Raymond Chandler

Joan Collins
She's common, she can't act – yet she's the hottest female property around these days. If that doesn't tell you something about the state of our industry today, what does?

Stewart Grainger (1984)

Jackie Collins is to writing what her sister Joan is to acting. *Campbell Grison*

Joan Collins career is a testimony to menopausal chic. *Erica Jong*

Joan Crawford
I'm a little repulsed by her shining lips, like balloon tyres in wet weather. *John Betjeman*

'*Rain*' *(1932)* – The reason that *Rain* failed with Miss Crawford is because Miss Crawford cannot act her way out of a paper bag. *Bette Davis*

There is not enough money in Hollywood to lure me into making another picture with Joan Crawford. And I like money.

Sterling Hayden

Poor old rotten egg, Joan . . . she was a mean, tipsy, powerful rotten egg lady.

Mercedes McCambridge

Miriam Davis
What annoys me most? Unused fireplaces, pink sweet peas, badly made beds . . . and Miriam Hopkins. *Bette Davis*

Doris Day
The only real talent Miss Day possesses is that of being absolutely sanitary – her personality untouched by human thought, her form unsmudged by the slightest evidence of femininity. *John Simon (1964)*

James Dean
I don't mean to speak ill of the dead, but he was a prick. *Rock Hudson*

Duilio del Prete
'*At Long Last Love*' *(1975)* – An Italian with no voice, makes the elegant English of Cole Porter sound like pig Latin.

Frank Rich – 'New Times'

'*At Long Last Love*' *(1975)* – He has as much charm as a broomstick with a smile painted on it. *John Simon – 'Esquire'*

'*At Long Last Love*' *(1975)* – Del Prete, an Italian discovery, sings as if he came to paint the mansion and stayed on to regale the company with wobbly impersonations of Louis Jordan and Maurice Chevalier.

Bruce Williamson – 'Playboy'

Bo Derek
Bo is a simple girl at heart, and only realists, puritans and most other sections of society would suggest that she is totally without charm and possesses an IQ slightly higher than her chest measurement.

Anne Billson – 'Time Out' (1984)

Kirk Douglas
Kirk would be the first to tell you that he's a difficult man, I would be the second.

Burt Lancaster

Richard Dreyfuss
'*Dillinger*' *(1973)* – Richard Dreyfuss draws attention to himself by overdoing it, as usual, playing Baby Face Nelson like a rabid pug dog. *Anon*

Faye Dunaway
She's a 20th-century fox, a calculating lady who repels even as she attracts. *Bart Mills*

'*The Wicked Lady*' *(1982)* – Even such natural activity as breathing now occasions in her a virtuoso display of over-acting. Her eyebrows quiver, her eyes pop, her nostrils dilate, and the skin over her cheek-bones tightens. When she actually utters a line, it is as if a battalion of signallers have gone simultaneously berserk and are semaphoring delirious messages. *Frank Walker*

Denholm Elliott
I amended the actor's cliché to 'Never work with children, animals, or Denholm Elliott!'
Gabriel Byrne

Douglas Fairbanks
On being pestered by a woman who asked him, 'Do you remember me, I met you with Douglas Fairbanks?' – Madam, I don't even remember Douglas Fairbanks! *Noël Coward*

Mia Farrow
On her marriage to Frank Sinatra – Hah! I always knew Frank would end up in bed with a boy! *Ava Gardner*

Eddie Fisher
The reason I drink is because when I'm sober I think I'm Eddie Fisher. *Dean Martin*

Jane Fonda
She didn't get that terrific body from exercise. She got it from lifting all that money. *Joan Rivers (1987)*

Zsa Zsa Gabor
A self-absorbed Barbie doll with a foreign accent.
Jeffrey Richards – 'Sunday Telegraph' (1992)

Greta Garbo
Excuse me, Ma'am, I thought you were a guy I knew in Philadelphia. *Groucho Marx*

Cary Grant
They are trying to show he's a great lover, but they'll never prove it to me.
Zsa Zsa Gabor

Charles Gray
Malvolio in 'Twelfth Night' (1974) – An actor whose perfection of suaveness is funny in itself, but who is therefore quite unable to play anyone with pretensions.
Clive James – 'The Observer'

Daria Halprin
'Zabriskie Point' (1970) – She tries to look cute, sexy and sweet – all at the same time – and turns in the kind of performance that might only appeal to fifty-five-year-old divorced men. *Michael Medved*

Cynthia Harris
'Edward and Mrs Simpson' (1978) – It is hard to tell whether she is acting badly or else giving a good impression of the kind of American woman who sounds like a bad actress. *Clive James – 'The Observer'*

Rex Harrison
If you weren't the best light comedian in the country, all you'd be fit for would be the selling of cars in Great Portland Street.
Noël Coward

Nigel Havers
'The Good Guys' – This might have been better if it didn't look quite so much like a Surrey Tourist Board promo. Oh, and if Nigel Havers could act.
Bruce Dessau – 'Time Out' (1992)

Goldie Hawn
The general squeaky-voiced persona of a vaguely disturbed chipmunk.
Sue Heal – 'Today'

'Deceived' (1992) – The actress who looked and squeaked like an unwaxed surfboard on *Rowan and Martin's Laugh-In.*
Jeff Sawtell – 'Morning Star'

Rita Hayworth
The worst lay in the world – she was always drunk and never stopped eating.
Peter Lawford

Katharine Hepburn
On auditioning for 'Gone with the Wind' (1939) – I can't imagine Rhett Butler chasing you for ten years. *David O. Selznick*

Charlton Heston
He's the only man who could drop out of a cubic moon, he's so square. *Richard Harris*

Helen Hobson
'Pygmalion (1992) – Though possessing a

pleasant enough voice, she is devoid of the gamine quality so necessary to the part and has the personality of a girl next door.

Beryl Bainbridge – 'The Oldie'

Dustin Hoffman

'Hook' (1992) – Hoffman, essaying Old Etonian, comes out like a poor take-off of Terry Thomas.

Hugo Davenport – 'Daily Telegraph'

Dustin Hoffman is the luckiest Jewish midget that ever lived. *Martin Rackin*

'Billy Bathgate' (1992) – He seems to have taken a correspondence course in playing gangsters from Al Pacino.

Christopher Tookey – 'Sunday Telegraph'

These drab looking people like Dustin Hoffman – can you believe any girl looks at Dustin Hoffman and gets a thrill? I can't!

Ruth Waterbury

Hulk Hogan

'Suburban Commando' (1991) – Hogan's timing makes Arnold Schwarzenegger look like Cary Grant.

Christopher Tookey – 'Sunday Telegraph'

Glenda Jackson

Quite aside from her age, Miss Jackson is not appealing in any part – face, body or limbs. Nothing she says or does stems from genuine feeling, displays an atom of spontaneity, leaves any room for the unexpected. It is all technique – and not the most intricate technique at that – about as good as computer poetry. *John Simon*

'The Music Lovers' (1970) – Her thunderous full-frontal, carpet-clawing caricature is a calamity of mistiming. *Mark Whitman*

Don Johnson

He wins the Eddie Murphy prize for milking celebrity as far as it will go.

Helen Fitzgerald (1986)

Charles Kean

Nothing would be more exasperating now than to sit through his performance of a part like [Shakespeare's] Richard, and hear his

wooden intonation in this fashion – 'Dow is the widter of our discotedt bade glorious subber by the sud of York.'

David Masson – 'Memories of London'

Edmund Kean

I went to see Mr Kean, and was thoroughly disgusted. This monarch of the stage is a little insignificant man, slightly deformed, strongly ungraceful, seldom pleasing the eye, still seldomer satisfying the ear – with a voice between grunting and croaking, a perpetual hoarseness which suffocates his words, and a vulgarity of manner which his admirers are pleased to call nature. *Mary Mitford (1814)*

Patsy Kensit

'Twenty-one' (1991) – Patsy Kensit trying to be raunchy reminded me irresistibly of all those awful films where Julie Andrews had to pretend to be a sex siren.

Christopher Tookey – 'Sunday Telegraph'

'Blame it on the Bell-boy' (1992) – Ms Kensit has all the comic timing and subtlety of an aircraft carrier.

Christopher Tookey – 'Sunday Telegraph'

Sylvia Kristel

'Lady Chatterley's Lover' (1981) – Kristel gives a boring performance and she plays it with the expression of a pall-bearer.

Jennifer Selway – 'Time Out'

Jessica Lange

'A Streetcar Named Desire' (1992) – Less a matter of deficient stage experience than of emotional timidity.

Frank Rich – 'New York Times'

Angela Lansbury

'The Three Musketeers' (1948) – Angela Lansbury wears the crown of France as though she had won it at a county fair.

'New Yorker'

George Lazenby

'On Her Majesty's Secret Service' (1969) – The Bond films were bad enough even with the partially ironic performances of Connery. Here, featuring the stunning nonentity Lazenby, there are no redeeming features.

Geoff Andrew – 'Time Out'

Jean-Pierre Leaud
An eternally callow, crashing bore.
John Simon

Dolph Lundgren
After Arnold Schwarzenegger, Dolph
Lundgren is a bit of a disappointment. At
least Arnold looks as if he comes supplied
with batteries. *Adam Mars-Jones (1987)*

John Lydon
'Order of Death' (1983) – The only
miscalculation is the casting of Lydon (aka
Johnny Rotten), who seems as threatening as
a wet poodle. *Chris Peachment – 'Time Out'*

Shirley MacLaine
She is Warren Beatty's older brother, not his
sister. *Andrei Konchalovsky (1987)*

I love her, but her oars aren't touching the
water these days. *Dean Martin*

On her autobiography 'Dance While You Can'
– Shirley MacLaine is 56 and this is her sixth
volume of autobiography. Even giant
egomaniacs usually stop short of dividing
their lives up into decade sized chunks, but
then to read Ms MacLaine is to encounter
one of the most inflated airheads ever to
break free of her moorings.
John Preston –
'Sunday Telegraph' (1992)

William Charles MacReady
'Othello' – He growls and prowls, and roams
and foams, about the stage, in every
direction, like a tiger in a cage, so that I never
know on what side of me he means to be; and
keeps up a perpetual snarling and grumbling
like the aforesaid tiger, so that I never feel
quite sure that he has done, and that it is my
turn to speak. My only feeling about my
acting it with Mr McReady is dread of his
personal violence. In Macbeth he pinched me
black and blue, and almost tore the point-lace
from my head. I am sure my little finger will
be re-broken. *Fanny Kemble (1848)*

Marie McDonald
A triple threat who can't sing, dance nor act.
Gene Kelly

Ian McKellen
'Scandal' (1988) – Less satisfying is
McKellen's Profumo, who looks more like a
samurai warrior than a war minister.
Steve Grant – 'Time Out'

Steve McQueen
A Steve McQueen performance just naturally
lends itself to monotony. Steve doesn't bring
much to the party. *Robert Mitchum*

Dean Martin
'The Ambushers' (1967) – Martin's acting is so
inept that even his impersonation of a lush
seems unconvincing. *Harry Medved*

Lee Marvin
'Paint Your Wagon' (1969) – Not since Attila
the Hun swept across Europe leaving 500
years of blackness has there been a man like
Lee Marvin. *Joshua Logan*

'The Great Scout and Cathouse Thursday'
(1976) – This dreary and eminently
forgettable Western has Marvin's
increasingly tedious hamming, matched, and
even topped, by Oliver Reed's hapless
mugging; not a pretty sight.
Chris Peachment – 'Time Out'

James Mason
'The Marriage Go Round' (1961) – An actor
who couldn't crack a joke if he was a lichee
nut. *'Time'*

Victor Mature
'Samson and Delilah' (1949) – Mature looks
as constipated as ever. *'Time Out'*

Ethel Merman
'Gypsy' (1959) – Brassy, brazen witch on a
mortgaged broomstick, a steamroller with
cleats. *Walter Kerr*

Bette Midler
She's got big tits but thank God she's got
them, because she hasn't got anything else.
Divine (1983)

'Jinxed' (1982) – In one scene I have to hit
her in the face, and I thought we could save
some money on sound effects here.
Ken Wahl (1982)

Imogen Milais-Scott

'Salome's Last Dance' (1987) – The petulant nymph, as incarnated by Milais-Scott – seemingly a graduate of the Toyah Wilcox School of Over-Emphatic-Diction and Hyperactive-Eyelids – is depressingly tiresome.   *Geoff Arnold – 'Time Out'*

Liza Minnelli

'Charlie Bubbles' (1968) – The supreme deadweight is Liza Minnelli, whose screen debut proves easily the most inauspicious since Turhan Bey's.   *John Simon*

'Stepping Out' (1991) – Putting on a sad show, courtesy of Liza with a zzzzz.
'Time Out'

Helen Mirren

'The Fiendish Plot of Dr Fu Manchu' (1980) – Co-star Helen Mirren continues her determined bid to give up acting for the role of ripest screen-tease object of the '80s.
Rod McShane – 'Time Out'

Marilyn Monroe

Next to her Lucrezia Borgia was a pussy-cat.
David Hall

Roger Moore

'Diane' (1956) – Lana Turner as Diane de Poitiers walked on screen in a clattering of heels and a fluttering of eyelashes, followed by a lump of English roast beef.   *'Time'*

Chesty Morgan

'Deadly Weapons' (1974) – Her efforts to perform the simplest operation (e.g. walking off without smiling at the camera) make her appear more pathetic than if she were to have posed in a freak show.   *David McGillivray*

Rebecca de Mornay

'The Hand that Rocks the Cradle (1992) – The performance is Cod de Mornay.
Anthony Lane – 'Independent on Sunday'

Hildegarde Neil

'Antony and Cleopatra' (1972) – Shakespeare's play . . . very nearly irretrievably sunk by Hildegarde Neil's petulant Cleopatra, a suburban schoolmarm having a fling on the Nile.
Tom Milne – 'Time Out'

Anthony Newley

'Mister Quilp' (1975) – Mr Newley's Quilp, a galvanized Quasimodo on a permanent high, is something of a strain to watch.
Michael Billington – 'Illustrated London News'

Nanette Newman

'International Velvet' (1978) – It's particularly sad that Elizabeth Taylor was unavailable to resume her role. Even at her latter-day worst, she's a far more compelling presence than Nanette Newman.   *Frank Rich*

Jack Nicholson

'The Shining' (1980) – In *Making 'The Shining'* Jack Nicholson told of how Stanley Kubrick had pushed him into an acting style beyond naturalism. Clips of Jack in action proved that there is no acting style beyond naturalism except ham.
Clive James – 'The Observer' (1980)

David Niven

'Bonnie Prince Charlie' (1948) – David Niven rallying his hardy Highlanders to his standard in a voice hardly large enough to summon a waiter.   *'New Yorker'*

'The Elusive Pimpernel' (1950) – Niven plays the Scarlet Pimpernel with the sheepish lack of enthusiasm of a tone deaf man called upon to sing solo in church. His companions lumber through their parts like schoolboys about to go down with mumps.
'Daily Express'

Kim Novak

Is Kim Novak a joke in her own time?
Robert Altman (1974)

Q. You just made *The Fifth Monkey*, and Kim Novak's comeback film *The Children*. Which is the most difficult to act with: monkeys or children?
A. Kim Novak.   *Ben Kingsley (1990)*

Margaret O'Brien

If that child had been born in the Middle Ages, she'd have been burned as a witch.
Lionel Barrymore

Michael Oliver

'Problem Child 2' (1992) – Oliver makes

Macaulay Culkin look like Gene Hackman.
Suzi Feay – 'Time Out'

Laurence Olivier
'Othello' – Larry's Othello looked like Al
Jolson with palsy. *Allison Pearson –*
'Independent on Sunday' (1992)

Tatum O'Neal
'Paper Moon' (1973) – All Tatum O'Neal did
was to remind me what a brilliant artist
Shirley Temple was. *Lindsay Anderson (1975)*

Peter O'Toole
'Rebecca's Daughter' (1992) – From Lawrence
of Arabia to Widow Twankey. This Carry-
On-Cross-Dressing marks the fall of Peter
O'Toole with a dull thud.
Tom Hutchinson – 'Mail on Sunday'

Al Pacino
'Scarface' (1983) – Pacino gives a monstrous
performance as the Cuban heel, clearly
aiming for role of the year, but the abiding
memory is of just another Method boy
chewing the scenery in his quiet way.
Chris Peachment – 'Time Out'

Pal (alias Lassie)
A vicious bastard. *Peter Lawford*

Jason Patric
'After Dark My Sweet' (1991) – Jason Patric
does a passable impersonation of Mickey
Rourke in one of Bruce Willis's sweatier T-
shirts. *Christopher Tookey – 'Sunday Telegraph'*

George Peppard
He's arrogant, the sort of man who expects
women to fall at his feet at the slightest
command; who throws his weight around.
He gives the impression that he's the star,
what he says goes and that nobody else is
very important. *Joan Collins*

Mandy Perryment
'Some Like It Hot' (1992) – Mandy
Perryment's Sugar (the Monroe film rôle),
while a great imitation, never quite rises to
the temperature at which some are supposed
to like it. *Rick Jones – 'Time Out'*

James Quin
Heavy and phlegmatic, he trod the stage,
Too proud for tenderness, too dull for rage.
Charles Churchill

Robert Redford
His acting is as close to neutral as any I
remember – he holds the camera for an
eternity with his level gaze and then doesn't
deliver anything. *David Denby*

Robert is adorable, but when they enriched
that handsome hunk of white bread, they
somehow left out the mythic minerals.
Richard Schickel (1978)

Burt Reynolds
'At Long Last Love' (1975) – He sings like
Dean Martin with adenoids and dances like a
drunk killing cockroaches.
John Barbour – 'Los Angeles'

Fiona Richmond
'Let's Get Laid' (1977) – Ms Richmond
displays the acting abilities of a chair and two
of the most suspiciously buoyant sachets of
flesh this side of Sainsbury's.
Giovanni Dadomo – 'Time Out'

Eric Roberts
'The Coca-Cola Kid' (1985) – Roberts, as the
kid from Coke, is well on his way to
becoming the world's worst actor.
Chris Peachment – 'Time Out'

Julia Roberts
As Tinkerbell in 'Hook' (1992) – J. M. Barrie's
Tinkerbell was all brains and no body,
whereas Julia Roberts . . .
Jill Parkin –
'Daily Express' (1992)

Anton Rodgers
'Some Singing for Blood' (1992) – As if
Dickens's Mr Pumblechook were cast in the
leading rôle in an advertisement for
Australian lager.
Benedict Nightingale – 'The Times'

Ginger Rogers
She was one of the worst, red-baiting,
terrifying reactionaries in Hollywood.
Joseph Losey

Katharine Ross

'*The Stepford Wives*' *(1974)* – It was hard to tell Katharine Ross playing a robot from Katharine Ross playing a normal housewife.
Les Keyser

Mickey Rourke

A fine actor with an unerring knack for choosing the wrong movies. *Peter Travers*

Misty Rowe

'*Goodbye, Norma Jean*' *(1975)* – Misty Rowe fails completely as a reincarnation of Monroe. *'Time Out'*

Rosalind Russell

'*Mrs Pollifax – Spy*' *(1970)* – Ros Russell, pseudonymously scripting as well as starring, was old enough to have known better, but did the honourable thing and retired immediately after. *Paul Taylor – 'Time Out'*

Theresa Russell

'*Whore*' *(1992)* – Her performance is like a bright public-schoolgirl's audition for RADA.
Christopher Tookey – 'Sunday Telegraph'

Ricky Schroder

'*Little Lord Fauntleroy*' *(1980)* – The unacceptable face of American child acting. Zzzzzz. *Chris Peachment – 'Time Out'*

Arnold Schwarzenegger

'*Conan the Destroyer*' *(1984)* – This new adventure is far closer to creator Robert E. Howard's preference for small minds in big bodies – a requirement Schwarzenegger fills wonderfully. *Giovanni Dodamo – 'Time Out'*

All that pumping iron seems to have given him an ethereal gaze and the toneless voice of an automaton. And it makes me wonder: is he really one of us? *Iain Johnstone*

He's the only man in the world that it is impossible to imagine having been a baby.
Penny Perrick – 'Sunday Times' (1992)

Paul Scofield

'*Heartbreak House*' *(1992)* – Scofield's captain, booming through the part with an exaggerated quaver, sounds like a small boy playing God – it is as obvious and irritating as an actress's lisping to show us that she thinks of herself as a little girl.
Rhoda Koenig – 'Punch'

George C. Scott

One of the best actors alive. But my opinion of him as an actor is much higher than my opinion of him as a man. *John Huston*

Peter Sellers

As a man he was abject, probably his own worst enemy, although there was plenty of competition. *Roy Boulting*

'*The Bobo*' *(1967)* – Even more embarrassing than Sellers' efforts to be funny is the realisation that he is trying to be moving too.
Tom Milne – 'Time Out'

Charlie Sheen

'*The Rookie*' *(1990)* – Only Sheen's hysterically inept handling of the godawful dialogue relieves the boredom.
Mark Kermode – 'Time Out'

'*Hot Shots*' *(1991)* – Sheen shows his usual acting ability and might do well to check which department stores need Santas next year.
Christopher Tookey – 'Sunday Telegraph'

Cybill Shepherd

'*At Long Last Love*' *(1975)* – As for Shepherd's dancing, the best that can be said is that it may not be recognisable as such: when this horsey ex-model starts prancing around, she tends to look as if she's fighting off a chronic case of the trots.
Frank Rich – 'New Times'

Christian Slater

'*Kuffs*' *(1992)* – The boy most likely to succeed has flunked out with this corny cop-spoof . . . he needs something extra special for real stardom. They call it talent.
Tom Hutchinson – 'Mail on Sunday'

Sylvester Stallone

His big asset: a face that would look well upon a three-toed sloth. If not the Incredible, Stallone is at least the Improbable Hulk.
Russell Davies (1977)

Signor Sylvester Stallone is not an actor or thespian in the normal sense, being monotonous to an extraordinary degree. He is, simply, 'the grunt'.
'Punch' (1992)

His career is more mysterious than cot death.
Rex Reed

'Rocky II' (1979) – This is the most solemn example of self-deification by a movie star since Barbra Streisand's *A Star Is Born*.
John Simon

Tommy Steele
'Some Like It Hot' (1992) – Made up as Josephine, he looks, eerily enough, more like Tommy Steele than he does in regular costume. Either that, or Minnie Caldwell.
Richard Cook – 'Sunday Times'

Meryl Streep
Oh God! She looks like a chicken.
Truman Capote (1986)

She seemed like a frozen, boring blonde, with ice water in her veins; from the Grace Kelly–Tippi Hedren School of Dramatic Art.
Rex Reed

Barbra Streisand
She's a real 'kvetch' – she's always moaning about something or other: a really hard-to-please lady.
Peter Bogdanovich

The Burt Lancaster Award that goes to the actor or actress whose performance most completely depends upon hair styling. This award is to be shared by Miss Streisand's hairdresser for *The Way We Were*.
Vincent Canby

'Hello Dolly!' (1969) – After she schlepped through *'Hello Dolly!'* I wrote her a telegram with just three words. 'What a pity!'
Barry Dennen

Her face looks as though a truck ran into it.
Divine (1983)

She overwhelms her material with vocal pyrotechnics.
Michael Feinstein (1984)

'Funny Girl' (1964) – An anthology of the

awkward graces, all knees and elbows, or else a boneless wonder, a seal doing a balancing act.
Ted Kalem – 'Time'

Filming with Streisand is an experience which may have cured me of movies.
Kris Kristofferson (1981)

I had no disagreement with Barbra Streisand. I was merely exasperated at her tendency to be a complete megalomaniac.
Walter Matthau

The most uninteresting person I have ever met. I just found her a bore. *Walter Matthau.*

I'm Number 10 at the box office. Right under Barbra Streisand. Can you imagine being under Barbra Streisand? Get me a bag, I may throw up.
Walter Matthau

She's a ball-buster. Protect me from her.
Nick Nolte (1992)

She's got the balls of a Russian infantry man.
Martin Ritt (1976)

Her speaking voice seems to have graduated with top honours from the Brooklyn Conservatory of Yentaism, and her acting consists entirely of fishily thrusting out her lips, sounding like a cabbie bellyaching at breakneck speed, and throwing her weight around . . . Miss Streisand is to our histrionic aesthetics what the Vietnam war is to our politics.
John Simon

Donald Sutherland
'Day of the Locust' (1974) – There's nothing specifically wrong with Donald Sutherland's performance. It's just awful. *Pauline Kael*

Elizabeth Taylor
'A Place in the Sun' (1951) – I got so sick of starry-eyed close-ups of Elizabeth Taylor that I could have gagged.
Raymond Chandler

'Suddenly Last Summer' (1959) – Katharine Hepburn as the matriarch trying to keep the lid on things by persuading Montgomery Clift to lobotomize her niece (Taylor, whose performance suggests that surgery has

already taken place).

Jennifer Selway – 'Time Out'

'The Comedians' (1967) – Elizabeth Taylor was a disaster. *Graham Greene* [Greene adapted the screenplay from his novel]

'Hammersmith is Out' (1972) – Wobbling her enormous derriere across the screen in a manner so offensive it would bring litigation from any dignified, self-respecting performer, and saying lines like: 'I'm the biggest mother of them all,' inspires pity instead of laughs. She has been announcing plans to retire from the screen. Now is as good a time as any. *Rex Reed (1972)*

Appearing at the 'Oscar' Ceremony – Elizabeth Taylor materialised in her new-found role as the Queen Mother, the crown jewels hanging down her throat and over a generous splash of bosom, and all in the service of Hollywood. *Andrew Sarris (1970)*

'The Comedians' (1967) – When they try to bring out her regal dignified qualities, nothing answers. Her dignity is simply stiff and ladylike, a little girl on her best behaviour. As for her woman of smouldering sexuality, one can only cry, in memory of the old days, 'Get on a horse!' Her off-screen personality may have developed in all these directions and more. But her acting ability closed up shop long ago. *Wilfred Sheed*

Lou Tellegen
On his autobiography 'Women Have Been Kind' – The book proper – and that adjective achieves an almost historical distinction as an example of unhappy selection – is written in a style that has all the elegance of a quirked little finger and all the glitter of a pair of new rubbers . . . It is a strange thing that for a few pages Lou Tellegen's book gives out a glamour. That is when he writes of Isadora Duncan (though, while we're up, I cannot recall, can you, any mention of him in her memoirs?). *Constant Reader [Dorothy Parker] –'New Yorker' (1931)*

Shirley Temple
'That Hagen Girl' (1947) – She acts with the

mopish dejection of a school-child who has just been robbed of a two-scoop ice-cream cone. *Bosley Crowther – 'New York Times'*

Jan Tunberger
'I Am Inexplicably Orange' – Tunberger should give celluloid a rest and ply his talents on Fifth Avenue where mugging is a fine art. *Bryan Forbes – 'Punch'*

Lana Turner
Probably the worst actress that ever made it to the top. *John Cromwell (1969)*

'The Three Musketeers' (1948) – As Lady de Winter, Lana Turner sounds like a drive-in waitress exchanging quips with hotrodders. *'New Yorker'*

She couldn't act her way out of her form-fitting cashmeres. *Tennessee Williams*

Liv Ullman
'St Joan' – It's just a story of Liv Ullman looking like George Peppard. *Anon*

'Lost Horizon' (1972) – Liv Ullman registers with all the impact of boiled ham on white bread. *Vincent Canby*

Jean-Claude Van Damme
'Double Impact' (1992) – The idea of two Van Dammes must have seemed workable on paper . . . but both exude the charisma of a packet of Cup-A-Soup.
Jonathan Romney – 'Time Out'

Rachel Ward
'After Dark My Sweet' (1991) – Her idea of how to play an alcoholic is to stand next to an empty wine bottle.
Christopher Tookey – 'Sunday Telegraph'

Raquel Welch
'The Legend of Walks Far Woman' – Not a very good singer or dancer, she is not a very good actress either . . . She looked like Sticks Out Woman.
Clive James – 'The Observer' (1980)

'Myra Breckenridge' (1970) – As an adaptation of Gore Vidal's novel, this is a major travesty. As a Hollywood comedy, it's

a major disaster . . . But as a Raquel Welch movie, it's better than most. *Tony Rayns – 'Time Out'*

I still don't believe that Raquel Welch exists. She has been manufactured by the media merely to preserve the sexless plasticity of sex objects for the masses. *Andrew Sarris*

Mae West

On being asked to 'sound a little sexier' when interviewing her – If I was endowed with the power of conveying unlimited sexual attraction through the potency of my voice, I would not be reduced to accepting a miserable pittance from the BBC for interviewing a faded female in a damp basement. *Gilbert Harding*

'Myra Breckenridge' (1970) – Mae West, close to eighty, resembles nothing less than a dressed-up corpse. *Michael Medved*

Pia Zadora

Mr Zadora pours money into Mrs Zadora as though she were an exotic nationalized industry, but the waning power of Pia shows no signs of reverse. *Julie Burchill*

COMEDIANS

Alternative Comediary

There is no alternative comedy. Either you're funny or you're not. *Bruce Forsyth (1992)*

Lenny Bruce

In the last year or six months Lenny Bruce had a nail tied to his foot and was going around in circles. *Phil Spector*

Andrew Dice Clay

'Adventures of Ford Fairlane' (1990) – Standing around like a spare prick at a wedding . . . the Diceman still comes over as a racist, homophobic, sexist ass-hole who mistakes sentimentality for true feeling. *Nigel Floyd – 'Time Out'*

Jack Dee

For a man being touted as the future of comedy, he's as up-to-date as a penny-farthing bike. *Garry Bushell – 'The Sun' (1992)*

Ben Elton

The old motormouth delivery has accelerated to the point where Elton's in grave danger of turning into the David Coleman of alternative comedy. *Allan Jones (1988)*

A humourless, crop-haired feminist. *'Punch' (1992)*

Simon Fanshawe

A 'comic' so dull that TV viewers experience a burning desire to go and check the dishwasher. *Gary Bushell – 'The Sun'*

Dawn French (and Lenny Henry)

Q. What do you call an elephant with a spade? A. Dawn French. *Anon*

Stephen Fry

He has the wit of an unflushed toilet. *Bernard Manning*

Stephen Fry and Hugh Laurie

If Vic Reeves and Bob Mortimer are the new Morecambe and Wise, this pair must be the new Little and Large. It could have been worse, they could be the new Cannon and Ball. *'Time Out' (1992)*

Bob Hope

Hope is not a comedian. He just translates what others write for him. *Groucho Marx*

Bob Hope homes into humour like a cornered heavyweight fighting for his laugh – and thereby uses more dead weight than discrimination. *John Pinkney – 'Melbourne Age' (1973)*

'Boy, Did I Get A Wrong Number!' (1966) – A store of one-line gags that often sound like a prelude to a friendly word from his sponsor. *'Time'*

Laurel and Hardy

'The Big Noise' (1944) – From any comic consideration, it represents the last stop on a dead-end street. *Howard Barnes – 'New York Herald-Tribune'*

'The Big Noise' (1944) – It has about as much humour in it as a six-foot hole in the ground. *Bosley Crowther – 'New York Times'*

Jerry Lewis

Lewis used to be one of my heroes . . . But, through the years, I've seen him turn into the arrogant, sour, ceremonial, piously chauvinistic egomaniac.　　　*Elliott Gould*

He hasn't made me laugh since he left Dean Martin.　　　*Groucho Marx*

Ernest P. Worrell (Jim Varney)

A twisted, cheap imitation of the young Jerry Lewis, whose comic turns make Paul Hogan's repertoire seem a galaxy of creativity.

Mark Kermode – 'Time Out' (1988)

Tony Slattery

He might be a very good actor but what possessed him to think he has a comic gift?

A. N. Wilson – 'Sunday Telegraph' (1991)

Norman Wisdom

'On the Beat' (1962) – The man's humour is of the most cretinous nature imaginable . . . Embarrassingly unfunny, it just shows that being a film comic is a most unsuitable job for a moron.　　　*Geoff Andrew – 'Time Out'*

IMPRESARIOS

Phineas T. Barnum

He will utterly take his stand in the social rank among the swindlers, blacklegs, pickpockets, and thimble-riggers of his day.

Anon

Sir Charles Blake Cochran

When things were good, he resembled a rooster; when bad, a benign bishop.

Vivian Ellis

AGENTS

An agent is a sort of Mack the Knife that does it with contracts.　　　*Anon*

An actor's agent is a guy who sometimes bites the ham that feeds him.　　　*Anon*

The theatrical press agent is a resilient amalgam of glue and guile, chutzpah and heartburn, optimism and imagination.

Robert Berkvist – 'New York Times'

Some are born great, some achieve greatness, and some hire public relations officers.

Daniel J. Boorstin

There's always a price to pay for fame. Today it's the salaries of your press agent and PR man.　　　*Edward F. Dempsey*

Little by little, the pimps have taken over the world. They don't make anything – they just stand there and take their cut.

Jean Giraudoux – 'The Madwoman of Chaillot' (1945)

The art of publicity is a black art.

Judge Learned Hand

A press agent is a guy who hitches his braggin' to a star.　　　*Horace G. McNab*

A Hollywood contact man is mostly all con with no tact.　　　*Rex Reed*

Agents do nothing for the good of football. I'd like to see them lined up against a wall and machine-gunned.

Graham Taylor (1983)

Kurt Frings

The Man who killed Hollywood.　　　*Anon*

MUSIC

CLASSICAL MUSIC

Composers are essentially a breed of men and women concerned with the arrangement of the same seven notes. *Richard Rodgers*

We now live in the Era of Incompetence; we have painters who can't paint, poets who can't rhyme and composers who whistle dissonance. *Dagobert Runes*

I don't think I shall ever become a convert to Italian music. It's such trash.
Richard Strauss (1886)

On his rôle as a music critic – I thought of myself as a species of knight errant attacking dragons single-handedly and rescuing musical virtue in distress.
Virgil Thomson –
'New York Times' (1981)
He later gave a revised version of his rôle – You explain how it went, and as far as you can figure out how it got that way . . . The description and explanation is the best part of music reviewing. There is such a thing, and you know it too, as a gift for judgement. If you have it, you can say anything you like. If you haven't got it, you don't know what you haven't got. And everything you say will be held against you. *Christian Science Monitor (1985)*

If you want to please only the critics, don't play too loud, too soft, too fast, too slow.
Arturo Toscanini

The immoral profession of musical criticism must be abolished.
Richard Wagner (1848)

You cannot have critics with standards; you can only have music with standards which critics may observe. *Alan Walker (1968)*

Criticism is the rationalism of intuitive musical experience. *Alan Walker (1968)*

STYLES

Baroque
Muzak for intelligentsia. *Anon (1970)*

Fugue
One damn fiddle after another.
H . L. Mencken

Any dolt can write a fugue a day; some do, but if, musically speaking, he is of feeble mind his best-made fugue will never be anything but a piece of doltish music.
Ernest Newman – 'Sunday Times' (1943)

Modern
Three farts and a raspberry, orchestrated.
John Barbirolli

Modern music is as dangerous as cocaine.
Pietro Mascagni (1927)

COMPOSERS

Thomas Arne
Arne had kept bad company: he had written for vulgar singers and hearers too long to be able to comport himself properly at the opera-house, in the first circle of taste and fashion. *Charles Burney (1779)*

J. S. Bach
Though full of great musical lore
Old Bach was a terrible bore
A fugue without a tune
He thought was a boon
So he wrote seventeen thousand more.
'Musical Herald' (1884)

Bela Bartok
Tonal chaos arising from the diabolical employment of unrelated keys simultaneously. *'Cincinnati Enquirer'*

'Fourth Quartet' – The opening allegory took me straight back to childhood and gave me in turn the rusty windlass of a well, the interlinking noises of a goods train that is

being shunted, then the belly-rumblings of a little boy acutely ill after a raid on an orchard, and finally the singular alarmed noise of poultry being worried to death by a Scotch terrier.

The second movement gave me continuously and throughout its short length the noise of a November wind in telegraph poles on a lonely country road.

The third movement began with a dog howling at midnight, proceeded to imitate the regurgitations of the less refined type of water-closet cistern, modulating thence into the mass snoring of a Naval dormitory around the dawn – and concluded with the cello reproducing the screech of an ungreased wheelbarrow.

The fourth movement took me straight back to the noises I made myself, on wet days indoors, at the age of six, by stretching and plucking a piece of elastic.

And the fifth movement reminded me immediately and persistently and vividly of something I have never thought of since the only time I heard it: the noise of a Zulu village in the Glasgow Exhibition – a hubbub all the more singular because it had a background of skirling Highland bagpipes. Both noises emerged in this the final movement of this Fourth Quartet of Bela Bartok. *Alan Dent (1945)*

If the reader were so rash as to purchase any of Bartok's compositions, he would find that they each consist of unmeaning bunches of notes, apparently representing the composer promenading the keyboard in his boots. Some can be played better with the elbows, others with the flat of the hand. None require fingers to perform, nor ears to listen to.
'Musical Quarterly' (1915)

Ludwig van Beethoven
His music always reminds one of paintings of battles. *Bertolt Brecht*

'*Symphony No. 9*' – The fourth movement is, in my opinion, so monstrous and tasteless and, in its grasp of Schiller's *Ode*, so trivial that I cannot understand how a genius like Beethoven could have written it.
Louis Spohr (1865)

'*Symphony No. 7*' – The extravagances of Beethoven's genius have reached the ne plus ultra in the *Seventh Symphony*, and he is quite ripe for the madhouse.
Carl Maria von Weber

Hector Berlioz
This is the way Berlioz composes – he splutters the ink over the pages of ruled paper and the result is as chance wills it.
Frederic Chopin

Musically speaking, he is a lunatic; a classical composer only in Paris, the great city of quacks. His music is simply and undisguisedly nonsense.
'Dramatic and Musical Review' (1843)

'*Leilo, ou le retour à la vie*' – This must be the craziest work ever sketched out by a composer not actually insane.
J. H. Elliot (1967)

He makes me sad because he is really a cultured, agreeable man and yet composes very badly. *Felix Mendelssohn (1831)*

'*Les Francs Juges*' – His orchestration is such an incongruous mess and so slapdash that you want to wash your hands after going through one of his scores.
Felix Mendelssohn (1834)

Berlioz is France's greatest composer, alas. A musician of great genius and little talent.
Maurice Ravel

Johannes Brahms
'*Four Serious Songs*' – Ungodly ditties.
Johannes Brahms (1896)

'*Motets for Double Chorus*' – I will not deny that there was a sort of broken thread of vocal tone running through the sound-fabric; but, for the most part, it was a horrible tissue of puffing and blowing and wheezing and groaning and buzzing and hissing and gargling and shrieking and spluttering and grunting and generally making every sort of noise that is incidental to bad singing, severe exertion, and mortal fear of losing one's place. It was really worse than influenza.
G. B. Shaw – 'The World'

'*Requiem*' – Brahms' *Requiem* has not the true funereal relish: it is so execrably and ponderously dull that the very flattest of funerals would seem like a ballet, or at least, a 'danse macabre', after it.

G. B. Shaw – 'The World' (1892)

'*Requiem*' – There are some sacrifices which should not be demanded twice from any man, and one of them is listening to Brahms' *Requiem*.

G. B. Shaw – 'The Star'

I played over the music of that scoundrel Brahms. What a giftless bastard!

Pyotr Tchaikovsky

He has no charm for me. I find him cold and obscure, full of pretensions, but without any real depth.

Pyotr Tchaikovsky

'*German Requiem*' – Schumann's last thought.

Richard Wagner (1879)

Benjamin Britten claims that he plays through 'the whole Brahms' at intervals to see whether Brahms is really as bad as he thought, and ends by discovering that he is actually much worse.

Colin Wilson – 'Brandy of the Damned' (1964)

In a single cymbal crash from a work of Liszt there is expressed more spirit and feeling than in all Brahms's symphonies and his serenades besides.

Hugo Wolf

Benjamin Britten

'*The Rape of Lucretia*' – Everywhere Mr Britten reminds us of his favourite composers.

William Glock – 'Time and Tide' (1946)

Anton Bruckner

'*Symphony No. 3*' – A vision of Beethoven's *Ninth* becoming friendly with Wagner's *Valkyries* and finishing up trampled under their hooves.

Eduard Hanslick

'*Symphony No. 8*' – It is not impossible that the future belongs to this nightmarish 'Katzenjammer' style, a future which we therefore do not envy. *Eduard Hanslick (1892)*

Frederic Chopin

'*Minute Waltz*' – Gives listeners a bad quarter of an hour.

Anon

The entire works of Chopin present a motley surface of ranting hyperbole and excruciating cacophony.

'Musical World' (1841)

'*Nocturne in E flat*' – Where John Field smiles Chopin makes a grinning grimace; where John Field sighs Chopin groans; where Field shrugs his shoulders Chopin twists his whole body; where Field puts some seasoning into the food Chopin empties a handful of cayenne pepper.

L. Rellstab – 'Iris' (1833)

Claude Debussy

'*La Mer*' – It is possible that Debussy did not intend to call it *La Mer* but, *Le Mal de Mer*, which would at once make the tone-pictures as clear as day. It is a series of symphonic pictures of sea-sickness. The first movement is 'Headache'. The second is 'Doubt', picturing moments of dread suspense, whether or no! The third movement, with its explosions and rumblings, has now a self-evident purpose. The hero is endeavouring to throw up his boot-heels!

'Boston Daily Advertiser' (1907)

Frederick Delius

'*Piano Concerto*' – Rarely has so wretched a plant been rescued and nourished; rarely has so great a composer written such drivel.

Arthur Hutchings – 'Delius'

The musical equivalent of blancmange.

Bernard Levin (1983)

Antonin Dvořák

'*Requiem*' – Dvořák's *Requiem* bored Birmingham so desperately that it was unanimously voted a work of extraordinary depth and impressiveness, which verdict I record with a hollow laugh, and allow the subject to drop by its own portentous weight.

G. B. Shaw

Edward Elgar

The Dream of Gerontius – Elgar might have been a great composer if he had thrown all that religious paraphernalia overboard. *Gerontius* is a nauseating work.

Frederick Delius

Gabriel Fauré

'*Romances sans Paroles*' – The sort of music a

pederast might hum when raping a choirboy.

Marcel Proust

Christoph Gluck
Gluck knew no more of counterpoint than my cook does. *George Frederick Handel*

Edvard Grieg
'*Piano Concerto*' – . . . as if the composer had resolved to use up all the melodies he had jotted down at various times in his sketchbook. *'Musical Times' (1877)*

'*Scenes from Olag Trygvason*' – I have no idea of the age at which Grieg perpetrated this tissue of puerilities; but if he was a day over eighteen the exploit is beyond excuse.

G. B. Shaw

George Frederick Handel
A tub of pork and beer. *Hector Berlioz*

Handel is only fourth-rate. He is not even interesting. *Pyotr Tchaikovsky*

Erich Korngold
'*Violin Concerto*' – More corn than gold.

Irving Kolodin

Franz Liszt
Liszt is a mere commonplace person, with hair on end – a snob out of Bedlam. He writes the ugliest music extant.

'Dramatic and Musical Review' (1843)

Mephistopheles dressed as an abbott.

Ferdinand Gregorovious

Composition, indeed! – decomposition is the proper word for such hateful fungi, which choke up and poison the fertile plains of harmony, threatening the world with drought. *'Musical World' (1855)*

Most of all he gives me the impression of being a spoilt child. I am very near to detesting him as a composer.

Clara Schumann (1841)

Gustav Mahler
'*Second Symphony*' – A detailed annotation of what the music would be like if only the composer could think of the right notes.

'Musical Times' (1931)

Felix Mendelssohn
'*Choral Symphony No. 2*' – I cannot think of any living conductor who could have ignited sparks with this material. *Hugh Canning*

Olivier Messiaen
'*Turangalila-Symphonie*' – Little more can be required to write such things than a plentiful supply of ink. *Igor Stravinsky*

Sergei Prokofiev
'*The Love of Three Oranges*' – Mr Prokofiev might well have loaded up a shotgun with several thousand notes of various lengths and discharged them against the side of a wall.

Edward Moore – 'Chicago Tribune' (1921)

Max Reger
Reger's name is the same backwards or forwards, and his music displays the same characteristic. *Irving Kolodin*

Rimsky-Korsakov
'*Scheherazade*' – It reminds me more of a bazaar than the Orient.

Claude Debussy (1906)

Camille Saint-Saëns
If he'd been making shell-cases during the war it might have been better for music.

Maurice Ravel

It is one's duty to hate with all possible fervour the empty and ugly in art; and I hate Saint-Saëns the composer with a hate that is perfect.

J. E. Runciman – 'Saturday Review' (1896)

Arnold Schoenberg
'*Five Orchestral Pieces*' – The music resembled the wailings of a tortured soul, and suggested nothing so much as the disordered fancies of delirium or the fearsome, imaginary terrors of a highly nervous infant.

'Globe' (1912)

Only a psychiatrist can help poor Schoenberg now . . . He would do better to shovel snow instead of scribbling on music paper.

Richard Strauss (1913)

Franz Schubert
Perhaps a more overrated man never existed.

'Musical Times' (1897)

Robert Schumann
'*Paradise and the Peri*' – Robert Schumann
has had his innings and has been bowled out
– like Richard Wagner. *Paradise and the Peri*
has gone to the tomb of the Lohengrins.
J. W. Davidson – 'Musical World' (1856)

Alexander Scriabin
'*Poem of Ecstasy*' – The obscenest piece of
music ever written. *Anon*

Dmitri Shostakovich
'*Lady Macbeth of Mtensk*' – It is a leftish
bedlam instead of human music. The
inspiring quality of good music is sacrificed
in favour of petty-bourgeois clowning. This
game may end badly. *'Pravda' (1936)*

Jean Sibelius
'*Symphony No. 6*' – I think he must have
been drunk when he wrote that.
Benjamin Britten

'*Violin Concerto*' – A polonaise for polar
bears. *Donald F. Tovey*

Louis Spohr
An academic pedant of the first rank.
Edvard Grieg

Richard Strauss
His absurd cacophony will not be music even
in the thirtieth century. *Cesar Cui (1904)*

'*Elektra*' – His Majesty does not know what
the [Grenadier Guards] Band has just played,
but it is never to be played again.
King George V

'*Domestic Symphony*' – A cataclysm of
domestic plumbing. *Henry L. Mencken*

He is no longer of the slightest artistic interest
to me, and whatever I may once have learned
from him, I am thankful to say I
misunderstood. *Arnold Schoenberg*

'*Salome*' – After its U.S. premiere, the critics
went up into the attic and dusted off
adjectives that hadn't been in use since Ibsen
was first produced in London. I remember
that 'bestial', 'fetid', 'slimy', and 'nauseous'
were among the more complimentary terms.
Deems Taylor – 'Men and Music'

'*Salome*' – I really like this fellow Strauss, but
Salome will do him a lot of damage.
Kaiser Wilhelm II

Igor Stravinsky
Stravinsky looks like a man who was potty-
trained too early and that music proves it as
far as I am concerned.
Russell Hoban – 'Turtle Diary' (1975)

'*Symphony for Wind – In Memory of Debussy*'
– I had no idea Stravinsky disliked Debussy
as much as this. *'Musical Times' (1921)*

'*Symphony for Wind – In Memory of Debussy*'
– If my own memories of a friend were as
painful as Stravinsky's seem to be, I would
try to forget it. *Ernest Newman*

'*Le Sacre du Printemps*' – The choreography
is ridiculous, the music is sheer cacophony . . .
It might be the creation of a madman.
Giacomo Puccini (1913)

Pyotr Tchaikovsky
'*First Piano Concerto*' – Tchaikovsky's *First
Piano Concerto*, like the first pancake, is a
flop. *Nicolai Soloviev (1875)*

Michael Tippett
'*The Mask of Time*' – . . . resembles a breech
delivery – one which is expressed in rhythmic
lurches, stabs of phrases and vocal
ornamentation designed to express agitation
rather than decorative grace.
Bernard Holland – 'New York Times' (1984)

Giuseppe Verdi
When I hear a work I do not like I am
convinced it is my own fault. Verdi is one of
those composers. *Benjamin Britten*

'*Ernani*'– It's organ-grinder stuff.
Charles Gounod

Heitor Villa-Lobos
Why is it, that whenever I hear a piece of
music I don't like, it's always by Villa-Lobos?
Igor Stravinsky

Antonio Vivaldi
Vivaldi is greatly overrated – a dull fellow
who could compose the same form over and
so many times over.
Igor Stravinsky – 'Craft' (1958)

Richard Wagner

The diabolical din of this pig-headed man, stuffed with brass and sawdust, inflated, in an insanely destructive self-aggrandizement, by Mephistopheles' mephitic and most venomous hellish miasma, into Beelzebub's Court Composer and general Director of Hell's Music – Wagner!   *J. L. Klein*

Is Wagner a human being at all? Is he not rather a disease? He contaminates everything he touches – he has made music sick. I postulate this viewpoint: Wagner's art is diseased.
Friedrich Nietzsche – 'Der Fall Wagner'

Sterile by nature like all monsters, Wagner is impotent to reproduce himself.   *H. Prevost*

Nietzsche was afraid of certain 'ands' – Goethe and Schiller, for example, or worse still, Schiller and Goethe. What would he say at seeing the spread of the cult of Nietzsche and Wagner or rather Wagner and Nietzsche.   *Jean Cocteau*

Wagner's works are long works which are long, and long-drawn-out because this old sorcerer looked upon boredom as a useful drug for the stupefaction of the faithful.
Jean Cocteau

Wagner is a man devoid of all talent.
Cesar Cui (1863)

Wagner drives the nail into your head with swinging hammer blows.
P. A. Fiorentino (1867)

Wagner, thank the fates, is no hypocrite. He says right out what he means, and he usually means something nasty.   *James Huneker*

There is no law against composing music when one has no ideas whatsoever. The music of Wagner, therefore, is perfectly legal.
'Paris National' (1850)
Is Wagner a human being at all? Is he not rather a disease?   *Friedrich Nietzsche*

Wagner was a monster. He was anti-Semitic on Mondays and vegetarian on Tuesdays. On Wednesday he was in favour of annexing Newfoundland, Thursday he wanted to sink Venice, and Friday he wanted to blow up the Pope.   *Tony Palmer (1986)*

A composer who had some wonderful moments, but awful quarter hours.
Gioacchino Rossini

For me Wagner is impossible . . . he talks without ever stopping. One just can't talk all the time.   *Richard Schumann*

'*Gotterdammerung*' – After the last notes of *Gotterdammerung* I felt as though I had been let out of prison.   *Pyotr Tchaikovsky*

I like Wagner's music better than anybody's. It is so loud that one can talk the whole time without people hearing what one says.
Oscar Wilde

Sir William Walton

'*Symphony No. 1*' – It has been pretty certain for some time that if Sibelius did not hurry up and write his *Eighth Symphony*, somebody else would write it for him.   *Neville Cardus – 'Manchester Guardian' (1935)*

OPERA AND ORATORIO

GENERAL

STOPERA! – Graffiti (outside proposed Dutch opera house.)

Nothing is capable of being set to music that is not nonsense.   *Joseph Addison*

An opera may be allowed to be extravagantly lavish in its decorations, as its only design is to gratify the senses and keep up an indolent attention in the audience.
Joseph Addison – 'The Spectator' (1711)

Opera is like a husband with a foreign title; expensive to support, hard to understand, and therefore a supreme social challenge.
Cleveland Amory (1960)

If an opera cannot be played by an organ-grinder, it is not going to achieve immortality.   *Sir Thomas Beecham*

Opera is a play representing life in another world whose inhabitants have no speech but song, no motions but gestures, and no postures but attitudes. All acting is simulation, and the word simulation is from simia, an ape; but in opera the actor takes for his model Simia audibilis (or Pithecanthropus stentor) – the ape that howls. *Ambrose Bierce*

Upon resigning from the Covent Garden Opera House – After two years' slogging, I came to the conclusion that opera as an artistic form was dead. *Peter Brook (1950)*

A magic scene contrived to please the eyes and ears at the expense of understanding. *Lord Chesterfield*

Tragic opera is just another disaster aria. *John H. Clark*

Opera is one of the strangest inventions of Western man. It could not have been foreseen by any logical process. *Sir Kenneth Clark*

People are wrong when they say that the opera isn't what it used to be. It is what it used to be. That's what's wrong with it. *Noël Coward*

I have sat through an Italian Opera, till, for sheer pain, an inexplicable anguish, I have rushed out into the noisiest places of the crowded streets, to solace myself with sounds, which I was not obliged to follow, and get rid of the distracting torment of endless, fruitless, barren attention! *Charles Lamb – 'Essays of Elia' (1823)*

In the final analysis, opera is a poor substitute for baseball. *'Los Angeles Herald' (1986)*

Opera is people singing when they should be talking. *'Mail on Sunday' (1992)*

On his own production of 'Porgy and Bess' (1985) – Critics complained it wasn't opera, it wasn't a musical. You give them something delicious to eat and they complain because they have no name for it. *Rouben Mamoulian – 'New York Times'*

Opera in English is, in the main, just about as sensible as baseball in Italian. *H. L. Mencken*

The genuine music-lover may accept the carnal husk of opera to get at the kernel of actual music within, but that is no sign that he approves the carnal husk or enjoys gnawing through it. *H. L. Mencken – 'Prejudices' (1920)*

The opera is to music what a bawdy house is to a cathedral. *H. L. Mencken (1925)*

Of all the noises known to man, opera is the most expensive. *Molière*

Going to the opera, like getting drunk, is a sin that carries its own punishment with it and that a very severe one. *Hannah More*

I sometimes wonder which would be nicer – an opera without an interval, or an interval without an opera. *Sir Ernest Newman*

If I had the power I would insist on all oratorios being sung in the costume of the period – with the possible exception in the case of the *Creation*. *Sir Ernest Newman – 'New York Post' (1924)*

The opera house is an institution differing from other lunatic asylums in the fact that its inmates have avoided official certification. *Ernest Newman*

There was a time when I heard eleven operas in a fortnight, which left me bankrupt and half-idiotic for a month. *J. B. Priestley (1923)*

Bel Canto is to opera what pole-vaulting is to ballet, the glorification of a performer's prowess and not a creator's imagination. *Ned Rorem – 'The New Republic' (1972)*

Though opera is a noble craft
Most operatic plots are daft! *Ron Rubin – 'How to be tremendously tuned in to Opera' (1959)*

Oratorios are unstaged operettas on scriptural themes, written in a style in which solemnity and triviality are blended in the right proportion for boring an atheist out of his senses. *G. B. Shaw*

Nothing can be more disgusting than an oratorio. How absurd to see five hundred people fiddling like madmen about the Israelites in the Red Sea. *Sydney Smith (1823)*

Sleep is an excellent way of listening to opera. *James Stephens*

In opera, anything that is too stupid to be spoken is sung. *Voltaire*

The battle of Crete [1941] was like German Opera, too long and too loud. *Evelyn Waugh*

An unalterable and unquestioned law of the musical required that the German text of French operas sung by Swedish artists should be translated into Italian for the clearer understanding of English speaking audiences.
Edith Wharton (1920)

OPERA SINGERS

Hark to the red-faced beeritone – gargling, gorgling, gurgling. *Anon*

El odio de los divos. *[Nowadays there are more divos than divas.]* *A non-Spanish newspaper*

I sometimes think I'd like opera better without the singing. *John Amis*

I do not mind what language an opera is sung in so long as it is a language I do not understand. *Sir Edward Appleton – 'The Observer' (1955)*

No good opera can be sensible – for people do not sing when they are feeling sensible.
W. H. Auden – 'Time' (1961)

No operatic star has yet died soon enough for me. *Sir Thomas Beecham (1958)*

Most sopranos sound like they live on seaweed.
Sir Thomas Beecham – 'Newsweek' (1956)

If you can strike a low G or F like a death rattle and a high F like the shriek of a little dog when you step on its tail, the house will resound with acclamation.
Hector Berlioz (1862)

When an opera star sings her head off, she usually improves her appearance. *Victor Borge*

The tenor's voice is spoilt by affectation
    And for the bass, the beast can only bellow;
    In fact, he had no singing education,
An ignorant, noteless, timeless, tuneless fellow. *Lord Byron (1824)*

    Yet I detest
Those scented rooms, where to a gaudy throng,
Heaves the proud harlot her distended breast
In intricacies of song. *Samuel T. Coleridge*

Swans sing before they die – 'twere no bad thing
    Should certain persons die before they sing. *Samuel T. Coleridge*

The lewd trebles squeak nothing but bawdy, and the basses roar blasphemy.
William Congreve (1700)

A German singer! I should as soon expect to get pleasure from the neighing of my horse.
Frederick the Great

Nobody really sings in opera. They just make loud noises. *Amelia Galli-Curci*

Opera is when a guy gets stabbed in the back and instead of bleeding he sings.
Ed Gardner – 'Duffy's Tavern'

The world, the flesh, and the devil lurk in the larynx of the soprano or alto.
James Huneker (1915)

Singers' husbands! Find me stones heavy enough to place around their necks and drown them all!
Andre Mertens – 'Time' (1960)

Canary birds have to demonstrate their ability to sing before they can be imported into this country. What a pity that doesn't apply also to imported opera singers.
'Nashville Southern Lumberman'

My own objection to the prima donna is that, as a rule, she represents merely tone and technique without intelligence.

Ernest Newman

How wonderful opera would be if there were no singers. *Gioacchino Rossini*

I am convinced that people applaud a prima donna as they do the feats of the strong man at a fair. The sensations are painfully disagreeable, hard to endure, but one is so glad when it is all over that one cannot help rejoicing. *Jean Jacques Rousseau – 'La Nouvelle Héloïse' (1761)*

Italian singers: of bestial howling, and entirely frantic vomiting-up of damned souls through their still carnal throats, I have heard more than, please God, I will never endure the hearing of again, in one of His summers.

John Ruskin

Tenors are usually short, stout men (except when they are Wagnerian tenors, in which case they are large, stout men) made up predominantly of lungs, rope-sized vocal chords, large frontal sinuses, thick necks, thick heads, tantrums and armour propre. It is certain that they are a race apart, a race that tends to operate reflexively rather than with due process of thought.

Harold C. Schonberg – 'Show' (1961)

I hate performers who debase great works of art: I long for their annihilation: if my criticisms were flaming thunderbolts, no prudent Life or Fire Insurance Company would entertain a proposal from any singer within my range, or from the lessee of any opera-house or concert-room within my circuit. *G. B. Shaw (1894)*

A tenor is not a man but a disease.

Hans von Bulow

Baritones are the born villains in opera.

Leonard Warren – 'New York World-Telegram and Sun' (1957)

Opera: it is a sham art. Large, plain, middle-aged women galumph around posing as pretty young girls singing to portly, plain,

middle-aged men posing as handsome young boys. *Woodrow Wyatt – 'To the Point' (1981)*

Anon
Soprano in 'Die Walkure' – Her singing reminds me of a cart coming downhill with the brake on. *Sir Thomas Beecham*

Baritone in 'Carmen'
He made a mistake, thinking himself to be the bull instead of the toreador.

Sir Thomas Beecham

Anon tenor
You sang like a composer. *Jules Massenet*

Maria Callas
I will not enter into a public feud with Madame Callas, since I am well aware that she has considerably greater competence and experience at that kind of thing than I have.

Rudolf Bing

When Callas carried a grudge, she planted it, nursed it, fostered it, watered it and watched it grow to sequoia size.

Harold C. Schonberg (1985)

Enrico Caruso
'Madame Butterfly' – Signor Caruso sang so well that his appearance was easily forgiven but when he was not actually singing, some of the audience were moved to observe that he looked like the Inspector of Police in the first act. *'The Times' (1905)*

Dame Kiri te Kanawa
A viable alternative to valium. *Ira Siff*

Jenny Lind
At the end of the first act we agreed to come away. It struck me as atrociously stupid. I was thinking of something else the whole time she was jugulating away, and O! I was so glad to get to the end and have a cigar.

William M. Thackeray (1850)

Dame Nellie Melba (Helen Porter Mitchell)
Melba's voice stirs me to almost passionate admiration, but admiration isn't joy; admiration doesn't satisfy; there is no ecstasy in admiration. *Selwyn Rider – 'Triad' (1919)*

MUSIC

Birgit Nilsson

Metropolitan Opera's 'Salome' – Salome was 16 and slinky-slim. Birgit Nilsson is 46 and boatswain-burly. As for casting the Swede in the title role of Richard Strauss's *Salome*, the idea seemed roughly comparable to starring Judith Anderson as Lolita.

'Time' (1965)

Luciano Pavarotti

What is or is not art is a matter for personal choice. If some people want to listen to an overweight Italian singing in his own language, so be it. *Terry Dicks*

Henrietta Sontag

We hang on every note Madame Sontag sings – This proves the lady's great power of execution. *'Musical Standard' (1870)*

Helen Traubels

On his tempestuous soprano – Nobody knows the Traubels I've seen. *Rudolf Bing*

OPERA COMPANIES

The Paris Opera

A stranger would take it for a railway station and, once inside, would mistake it for a Turkish bath. They continue to produce curious noises which the people who pay call music, but there is no need to believe them implicitly. *Claude Debussy (1921)*

COMPOSERS

Anon

I liked your opera. I think I will set it to music. *Ludwig van Beethoven*

Ludwig van Beethoven

'Fidelio' – All impartial musicians and music lovers were in perfect agreement that never was anything as incoherent, shrill, chaotic and ear-splitting produced in music.

August von Kotzebue (1806)

Vincenzo Bellini

'La Somnambula' – . . . dull enough to send the most athletic sleepwalker back to bed.

'Newsweek' (1963)

Georges Bizet

'Carmen' – The melodies lack distinction . . .

the piece is not dramatic . . . it lacks sincerity and truth. *Oscar Comettant*

'Carmen' – In *Carmen* the composer has made up his mind to show us how learned he is, with the result that he is often dull and obscure. *Leon Escudier*

'Carmen' – Take the Spanish airs and mine out of the score, and there remains nothing to Bizet's credit but the sauce that masks the fish. *Charles Gounod (1875)*

Johannes Brahms

'The Peasant a Rogue' – There may be people who are serious enough to find this opera comic, just as there are people comical enough to take Brahms's symphonies seriously. *Hugo Wolf (1885)*

Charles Gounod

'La Redemption' – If you will only take the precaution to go in long enough after it commences and to come out long before it is over, you will not find it wearisome.

G. B. Shaw (1882)

Hans Werner Henze

A Beatles record is shorter and cleverer than a Henze opera. *Pierre Boulez*

Wolfgang A. Mozart

'The Marriage of Figaro' – Far too noisy . . . Far too many notes.

Emperor Ferdinand of Austria (1786)

Stephen Oliver

'Timon of Athens' – Opera for the John Major era. *'Time Out' (1991)*

Giacomo Puccini

'Tosca' – The opera, the public is informed, has been produced with great success in Italy and South America, and as far as I am concerned, the places are welcome to keep it.

'Morning Post' (1906)

Wagner is the Puccini of music.

J. B. Morton

'Tosca' – Puccini represents evil art – Italian music, to wit – and his success would have meant the preponderating influence in England of that evil art. Wherefore, it has

been my duty to throw back the score of Tosca at him. Puccini: may you prosper, but in other climes! Continue, my friend, to sketch in scrappy incidental music to well-known plays.   *J. F. Runciman –*
The Saturday Review' (1990)
Dimitri Shostakovich: What do you think of Puccini?
Benjamin Britten: I think his operas are dreadful.
Shostakovich: No, Ben, you are wrong. He wrote marvellous operas, but dreadful music.

Gioacchino Rossini
Royal Opera House's 'William Tell' (1992) – A case of apple crumble . . .
David Gillard – 'Daily Mail' (1992)

'*The Barber of Seville*' – Mozart minus the brains.   *Clive James – 'The Observer' (1976)*

Igor Stravinsky
'*The Rake's Progress*' – I liked the opera very much. Except the music.   *Benjamin Britten*

Giuseppe Verdi
'*Rigoletto*' – Verdi's inexpressive and frightfully ugly music fell flat upon the audience . . . Our opinion of Signor Verdi's powers is well known, and his present work is rather worse better than his previous productions . . . it will be unnecessary to enter into painful details.
'The Morning Post' (1853)

Richard Wagner
Wagner has done undeniably good work in humbling the singer.   *Max Beerbohm*

'*Tristan and Isolde*' – A sort of chromatic moan.   *Hector Berlioz (1862)*

His opera style recognises only superlatives, but a superlative has no future. It is the end, not the beginning.   *Eduard Hanslick*

'*Tristan und Isolde*' – The prelude to *Tristan und Isolde* reminds me of the old Italian painting of a martyr whose intestines are slowly unwound from his body on a reel.
Eduard Hanslick (1868)

Bavarian State Opera's 'Lohengrin' (1978) – It

was just as boring as every other production of *Lohengrin* I have ever seen, but that was inevitable, because *Lohengrin* simply happens to be a bore.   *Clive James – 'The Observer'*

'*Tristan und Isolde*' – This is not music – believe me! I have always flattered myself I know something about music – but this is chaos. This is demagogy, blasphemy, insanity, madness! It is perfumed fog, shot through with lightning! It is the end of honesty in art.
Thomas Mann – 'Buddenbrooks' (1901)

'*Tannhäuser*' – The latest bore – but it is colossal – is *Tannhäuser*. I think I could compose something like it tomorrow, inspired by my cat scampering over the keys of the piano.   *Prosper Mérimée (1861)*

This man, this Wagner, this author of *Tannhäuser*, of *Lohengrin*, and so many other hideous things – and above all, the overture of *Der Fliegende Hollander*, the most hideous and detestable of the whole – this preacher of the '*Future*', was born to feed spiders with flies.   *'Musical World' (1855)*

'*Die Meistersinger*' – German beer-music.
Frederick Nietzsche

'*Parsifal*' – The kind of opera that starts at six o'clock. After it has been going three hours you look at your watch and it says 6.20.
David Randolph

'*Lohengrin*' – One cannot judge Wagner's opera after a first hearing, and I certainly have no intention of hearing it a second time.
Gioacchino Rossini

'*Die Meistersinger*' – Of all the bete, clumsy, blundering boggling, baboon-blooded stuff I ever saw on a human stage, that thing last night beat – and as far as the story and acting went – and all of the affected, sapless, soulless, beginningless, endless, topless, bottomless, topsituriest, tuneless, scrannelpipiest – tongs and boniest – doggerel sounds I ever endured the deadliness of, that eternity for nothing was deadliest, as far as it sounds went. I never was so relieved, so far as I can remember, in my life, by the stopping of any sound – not excepting railroad whistles – as I was by the cessation of the cobbler's bellowing.

John Ruskin (1882)

'*Tristan und Isolde*' – The prelude to *Tristan und Isolde* sounded as if a bomb had fallen into a large music factory, and had thrown all the notes into confusion.

'The Berlin Tribune' (1871)

'*Lohengrin*' – The banging and slamming and booming and crashing were something beyond relief. The racking and pitiless pain of it remains stored up in my memory alongside the memory of the time that I had my teeth fixed.   *Mark Twain (1880)*

Once you know one Wagner opera thoroughly, there can be no fresh surprises from the others. There is great magnificence, but it is all of a kind, like the same mountain scenery going on for four hundred miles.

Colin Wilson – 'Brandy of the Damned' (1964)

Kurt Weill
'*The Beggar's Opera*' – Compare the music of *The Beggar's Opera* with the music of a contemporary revue. They differ as life in the Garden of Eden differed from life in the artistic quarter of Gomorrah.

Aldous Huxley – 'All Along the Road'

CONDUCTORS

There are no bad orchestras, only bad conductors.   *Anon*

Show me an orchestra that likes its conductor and I'll show you a lousy conductor.

Goddard Lieberson

Sir Thomas Beecham
A pompous little duckarsed bandmaster who stood against everything creative in the art of his time. *John Fowles – 'The Collector' (1963)*

Leonard Bernstein
His conducting has a masturbatory, oppressive and febrile zeal, even for the most tranquil passages. (Today he uses music as an accompaniment to his conducting.)

Oscar Levant – 'The Memoirs of an Amnesiac' (1965)

He has been disclosing musical secrets that have been known for over four hundred years.   *Oscar Levant*

I think a lot of Bernstein – but not as much as he does.   *Oscar Levant*

Signor Costa
Costa does not beat time, he threshes it.

Felix Mendelssohn

Herbert von Karajan
A sort of musical Malcolm Sargent.

Sir Thomas Beecham

Sir Landon Ronald
There was one respect in which Ronald outshone all other conductors. This was in the gleam of his shirtfront and the gloss of his enormous cuffs, out of which peeped tiny, fastidious fingers. He made music sound as if it, too, was laundered.

James Agate – 'Ego 4' (1940)

Sir Malcolm Sargent
The BBC Symphony Orchestra can best be described as the 'Sargent's Mess!'

Sir Thomas Beecham

I didn't know that he'd been knighted. It was only yesterday he was doctored.

Sir Thomas Beecham (1947)

Sir Georg Solti
'*Figaro*' – He conducted the second act finale with a smile on his face – it would have been better if he had cut his throat.   *Anon*

George Szell
He has an enormously wide repertory. He can conduct anything provided it's by Beethoven, Brahms, or Wagner. He tried Debussy's *La Mer* once. It came out as *Das Merde*.   *Anon*

Arturo Toscanini
A glorified Italian bandmaster.

Sir Thomas Beecham

I hate Toscanini. I've never heard him in a concert hall, but I've heard enough of his recordings. What he does to music is terrible . . . He chops it up into a hash and then pours a disgusting sauce over it . . . I think it's outrageous.   *Dimitri Shostakovich*

MUSICIANS

These three take crooked ways: carts, boats and musicians.   *Hindu proverb*

Anonymous musician at rehearsal – We cannot expect you to be with us all the time, but perhaps you could be good enough to keep in touch now and again.   *Thomas Beecham*

Musicians are ordinarily the least sophisticated of political animals, perhaps because for so many of their formative years they are shut up in practice rooms communicating with the dead.
   Donal Henahan (1970)

To a colleague – Oh, well then, you play Bach your way; and I'll play him his.
   Wanda Landowska

Said Oscar Wilde – 'Each man kills the thing he loves.' For example, the amateur musician.   *H. L. Mencken*

To a musician who had just played the first of two self-composed pieces – You need not play any more. I prefer the other.
   Gioacchino Rossini

Artists who say they practise eight hours a day are liars or asses.   *Andres Segovia (1980)*

Most of our women pianists and violinists have physiques that can only be described as miserable, narrow-chested, shallow bodies, bad carriage, emaciated arms, underdeveloped muscles, feeble tissues; they look like the poor, mean, thin, parched, anaemic sounds they produce from their instruments – pale, wan changelings of tone.
   Kaikhosru S. Sorabji – 'Around Music' (1932)

Orchestras

Each of its members is a poor disappointed devil. Collectively they are like a suppressed crowd of rebels, and, as an official 'body', they are bumptious and vain. Routine gives their playing the varnish of perfection and assurance. For the rest, they loathe their work, their job, and most of all, music.
   Ferruccio Busoni

Pianists

There are three kinds of pianists: Jewish pianists, homosexual pianists, and bad pianists.   *Vladimir Horowitz*

Johannes Brahms

Brahms – what a pianist! One of ten thumbs!
   Philip Hale – 'Boston Herald'

Ignacy Paderewski

Regarded as an immensely spirited young harmonious blacksmith, who puts a concerto on the piano as upon an anvil, and hammers it out with an exuberant enjoyment of the swing and strength of the proceedings.
   G. B. Shaw – 'Music in London' (1890)

Strings

Most string quartets have a basement and an attic, and the lift is not working.
   Neville Cardus – 'The Delights of Music'(1966)

In came a fiddler – and tuned like fifty stomach-aches.
   Charles Dickens – 'A Christmas Carol' (1843)

Viola players are horn players who have lost their teeth.   *Hans Richter*

Harpists spend half their time tuning and the other half playing out of tune.
   Igor Stravinsky

He was a fiddler, and consequently a rogue.
   Jonathan Swift (1711)

It was loud in spots and less loud in other spots, and it had that quality which I have noticed in all violin solos of seeming to last much longer than it actually did.
   P. G. Wodehouse (1942)

To an anonymous cellist – Madam, you have between your legs an instrument capable of giving pleasure to thousands – and all you can do is scratch it.   *Sir Thomas Beecham*

To an anonymous violinist – Difficult you call it, Sir? I wish it were impossible.
   Samuel Johnson

*On being told that a string quartet he was
listening to had been together for twelve years –
Surely, we've been here longer than that?*
G. B. Shaw

Nigel Kennedy
He attempts to achieve with his dress and
platform manner what he cannot obtain
through pure musical results.
*Dennis Rooney –
'The Strad'*

Detroit String Quartet
The Detroit String Quartet played Brahms
last night. Brahms lost. *Bennett Cerf*

Hollywood String Quartet
How could a New Yorker possibly take
something called the Hollywood String
Quartet seriously? *Leonard Slatkin*

Wind
All first oboists are gangsters. They are
tough, irascible, double-reed roosters, feared
by colleagues and conductors.
*Harry E. Dickson – 'Gentlemen, More Dolce
Please' (1969)*

The chief objection to playing wind
instruments is that it prolongs the life of the
player. *G. B. Shaw*

INSTRUMENTS

Accordion
An accordion is an instrument with the
sentiments of an assassin. *Ambrose Bierce*

The vile belchings of lunatic accordions.
Arthur Honegger (1951)

It's nothing to play an accordion. Anyone
who can fold a road map can play the
accordion. *Robert Orben*

Bagpipes
A true gentleman is a man who knows how to
play the bagpipes – but doesn't. *Anon*

The bagpipes sound exactly the same when
you have finished learning them as when you
started.
Sir Thomas Beecham

I find distance lends enchantment to
bagpipes – for example, the piper on one
mountain, the listener on another.
William Blezard

The churl did blow a grating shriek,
The bag did swell and harshly squeak,
As does a goose from nightmare crying,
Or dog, crushed by chest when dying . . .
Its sound is like a crane's harsh moan,
Or like a gosling's latest groan;
Just such a noise a wounded goat
Sends forth from her hoarse and gurgling
throat. *Lewis Glyn Cothi –
'The Saxons of Flint' – (c.1480)*

I got to try the bagpipes. It's like trying to
blow an octopus. *James Galway (1978)*

These are bagpipes. I understand the
inventor of the bagpipes was inspired when
he saw a man carry an indignant, asthmatic
pig under his arm. Unfortunately, the man-
made sound never equalled the purity of the
sound achieved by the pig. *Alfred Hitchcock*

Professor Saunders asserts that the bagpipes
have been played since 8000 B.C. Quite long
enough. *'Punch'*

Others, when the bag-pipes sings i' the nose,
Cannot contain their urine.
*William Shakespeare –
'The Merchant of Venice'*

Cello
I am not fond of the violoncello: ordinarily I
had just as soon hear a bee buzzing in a stone
jug. *G. B. Shaw – 'The World' (1890)*

The cello is not one of my favourite
instruments. It has such a lugubrious sound,
like someone reading a will. *Irene Thomas*

Clarinet
A clarinet is an instrument of torture
operated by a person with cotton in his ears.
There are only two instruments worse than a
clarinet – two clarinets. *Ambrose Bierce*

Clavichord
The clavichord gives a fretful waspish sound,

not at all suited to tender expression.

John Robison (1801)

Double bass

The double bass is a dangerous rogue elephant.   *Charles Villiers Stanford (1911)*

Fife

The vile squealing of the wry-neck'd fife.

William Shakespeare –
'The Merchant of Venice' (1596)

Harpsichord

The sound of the harpsichord resembles that of a bird-cage played with toasting-forks.

Anon

Sounds like two skeletons copulating on a corrugated tin roof.   *Sir Thomas Beecham*

The harpsichord, however it may sound in a small room – and to my mind it never has a pleasant sound – in a large concert room sounds just like the tickling of a sewing machine.   *Ralph Vaughan Williams (1950)*

Jew's harp

A Jew's harp is an unmusical instrument, played by holding it fast with the teeth and trying to brush it away with the finger.

Ambrose Bierce

Oboe

The oboe is an ill woodwind that blows no good.   *Anon*

Organ

The Winchester Cathedral organ is audible at five miles, painful at three and lethal at one.

Anon

The organ is a mechanical box of whistles.

Sir Thomas Beecham

[*N.B. Christopher Wren was reputed as saying that the St Paul's Cathedral organ was a confounded box of whistles.*]

With the advent of electronic organs – the wonderful old paaah and chaah became just plain aaah.   *E. P. Biggs – 'Newsweek' (1977)*

Piano

The upright piano is a musical growth found adhering to the walls of most semi-detached houses in the provinces.

Sir Thomas Beecham

A piano is a parlour utensil for subduing the impenitent visitor. A piano is operated by depressing the keys of the machine and the spirits of the audience.   *Ambrose Bierce*

I wish the Government would put a tax on pianos for the incompetent.   *Edith Sitwell*

Saxophone

The evil that men do lives after them. The saxophone was made in 1846.

'Asheville Times'

The saxophone is a long metal instrument bent at both ends. It is alleged to be musical. The creature has a series of tiny taps stuck upon it, apparently at random. These taps are very sensitive; when touched they cause the instrument to utter miserable sounds, suggesting untold agony. At either end there is a hole. People, sometimes for no reason at all, blow down the small end of the saxophone, which then shrieks and moans as if attacked by a million imps of torture.

'London Daily News' (1927)

The worst is yet to come. A saxophone endurance contest is proposed.

'Vancouver Province'

I do not like the saxophone, it sounds like the word: 'Reckankreuzungsklankwerkzeuge'.

Richard Wagner

Tuba

The tuba is certainly the most intestinal of instruments, the very lower bowel of music.

Peter de Vries

Ukulele

The ukulele is a so-called musical instrument which, when listened to, you cannot tell whether someone is playing it or just monkeying around.   *Anon*

The inventor of the ukulele has just died in Hawaii. As he reached the age of almost eighty, he seems nearly to have lived down his crime.   *'Manchester Union'*

MUSIC

Violin
A violin is an instrument to tickle the human ears by friction of a horse's tail on the entrails of a cat. *Ambrose Bierce*

A squeak's heard in the orchestra,
The leader draws across
The intestines of the agile cat
The tail of the noble hoss. *George T. Lanigan – 'The Amateur Orlando' (c.1880)*

Is it not strange that sheep's guts should hale souls out of men's bodies?
William Shakespeare – 'Much Ado About Nothing' (1598)

When a man is not disposed to hear musick, there is not a more disagreeable Sound in Harmony than that of a violin.
Richard Steele – 'Tatler' (1710)

POPULAR MUSIC

GENERAL

Pop music is the kind played so fast that you can't tell what classical composer it was stolen from. *Anon*

Songs used to have rhymes without reason. Now they have reason without rhymes.
Sammy Cahn

Popular music in the USA is one of the few things in the twentieth century that have made giant strides in reverse. *Bing Crosby*

Sweet popular music is claptrap in the main, and in the main is where it belongs.
Peter de Vries

The kids today are quite right about the music their parents listened to; most of it was trash. The parents are quite right about what their young listen to: most of it is trash too.
Gene Lees – 'High Fidelity' (1967)

Every popular song has at least one line or sentence that is perfectly clear – the line that fits the music. *Ezra Pound*

The lyrics of pop songs are so banal that if you show a spark of intelligence they call you a poet. *Paul Simon (1968)*

One never realizes the vulgarity of human beings so acutely as when listening to the mindless bawling of popular songs.
John Sullivan – 'But for the Grace of God'

Those whites can play instruments real fine. But there's something missing in their singing. They just don't eat enough pinto beans; they haven't had enough hard times.
Muddy Waters

COMPOSERS

George Gershwin
'*Rhapsody in Blue*' – How trite and feeble and conventional the tunes are; how sentimental and vapid the harmonic treatment, under its disguise of fussy and futile counterpoint! Weep over the lifelessness of the melody and harmony, so derivative, so stale, so inexpressive.
Lawrence Gilman – 'New York Tribune' (1924)

George's music gets around so much before an opening that the first night audience thinks it's at a revival. *George S. Kaufman*

Cole Porter
He sang like a hinge. *Ethel Merman*

PERFORMERS

Charles Aznavour
Charles as no voice! *Anon*

Ray Charles
He is nothing but a blind, ignorant nigger.
Elvis Costello (1979)

Perry Como
Perry gave his usual impersonation of a man who has been simultaneously told to say 'Cheese' and shot in the back with a poisoned arrow. *Clive James – 'The Observer' (1978)*

Neil Diamond
'*The Jazz Singer*' (1980) – The performance is okay . . . but then Diamond never attempts anything so difficult as chewing gum and walking at the same time.
Rod McShane – 'Time Out'

Mary Hopkin

On the Beatles launching Apple Records – I wouldn't get any satisfaction out of creating a Mary Hopkin.   Mick Jagger

Julio Iglesias

'*1100 Bel Air Place*' – Julio goes to Hollywood . . . but to little avail, the assistance of two 'dialect coaches', the quavering tones and husky accent of the suave Latin crooner remain frighteningly reminiscent of an over-attentive Spanish waiter who's coming on a bit amorous.   *Tom Hibbert (1984)*

Tom Jones

His triumphs in singles like *It's Not Unusual* and *Delilah* have earned him a permanent niche in the annals of nursing-home rock.
John Swenson – '*Rolling Stone*'

Billy La Bounty

It's only when you hear a pop singer this bad that you can completely appreciate how skilful – I didn't say good – hacks like Barry Manilow and Tony Orlando are.
Dave Marsh – '*Rolling Stone*'

Liberace

On bad reviews for his 1954 Madison Square concert – What the critics said hurt me very much. I cried all the way to the bank. [*Later he added* – . . . and then I bought the bank.]

A deadly, winking, sniggering, snuggling, chromium-plated, scent-impregnated, luminous, quivering, giggling, mincing, heap of mother love.
William Connor – '*Daily Mirror*' *(1956)*

'*The Liberace Show*' – Such dimpling and winking! Such tossing of blond curls, and fluttering of eyelashes and flashing of teeth! Such nausea.   *Faye Emerson* – '*New York World/ Telegram*' *(1952)*

Did you see Liberace's *Valentine Night Special*? It was like being forcibly fed with warm peppermint creams.
Clive James – '*The Observer*' *(1980)*

Barry Manilow

The USA '94 World Cup mascot is a footballing mutt . . . USA '94 are still looking for a name for the dribbling dawg. Dare we suggest Barry Manilow?   '*Time Out*'

Liza Minnelli

BBC TV's '*Love from A to Z*' *(1974)* – Liza can't even walk up a flight of stairs sincerely (a flight of stairs was wheeled on for the specific purpose of allowing her to prove this).   *Clive James* – '*The Observer*'

Olivia Newton-John

Olivia looks as antiseptic as an intensive care unit in a maternity hospital.
Clive James – '*The Observer*' *(1974)*

The Osmonds

On stage their act is pure corn – laborious mimes to playback, sub-Motown choreography and mirthless humour. Merrill looks like Philip Jenkinson and little Jimmy (once again the Bad Sight of the Week) must appeal only to children so young they can't cut up their own food.
Clive James – '*The Observer*'

Donnie Osmond

Prima Donny . . . all eyes, sob and slop. He couldn't open his yap without referring to his tender years; he had teeth like so many well-kept tombstones, and all the soul of one.
Julie Burchill

Well crafted garbage – trash is too elevated a description.   *Dave Marsh* – '*Rolling Stone*'

Marie Osmond

She is so pure, Moses couldn't even part her knees.   *Joan Rivers*

The Osmond Boys

'*Show Me the Way*' – Shit! it had to happen didn't it. Yes, they're the sons and the record sounds like New Kids doing a Canadian beer ad. Don't they have family planning over there?   *Laura Lee Davies* – '*Time Out*' *(1991)*

Johnnie Ray

He was the Jayne Mansfield of pop, totally dumb and unautonomous and out of control with no redeeming merit whatsoever – no voice, no songs, no music.   *Julie Burchill*

Helen Reddy
The queen housewife of rock.   *Kim Fowley*

Cliff Richard
I think Cliff Richard is controversial. Anyone who's lived with his mum for that long is definitely suspicious.   *Johnny Rotten (1986)*

'*This New Year*' *(1992)* – Cliff, luv, you've got to stop. It would be infinitely more honest if you opened a squat shop at seasonal times.   *Gill Whyte – 'Time Out'*

Demis Roussos
Roussos – fat, shaggy, rich, dynamic – is a Phenomenon . . . Common sense dictated that the Phenomenon's appeal could not lie in his music, which is derivative to the point of putrefaction. But it seemed even less likely that the appeal could lie in the man himself, since the larger than lifesize entertainer was quickly revealed as one of the least attractive showbiz Phenomena since Jimmy Boyd, the delinquent who saw mommy kissing Santa Claus . . . His singing is done in an unrelenting ying-tong tremolo which would curdle your brains like paint-stripper if you gave it time.
        Clive James – 'The Observer' (1976)

Frank Sinatra
He's an ugly bastard with huge flapping ears.
        Robbie Coltrane

Frankie Valli
'*Frankie Valli is The Word*' – In plain English, that word means garbage.
        Dave Marsh – 'Rolling Stone'

Crystal Waters
'*Megamix!*' *(1992)* – The exclamation mark is symbolic of the ill conceived guilt over this audacious production – a sort of apology.
        Gill Whyte – 'Time Out'

BAND MUSIC

Brass bands are all very well in their place – outdoors and several miles away.
        Sir Thomas Beecham

On an anonymous big band – This excruciating medley of brutal sounds is subordinated to a barely perceptible rhythm. Listening to this screaming music for a minute or two, one conjures up an orchestra of madmen, sexual maniacs, led by a man-stallion beating time with an enormous phallus.   *Maxim Gorky*

Big Band music is twenty men who take it in turns to stand up – plus a drummer.
        'Mail on Sunday' (1992)

I'll make two predictions: big bands won't make a comeback and Dolly Parton will continue to be the only girl with big tits to sell records.   *Artie Mogull*

COUNTRY AND WESTERN

GENERAL

There's nothing like a hardship song to set my toes a-tappin'.   *Roseanne Barr*

I have long harboured a suspicion that most country songwriters moonlight as speechwriters for President Reagan or scriptwriters for *Dallas* since they share a desire to reduce all life to the dimensions of a B-movie.
        Paul Lashmar – 'The Observer' (1986)

You don't understand country and western music. It's about the real things in life – murder, train wrecks, amputations, faucets leakin' in the night – all stuff like that.
        'Mary Hartman, Mary Hartman' (U.S. T.V.)

Country – doesn't that mean singing between your teeth?   *James McGibbin (1992)*

PERFORMERS

The Bellamy Brothers
Pop without the snap or crackle.
        Dave Marsh – 'Rolling Stone'

Garth Brooks
How Brooks achieved superstar status remains as much a mystery as the Marie Celeste.
        Fred Dellar – 'Melody Maker' (1992)

John Denver

I'm a John Denver freak, and I don't give a shit that he looks like a f***ing turkey.

Grace Slick

Willie Nelson

Q. What has 300 legs and seven teeth?
A. The front row at a Willie Nelson concert.

'Playboy' (1988)

Kenny Rogers

The musical equivalent of a black-velvet Elvis, the embodiment of schlock art.

Alanna Nash (1990)

DANCE, DISCO, RAP AND SOUL

Rap music is people talking when they should be singing.   *'Mail on Sunday' (1992)*

PERFORMERS

Bananarama

I met Bananarama once. They are living proof that make-up works.

Chesney Hawkes (1990)

Bananarama display the discrete choreography of a herd of clubfooted elephants.   *'Melody Maker' (1983)*

The Bee Gees

Why do they sing like that?   *Roger Daltrey*

Boney M

'Rivers of Babylon' – This song does to reggae what some listeners might like to do to the group: drowns it. *Dave Marsh – 'Rolling Stone'*

Johnny Bristol

His speciality is a kind of post-feminism seduction, encouraging women to improve themselves flat on their back. To which one can only respond: 'Get f***ed!'

Dave Marsh – 'Rolling Stone'

Carter USM

The Steptoe and Son of technopop.

Laura Lee Davies – 'Time Out' (1992)

Color Me Badd

'Heartbreaker' (1992) – Color Me Beige more

like. Burbling dance pop music more watered down than a pint at my local.

Laura Lee Davies – 'Time Out'

Julee Cruise

'Summer Kisses, Winter Tears' – Cotton-wool tonsils is back with another piece of corny, cabaret pop Hank Marvin would be proud of.   *Laura Lee Davies – 'Time Out' (1992)*

Chris de Burgh

'Spanish Train and Other Stories' – It sounds almost like the Cat Stevens score to Ingmar Bergman's first rock musical.

Bart Testa – 'Rolling Stone'

Des'ree

'Mind Adventures' (1992) – There's a kind of grim tenacity to the way the songs on *Mind Adventures* hang on for your approval . . . Approval has to do with the purchase of furniture, not pop records, and this one's a sofa-bed.   *Nick Coleman – 'Time Out'*

Sheena Easton

'The Best Kept Secret' – The only trouble is this collection of divine melodies leaves an absolute blank on the brain . . . like afternoon Radio 2. The sort of music that won't disturb your grandmother.

Claire Sheaff – 'Rolling Stone'

Floaters

'Float On' – A leading contender in the Dumbest Popular Record in the Universe Sweepstakes.   *Dave Marsh – 'Rolling Stone'*

Freez

'Gonna Get You' – Music for shopping.

Josephine Hocking (1984)

Eddie Grant

'Paco and Ramone' (1992) – Much like a modernised version of Rolf Harris' seminal *Two Little Boys* – but obviously not as good.

Gill Whyte – 'Time Out'

Robert Hazard

'Wing of Fire' – Chockablock with draggy tempos, histrionic lyrics and the least effective hooks to come out of Philadelphia since Marvis Frazier's . . . a mishmash of dopey quasi-reggae, saggy limp-rock, and

MUSIC

droopy tavern technopop.
Christopher Connelly – 'Rolling Stone' (1984)

Janice
'*Janice*' – Nice girls finish last, too.
Dave Marsh – 'Rolling Stone'

Kris Kross
A rap duo whose gimmick is to wear all their clothes backwards. It's a relief to see the front of them.
Dermot Purgavie – 'Daily Mail' (1992)

Alison Limerick
There was a young singer of soul
Who just won a 'Billboard' dance poll
With such predictable pop
She's on her way to the top
What's happened to good rock 'n' roll?
Gill Whyte – 'Time Out' (1992)

Madonna
I have seen her up close! Neither the music nor the image inspires my loins.
David Coverdale (1988)

'*Who's That Girl*' – Who's that girl? Who cares? *Alan Frank*

Armed with a wiggle and a Minnie Mouse squawk, she is coarse and charmless.
Sheila Johnston (1987)

She is closer to organized prostitution than anything else. *Morissey (1986)*

Robert Palmer
The Fraud of Funk.
Dave Marsh – 'Rolling Stone'

Why do I always get the impression that in a past life Robert Palmer was a garden gnome? . . . Is it perchance, the way he sings? Kinda like he passed away in an armchair three days ago while attempting to squeeze the juice from a lemon, with the sole aid of his buttocks.
Andrew Smith – 'Melody Maker' (1992)

The Pasadenas
'*Yours Sincerely*' (1992) – If Bob Marley or Marvin Gaye have any sway with the Big Man Upstairs, then the Pasadenas will be

condemned to Majorcan casinos in winter and the Butlins circuit in the summer. And this offering can only be construed as a worthy audition for such places.
Dave Faulkner – 'Time Out'

Pet Shop Boys
'*It Couldn't Happen Here*' (1987) – Director John Bond's attempt at a narrative stringing together the Pet Shop Boys' pop themes is witless, aimless and pretentious. If this sickbag of kitsch communicates anything it's the anguish of a young aesthete on discovering that flying ducks still adorn the walls of his mother's house.
Elaine Paterson – 'Time Out'

They are duller than the mud-caked hub-cap of a record company MD's roller. They sound like Frankie [*Goes to Hollywood*] with a ball and chain. *Sandy Robertson (1986)*

Michelle Phillips
'*Victim of Romance*' – I liked her better when she was married to Dennis Hopper – but then that only lasted a week.
Dave Marsh – 'Rolling Stone'

P.M. DAWN
'*Reality Used to Be a Friend of Mine*' (1992) – Enough to bore the saddle off a donkey.
Gill Whyte – 'Time Out'

Prince
He looks like a dwarf who's been dipped in a bucket of pubic hair. *Boy George (1986)*

'*For You*' (1978) – Rubbish from the days when he used to spell things properly and wear suspenders. *'Melody Maker' (1992)*

Rave Nation featuring Juliette
'*Stand Up*' (1992) – Be honest. If you were given a record entitled 'Stand Up' by someone called Rave Nation featuring Juliette, would you play it?
Nick Coleman – 'Time Out'

Lionel Richie
He's got a chin like an ironing board.
Pete Burns (1984)

Satellite of Undying Love
Promoting themselves as 'spiritual disco' . . .

S.O.U.L. are in fact about as spiritual as a copy of *Bunty*.   *Gill Whyte – 'Time Out'*

Shakatak
A group that must fall into the dreaded category of 'coffee table music' to be filed alongside the likes of James Last. And that's a crime.   *Linda Duff (1984)*

Shut Up and Dance
'The Green Man' (1992) – Ultimately unlistenable. Probably something akin to a *Blue Peter* DIY project – fun to make but crap to use afterwards.
                Gill Whyte – 'Time Out'

Silje
'I Need Your Love' (1992) – Neurotic pop with screechy guitar and raspy Bonnie Tyler vocal. Please, someone shag her and put her out of her misery.
                Elaine Roylance – 'Time Out'

Simply Red
Simply Red are just music for chartered accountants to court to in wine bars.
                'Melody Maker' (1992)

Soul II Soul
'Volume 3: Just Right' (1992) – Funki dead.
                Nick Coleman – 'Time Out'

St Etienne
'Join My Club' (1992) – Utterly, utterly weak and weedy rave pop; you couldn't dance to this, but you could try skipping.
                Nick Hornby – 'Time Out'

Wet, Wet, Wet
There is a case for Wet, Wet, Wet – at the Baker Street lost property office.
                Laura Lee Davies – 'Time Out'

Barry White
'Just the Way You Are' – One thing worse than Billy Joel singing a Billy Joel song, is Barry White singing a Billy Joel song. The fat prat.   *Gary Bushell (1978)*

Mr Love Walrus.   *Gill Whyte – 'Time Out'*

Zucchero
'Diamante' (1992) – Sex mood music,

performed by and for amorous courgettes and other gourds.   *Gill Whyte – 'Time Out'*

FOLK MUSIC

GENERAL

A folksinger is someone who sings through his nose by ear.   *Anon*

A folksinger is an intellectual who sings songs that nobody ever wrote.   *Anon*

Folk singing is just a bunch of fat people.
                Bob Dylan

In the USA real folk music long ago went to Nashville and left no survivors.
                Donal Henahan – 'New York Times' (1977)

Endless songs about shipwrecks in the 19th century.   *'Mail on Sunday' (1992)*

PERFORMERS

Ravi Shankar
I don't want to manage Ravi Shankar. If hymns were hits, I'd be managing Moses.
                Dee Anthony

HEAVY METAL

GENERAL

Why do all heavy metal guitarists look like Joan Jett?   *Boy George*

Heavy Metal is the transformation of precious jewels and gold into lead.
                Charles Shaar Murray (1984)

PERFORMERS

AC/DC
AC/DC is an Australian hard-rock band whose main purpose on earth apparently is to offend anyone within sight or earshot. They succeed on both counts.
                Billy Altman – 'Rolling Stone'

Alice Cooper
Alice Cooper are the worst, most disgusting side of rock music.   *Lou Reed*

Kiss

Rock 'n' roll is just mindless fun, the whole f***ing thing is a poetic invention, a grandchild of the whole Dada/Surrealist movement. Rock 'n' roll thrives on negative energy. Those guys in Kiss couldn't wipe their ass by themselves. *Alan Lanier*

La Guns

'The Ballad of Jayne' (1992) – Like unhealthy cereal which is foisted upon the public with the allure of a 'free gift', the Guns have taken the measure of including a 'free giant poster/calendar' with this abysmal rock ballad. Strangely, I am not tempted by a year spent with the boys. Is nothing in life for free?
Gill Whyte – 'Time Out'

Led Zeppelin

They may be world famous but four shrieking monkeys are not going to use a privileged family name without permission.
Eva von Zeppelin

Megadeath

The gruesome noise of corpses in the machinery. *David Stubbs (1988)*

Motley Crüe

Their version of rock 'n' roll is such a careful distillation of Black Sabbath, Kiss and other arena giants that you'd almost think it was developed by MTV's marketing staff.
J. D. Considine – 'Rolling Stone'

Ozzy Osborne

He couldn't carry a tune around in a suitcase.
Ronnie James Dio (1982)

JAZZ AND BLUES

GENERAL

Some happy day we shall beat our swords into plowshares and our jazz bands into unconsciousness. *'Baltimore Sun'*

Jam sessions, jitterbugs and cannibalistic rhythmic orgies are wooing our youth along the primrose path to Hell.
Rev. F. J. Blackman (1938)

I don't like the word 'Jazz' that the white people dropped on us. *Miles Davis*

Jazz is music invented for the torture of imbeciles. *Henry van Dyke*

I don't write Jazz, I write Negro folk music.
Duke Ellington

Playing 'bop' is like playing Scrabble with all the vowels missing. *Duke Ellington*

For the most part jazz criticism has been conducted by those whose passionate love of music was never quite passionate enough for them to learn the rudiments of jazz making.
Benny Green (1974)

Jazz is strictly for the stay-at-home types.
Buddy Holly

A prominent composer of popular music says, 'Jazz is still in its infancy.' Or, to be more exact, it is still at the colic stage.
'Kansas City Star'

'Jazz is dying!' Well, it always sounded that way. *'Greenville Piedmont'*

Giving jazz the Congressional seal of approval is a little like making Huck Finn an honorary Boy Scout.
Melvin Maddocks –
'Christian Science Monitor' (1986)

Jazz is five men on the same stage all playing a different tune. *'Mail on Sunday' (1992)*

Blues is played exclusively by people who woke up this morning.
'Mail on Sunday' (1992)

Rhythm and blues is not music, it's a disease.
Mitch Miller

The Negro, with his unusual sense of rhythm, is no more accurately to be called musical than a metronome is to be called a Swiss music-box.
George J. Nathan – 'Comedians All' (1919)

Jazz music is rendered; cubist pictures are executed; the perpetrators should be both.
'Newspaper Enterprise Association'

We can't see why jazz musicians should be paid $15 a day. Riveters, who get only $10, make almost as much noise and do something useful besides. *'New York Tribune'*

A terrible revenge by the culture of the Negroes on that of the Whites.
Ignacy Paderewski

Jazz music seems to be improving. At a jazz-band performance the other night it was so quiet that the audience could almost have heard a revolver fired. *'Punch'*

It must be true as reported that jazz is dying. There is no other way to account for the weird noise it makes. *'Toledo Blade'*

Today you play jazz, tomorrow you will betray your country. *Stalinist poster*

PERFORMERS

Harry Connick Jr
'We Are In Love' – Connick sings with more than a little charm. But it is the charm of a used-car salesman who hopes you won't notice how rusty the autos on his lot really are. *'Entertainment Weekly' (1990)*

Miles Davis
I saw him standing in snakeskin trousers with an electrified orange trumpet, playing a series of screeching notes that meant f*** all – I thought, why don't you just drive a red-hot nail through your balls? *Spike Milligan (1988)*

Duke Ellington
A Harlem Dionysus drunk on bad bootleg liquor. *Ernest Newman*

Hugues Panassie
Who does that Frog think he is to come over here and try to tell us how to play? We don't go over there and tell them how to jump on a grape. *Eddie Condon*

NEW WAVE

GENERAL

The New Romantics of the early eighties . . . built their house on nothing but nerky clothes and even nerkier music. The Romantics were all a good two stone too heavy ever to look exquisite or elegant; it would have been easier to feel romantic about a waste disposal unit. The New Romantics' contribution to humanity was boys in frocks, hardly cause for streetparties and celebrations.
Julie Burchill – 'The Method Rhythm'

Punk Rock: A style of simple rock music played with great vigour but lacking polish. *'Concise Oxford Dictionary'*

Punk rock is a bad scene and I don't understand why it has to exist when there's so much in life. *Frank Sinatra*

PERFORMERS

The Clash
The sheets of sound they let loose have the cumulative effect of mugging.
'The Times' (1979)

Cherie Curry of The Runaways
Handling Cherie Curry's ego is like having a dog urinate in your face. *Kim Fowley*

Elvis Costello
Looks like Buddy Holly after drinking a can of STP Oil Treatment.
Dave Marsh – 'Rolling Stone'

Devo
The five vegetables of the apocalypse.
'New Musical Express' (1978)

Generation X
The only 'punk' band with a zero credibility rating . . . They were no more rebellious than Jason Donovan.
Caren Myers – 'Melody Maker' (1992)

Boy George
He reminds me of an aubergine – all shiny and plump. *Paul Young (1985)*

He's just an old soddin' queen mincing around like some sickening Danny La Rue.
Ian McCulloch (1985)

Billy Idol
The Perry Como of Punk *Johnny Rotten*

John Lydon (aka Johnny Rotten)
John Lydon's a has-been. An also-ran. A pitiful pathetic poseur who once sounded righteously angry and now sounds pathetically drained.

Craig Zeller – 'Rolling Stone'

Morrissey (The Smiths)
'*The Smiths*' – Morrissey lays out his life like a shoebox full of faded snapshots.

'Rolling Stone'

Sex Pistols
After a concert – I felt unclean for about forty-eight hours.　　　*Anon GLC Councillor*

Feargal Sharkey (The Undertones)
A face like a bucket with a dent in it.

Allan Jones (1988)

The Smiths
Drab music for drab people.

Tony James (1985)

Spandau Ballet
'*Parade*' – Even if Spandau Ballet were to become great at what it does, what it does would still be the most cretinous sort of Anglo-yuppie muzak imaginable.

Kurt Loder – 'Rolling Stone'

Stranglers
Hippies with their hair cut off to make some money.　　　*Boy George (1983)*

'*Golden Brown*' – A record to make Stranglers cult-heroes with Julio Iglesias fans.

Colin Irwin (1982)

Joe Strummer (The Clash)
He makes Andy Capp look like a radio announcer.　　*Dave Marsh 'Rolling Stone'*

Fee Waybill (The Tubes)
He had the most unique range in rock: two notes, both flat.

Dave Marsh – 'Rolling Stone'

RAGTIME

A wave of vulgar, filthy and suggestive music has inundated the land. The pabulum of theatre and summer hotel orchestra is coon music. Nothing but ragtime prevails and the cake-walk with its obscene posturings, and lewd gestures. It is artistically and morally depressing and should be suppressed by press and pulpit.　　*'Musical Courier' (1899)*

REGGAE

Reggae is the most racist music in the world. It's an absolute total glorification of black supremacy.　　*Morrisey (1986)*

PERFORMERS

Bob Marley
'*Time Will Tell*' (1992) – No amount of rare concert and rehearsal footage can conceal that Marley's music in bulk is an exercise in monotony and that as a socio-political thinker he is slightly less interesting than Cilla Black.　　*Christopher Tookey –*
'Sunday Telegraph' (1992)

Ziggy Marley
It is simply not enough to look and sound like a bad *Spitting Image* puppet of your dad – you have to have something of comparable significance to say. If you don't, you look like a nance and an opportunist and a victim of bad parenting . . . He has all the weight but none of the significance.

Nick Coleman – 'Time Out' (1992)

ROCK 'N' ROLL

Rock 'n' Roll at its core is merely a bunch of raving shit.　　*Lester Bangs – 'Cream'*

Rock 'n' Roll is a means of pulling down the white man to the level of the Negro. It is part of a plot to undermine the morals of youth of our nation. It brings people of both races together.　　*Asa Carter – North Alabama*
Citizens' Council (1956)

Poison put to sound – a brutalization of both life and art.　　*Pablo Casals*

Rock is music that requires very little knowledge and not much talent.

Harry Connick Jr (1990)

If Rock 'n' Roll is here to stay I might

commit suicide. *Sammy Davis Jr*

Commercial Rock and Roll music is a brutalisation of the stream of contemporary Negro church music – an obscene looting of a cultural expression.
Ralph Ellison – 'Shadow and Act' (1964)

Rock 'n' Roll is instant coffee. *Bob Geldof*

You have to blame Thomas Alva Edison for today's Rock 'n' Roll. He invented electricity.
Stan Getz

More happens in two bars of great music than in two minutes of Rock 'n' Roll.
Paul Goodman – 'New York Review of Books' (1971)

The kids that go to Rock festivals lie around in mud listening to a shitty sound system, eating day-old garbage, and they think they're having a good time. They're just being had. *Bill Graham*

Rock 'n' Roll is a corruption of Rhythm and Blues which was a dilution of the blues, so that today's mass-marketed noise is a vulgarisation of a vulgarisation.
Benny Green (1976)

The British Rock and Pop Awards – So inconsequential that it wasn't even offensive, it had the lasting importance of someone breaking wind in the middle of a hurricane.
Clive James – 'The Observer'

Rock 'n' Roll drummers should be put in a capsule and their asses lost in outer space.
Elvin Jones

'Rock Against Drugs' is like Christians against Christ – Rock created drugs.
Sam Kinison (1989)

All Rock and Roll is about is having a good time and getting laid, it'd be stupid to pretend otherwise. *Lemmy*

Youth has many glories, but judgement is not one of them, and no amount of electronic amplification can turn a belch into an aria.
Alan Jay Lerner (1978)

Rock lyrics are doggerel, maybe.
Dave Marsh and Kevin Stein (1981)

Rock and roll is a communicable disease.
'New York Times' (1956)

Some Rock music is a help to the devil.
Archbishop John O'Connor (1990)

All Rock 'n' Roll singers sound like a nudist backing into a cold-nosed dog – set to music.
Robert Orben

Rock 'n' Roll might best be summed up as a monotony tinged with hysteria.
Vance Packard – 'Testimony to US Senate' (1958)

Rock critics are full of shit. If they weren't they'd be out playing and they wouldn't have time to criticise anybody. *Felix Pappalardi*

Rock began as a scandal. It was underclass music. *Abe Peck – 'New York Post'*

Rock music has become the devil's playground. *Dan and Steve Peters – 'Why Knock Rock?' (1984)*

Rock and Roll songs are junk; in many cases they are obscene junk much on the level with dirty comic magazines. *Billy Rose*

The Sex Pistols finished Rock 'n' Roll. This was the last Rock 'n' Roll band. It's all over now [sic] Rock 'n' Roll's shit. It's dismal. Grandads dance to it.
Johnny Rotten (1978)

Rock 'n' Roll fosters almost totally negative and destructive reactions in young people. It smells phoney and false. *Frank Sinatra*

Rock 'n' Roll is the most brutal, ugly, vicious form of expression it has been my misfortune to hear – sly, lewd, in plain fact dirty. It manages to be the martial music of every sideburned delinquent on the face of the earth. This rancid smelling aphrodisiac I deplore.
Frank Sinatra – 'New York Post' (1957)

Rock 'n' Roll is sung, played, and written for

the most part by cretinous goons.
Frank Sinatra – 'Western World' (1958)

Rock 'n' Roll is not meant to be criticised. If you can find someone who's willing to pay you to be a critic, then you've found a sucker. *Paul Stanley*

Rock and Roll is dull, ugly, amateurish, immature, trite, banal and stale. It glorifies the mediocre, the nasty, the bawdy, the cheap, the tasteless. *Meredith Willson*

Rock 'n' Roll is the hamburger that ate the world. *Peter York – 'Style Wars' (1980)*

Most people wouldn't know good Rock music if it came up and bit them in the ass.
Frank Zappa

PERFORMERS

ABC
'*Beauty Stab*' – It seems that Martin Fry has only succeeded in shooting a poison arrow into his own foot.
Errol Somay – 'Rolling Stone'

Brian Adams
As far as his love numbers go, I'm afraid someone who sings like he's got a throat infection is not going to get me smooching.
Laura Lee Davies – 'Time Out'

'*Though I'd Died and Gone to Heaven*' *(1992)* – Another roaring rock song for those who live in the service station.
Laura Lee Davies – 'Time Out'

Gregg Allman and Cher
Allman and Woman: 'Two the Hard Way" – It's hard to imagine a more inappropriate combination than Gregg Allman and Cher. This record may as well be a copy of the latest scandal sheet about Hollywood's odd couple as an attempt at music.
John Swenson – 'Rolling Stone'

The Animals
'*Ark*' – The group's second reunion album . . . more thud-thud than 'Boom-Boom', *Ark* is a good idea that should have stayed in dry dock. *David Fricke – 'Rolling Stone'*

The Art of Noise
'*Who's Afraid of . . .*' – It gets about as tedious as mowing the lawn.
Parke Puterbaugh – 'Rolling Stone'

'*Shades of Paranoia*' – . . . just another strain on the National Grid.
David Stubbs – 'Melody Maker' (1992)

Bay City Rollers
I lost all my friends in the Bay City Rollers disaster of '74, it was like some plague, a complete wipe-out . . . from their moronic prancing and chanting, from their gormless unformed Pools-winner faces, from their tartan trimmings and short pants.
Julie Burchill – 'The Face' (1984)

Whoever is doing the Bay City Rollers' publicity has no sense of shame.
John Peel on Radio 1

Chuck Berry
I think for the life span he's lasted, Chuck Berry's productivity has been nil, more or less. *Elton John*

David Bowie
The thin white duke changed musical styles like clothes, seeing rock more as a pose than as internal combustion.
John Milward – 'Rolling Stone'

Kate Bush
Sort of like the consequences of mating Patti Smith with a Hoover vacuum cleaner.
Dave McGee – 'Rolling Stone'

Cabaret Voltaire
They sound like a Hoover with an old bag screaming over it. *Pete Burns (1987)*

Captain and Tennille
Toni Tennille looks like a toothpaste-commercial reject and acts the part.
Ken Tucker – 'Rolling Stone'

The Charlatans
'*Weirdo*' – This is as redundant as a pudding bowl haircut.
Andrew Smith – 'Melody Maker' (1992)

Ingrid Chavez
'*May 19 1992*' – If this flaccid hash of

techno-gurgles and choccy bar ad copy makes for shopping music, never mind poetry, then the sooner we all start doing Performance Art at home instead of watching telly the better . . . Drivel and hum.

Nick Coleman – 'Time Out' (1992)

Eric Clapton

If I go round to someone's house and there's an Eric Clapton record, I just walk out.

Jon Moss (1985)

The Cult

'Heart of Soul' – Ian Astbury is scurrying about bare-chested among these tenth-hand rock riffs like a Jap soldier in the jungle who hasn't been told the war's over.

David Stubbs – 'Melody Maker' (1992)

Roger Daltrey

'Parting Should be Painless' – Parting with this album should not only be painless, but pleasurable.

Parke Puterbaugh – 'Rolling Stone'

Dire Straits

'On Every Street' (1991) – A pot-plant among rock records.   *'Time Out'*

Dr Feelgood

They sound like sparse backing for a lead singer who never appears.

Charley Walters – 'Rolling Stone'

Bob Dylan

I am unable to see in Dylan anything other than a youth of mediocre talent. Only a completely non-critical audience, nourished on the watery pap of pop music could have fallen for such tenth-rate drivel.

Ewan MacColl – 'Sing Out' (1965)

Actually, I never liked Dylan's kind of music before; I always thought he sounded just like Yogi Bear.   *Mike Ronson*

Echo and the Bunnymen

'Ocean Rain' – A monochromatic dirge of banal existential imagery cloaked around the mere skeleton of a musical idea.

Parke Puterbaugh – 'Rolling Stone'

Emerson, Lake and Palmer

'Works' – Appropriately titled, like a tuna-fish hero sandwich with so much glop on it you forget what you're eating.

Bruce Malamut – 'Rolling Stone'

Energy Orchard

'Stop the Machine' (1992) – Nonsense rock for grown-up people with sensible jobs, this is music without anger, edge, excitement, talent, originality or flair . . . When God invented rock 'n' roll this wasn't really what he had in mind.   *Ross Fortune – 'Time Out'*

Fabian

This instant asphalt Elvis from Philadelphia.

Fred Schruers – 'Rolling Stone'

Bryan Ferry

He sings like he's throwing up.

Andrew O'Connor

Flying Picketts

'Lost Boys' – They should be banished to Blackpool (preferably chained to the rocks as the tide's coming in). Really, it's that bad.

Kimberley Leston – 'Rolling Stone'

Art Garfunkel

He makes Paul Simon look like LL Cool J.

Ian Gittins (1988)

Gerry and the Pacemakers

'Ferry Cross the Mersey: The Movie' (1964) – A little glimpse into hell.

Kenneth Tynan – 'The Observer'

Haircut One Hundred

'Paint & Paint' – Haircut One Hundred have almost everything – but tunes to help you breathe more easily.   *Tom Hibbert (1984)*

George Harrison

On the Natural Law Party concert – George Harrison sounded as cocky as a Mersey tugboat.   *Ian Lyness – 'Daily Express' (1992)*

If you see George Harrison, you can tell him that I think he's a load of old rope.

Cliff Richard

Lisa Hartman

'Lisa Hartman' – She is that rarity, a

completely talentless singer.

John Swenson – 'Rolling Stone'

Jimi Hendrix
Played guitar like a man possessed but you wished he'd put it back in his pants and have a cup of tea or something . . . The guitar-asphallus technique never struck me as graceful or beguiling. And, yes he was dextrous, but so presumably is Paul Daniels.

Chris Roberts –
'Melody Maker' (1992)

Herman's Hermits
'Henry the Eighth' – It would be cheaper, and no more unpleasant, to record yourself in the shower while holding your nose.

Dave Marsh – 'Rolling Stone'

Honeymoon Suite
Musical junk food.

J. D. Considine – 'Rolling Stone'

Human League
'Hysteria' – This album is a turkey – USDA prime self-basting Butterball.

Crispin Sartwell – 'Rolling Stone'

Icehouse
'Sidewalk' – Most of *Sidewalk* is pedestrian.

J. D. Considine – 'Rolling Stone'

Michael Jackson
'Moonwalker: the Movie' (1988) – Altogether a ghastly experience, which even the rabid 11-year-old in your life might well find patronizing and unimaginative.

Nick Coleman – 'Time Out'

'Remember the Time' (1992) – Remember The Time when you used to make decent f***ing records?

'Melody Maker'

The beige chanteur, the Caucasian Diva.

'Punch' (1992)

Mick Jagger
I think Mick Jagger would be astounded and amazed if he realized to how many people he is not a sex symbol.

Angie Bowie

He moves like a parody between a majorette girl and Fred Astaire.

Truman Capote

It really bothers me that a twerp like Jagger can parade around and convince everyone that he's Satan.

Ry Cooder

Mick Jagger – isn't he that motorcycle rider?

Gerald Ford

Elton John
He was probably born to be chairman of Watford Football Club, and now he's beginning to look like the chairman of Watford Football Club.   *Rod Stewart (1977)*
[*Elton replied:* Rod should stick to grave-digging, 'cos that's where he belongs, six feet under. *(1977)*]

Grace Jones
No-talent singer whose camp posturing made her a Bette Midler-style favourite with the gay community. You had to be there, I guess.

John Swenson – 'Rolling Stone'

Howard Jones
'Human's Lib' – Although *Human's Lib* has its moments, Howard Jones seems a little blinded by science.

Christopher Connelly – 'Rolling Stone'

Janis Joplin
I'm tired of Janis Joplin stories. It's always the same old thing.   *'Esquire'*

I couldn't stand Janis Joplin's voice . . . She was just a screaming little loudmouthed chick.   *Arthur Lee*

Nick Kamen
Can't WEA lose him down an alleyway or something?   *Laura Lee Davies – 'Time Out'*

Paul Kanter
Strictly for Jefferson Airplane completists and bong aficionados.

Parke Puterbaugh – 'Rolling Stone'

The Katydids
'Shangri-la' – Rings about as true as the sound of a piece of Ratners crystal. Thud!

Sharon O'Connell – 'Melody Maker' (1992)

Nik Kershaw
'Human Racing' – An offensively bland collection notable only for making Howard

Jones sound like Twisted Sister.

Ian Cranna (1984)

Kraftwerk

'*Autobahn*' – Valuable as both a musical oddity and background music for watching tropical fish sleep.

Alan Niester – 'Rolling Stone'

John Lennon

'*Imagine: The Movie*' *(1988)* – It's a lesson in how to use celluloid to create your own personal version of reality. But then, when did Lennon ever truly deal with reality?

Mal Peachey – 'Time Out'

'*Imagine*' – If you want to hear pretentiousness, just listen to *Imagine*. All that 'possessions' crap.   *Lou Reed*

Annie Lennox

Annie Lennox is the most annoying singer in pop music right now, as histrionic as Crystal Gayle . . . At her most memorable, Lennox moans. *James Hunter – 'Rolling Stone' (1984)*

Lords of the New Church

'*Is Nothing Sacred?*' – Lords of the New Garage is more like it. *Is Nothing Sacred?* is nothing special.

David Fricke – 'Rolling Stone'

Linda McCartney

Having Linda McCartney on stage in a multi-million dollar tour is like hiring a good black construction worker to edit the *New York Times*.   *Lester Bangs*

I don't think Linda is any substitute for John Lennon.   *George Martin*

Paul McCartney

I'd join a band with John Lennon any day, but I wouldn't join a band with Paul McCartney.   *George Harrison*

Do you think Paul McCartney makes records just to annoy me personally, or does he want to get up everyone's f***ing nose with his f***ing antics?   *Alex Harvey*

Freddie Mercury (Queen)

'*Freddie Mercury Memorial Concert*' *(1992)* –

It went on for four hours, and even television critics need to eat, relieve themselves and answer the telephone. I must say that I found all these activities more interesting than the 'concert' which was the usual parade of show-offs who turn up for these occasions.

A. N. Wilson – 'Sunday Telegraph'

'*Freddie Mercury Memorial Concert*' *(1992)* – A lovely tribute to Freddie, though I never saw his live performances, but he sounds absolutely terrible.

A. N. Wilson – 'Sunday Telegraph'

'*Freddie Mercury Memorial Concert*' *(1992)* – As a tribute to Freddie Mercury, the concert could scarcely have been more complimentary. But as an attempt to promote AIDS awareness it made about as much sense as an animal rights convention in a knacker's yard.   *Toby Young – 'Daily Mail'*

Mink DeVille

'*Where Angels Fear to Tread*' – Where talent fears to tread.   *Kurt Loder – 'Rolling Stone'*

The Monkees

You can't get the Monkees back together as a rock 'n' roll group. That would be like Raymond Burr opening up a law practice.

Mike Nesmith

Nena

'*99 Red Balloons*' – A swirl of routine synth-pop topped with the flavourless cherry of Nena's singing, immaculately free of personality and substance.

Don Sheway (1984)

'Never Too Young to Rock: The Movie'

(1975) featuring Mud, Slick and The Glitter Band – Despite the title, it makes you feel at least 102.   *Geoff Brown – 'Time Out'*

Yoko Ono

The Beatles' Movie 'Let It Be' (1970) – A sullen portentous compendium dogged by the baleful presence of Yoko Ono.

Clive James – 'The Observer' (1979)

If I found her floating in my pool, I'd punish my dog.   *Joan Rivers (1983)*

Pavlov's Dog

Blue Oyster Cult on laughing gas.

John Milward – 'Rolling Stone'

Pink Floyd

'The Wall: The Movie' (1982) – Crossing *Privilege* with *Tommy* couldn't result in anything shallower. All in all, it's just another flick to appal. *Paul Taylor – 'Time Out'*

The Pogues

'Completely Pogued: The Movie' (1989) – Even if you have absolutely no interest in the music, the vast array of pasty-faced uglies is really quite stunning.

Laura Lee Davies – 'Time Out'

Elvis Presley

I've found someone to replace Tony Curtis as the world's worst actor – Elvis Presley.

Anon

'Wild in the Country' (1961) – As wild as a glass of milk. *Geoff Brown – 'Time Out'*

Presley sounded like Jayne Mansfield looked – blowsy and loud and low. *Julie Burchill*

He never contributed a damn thing to music.

Bing Crosby

'Spinout' (1966) – For Presley immobility may signify maturity. He is pitching his act at some sort of adult audience – possibly adult chimpanzees . . . about all he does on the screen is waggle an aggressive guitar and, in an electronically reconstituted baritone, belt out a series of steamy lyrics. *'Time'*

'Kid Galahad' (1962) – A musical remake of the 1937 boxing drama . . . the flabby Presley, recently demobbed from the army, looks as if he couldn't survive a round with Donald Duck. His songs aren't exactly knockouts either. *Adrian Turner – 'Time Out'*

Queen

'Freddie Mercury Memorial Concert' (1992) – Throughout the Eighties, Queen were regarded by most pop fans as naff, bombastic second-raters. Now, all of a sudden, everyone from David Bowie to Liza Minnelli speaks of the group as if it were one of the greatest phenomena of all time; I even heard someone at the concert refer to dear old Freddie Mercury as a 'genius'.

'The Weasel' – 'The Independent'

Lou Reed

On finishing the production for the album 'Berlin' – Alright, wrap up this turkey before I puke. *Bob Ezrin*

Keith Richard

Even the deaf would be traumatised by prolonged exposure to the most hideous croak in Western culture. Richard's voice is simply horrible. *Nick Coleman – 'Time Out'*

Rolling Stones

The band is now basically a T-shirt selling machine. Jumping Jack Flash no more – more like Limping Hack Flash.

Julie Burchill – 'Mail on Sunday' (1992)

You walk out of the Amphitheatre after watching the Rolling Stones perform and suddenly the Chicago stockyards smell clean and good by comparison.

Tom Fitzpatrick – 'Chicago Sun-Times'

Sting

Somebody should clip Sting around the head and tell him to stop singing in that ridiculous Jamaican accent. *Elvis Costello*

Talk Talk

Talk Talk are yet another white synthesizer pop group complete with singer (Mark Hollis) who wants to be Brian Ferry.

Josephine Hocking

Tears For Fears

If honesty were compulsory, every TFF song would be called 'Laughing and Singing All The Way To The Bank'.

David Stubbs – 'Melody Maker' (1992)

Tanita Tikaram

'You Make the Whole World Cry' – She always sings about two octaves below her natural range . . . She couldn't come on dafter if she wore a false beard in the hope that people would think she was a man and take her more seriously.

David Stubbs – 'Melody Maker' (1992)

The Hypnotic

'*Coast to Coast*' *(1992)* – Dippy, strung-out, phased, thrashy, droning and self-indulgent. It is boring both within and without itself.

Gill Whyte – 'Time Out'

Thompson Twins

'*The Saint*' *(1992)* – They've gone house. They should have gone home.

Gill Whyte – 'Time Out'

Tin Machine

Loud clanking noises.   '*Time Out*' *(1991)*

Toto

Formula pop singing that wouldn't go over in a Holiday Inn cocktail lounge.

Dave Marsh – 'Rolling Stone'

Pete Townshend (The Who)

He is so talentless, and as a lyricist he's so profoundly untalented and philosophically boring to say the least.   *Lou Reed*

Tina Turner

All legs and hair with a mouth that could swallow the whole stadium and the hot-dog stand.   *Laura Lee Davies – 'Time Out'*

U2

Music for plumbers and bricklayers.

Ian McCulloch (1984)

Voice of the Beehive

'*Perfect Place/Sit Down*' *(1992)* – The A-side is the stuff of advertisers' dreams – burning corn fields and building societies – you know, the ideal world. The B-side, depending whether you play it at 33 or 45, is either a drunken karaoke chorus or the three piggies.

Gill Whyte – 'Time Out'

Roger Waters

'*The Pros and Cons of Hitch-Hiking*' – Even the most exalted English rock legend shouldn't try to sell swill to a public that's demonstrably less piggish than the pop-star himself.   *Kurt Loder – 'Rolling Stone'*

Burt Weedon

I thought he was a tailor or something.

Mick Jones (The Clash)

Frank Zappa

Frank Zappa is probably the single most untalented person I've heard in my life. He's two-bit, pretentious, academic and he can't play his way out of anything. He can't play rock 'n' roll, because he's a loser. And that's why he dresses so funny. He's not happy with himself and I think he's right.   *Lou Reed*

Frank Zappa couldn't write a decent song if you gave him a million and a year on an island in Greece.   *Lou Reed*

ZZ Top

'*Fandango*' – Rock and roll can be mindless fun, but it never deserved to be this empty-headed.   *Dave Marsh – 'Rolling Stone'*

MISCELLANEOUS

GENERAL

Yodelling is nothing but hogcalling with frost on it.   *George M. Cohan*

Canned music is like audible wall-paper.

Alistair Cooke

The music at a marriage procession always reminds me of the music of soldiers entering a battle.   *Heinrich Heine*

World music is a dozen different types of percussion all going at once.

'*Mail on Sunday*' *(1992)*

Music-hall songs provide the dull with wit, just as proverbs provide them with wisdom.

W. Somerset Maugham (1949)

Let a short Act of Parliament be passed, placing all street musicians outside the protection of the law, so that any citizen may assail them with stones, sticks, knives, pistols, or bombs with incurring any penalties – except, of course, in the case of the instrument itself being injured, for Heaven forbid that I should advocate any disregard of the sacredness of property.

G. B. Shaw – 'Morning Leader' (1893)

I don't give a damn about 'The Missouri Waltz' but I can't say it out loud because it's the song of Missouri. It's as bad as *The Star Spangled Banner* so far as music is concerned.

Harry S. Truman (1958)

NATIONAL ANTHEMS

British

On hearing the National Anthem being played before a televised F.A. Cup Final – Oh, do turn it off, it is so embarrassing unless one is there – like hearing the Lord's Prayer when one is playing canasta.

Queen Elizabeth the Queen Mother

The tune is appalling and the words banal.

Michael Foot

Russian

'*The Red Flag*' – The funeral march of a fried eel.

G. B. Shaw

MEDIA

GENERAL

Each day a few more lies eat into the seed with which we are born, little institutional lies from the print of newspapers, the shock waves of television, and the sentimental cheats of the movie screen.

*Norman Mailer –
'Advertisements for Myself' (1959)*

THE PRESS

GENERAL

I keep reading between the lies.

Goodman Ace

Whole forests are being ground into pulp daily to minister our triviality.   *Irving Babbitt*

I am unable to understand how a man of honour could take a newspaper in his hands without a shudder of disgust.

Charles Baudelaire

It's the duty of a newspaper to comfort the afflicted and afflict the comfortable.

'*Inherit the Wind*'

The man who never looks into a newspaper is better informed than he who reads them, inasmuch as he who knows nothing is nearer to truth than he whose mind is filled with falsehoods and errors.

Thomas Jefferson (1807)

On the whole I would not say that our press is obscene. I would say that it trembles on the brink of obscenity.   *Lord Longford (1963)*

All successful newspapers are ceaselessly querulous and bellicose. They never defend anyone or anything if they can help it; if the job is forced upon them, they tackle it by denouncing someone or something else.

H. L. Mencken (1919)

What priestcraft was to the fourteenth century, presscraft is to the twentieth.

William G. Sumner

How many beautiful trees gave their lives that today's scandal should, without delay, reach a million readers?   *Edwin Way Teale –
Circle of the Seasons' (1953)*

NEWSPAPERS

Sunday papers

The Sunday papers are the same every week . . . those ghastly obligatory articles by women on how awful it is to be a woman.

Jeffrey Bernard

Tabloids

Daily fun magazines – things resembling the stained sheets of the famous rather than the news sheet of the citizen.

Julie Burchill – 'Damaged Goods'

The British tabloid newspaper is as British as

the football hooligan – and just as welcome.
Julian Critchley

Tass – *official Soviet news agency*
It's always a compliment to be denounced by
Tass. *Ed Koch*

'The Daily Express'
All Fools' Day is traditionally used by
newspapers for the publication of spoof
stories to mislead the reader. I searched the
Daily Express yesterday for its spoof and then
suddenly realised what it was. The whole
paper was the joke.
Joe Haines – 'Daily Mirror' (1992)

The *Daily Express* is a bloody awful
newspaper full of lies, scandal and
imagination. It is a vicious newspaper.
Prince Philip

'The Daily Mail'
If I blow my nose they would say I'm trying
to spread germ warfare.
Ken Livingstone (1992)

'New Musical Express'
I look at *NME* and I see about half a dozen
mistakes every week. I know for a fact that 95
per cent of the people who work on music
papers know less about music than I do.
Terry Christian (1992)

'The New York Post'
I wish I could sue the *New York Post* but it's
awfully hard to sue a garbage can.
Paul Newman (1983)

'The New York Times'
On returning from New York – Newspapers
too thick, lavatory paper too thin.
Sir Winston Churchill

Viewing with dismay the conditions in
somebody else's backyard is a great specialty
of the *New York Times*. *John Crosby (1966)*

New York newspapers go on forever about
nothing. *Brendan Behan*

MAGAZINES

'Hello'
Hello is to serious issues what the World

Wrestling Federation sticker album is to
children's literature.
Mary Riddell – 'Daily Mirror' (1992)

'Playboy'
Playboy magazine is simply the house
magazine of the fundamentalists of sexiosity.
It shouts so loud that you wonder whether it
believes itself. *Reverend Earl Brill (1966)*

'Punch'
On its announced closure – I am a little
surprised, I didn't know it was still going. . . .
Terminal boredom has finally caught up with
it. *Ian Hislop (1992)*

JOURNALISTS

No news is good news; no journalists is
better. *Nicolas Bentley*

I hesitate to say what the functions of the
modern journalist may be; but I imagine that
they do not exclude the intelligent
anticipation of facts before they occur.
Lord Curzon (1989)

Never trust a smiling reporter. *Ed Koch*

Journalists are born. Why, nobody knows.
Lennie Lower (1963)

Journalists are a species of foul vermin. I
mean I wouldn't hire people like you to guard
my sewer. Journalists are morons, idiots . . .
ignorant and stupid. *Lou Reed*

Julie Burchill
She's just the Glenda Slag of modern pop-
writing. *Elvis Costello (1983)*

Peter McKay
He would cut your throat and destroy all
chance of friendship for two lines in the
Daily Express. *Auberon Waugh*

Elsa Maxwell
She was built for crowds. She has never
come any closer to life than the dinner table.
Janet Flanner

Jack Newfield
His style could be characterized as mis-

statement, omission and sleight of hand. For him, truth is putty, to be twisted and squeezed into one fantastic shape or another. The result is an ugly self-portrait of the artist as a bitter man. *Ed Koch*

Jean Rook

Jean Rook, who is reported to earn more money than any woman in Fleet Street, for reasons which escape me. Probably she draws the bulk of her massive screw in danger money, to offset the lacerating cortical damage she must sustain when reading her own prose.

Clive James – 'The Observer' (1975)

Israel Zangwill

He is an old bore; even the grave yawns for him. *Herbert Beerbohm Tree*

EDITORS AND PUBLISHERS

It is with publishers as with wives: one always wants somebody else's. *Norman Douglas*

In a way it's a comfort to know that British newspaper editors don't believe everything they read in the newspapers. *Prince Philip*

William F. Buckley Jr – *Editor of 'New Republic'*

Looks and sounds not unlike Hitler – but without the charm. *Gore Vidal*

Hugh Hefner – *Editor of 'Playboy'*

This physically disgusting, emotionally incontinent, dirty old (subhu)man.

Julie Burchill

Mocking Hefner is easy to do, and in my view should be made even easier.

Clive James – 'The Observer' (1974)

Richard Ingrams – *Editor of 'Private Eye' and 'The Oldie'*

The most vain man I have ever met. He's got that supreme vanity of people who never wash. *Peter McKay*

He looks like the painting in Wedgwood Benn's attic. *Willy Rushton*

Andrew Neil – *Editor of 'The Sunday Times'*

The triple-wheat crimped, Sabbath publication editor. *'Punch' (1992)*

Sydney Rosenfeld – *Editor of 'Puck'*

His distinguishing physical feature is an umbrageous hirsute thatch à la Pompadour.

Harry B. Smith

Delmore Schwartz – *Editor of 'Partisan Review'*

He thinks that Schiller and St Paul were just two *Partisan Review* editors. *Randall Jarrell*

David Sullivan – *Publisher of 'The Sunday Sport'*

There's one porn every minute. *'Today'*

BROADCASTING

GENERAL

Photography is going to marry Miss Wireless, and heaven help everybody when they get married. Life will be very complicated.

Marcus Adams – 'The Observer' (1925)

Everything is for the eye these days – TV, *Life*, *Look*, the movies. Nothing is just for the mind. The next generation will have eyeballs as big as cantaloupes and no brain at all.

Fred Allen

What the mass media offer is not popular art, but entertainment which is intended to be consumed like food, forgotten and replaced by a new dish.

W. H. Auden – 'The Dyer's Hand' (1962)

Broadcasting is too important to be left to the broadcasters. *Tony Benn (1969)*

The only thing movies and TV leave to the imagination these days is the plot.

Paul Harwitz

Children watch too much television not only because indolent parents allow them to, but because the standard of most programmes is pitched at their level. *Richard Ingrams (1977)*

The marvels – of film, radio and television –

are marvels of one-way communication, which is not communication at all.
Milton Mayer

Radio and television as entertainments are fine, but they bear as much relation to books as airline meals to food.
Frank Muir – 'The Guardian' (1973)

The gift of broadcasting is without question the lowest human capacity to which any man could attain.
Harold Nicolson – 'The Observer' (1947)

TELEVISION

Television will never replace the old-fashioned keyhole. *Anon*

A spirit of national masochism prevails, encouraged by an effete corps of impudent snobs who characterise themselves as intellectuals. *Spiro Agnew (1966)*

Working on television is like being shot out of a cannon. They cram you all up with rehearsals, then someone lights a fuse and – *bang* – there you are in somebody's living-room. *Tallulah Bankhead*

Three-quarters of television is for half-wits. The boxing's all right. *Sir Thomas Beecham*

All the music I have ever seen on television looks grotesque. You see right down the larynx, almost into the tummy, the eyes go this way, the nose goes that way, and the mouth is twisted round. The whole thing is revolting. That's television, so far as music is concerned. *Sir Thomas Beecham*

TV performers for the most part fall into two groups – those who have been dropped and those who are going to be dropped.
Leslie Bell

I began in 1952 by thinking of television as a window on the world, then as a mirror in the corner, finally as the biggest aspidistra in the world. *Peter Black (1974)*

Television is an evil medium, it should never have been invented, but since we have to live

with it, let us try and do something about it.
Richard Burton (1967)

TV is the longest running amateur night in history. *Robert Carson*

Television is democracy at its ugliest.
Paddy Chayefsky

Books and plays are diversions about which most of us exercise some decision, even if our selection is based totally on misleading publicity. The movies are in a twilit zone. Television is even lower down the scale of human choice. We nearly always see it by default. *Quentin Crisp (1981)*

Why should people go out and pay to see bad films when they can stay at home and see bad television for nothing? *Samuel Goldwyn*

I'll believe in colour television when I see it in black and white. *Samuel Goldwyn*

In the age of television, image becomes more important than substance. *S. I. Hayakawa*

The vast British Empire built up over hundreds of years has been reduced to ruins largely through the influence of television.
Albert Herzog (1966)

Television has done much for psychiatry by spreading information about it, as well as contributing to the need for it.
Alfred Hitchcock

TV has proved that people will look at anything rather than at each other.
Ann Landers

So now there's a National Heritage ministry responsible for the arts, sport, broadcasting and the national lottery. Funny – I thought broadcasting was the national lottery.
Jack Hughes – 'The Independent on Sunday' (1992)

Television is another kind of car, a windshield on the world. We climb inside, drive it, and it drives us, and we all go in the same direction, see the same thing. It is more than a mobile home, it is a mobile nation. It has become, then, our common language, our ceremony, our style, our entertainment and anxiety, our sympathetic magic, our way of celebrating, mourning, worshipping. It's flimsy glue, but for the moment it's the only thing holding America together.

John Leonard – 'Playboy' (1976)

TV is an object proving that sight has a definite odour. *Gerald F. Lieberman*

Television, if unchecked, may carry us back to a pre-tribal state of social development where the family was the largest conversational unit.

A. J. Liebling – 'The Sweet Science'

Television is the literature of the illiterate, the culture of the low-brow, the wealth of the poor, the privilege of the underprivileged, the exclusive club of the excluded masses.

Lee Loevinger (1966)

TV is the golden goose that lays scrambled eggs; and it is futile and probably fatal to beat it for not laying caviar. *Lee Loevinger (1966)*

Television is simply automated day-dreaming. *Lee Loevinger – 'Vogue' (1967)*

Television is summer stock in an iron-lung.
'The Manchester Guardian' (1959)

I find television very educating. Every time someone turns on the set I go into the other room and read a book. *Groucho Marx*

Television is of great education value. It teaches you while still young how to (a) kill, (b) rob, (c) embezzle, (d) shoot, (e) poison.
George Mikes

Television is simply a hole through which you push various communications.
Jonathan Miller

There are no special virtues about television, apart from the fact that it is in the home.
Jonathan Miller – 'Evening Standard' (1970)

When television is good, nothing is better. When it's bad, nothing is worse.
Newton N. Minow

This medium is bound to deceive. Even if you put truth into it, it comes out a deception. *Malcolm Muggeridge*

Something inferior, cheap, horrible about television as such; it's a prism through which words pass, energies distort, false. The exact converse of what is commonly believed – not a searcher out of truth and sincerity, but rather only lies and insincerity will register on it. *Malcolm Muggeridge – 'Diaries' (1981)*

On some occasions, the most effective way to improve the flavour of a TV dinner is to turn off the television. *Robert Orben*

A TV set is a machine with a picture in front, tubes in the middle and an instalment behind. *Robert Orben*

I have never seen a bad television program, because I refuse to. God gave me a mind, and a wrist to turn things off.
Jack Paar – 'TV Guide'

Television is an entertainment which flows like tap-water. *Dennis Potter (1967)*

TV is the stage for plays about psychopathic adolescents and homicidal nymphomaniacs who are tragically trapped in immense riches.
Leo Rosten

Television has lifted the manufacture of banality out of the sphere of handicraft and placed it in that of a major industry.
Nathalie Sarraute

Television is a nightly national seance.
Daniel Schorr

TV is a medium made to order for those with aptitudes for stage acting and synthetic sincerity. It has encouraged the development of thespian talents where none had been previously known to exist.
Daniel Schorr – 'Esquire' (1977)

TV often cannot cover the passing of the torch without fanning the flames in the process. *Martin Schramm (1984)*

TV is the device that brings into your living

room characters you would never allow in your living room. *Red Skelton*

Some performers on television appear to be horrible people, but when you finally get to know them in person, they turn out to be even worse.
Allen Smith – 'Let the Crabgrass Grow' (1960)

Television is such an ugly piece of furniture.
John Walters (1990)

In this business the sign of creativity is to have a trenchcoat that outdoes all the others, to dress like Hemingway coming out of the tundra. *Ed Warren (1976)*

The television screen is the finest medium ever devised for showing old films.
Keith Waterhouse – 'Radio Times' (1979)

I hate television. I hate it as much as peanuts. But I can't stop eating peanuts.
Orson Welles – 'New York Herald/ Tribune' (1956)

The danger of television is repetition.
Robin Williams

Television is the plug-in drug. *Marie Winn*

Television is chewing gum for the eyes.
Frank Lloyd Wright

I can't understand why anybody would want to devote their life to a cause like dope. It's the most boring pastime I can think of. It ranks a close second to television.
Frank Zappa

TV CRITICS

A TV critic is a man forced to be literate about the illiterate, witty about the witless and coherent about the incoherent.
John Crosby (1955)

TV critics are those who roam the channels after dark, searching for buried treasure.
Harriet van Horne – 'New York World-Telegram & Sun' (1958)

The greatest risk to the television critic is

bedsores, or a sprained wrist as he reaches too suddenly for the thin mints.
Clive James – 'The Observer'

On 'Fawlty Towers' – Statistical surveys reveal that only the television critic of the *Spectator* is incapable of seeing the joke, which is that Basil Fawlty has the wrong temperament to be a hotel proprietor, just as some other people have the wrong temperament to be television critics.
Clive James – 'The Observer' (1981)

In writing about TV you are really writing about everything. TV is like the sea we swim in. The trouble is that, like fish, we would be the last ones to notice that we were wet, or ask questions about the nature of wetness.
John Leonard – 'Playboy' (1976)

You can no more review television than you can review old girlfriends. *John Leonard*

Television is like a station bookstall. Something we might pick up to titillate the brain very gently ought not to be observed with the same critical standards as something designed to feed the mind.
Kenneth Robinson – 'Listener' (1978)

TV exposure has done wonders for my book sales, but it has had a strange effect on the critics. *Irwin Shaw (1977)*

PROGRAMMING

If we think of programming as an all-American menu, then the detective show is definitely the hamburger.
Martha Bayles – 'Wall Street Journal' (1984)

On the three rival US networks – Unlike productions in the other arts, all television shows are born to destroy two other shows.
Les Brown – 'Harpers' (1985)

Reporting the news on television is like writing with a one-ton pencil. *'Esquire' (1971)*

Most American television stations reproduce all night long what only a Roman could have seen in the Coliseum during the reign of Nero. *George Faludy*

The news is the one thing the networks can point to with pride. Everything else they do is crap – and they know it.

Fred Friendly (1980)

If TV were to do the Second Coming of Christ in colour for a full hour, there would be a considerable number of stations which would decline to carry it on the grounds that a Western or a quiz show would be more profitable. *Edward R. Murrow (1964)*

This season the only things worth watching on TV seem to be the tragedies and the comedies – the news and the commercials.

Angie Papadakis

Dealing with network executives is like being nibbled to death by ducks. *Eric Sevareid*

Television networks are concerned by what appears to be a diminishing audience. Some alarmists are even predicting that the country is about to be engulfed in a wave of literacy.

Edward Stevenson

BBC TV

It is true that a joke in the BBC's mouth is no laughing matter. *Brendan Bracken*

The BBC is a great quivering mess creeping into the 1940s out of the 1920s.

John Peel (1967)

A home for distressed gentlefolk – or, as it is better known, the BBC Television Centre.

Barry Took and Marty Feldman

The BBC was known as 'Auntie' – suggesting someone prudish and Victorian – and she still is on some days. On others she's a champagne-soaked floozie, her skirts in disarray, her mind in the gutter.

Morley Safer

Channel 4

Beats me how a channel watched by five per cent of the population can offend ninety-five per cent. *Spencer – 'Punch'*

MTV (Music Television)

A videot's delight. *Anon*

MTV is the lava lamp of the 1980s.

Doug Ferrari

Watching three hours of one type of music, you lose your f***ing mind.

Ozzy Osborne (1989)

PBS (Public Broadcasting Service)

I know it's public television if:
1. Bert and Ernie are performing,
2. Julia Child is cooking,
3. Mr Rogers is talking to small children,
4. Beverly Sills is introducing Luciano Pavarotti,
5. Leo Buscaglia is lecturing on the value of love,
6. the Monty Python company is satirizing the BBC,
7. mulch is being discussed on the Victory Garden or, what is more likely,
8. I am watching the 10th rerun of any of the above.

Russell Baker – 'New York Times' (1986)

What would public television be if the British didn't speak English? *Laurence Grossman*

Public television is for the humour-impaired.

Alan Goldberg

Chat shows

Conversation is killing the art of television.

A. E. Beard – 'Punch'

Cop shows

Perhaps the crime situation would be improved if we could get more cops off television and onto the streets.

Bill Vaughan – 'Kansas City Star'

Disaster/biopics

Should you ever find yourself in a jet about to crash or a skyscraper about to explode, take comfort in the thought that in a few short months you could be portrayed by Karen Allen.

Jay Martell – 'Rolling Stone' (1990)

Educational TV

Educational television is the bright gray blackboard. *Henri Dieuzeide (1963)*

All TV is educational TV. The only question is what is it teaching?

Nicholas Johnson – 'Life' (1971)

Educational TV should be absolutely

forbidden. It can only lead to unreasonable expectations and eventual disappointment when your child discovers that the letters of the alphabet do not leap up out of books and dance around the room with royal-blue chickens. *Fran Lebowitz (1981)*

I read in the newspapers they are going to have 30 minutes of intellectual stuff on TV every Monday from 7:30 to 8 to educate America. They couldn't educate America if they started at 6:30.
Groucho Marx – 'Boston Globe' (1960)

Game shows
Game shows are for people who expose their innermost secrets for a bag of luggage.
Johnny Carson (1989)

Health shows
Contrary to popular cable TV-induced opinion, aerobics have absolutely nothing to do with squeezing our body into hideous shiny Spandex, grinning like a deranged orang-utan, and doing cretinous dance steps to debauched disco music.
Cynthia Heimel – 'Sex Tips for Girls' (1983)

Music shows
A lot of pop TV is like nouvelle cuisine. It looks great, but tastes shite.
Malcolm Gerry (1988)

News magazine shows
They favour flashy packages of bite-sized stories that are to serious journalism what McNuggets are to a full-course meal.
Henry F. Waters – 'Newsweek' (1982)

Soap operas
According to Sky TV, the 'environmentally aware' cast of *East St* toss all their old scripts into a huge sack which they send off for recycling. This gives *East St* the edge over *Neighbours* and *Home and Away*, whose scripts have already been recycled from something else.
Charlie Catchpole – 'News of the World' (1992)

Soap opera producers have tourniquets on their brains. *Robert Duvall (1986)*

Other shows
Andy Pandy (BBC TV)

An effete prancing boy doll plastered in rouge and swathed in satin rompers – a great male role model. The most decisive, dynamic thing Andy Pandy ever did was to raise a wooden hand and wave goodbye after the allotted ten minutes of torture by boredom.
Julie Burchill – 'Are You Sitting Comfortably?'

Are You Being Served? (BBC TV)
Reviewing the movie spinoff – Woefully unfunny and extremely objectionable big-screen spin-off from the woefully and extremely objectionable TV sit-com series set in a none too realistic department store. Crap of the lowest order.
Geoff Andrew – 'Time Out' (1977)

'Mrs Slocombe gets a surprise' . . . perhaps someone tells a non-smutty joke. *'Time Out'*

Bodyline (BBC TV)
Silly lies and bunkum. *Harold Larwood*

The Brian Conley Show (ITV)
If you find yourself watching this on Saturday night, call the Samaritans.
Elaine Patterson – 'Time Out' (1992)

The Camomile Lawn (Channel 4)
Camomile Porn. *'Time Out' (1992)*

CBS News (US TV)
The biggest bunch of party-pooping stuffed shirts you'd find outside the Federal government. *Tom Shales*

Cop Rock (US TV)
The *Cop* stuff was warmed-over *Hill Street Blues*; the *Rock* made Milli Vanilli seem like models of authenticity.
Ken Tucker – 'Entertainment Weekly' (1990)

Coronation Street (ITV)
So the Americans and Russians are both developing 'nerve-gas' which will paralyse the population of cities for a short period but leave them uninjured afterwards. Britain has had a weapon of this kind for a couple of years now; it's called *Coronation Street*.
'Punch' (1962)

The Cosby Show (US TV)
A show that makes daffy humour out of all

the negative aspects of aging, but cannot effectively point up the positive.

'New York Times'

The family isn't only well-off, but affluent – they may boast the largest, most tastefully decorated home in sit-com history. This family, quite determinedly, isn't black in anything but their skin colour. I don't mean just in their lifestyle – even their cultural background, and their whole context of reference, is that of American Caucasian.

'Village Voice'

Crossroads (ITV)
The TV soap opera whose acting gives trees a bad name.   *Tim Satchell – 'Daily Mail'*

The Darling Buds of May (ITV)
Pastoral poppycock . . . undemandingly frothy. . . . Far from perfick.   *'Time Out'*

EastEnders (BBC TV)
Save *EastEnders*. Act now!

Graffiti (outside BBC TV studios)

Eldorado (BBC TV)
The setting has all the history and glamour of Stevenage and Essex, and the plot was as interesting as a crushed snail. It would rot children's brains faster than heroin.

Lynette Burrows – 'Daily Mail' (1992)

I really wanted to be able to give this sunshine soap the thumbs up instead of the usual selection of fingers . . . the characters are such a rip-off of Albert Square and other soap hits that viewers risk being done for receiving stolen goods.

Garry Bushell – 'The Sun' (1992)

Wish we were there do we, in Eldorado, on the Costa Lotsalicencefees?

Hilary Kingston – 'Daily Mirror' (1992)

What is the BBC doing spending money on this shambles?   *Mary Whitehouse (1992)*

Falcon Crest (US TV)
If you scoop up *Dallas* and *Flamingo Road* together, move them north to *Knot's Landing*, and then transport the whole to San

Francisco, you've got *Falcon Crest* and you're welcome to it.

Clive James – 'The Observer' (1982)

George and Mildred (ITV)
Reviewing the movie spinoff – It's the same ageist, sexist class structure you know and loathe. Feeble humour even in its half-hour slot, and desperately unfunny at three times the length.

Martyn Auty – 'Time Out' (1980)

The Golden Girls (US TV)
What we're offered here is a group of women reduced to their aging, and obsessed by it, firing off volleys of tired banter about dentures, weakening bladders, 'hearts that only beat a few times a week', and dates who are wildly attractive because 'he doesn't talk loudly in the movies, doesn't take his own pulse, and he's – nudge, nudge – still interested'.   *'Village Voice'*

Goodbye, Darling . . . (BBC TV)
The first part suggested that the three dots in the title portend a steadily accelerating build-up of tension in the viewer, possibly leading to migraine. There is a limit to how much drama the brain can take in before the cerebral cortex starts to boil.

Clive James – 'The Observer' (1981)

The Good Guys (ITV)
This might have been better if it didn't look quite so much like a Surrey Tourist Board promo.   *Bruce Dessau – 'Time Out' (1992)*

Grace and Favour (BBC TV)
More antique antics from the ageing survivors of *Are You Being Served?*

'Time Out' (1992)

Happy Days (US TV)
As for the '50s, they are feebly re-created. Token details are trotted in – white socks, penny loafers, baggy pants and high school jackets – without much conviction or effect. Extracts from '50s pop are used haphazardly on the soundtrack; though *The Song from the Moulin Rouge* was a '53 hit, Elvis's *Hound Dog* a '56 hit, the Crew-Cuts' *Sh-Boom* a '54 hit and Bobby Darin's *Splish-Splash* vintage '58, they all pop up on the opening show.

During the '50s, nobody listened to last year's songs.

Tom Shales – 'Washington Post' (1974)

Hollywood Squares (US TV)
Since the squares are at all times occupied by the likes of Vince Edwards, the Hudson Brothers, the Gabor Sisters and Margaret Truman, the viewer often feels as if he has stumbled into a video black-hole full of fame's has-beens and never-weres.

Frank Rich – 'Time' (1980)

Inspector Morse (ITV)
Overlong, cringingly obvious, it moves with the speed and agility of a tortoise with a groin strain. . . . One is asked to indulge the ponderous pomposity of a paunchy detective with a gammy leg and the charm of a costive dobermann. He is rude, without being funny, he is dyspeptic, grumbling, irritable – W. C. Fields without the one-liners.

Sean Macaulay – 'Punch' (1992)

The Jewel in the Crown (ITV)
If we are told of some four-volume epic we're apt to say 'How interesting', but we never will read it unless we have both legs in traction.

Martha Bayles – 'Wall Street Journal' (1984)

Love from A to Z (BBC TV)
Bad Sight and Bad Sound of the Week were twin titles both won by *Love from A to Z*, a river of drivel featuring Liza Minnelli and Charles Aznavour. Right up there beside the Tom Jones specials in the bummer stakes.

Clive James – 'The Observer' (1974)

The Male Menopause (BBC TV)
A sub-sociological drone-in fronted by Michael Parkinson, was the mental equivalent of navel fluff.

Clive James – 'The Observer' (1975)

The Morning Show (US TV)
It's the *Mourning Show*. Is it true that the theme song is going to be 'Taps'?

Steve Friedman (1987)

Muffin the Mule (BBC TV)
Muffin the Mule, an inane, capering quadruped who danced gracelessly on a piano played by his chair-bound cheerleader, an unfortunate Joyce Grenfell impersonator, who trilled a never-changing song of rhetorical revelry and self-celebration.

Julie Burchill – 'Are You Sitting Comfortably?'

Noddy (BBC TV)
A sort of grinning, kerb-crawling Cecil Rhodes.

Julie Burchill – 'Are You Sitting Comfortably?'

Noel's House Party (BBC TV)
Tiswas without the jokes.   'Time Out' (1991)

The Old Grey Whistle Test (BBC TV)
The Old Dead Squirrel Nest.   Nickname

On the Buses (ITV)
Reviewing the movie (1971) – Dire spin-off from the stultifyingly unfunny TV series.

Geoff Andrew – 'Time Out'

Mutiny on the Buses: The Movie (1972)
Much lower than these cretinous larks among London's bus crews comedy cannot get. The sole interest in this truly appalling spin-off from the TV sitcom series lies in wondering why the sweaty [Reg] Varney – trying to play half his age – never got a better haircut to stop the greasy locks falling over his face.

Geoff Andrew – 'Time Out'

People's Court (US TV)
Titanic clashes in this video courtroom are likely to swirl around botched paint jobs, unshoveled sidewalks, defective toasters, aggressive guard dogs, and every conceivable, and sometimes inconceivable, mishap involving a vacuum cleaner.

Henry F. Waters – 'Newsweek' (1986)

Poldark (BBC TV)
A wall of corn from Cornwall, BBC 1's new thriller serial *Poldark* is aptly branded with a title which turns out to be an anagram for old Krap. I rest my case.

Clive James – 'The Observer' (1975)

Private Schulz (BBC TV)
A supposedly comic series like *Private Schulz* would be an offence if it were funny. In fact, it is no funnier than a cold sore on the lip.

Clive James – 'The Observer' (1981)

Resnick (BBC TV)
Makes [*Inspector*] *Morse* seem cheery and
Spender look lively. The pace is so leaden it
might as well be shown in slow motion.
                    Gary Bushell – 'The Sun' (1992)

Terrible title – how about Inspector Morose?
        Compton Miller – 'Daily Express' (1992)

60 Minutes (US TV)
They'll leave anything incompatible with
their view on the cutting-room floor. *60
Minutes* is to journalism what *Charley's Aunt*
is to criminology.   *John McNulty*

Specials (BBC TV)
The hobby bobby series which made
Neighbours sound like Dostoevsky.
                    'Time Out' (1991)

Star Trek (US TV)
As surely as Brunnhilde's big moments are
accompanied by a few bars of the Valkyries'
ride, Spock will say that the conclusion is
logical . . . Chekhov will act badly, Bones . . .
will act extremely badly. Kirk employs a
thespian technique picked up from
somebody who knew Lee Strasberg's sister.
                    Clive James – 'The Observer'

Surgical Spirit (ITV)
It didn't have this reviewer in stitches.
        Elaine Patterson – 'Time Out' (1992)

Sweeney! (ITV)
'*Sweeney!: The Movie' (1976)* – For a piece of
shitty incompetence, this spin-off from the
TV cop series would be hard to outdo.
                    Andrew Nickolds

Take Your Pick (ITV)
The most fatuous vehicle of yelping greed
and imbecile banter ever devised.
        John Walsh – 'The Sunday Times' (1992)

That's Life (BBC TV)
The whole style of Esther Rantzen's *That's
Life* affects me like being trapped in a lift with
a warm-up man.
        Clive James – 'The Observer' (1982)

Top of the Pops (BBC TV)
Looking at *Top of the Pops* is like putting my
head in the fridge in the middle of the night
hoping that there's gonna be a couple of cans
of beer in there, and all I can find is a couple
of old, dead fish.   *Tony James (1985)*

Twin Peaks (US TV)
Twin Peaks more and more resembles a
freak-show version of *Dynasty*.
                    'Rolling Stone' (1990)

The Woodentops (BBC TV)
A horrific mutant nuclear family of skittles
who went about their daily round of domestic
drudgery with amazing placidity, never
seeming to notice the terrible trick that
Nature had played on them.
        Julie Burchill – 'Are You Sitting Comfortably?'

TV PERSONALITIES

Kate Adie
She never hesitates in insulting and scolding
our representatives as if they are her personal
slaves. We are demanding the BBC never
ever send Kate Adie back to Libya.
                    Mahmoud al-Busifi

Cilla Black
Miss Priscilla Black 'may have plastic surgery
to improve her looks'. Guttersnipe does not
wish to appear ungallant but might not a
carrier-bag serve her avowed purposes at a
mere fraction of the cost?
        *'Guttersnipe' (Mitchell Symons) – 'Punch'
                                (1992)*

Terry Christian
I can't stand people from Manchester like
Terry Christian. Makes you wish Myra
Hindley had been given a few more years of
freedom.   *Rob Newman (1992)*

Julian Clary
He's built his career on recycling garbage.
                    Gary Bushell – 'The Sun'

David Dimbleby
If degrees were handed out for
bumptiousness, he would emerge with first-
class honours.
        John Junor – 'The Mail on Sunday' (1992)

Richard Drecker
A forthright young man with the identikit

face of a loan shark.
Allison Pearson – 'Independent on Sunday'
(1992)

Bruce Forsyth
He'll be a riot at your friend's wedding, but not on Broadway.
Anonymous US critic (1979)

Nice to see you, Brucey – but to hear you sing, not so nice. *Gary Bushell – 'The Sun'*

David Frost
One cannot open one's mouth without you jumping into it. *Robin Cook (1992)*

The man who wears his hair back to front.
Frankie Howerd (1963)

Gilbert Harding
Dear Gilbert Harding. One o'clock on December the third is the time. Insults will be worn. Sincerely, Cassandra.
Sir William Connor

Jonathan King
Q. What does Jonathan King use for contraception?
A. His personality. *Anon*

Malcolm Muggeridge
Lord Buggeridge of Snide.
Nickname in 'Private Eye'

Jeremy Paxman
A nonentity with a paunch.
Geoffrey Aquilina-Ross –
'For Him' (1992)

Paxman has the apologetic air of a compromised man who is unwilling to say any very rude things about his employers.
Richard Ingram – 'The Oldie' (1992)

Katie Puckrik
Isn't her name a gift to rhyming slang!
Gary Bushell – 'The Sun' (1992)

Magnus Pyke
Coiling and uncoiling around the studio like one of those wire toys that walk down stairs.
Clive James – 'The Observer'

Shane Richie
Rentagob Shane Richie is an even more odious host than Jeremy Beadle. *'Time Out'*

Esther Rantzen
On critics comparing his show to 'That's Life' –
I'm not a woman and I haven't got buck teeth. *Michael Barrymore*

David Vine
The boy who learned his enunciation from Eddie Waring on *It's a Knockout*.
Clive James –
'The Observer' (1972)

Dr Ruth Westheimer
The strident pygmy . . . the pipsqueak guru.
David Sexton –
'The Sunday Telegraph' (1992)

Mary Whitehouse
Q. What are the three best things about Mary Whitehouse?
A. 1. She's knocking on a bit and will probably be dead soon.
2. She's knocking on a bit and will probably be dead soon.
3. She's knocking on a bit and will probably be dead soon. *Anon*

Bob Wilson
The former goalkeeper, who always shows signs of having dived head first at flying feet too often. *Stafford Hildred – 'The Daily Star'*

Jodie Wilson
The last bimbo assistant in the world – a toothy lip-gloss dream.
John Walsh –
'The Sunday Times' (1992)

Terry Wogan
Wogan's is a bionic smile if I ever saw one. My guess is that the BBC built him in their own workshops, under licence from General Dynamics. Unfortunately they had to skimp slightly on the brain. Hughes Electronics wouldn't come through with the advanced technology for anything else but cash on the nail, so the Beeb's engineers had to solder together their own version on a restricted budget.
Clive James –
'The Observer' (1976)

RADIO

RADIO STATIONS

Radio One

A station that is often little more than one long commercial – a commercial for the DJs themselves, begging letters to be whisked away into the lush hinterlands of the small screen. *Julie Burchill*

Sometimes listening to Radio One is like being a teenager at a party organised by well-meaning grown-ups where everyone is trying to be having a fantabulous time.
Helen Fielding – 'The Sunday Times' (1992)

The character of Radio One is still firmly based in the weird self-important world of the daytime DJ, a world which suggests wine bars, white GTis, personal appearances and the thrill of bumper-stickers.
Helen Fielding – 'The Sunday Times' (1992)

RADIO SHOWS

ITMA – *BBC Radio*

ITMA is the average man's equivalent of *Finnegan's Wake*.
Arthur Calder-Marshall – 'Tribune'

Soap operas

Between 9am and 10am the American radio is concerned almost exclusively with love. It seems a little like ending breakfast with a stiff bourbon. *Dean Acheson – 'Reporter' (1957)*

DISC JOCKEYS

Failed film-extras, tanned and teethed, voltaic with manic enthusiasm, spurting their vacuous encomia (the simulated orgasms of the impotent), knowledgeable in the brief pathetic chronicles of the shag-haired twangers, bright and kidding and empty-eyed, their mean little slogans like potato crisps. . . . For this they stink to heaven. . . . Do they merit vitriol, even a drop of it? Yes, because they corrupt the young, persuading them that the mature world, which produced Beethoven and Schweitzer, sets an even higher value on the transient anodynes of

youth than does youth itself. . . . They are the Hollow Men. They are electronic lice.
Anthony Burgess – 'Punch' (1967)

On BBC local radio DJs – An endless succession of DJs with mouths so big that they have child-bearing lips. . . . They had IQs so low they thought Noam Chomsky was the sound a horse makes on its bit. . . . Their mouths moved in gear while their brains were still in neutral; they spouted half an inch of meaning to every fifty feet of noise.
Victor Lewis-Smith – 'The Mail on Sunday' (1992)

We think that pop-stars should stick to posing for photographs and DJs should stick to playing charity football.
'Melody Maker' (1983)

Simon Bates

I'm just grateful that Simon Bates is too hideous for TV.
Gary Bushell – 'The Sun' (1992)

Simon Dee

Dee comes over as a cross between Confucius and Baden-Powell. *'Daily Mirror'*

Rick Dees

'Into the Night with Rick Dees' (ABC TV) – Every week his jokes bomb, his interviews go nowhere, he laughs too loudly at guests' mild remarks; it's horrifying. Dees is a perfectly good radio DJ; ABC should let him go back to his day job.
Ken Tucker – 'Entertainment Weekly' (1990)

Wolfman Jack

'Fun 'n' Romance' – Disc jockeys should be heard and not seen. Disc jockeys should play records, not make them.
Dave Marsh – 'Rolling Stone'

John Peel

A very dangerous man to have on the airwaves. *Geoffrey Dickens*

Mike Read

We called the single *Come Back* because we hoped, with 'come' in the title, that Mike Read would ban it. *Pete Wylie (1984)*

POLITICS

UNITED KINGDOM

PARLIAMENT

General
Parliament is nothing less than a big meeting of more or less idle people. *Walter Bagehot*

Parliament is the longest running farce in the West End. *Cyril Smith (1973)*

When we have finally stirred ourselves to hang them all, I hope our next step will be to outlaw political parties outside Parliament on the grounds that, like amusement arcades, they attract all the least desirable members of society. *Auberon Waugh – 'Spectator' (1984)*

The House of Commons
A Palace of Illogicalities.
Lord George Brown – 'In My Way' (1971)

Television has greatly enhanced the prestige and influence of the House of Lords, which presents an intelligent and informed contrast to the monkey-house noises emanating from Prime Minister's question time in the commons. *Lord Hailsham*

The Commons, faithful to their system, remained in a wise and masterly inactivity.
James MacKintosh

On the role of 'Speaker of the House' – It is nine-tenths utter boredom.
Bernard Weatherill

Only people who look dull ever get into the House of Commons, and only people who are dull ever succeed there.
Oscar Wilde (1895)

It's not so much a gentleman's club as a boys' boarding school. *Shirley Williams*

The House of Lords
The House of Lords is like a glass of champagne that has stood for five days.
Clement Attlee

The House of Lords is the British Outer Mongolia for retired politicians.
Aneurin Bevan (1962)

The House of Lords is a model of how to care for the elderly. *Frank Field (1981)*

The House of Lords is the only club in the world where the proprietor pays for the drinks. *Michael Foot*

Five hundred men, ordinary men, chosen accidentally from among the unemployed.
David Lloyd George

The dust and silence of the upper shelves.
Thomas Macaulay

The House of Lords must be the only institution in the world which is kept efficient by the persistent absenteeism of its members.
Viscount Samuel

The House of Lords has a value – it is good evidence of life after death.
Lord Soper (1978)

The House of Lords is a perfect eventide home. *Baroness Mary Stocks*

We in the House of Lords are never in touch with public opinion. That makes us a civilised body.
Oscar Wilde – 'A Woman of No Importance'

The Civil Service
A difficulty for every solution. *Herbert Samuel*

Britain has invented a new missile. It's called the civil service – it doesn't work and it can't be fired. *Sir Walter Walker (1981)*

The British Civil Service is a beautifully designed and effective braking system.
Shirley Williams (1980)

POLITICS

POLITICAL PARTIES

Vote Labour and you build castles in the air.
Vote Conservative and you can live in them.
David Frost – 'That Was The Week That Was' (1962)

On the Opposition's EC policies – A United States of Europe, Lib hook, Lab line, and socialist sinker.   *John Major (1992)*

Conservative Party

Conservative Party Poster – Labour In. Everybody Out.
Graffiti added: Celebrating.

If capitalism depended on the intellectual quality of the Conservative Party, it would end about lunchtime tomorrow.
Tony Benn (1989)

The Tory Party, in so far as I am concerned, are lower than vermin.   *Aneurin Bevan*

Tories are not always wrong, but they are always wrong at the right moment.
Lady Violet Bonham Carter

People are beginning to wish that the voters had been given breathometer tests when they voted in the present Conservative government.
William F. Buckley Jr – 'On the Right' (1967)

There never was a more bloody-minded set of thugs than the British ruling class.
Barbara Castle

The Conservative Party is an organised hypocrisy.   *Benjamin Disraeli*

The Conservatives are nothing else but a load of kippers – two-faced and gutless.
Eric Heffer

On their lack-lustre 1992 General Election campaign – It is as if Dickens's Mr Micawber is left hanging around with Beckett's Godot.
Neil Kinnock

On their transportation policy – Fare-hiking, cost-cutting, congestion-creating, life-threatening, traffic fuming, steam-powered.
John Prescott (1992)

Kick the Tories out . . . and keep on kicking.
'Socialist Worker' (1992)

Labour Party

That bunch of rootless intellectuals, alien Jews and international pederasts who call themselves the Labour Party.
Alan Bennett – 'Forty Years On' (1968)

The Socialist movement in England has never been remarkable for the possession of first-class brains.   *Lord Birkenhead*

What a genius the Labour Party has for cutting itself in half and letting the two parts writhe in public.
'Cassandra' – 'The Daily Mirror'

On continued rationing under the Labour government – The Socialist dream is no longer Utopia, but Queuetopia.
Sir Winston Churchill

They are not fit to manage a whelk stall.
Sir Winston Churchill

Socialism is the philosophy of failure, the creed of ignorance and the gospel of envy.
Sir Winston Churchill

A Labour Government is government of the duds, by the duds, and for the duds.
Sir Winston Churchill

The inherent vice of socialism is the unequal sharing of miseries.
Sir Winston Churchill (1945)

The American declaration of Independence said 'All men are created equal', but the British Socialist party says 'All men shall be kept equal'.   *Sir Winston Churchill*

The style of Labour's politics is a turn-off to many women – and probably to many men as well.   *Bryan Gould (1992)*

It's no use saying that the Labour Government works if one and a half million [*unemployed*] do not.
Joe Haines – 'The Daily Mirror' (1977)

The things that divide the Party are much

greater than the things that unite them.
Frank Johnson – 'The Times' (1984)

Every time the Labour Party are asked to name their weapons they pick boomerangs.
Iain MacLeod

On Labour's continued Socialism – When they are kicking out Big Brother everywhere else in the world, we're not going to let little brother come creeping back here.
John Major (1992)

On Labour's education policy – Finding the blunders in it wouldn't tax the collective mind of a kindergarten.   *Chris Patten (1992)*

If they win power they will turn a Grimm fairy-tale into a grim scary tale.
Tim Rice (1992)
[*He also 'politicized' the Seven Dwarfs* –
Happy: Brian Gould seems to be smiling all the time, and a little like the lead singer of Wet, Wet, Wet.
Sneezy: Robin Cook, he'll catch a cold when he finds he can't cure problems by flinging money at them that he hasn't got.
Doc: John Smith, because he doctors the figures.
Bashful: Gerald Kaufman.
Sleepy: Roy Hattersley.
Grumpy: John Prescott.
Dopey: The Dwarf who takes up the rear would be the leader. I need say no more.]

Scotland needs the Labour Party as much as Sicily needs the Mafia.
Malcolm Rifkind (1992)

The Labour Party is not dead, just brain-dead.   *Norman Tebbitt*

The Labour Party is like a stage-coach. If you rattle along at great speed everybody inside is too exhilarated or too seasick to cause any trouble. But if you stop, everybody gets out and argues about where to go next.
Harold Wilson

Liberal Party
The truth is that the Liberals do not want to abolish the House of Lords when it opposes the people – but wish to abolish the people

when they oppose the Liberal Party.
Lord Birkenhead

The Liberal Government has turned its back on the country, and now has the impertinence to claim the country is behind it.   *Lord Birkenhead*

Basically the Liberal Party is divided between wispy beards and others. Wispy beards wear T-shirts with slogans on, ill-fitting jeans and those heavy shoes which look like Cornish pasties.   *Simon Hoggart (1981)*

As usual the Liberals offer a mixture of sound and original ideas. Unfortunately, none of the sound ideas are original and none of the original ideas are sound.
Harold Macmillan (1961)

The Liberals are now just a shadow of a splinter.   *Sir Gerald Nabarro (1972)*

The small troupe of exhibitionists, failed vaudeville artists, juicy young Boy Scouts and degenerate old voluptuaries which is the Liberal Party.   *Auberon Waugh – 'Private Eye'*

Liberal-Democratic Party (LDP)
Woolly-hatted, muesli-eating, Tory lick-spittles.   *Tony Banks*

To expect the Liberals to control Labour would be like asking Dad's Army to restrain the Mongol hordes.   *Douglas Hurd (1992)*

One week before the election, the Labour Party start cuddling up to the Liberal-Democrats for support. It is like leaning on candy-floss.   *John Major (1992)*

The Liberal-Democrats are a Trojan horse to the Labour Party.   *John Major (1992)*

The popularity of the Liberal Democrats has sunk so low in the opinion polls that they are considering employing the services of Jacques Cousteau to see whether anything can be done to resuscitate it. *Andrew Mitchell*

The Liberal-Democrats couldn't survive a moment's scrutiny of their policies. At local level they back four routes for a by-pass –

North, South, East and West. At national level, they are just as bad.
Chris Patten (1992)

Liberals are Enid Blyton Socialists – a dustbin for undecided votes. *Norman Tebbitt*

They have a new colour. They call it gold; it looks like yellow to me. *Margaret Thatcher*

'Loony Left'
In close-up the British revolutionary Left seethes with such repulsive self-righteous dogmatists that it practically drives one to enlist as a deck-hand on 'Morning Cloud'.
Richard Neville (1972)

The Loony Left have become so politically pure as to make Snow White look like a vamp. *Robert Kilroy-Silk –*
'The Daily Express' (1992)

Natural Law Party
I don't really know what they stand for. I saw George Harrison and he wasn't sure what they stood for either. *Ringo Starr (1992)*

Social-Democrat Party (SDP)
The heterosexual wing of the Labour Party.
George Foulkes

They have policies like liquid grease.
Neil Kinnock

Stale claret in new bottles – it is a confidence trick not to be mistaken for the elixir of life.
Francis Pym

Political manifestos
After the 1992 Conservative manifesto had sold 70,000 copies – twice as many as the other parties combined – On these figures, ours should be in the non-fiction bestseller list; the others are the fiction also-rans. *Anon Tory*

Political opinion polls
I got more egg on my face during the election than anyone – except the pollsters.
John Major (1992)

Opinion polls are about as scientific as looking at the entrails of a chicken.
Jim Sillars (1992)

POLITICAL FIGURES

Anonymous Irish MP
He rose without a friend and sat down without an enemy. *Henry Grattan*

Jeffrey Archer
John Major thinks this man is a serious political figure. *Alastair Campbell –*
'The Sunday Mirror' (1992)

Paddy Ashdown
Prattling Paddy Ashdown.
'The Daily Star' (1992)

Don't vote for Paddy LETdown . . . There is one party you should scrap off the slate in this election. That's Paddy Ashdown and his prigs. Captain Ashdown hasn't got enough 'trained troops' to run the taps in a toilet.
'The Daily Star' (1992)

I'd rate him nine out of ten. But he loses a point because of the shifty way he touches his nose.
Dr Michael Durtnard – Chiropractor (1992)

A one-man band who had transformed a party without a leader into a party without a party . . . And he was a leader with more answers than there were questions, and more news conferences than there were newspapers. *Michael Heseltine (1992)*

After losing seats at the General Election –
Paddy Crashdown. *'The Daily Mirror' (1992)*

I nominate him for the Greta Garbo Award for the leader who wants to be alone.
Norman Tebbitt (1992)

Kenneth Baker
He lies on his back with his legs waggling in the air. I've never heard such a weak-kneed response. *Anthony Beaumont-Dark.*

Stanley Baldwin
His successive attempts to find a policy remind me of a chorus of a third-rate review. His evasions reappear in different scenes and in new dresses, and every time they dance with renewed and despairing vigour. But it is the same old jig. *Lord Beaverbrook*

Not dead. But the candle in that great turnip has gone out. *Sir Winston Churchill*

Tony Banks
He is a man whose contribution to the arts is about the same as Bluebeard's contribution to the institution of marriage. *Terry Dicks*

He reminds me of Henry VIII – not with all the doublet and hose, but at least well-fed. *Terry Dicks*

Anthony Beaumont-Dark
He has a knee-jerk response to everything. *Alastair Campbell – 'The Daily Mirror'*

Margaret Beckett
She looks like a woman resigned to walk home alone to an empty bedsit after Grab-a-Granny night at the local disco. *Richard Littlejohn – 'The Sun' (1992)*

Tony Benn
He did more harm to British Industry in one speech than the combined efforts of the Luftwaffe and U-Boats did in the whole of the last War. *Cyril Smith*

Lord Charles Beresford
He can best be described as one of those orators who, before they get up, do not know what they are going to say; when they are speaking, do not know what they are saying; and when they have sat down, do not know what they have said. *Sir Winston Churchill*

Aneurin Bevan
A debate on the NHS without the Right Honourable Gentleman would be like putting on *Hamlet* with no one cast in the part of the first grave-digger. *Iain MacLeod*

Paul Boateng
Far from being a loony left in sheep's clothing, Paul Boateng comes across as a sheep who used to dress in wolf's clothing to keep up with the fashions. He gets more sheepish by the day . . . if Labour wins the General Election, he will probably bleat out loud in celebration. *Joe Joseph – 'The Times' (1992)*

Virginia Bottomley
A thug in twin-set and pearls *Anne Robinson – 'The Daily Mirror' (1992)*

Sir Rhodes Boyson
He looks like a character out of an unpublished novel by Charles Dickens. *Anon*

George Brown
A pimp and a bastard. *Aneurin Bevan*

James Callaghan
He suffers from what you may regard as a fatal defect in a Chancellor. He is always wrong. *Iain MacLeod*

As Moses he would have mistimed his arrival at the parting of the waves. *Austin Mitchell*

John Campbell
Edinburgh is now celebrated for having given us the two greatest bores that have ever been known in London, for Jack Campbell in the House of Lords is just what Tom Macaulay is in private society. *Lord Henry Brougham*

Henry Campbell-Bannerman
He is a mere cork, dancing on a current which he cannot control. *Arthur Balfour*

He is remembered chiefly as the Prime Minister about whom all is forgotten. *Nicolas Bentley*

Barbara Castle
Mrs Castle is an inverted version of Lord Kitchener. *Jeremy Thorpe (1975)*

Neville Chamberlain
A good mayor of Birmingham in an off-year. *David Lloyd George*

Randolph Churchill
He should not be allowed out in private. *Anon*

He is like a minute insect which bites without being felt. *Benjamin Disraeli*

Sir Winston Churchill
The trouble with Winston is that he nails his trousers to the mast and can't climb down. *Clement Attlee*

He is a man of simple tastes – he's always prepared to put up with the best of everything. *Lord Birkenhead*

In private conversation, he tries on speeches like a man trying on ties in his bedroom to see how he would look in them.
Lionel Curtis (1912)

He would kill his own mother just so that he could use her skin to make a drum to beat his own praises. *David Lloyd George*

He has half a dozen solutions to any problem and one of them is right – the trouble is he does not know which it is.
David Lloyd George

Sir Stafford Cripps

He was not a good judge of men, nor had he enough experience to temper his enthusiasm. He was a political goose. *Clement Attlee*

Richard Crossman

He is one of the most unfaithful deceivers, with a coating of intellectual cheap glitter.
Hugh Dalton

Utterly unscrupulous. Moral principle was not his strong suit. *Lord Hailsham*

He had a heavyweight intellect with a lightweight judgement. *Denis Healey*

Edwina Currie

When she goes to the dentist, he's the one who needs the anaesthetic. *Frank Dobson*

Edwina Currie is to the Conservative Party what the Bishop of Durham is to the Church of England. *Richard Holt*

She has done for our party what King Herod did for babysitting. *Andrew MacKay*

Lord Curzon

Curzon has changed sides on almost every issue during his career. He is often undecided whether to desert a sinking ship for one that might not float. *Lord Beaverbrook*

Earl of Derby (Edward Stanley)

A harpooned walrus. *David Lloyd George*

Geoffrey Dickens

He rarely says anything intelligent.
Sarah Baxter – 'New Statesman'

Terry Dicks

Listening to him opining on the arts is rather like listening to Vlad the Impaler presenting *Blue Peter*. *Tony Banks*

Alf Garnett's vicar on earth – if ignorance is bliss, he must be an extremely happy man.
Patrick Cormack

Frank Dobson

He behaves like an agitated parrot with constipation. He is more funny than wise.
John Major

Alec Douglas-Home

He appeared honourably ineligible for the struggle of life. *Cyril Connolly*

He created the impression of being rather dated, rather fuddy-duddy, rather aristocratic, indifferent in health and altogether too well-mannered for politics in the age of Harold Wilson.
Sir Gerald Nabarro (1963)

Sir Alec is the first recorded case in history of a man who not only thinks he owns a Moss Bros. suit, but he owns Moss Bros. as well.
Harold Wilson

Tom Driberg MP (William Hickey)

He is driven by malice and hatred. Man has been falling ever since the birth of Adam, but never in the whole course of human history has any man fallen quite so low as Driberg.
Lord Beaverbrook

To have published an obituary of Tom Driberg without mentioning homosexuality would have been like published an obituary of Maria Callas without mentioning opera.
William Rees-Mogg – 'The Times' (1980)

He was a man who never managed to do much harm despite being an MP for 32 years. *Auberon Waugh – 'Private Eye'*

Henry Dundas

The Right Honourable gentleman is indebted

to his memory for his jests and his imagination for his facts. *Richard B. Sheridan*

Anthony Eden
Not a gentleman; dresses too well.
Bertrand Russell

Andrew Faulds
In debate, his method is rather akin to the manner of a Shakespearian actor auditioning for a crowd scene at a football match.
Greg Knight

Michael Foot
His idea of policy is to spend, spend, spend. He is the Viv Nicholson of politics.
John Major

His knowledge of industry could be accommodated on the back of a four-penny stamp. *Sir Gerald Nabarro*

Michael Forsyth
END THE FORSYTH SAGA. *SNP Banner (1992)* [*The Conservative Scottish Office Minister retaliated with his own banner –* COMING SOON: FORSYTH III.]

Norman Fowler
Norman Fowler looks as if he is suffering from a famine and Nigel Lawson looks as though he caused it. *Neil Kinnock*

Hugh Gaitskell
He is Mr Rising Price himself. *Iain MacLeod*

Lord Gladstone (Jnr)
The best living embodiment of the Liberal doctrine that quality is not hereditary.
David Lloyd George

A pigmy posturing before the footlights in the road of a giant. *David Lloyd George*

Teresa Gorman
Small, short-sighted, blonde, barbed – she reminds me of a bright little hedgehog.
Edwina Currie

Bernie Grant
A meddling loony. *Anthony Beaumont-Dark*

Keir Hardie
On being told that Hardie would be in heaven

before he would – If heaven is going to be filled with people like Hardie, well the Almighty can have them to Himself.
Sir Winston Churchill

Roy Hattersley
He can only be described as an area of outstanding national humbug. *Anon*

The only true spitting image in politics. *Anon*

I don't think he is a particularly nice man.
Barbara Castle (1969)

He is the acceptable face of opportunism.
David Owen

I don't hate Roy Hattersley, but he's the person I dislike the most. *Kim Wilde (1987)*

Edward Heath
He has no place in the Party. He has no future in Parliament. He has no place, for Parliament is a generous place; democracy a generous thing. May I suggest he pursues his alternative career and conducts orchestras, since he does not know how to conduct himself. *Nicholas Fairbairn*

Receiving support from Ted Heath in a by-election is like being measured by an undertaker. *George Gardiner*

I am sure Mr Heath thinks he is so honest. But I wish he didn't have to have his friends say it so often. *Roy Jenkins (1970)*

That grammar school twit.
Johnny Speight – 'Till Death Do Us Part'

Michael Heseltine
Michael Heseltine is to accuracy what Gary Glitter is to good taste. *Bryan Gould (1992)*

Arriving with all the urgency of Dyno-Rod to the scene of a drain-clearing emergency, the Smiling-Talking-Greeting-Walking-Living-Photo-Opportunity Mr Heseltine descended on Forest Hill . . . A rising conservative star should think twice before acting with children, animals, and Michael Heseltine.
Joe Joseph – 'The Times' (1992)

Michael Heseltine put the con into conservative and John Major put the er . . . er in.
Neil Kinnock (1992)

I like the Tyrannosaurus Rex with his big teeth. It looks a bit like Michael Heseltine.
Neil Kinnock (1992)

The Archie Rice performances of Michael Heseltine have become embarrassing.
'The Times' (1992)

Denis Howell
On his appointment as Labour 'Minister for Emergencies' – It is an alarming thought that if we are ever invaded by monsters from outer space, the man who will be appointed to save us as Minister for Monsters will be this joke yobbo who could easily be mistaken for the traditional plumber with a cleft palate who has lost his dentures down the lavatory.
Auberon Waugh – 'Private Eye'

Roy Jenkins
He tended to knock off at seven o'clock – not so much a Socialist but a socialite.
Harold Wilson

Robert Jenkinson (Earl of Liverpool)
His lack of originality was such that, had he been present at the Creation, he would have begged God not to disturb the chaos.   *Anon*

The Arch-Mediocrity who presides, rather than rules, over a Cabinet of Mediocrities – not a statesman, a statemonger.
Benjamin Disraeli – 'Coningsby'

Keith Joseph
He is a mixture of Hamlet, Rasputin and Tommy Cooper.   *Denis Healey*

Gerald Kaufman
On his absence from Labour's election campaign – I've heard of a shadow foreign minister, but never an invisible one.
Jerry Hayes (1992)

He has crawled so far up the backside of NATO that you can't see the soles of his feet.
Ken Livingstone

On his absence from Labour's election campaign

– Who cares what they've done with Gerald Kaufman, as long as we don't have to look at him.
Andrew Rawnsley – 'The Guardian' (1992)

Neil Kinnock
Kinnock is capable, intelligent, forceful, charming, attractive. Kinnock would make an excellent prime minister. But we're stuck with her wretched husband instead.
Anon Labour MP (1990)

On proportional representation – He had shifted his bottom along the fence, but he's still sitting on it.   *Paddy Ashdown (1992)*

Get stuffed Boyo.
Brian Bateson – Aero-Banner (1992)

A swaggering boyo.   *Kenneth Baker (1992)*

Kinnock's Sheffield rally looked like a cross between the Nuremberg rallies and an Oscar ceremony.   *Rosie Barnes (1992)*

A vote for Kinnock is a vote against Christ.
Barbara Cartland (1992)

He is ruled by the person who makes him breakfast.   *Edwina Currie*

However much he has been posturing about behaving like a leader he doesn't have a leader's posture. Mr Kinnock is very chunky and slumpy, with poor muscle tone, and his body language shows that he is mega-aggressive. He has a way of jabbing his finger at people, which is very unpleasant . . . His body language shows that in the back of his mind he's not sure he's up to the job. I'd rate him only two out of ten.
Dr Michael Durtnard – Chiropractor (1992)

A dodgy leader of a dodgy party, not quite 100p to the pound.   *Michael Heseltine (1992)*

The Labour Manifesto – it's all Kinnock's – a great big load of Kinnocks.
Michael Heseltine (1992)

The not very bright Mr Kinnock, the famous Welsh windbag.
Anthony King – 'The Daily Telegraph' (1992)

On Anthony Hopkins' Oscar-winning portrayal of 'Hannibal' Lechter in 'Silence of the Lambs' – Isn't it enough to have one Welshman who's terrified half the country?
Norman Lamont (1992)

Karaoke Kinnock, the man who'll sing any song you want him to. *Ian Lang (1992)*

He has an infallible knack for getting the wrong end of every stick. *Nigel Lawson*

It's a choice between John Major's magic soap-box or Neil Kinnock's soft soap.
Richard Littlejohn – 'The Sun' (1992)

He craves the highest office in the land like a derelict needs his first Special Brew of the morning. *Richard Littlejohn – 'The Sun' (1992)*

Kinnock swans around in a Red Rover Sterling claiming to be the champion of people who can barely afford a Red Rover bus pass.
Richard Littlejohn – 'The Sun' (1992)

He is a shouter. What he does to his voice is like putting paraffin into the engine of a sports car.
Victor Maddern – Voice Coach (1992)

I'm as Welsh as nutty slack but I can see through Neil Kinnock's red mist of deceit easily. I know histrionics when I see them.
Ruth Madoc (1992)

There are just three words in Labour's vocabulary for Europe – oui, si and jahwohl. Well, let me offer you a fourth, absolutely vital word to defend Britain's interest – no. Can anyone imagine Mr Kinnock saying anything so short? *John Major (1992)*

Nodding and winking and grinning, a foot-in-the-door salesman trying to sell you a gentle, harmless, semi-demi socialism.
John Major (1992)

A Labour government will mean a nightmare on Kinnock street. *John Major (1992)*

The chameleon of politics, consistent only in his inconsistency. *John Major (1992)*

If I accurately recall my Shakespeare: you draweth out the thread of your verbosity finer than the staple of your argument – appropriately from *Love's Labour's Lost*, and Labour will lose. *John Major (1992)*

'Hannibal' Kinnock is the greatest serial-spender in history. His policies will eat you alive. *David Mellor (1992)*

The policy has become almost indistinguishable from the Tories with Kinnock performing more double somersaults than Major's father ever did in his chosen profession. *Arthur Scargill (1992)*

I would say Neil Kinnock, to get into Downing Street, would boil his granny for glue. *Jim Sillars – SNP (1992)*

A nice man but someone who could be drawn into a punch up in a curry-house.
'The Sun' (1992)

If you want to make it, don't fake it with Kinno the Commo Kid. *'The Sun' (1992)*

A man with a short fuse who shoots from the lip. *'The Sun' (1992)*

On the dangers of voting in his mortgage policy – He'll have a new home, you won't!
'The Sun' (1992)

He's the LAB-err leader. *'The Sun' (1992)*

Front-page headline on the morning of the general election – If Neil Kinnock Wins Today Will the Last Person To Leave Britain Please Turn Out the Lights. *'The Sun' (1992)*

He has a boyo look and he will never look good no matter what he wears.
John Taylor – 'British Style' (1992)

He does have the air of a chicken pecking at a lot of corn on the ground when he is speaking. *Norman Tebbitt (1992)*

I have never rated Neil Kinnock as anything but a windbag whose incoherent speeches spring from an incoherent mind.
Norman Tebbitt

He is a crypto-communist. *Margaret Thatcher*

When it comes to constitutional issues in Wales, we trust Neil Kinnock about as far as we could drop-kick him.
Dafydd Wigley – Plaid Cymru (1992)

Norman Lamont
Vatman! *Labour poster (1992)*

On Budget day – I should have played something by Lamont-Dozier, because there isn't anyone dozier than Lamont!
Peter Young: Jazz FM (1992)

Nigel Lawson
A fat slug. *Andrew Faulds*

He reminds me of King Canute. *Cyril Smith*

Peter Lilley
As Trade and Industry Secretary – He must have one of the easiest jobs around because there's not much trade and very little industry.
Anon member of BBC TV's 'Question Time' audience (1992)

Ken Livingstone
He plays the jilted Miss Havisham of the party, entangled in his own time-warp, all dressed up with nowhere to go.
Joe Joseph – 'The Times' (1992)

David Lloyd George
If only I could piss the way he talks.
Georges Clemenceau

Ian Mikardo
Not as nice as he looks. *Sir Winston Churchill*

Ramsay MacDonald
I remember, when I was a child, being taken to the celebrated Barnum's circus, which contained an exhibition of freaks and monstrosities, but the exhibit . . . which I most desired to see was the one described as 'The Boneless Wonder'. My parents judged that spectacle would be too revolting and demoralising for my youthful eyes, and I have waited 50 years to see the boneless wonder sitting on the Treasury Bench.
Sir Winston Churchill (1931)

Harold Macmillan
After sweeping changes to his cabinet – Greater love hath no man than this, that he lay down his friends for his life. *Jeremy Thorpe*

Alice Mahon
The Madame Defarge of the Labour Party.
Nicholas Bennett

John Major
He acted less like a Prime Minister than a little boy caught out fibbing at school.
'The Daily Mirror' (1992)

He leans his head too far forward. If you mentally cut off his head it would fall to the ground without touching his body.
Dr Michael Durtnard – Chiropractor (1992)

Not so much a wet, but a wimp.
Denis Healey (1992)

Poor John Major. What can you say except he will always look grey like his *Spitting Image* puppet. *Peter Howarth – 'GQ' (1992)*

He is a ditherer and a dodger, a ducker and weaver. *Neil Kinnock (1992)*

Replying to the Shakespeare insult – You read a quote from Shakespeare. Let me give you one from Mrs Thatcher, 'You are frit!'
Neil Kinnock (1992)

On his soap-box approach to the election – Mr Kinnock does not need a soap-box to increase his stature.
M. G. Pattison – Letter to 'The Times' (1992)

He is a box-office disaster, who has failed to win any awards for his production – *Honey, I Shrunk the Economy.* *John Smith (1992)*

I do not accept the idea that all of a sudden Major is his own man . . . There isn't such a thing as Majorism. *Margaret Thatcher (1992)*

I'm absolutely fed up with hearing how 'nice' Mr Major is. Nice is not necessarily an asset. In a politician, it's probably a menace. I looked up 'nice' in my dictionary. The first definitions were: 'Foolishly simple, wanton, coy, over-particular.' Yeah, that'll bring in the votes. *Michael Winner (1992)*

David Mellor

On becoming National Heritage Minister – If the Conservatives want to make the arts more popular and less nancy, well, I have my doubts about whether David Mellor is the one for the job.

    Kenneth Branagh – *'Evening Standard' (1992)*

Nature has deigned him along the lines of a professional mourner, a fourth form sneak or one of those woeful Victorian clerks who sat at their ledgers from dawn to dusk.

    Jill Parkin – *'The Daily Express' (1992)*

On becoming National Heritage Minister – The acronym of his remit Broadcasting, Arts, Sports, Television, Architecture, Recreation, Drama – adds up to BASTARD. So what does that make him?

    'The Sunday Telegraph' (1992)

John Moore

His delivery at the dispatch-box has all the bite of a rubber duck.   *Lady Falkender*

Tom O'Brien – *Leader of the N.A.C.E.*

He suffered more than any other trade union leader from the malady known as enuresis – a propensity for leaking when Pressmen are present.   *Harold Wilson*

Dr David Owen

On backing the Conservatives in the 1992 General Election – It is only fair to the other parties. It is the Tories' turn after all.

    Paddy Ashdown (1992)

[*Neil Kinnock enthused* – Probably the most brilliant of all that has been offered about somebody who switches parties. I think Paddy deserves ten out of ten.]

On backing the Conservatives in the 1992 General Election – A case of the doc calling the kettle black.

    Jane Gordon – *'Today' (1992)*

He is incapable of working in a team. He's like an upas tree which poisons the ground for miles around.   *Denis Healey*

On backing the Conservatives in the 1992 General Election – Dr Owen's intention is marvellous news for us. That man is the kiss of death for any party unlucky enough to attract his support.

    David Jamieson – *Labour (1992)*

Labour's Dr Smug.   *'The Sun' (1979)*

Rev Ian Paisley

If the word 'No' was removed from the English language, he would be speechless.

    John Hume (1992)

Cecil Parkinson

Parkinson's red face looming over the dispatch-box is a pretty terrifying sight. I was not sure at one stage whether it was indignation, claret, or a faulty sun-lamp.

    Peter Snape

Chris Patten

Anon Marxist: I'm from *Living Marxism*. Chris Patten: I didn't know it was still alive. Anon Marxist: It's more alive than your election campaign.

Chris Patten was like a teetotaller who had suddenly taken to drink and it had gone to his head.

    Lord Jenkins

Arthur Scargill – *President of the N.U.M.*

He appears in the tradition of Hereward the Wake, fighting on against the Normans though all can see the cause is hopeless.

    Lord Wyatt

Emmanuel (Manny) Shinwell

'Shinbad the Tailor' is by far the least attractive member of the government, always looking round for someone to whom to pass the blame. He will not face facts squarely. He is a coarse-grained shit and a low cur.

    Hugh Dalton

Lord Roseberry

He outlived the future by ten years and his past by more than twenty.

    Sir Winston Churchill

Denis Skinner

The Beast of Bolsover.   *Anon*

Cyril Smith

He would be quite brilliant if he retained as

much of what he reads as of what he eats.
Anon

In Rochdale, we've got Cyril Smith who's so fat he takes up most of the f***ing town.
Lisa Stansfield

John Smith
He's like Fagin – 'You gotta pick a pocket or two' – the battle hymn of any aspiring Labour chancellor. *Michael Heseltine (1992)*

I always knew that Neil Kinnock belonged in the economic nursery. Now, God help us, we've got twins. *Michael Heseltine (1992)*

He has as much likelihood of understanding how the economy works as Donald Duck has of winning Mastermind. *John Major*

Nicholas Soames
He can trace his ancestry back to royalty – King Kong. *Anon*

Viscount Stansgate
He is the world's best-known political featherweight. *Lord Birkenhead*

John Stonehouse
Old politicians never die, they simply wade away. *Malcolm Rifkind*

John Taylor
He is said to be Cabinet material; we don't want Cabinet material. There are too many toss-pots in the Cabinet already. He should have been a candidate in Wolverhampton, where his colour would have been more appropriate.
Dudley Aldridge – former Mayor of Cheltenham (1992)

I don't think we want a bloody nigger to represent us. *Bill Galbraith (1992)*

Teddy Taylor
He would swim through shark-infested waters to get near a microphone.
Jeremy Paxman

Norman Tebbitt
He is the most stupendously offensive man in the House. *Michael Foot*

The American adage 'don't get mad, get even' doesn't apply to Norman. He gets mad and even. *'The Observer'*

Putting him in charge of industrial relations is like appointing Dracula to take charge of the blood transfusion service. *Eric Varley*

Margaret Thatcher
I wouldn't say she was open-minded on the Middle-East so much as empty-headed. She probably thinks that Sinai is the plural of sinus. *Jonathan Aitken*

An ex-spam hoarder from Grantham presiding over the social and economic decline of our country. *Tony Banks*

Mrs Thatcher is a very tough lady – you could bounce golf balls off her and she wouldn't notice. *Sir Rhodes Boyson (1990)*

The dominatrix in the pussy-cat bow, the Darwinian Dresden doll. *Julie Burchill*

I am not prepared to accept the economics of a housewife. *Jacques Chirac (1987)*

She adds the diplomacy of Alf Garnett to the economics of Arthur Daley. *Denis Healey*

She is not just a female Franco, but a Petain in petticoats. *Denis Healey*

She behaves like a superannuated Sumo-wrestler. *Denis Healey*

She should be a pom-pom girl for Ronnie.
Mick Jones (1987)

In ten years, she'll probably replace Guy Fawkes as an effigy. *Ken Livingstone (1992)*

She has the mouth of Marilyn Monroe, and the eyes of Caligula. *Francois Mitterand*

I note with alarm that the former PM now refers to herself in the third person ('Thatcherism will live. It will live long after Thatcher has died'). This is a habit she shares with Colonel Oliver North and Arthur Scargill. I fear the worst.
'The Weasel' – 'The Independent' (1992)

POLITICS

William Waldegrave
On the absence of certain key party figures from the election campaign – Where's Gerald Kaufman? He's on the search party for William Waldegrave.
Anon Labour MP (1992)

Absolutely ghastly. The trouble with brains is they don't breed common sense.
Anthony Beaumont-Dark (1992)

Horace Walpole
The little thin man wears a shocking hat.
Duke of York

Shirley Williams
You'll never get on in politics, my dear, with that hair.
Nancy Astor

Harold Wilson
Most of his speeches are cheap, but he gets away with it. He is an old entertainer – the Archie Rice of the Labour Party.
Tony Benn

Harold Wilson was the first Labour leader without a dream; his only dream was realised the day he became Labour leader.
Julie Burchill

Double-talk is his mother tongue. He is a man whose vision is limited to tomorrow's headlines.
Iain MacLeod

He's a waste-paper basket, filled with lightly given promises and pledges.
Iain MacLeod

John F. Kennedy has described himself as an idealist without illusions. Harold Wilson is an illusionist without ideals.
Iain MacLeod

When it comes to naked party politics, no Prime Minister has ever made such an idiot of himself by flagrantly broken promises as Mr Harold Wilson.
Sir Gerald Nabarro

George Brown drunk is a better man than the Prime Minister sober.
'The Times'

David Winnick
He greets every problem head on – with an open mouth and a closed mind. He gives an impression of a mixture between Uriah Heep and Jaws. He has about as much charm as a

puff adder.
John Major

UNITED STATES OF AMERICA

GENERAL

Is America ready for self-government?
New York graffiti

During an election campaign the air is full of speeches and vice versa.
Henry Adams

If I were to go over my life again, I would be a shoemaker rather than an American statesman.
John Adams

On the call to impeach President Nixon – A group of politicians deciding to dump a President because his morals are bad is like the Mafia getting together to bump off the Godfather for not going to Church on Sunday.
Russell Baker – 'New York Times' (1974)

Criticism of government finds sanctuary in several portions of the 1st Amendment. It is part of the right of free speech. It embraces freedom of the press.
Hugo L. Black (1961)

Politics, where fat, bald, disagreeable men, unable to be candidates themselves, teach a president how to act on a public stage.
Jimmy Breslin – 'Table Money' (1986)

I'd rather trust the government of the USA to the first 400 people listed in the Boston telephone directory than to the faculty of Harvard University.
William F. Buckley Jnr

No man should be in public office who can't make more money in private life.
Thomas E. Dewey

I was ashamed of being a Republican and afraid of being a Democrat. *Robert W. Kenny*

America is still a government of the naive, for the naive, by the naive.
Christopher Morley – 'Inward Ho!' (1923)

American politics is a form of socialism for the rich.
Gregory Nunn

Lobbyists are people who go to Washington to mix business with pressure.

Lane Olinghouse

You can always get the truth from an American statesman after he has turned seventy or given up all hope of the Presidency. *Wendell Phillips*

The State, that cawing rookery of committees and sub-committees. *V. S. Pritchett*

Ninety-eight per cent of the adults in this country are decent, hard-working, honest Americans. It's the other lousy two per cent that gets all the publicity. But then – we elected them. *Lily Tomlin*

THE PRESIDENCY

Presidential timber is mostly bark. *Anon*

Thank God Only One Of Them Can Win!
Bumper sticker during Kennedy/Nixon Presidential Campaign (1960)

Trying to make the presidency work these days is like trying to sew buttons on a custard pie. *James D. Barber*

Take our presidency; they're a bunch of yo-yos. The presidency is now a cross between a popularity contest and a high school debate, with an encyclopaedia of clichés the first prize. *Saul Bellow*

Presidency – the greased pig in the field game of American politics. *Ambrose Bierce*

The office of President is such a bastardised thing, half royalty and half democracy, that nobody knows whether to genuflect or spit.
Jimmy Breslin

Anyone that wants the presidency so much that he'll spend two years organising and campaigning for it is not to be trusted with the office. *David Broder*

If Presidents don't do it to their wives, they do it to the country. *Mel Brooks*

Have you ever seen a candidate talking to a rich person on television? *Art Buchwald*

The US Presidency is a Tudor monarchy plus telephones. *Anthony Burgess (1977)*

Carter, Ford and Nixon – See No Evil, Hear No Evil and Evil. *Robert J. Dole (1983)*

Roosevelt – a false witness.
Truman – a merchant.
Eisenhower – I am told that on the golf links he is better with a putter than he is with the long shots and that doesn't surprise me.
Kennedy – the style of a hairdresser's assistant – he combed his way through problems.
Johnson – a truck driver or a stevedore – or a legionnaire.
Charles de Gaulle – 'Time' (1969)

Oh, that lovely title, ex-president.
Dwight D. Eisenhower (1959)

I can't wait to run against a President who owns more tuxedos than books. *Gary Hart*

No man will every bring out of the Presidency the reputation which carries him into it. *Thomas Jefferson*

Being president is like being a jackass in a hailstorm. There's nothing to do but stand there and take it. *Lyndon B. Johnson*

There should be more in American liberty than the privilege we enjoy of insulting the President with impunity. *Austin O'Malley*

The Constitution provides for every accidental contingency in the Executive – except a vacancy in the mind of the President. *John Sherman*

The power to blow up the world cannot be entrusted to anyone sick enough to seek it.
Philip Slater

This country is full of dignified, self-contained politicians who will refuse to accept the Presidency unless they are elected.
'Stamford Advocate'

In America any boy may become President

and I suppose that's just the risk he takes.
Adlai Stevenson (1952)

On the 1980 Presidential candidates (Reagan and Mondale) – God! The country that produced George Washington has got this collection of crumb-bums!
Barbara Tuchman (1980)

All the President is, is a glorified public relations man who spends his time flattering, kissing, and kicking people to get them to do what they are supposed to do anyway.
Harry S. Truman

Why in hell does anybody want to be head of state? Damned if I know. *Harry S. Truman*

The American Presidency is merely a way station en route to the blessed condition of being ex-President. *John Updike*

These presidential ninnies should stick to throwing out baseballs and leave the important matters to serious people.
Gore Vidal

Any American who is prepared to run for President should automatically, by definition, be disqualified from ever doing so.
Gore Vidal

The US brags about its political system, but the president says one thing during the election, something else when he takes office, something else during mid-term and something else when he leaves.
Deng Xiaoping

VICE-PRESIDENCY

My country has contrived for me the most insignificant office that ever the invention of man contrived or his imagination conceived.
John Adams

Th' prisidincy is th' highest office in th' gift iv th' people. Th' vice-prisidincy is th' next highest an' th' lowest. It isn't a crime exactly. Ye can't be sint to jail f'r it, but it's a kind iv disgrace. *Finlay Peter Dunne*

The Vice-Presidency of the USA isn't worth

a pitcher of warm spit. *John Nance Garner*

The Vice Presidency is a spare tyre on the automobile of government.
John Nance Garner

Should have stuck with my old chores as Speaker of the House. I gave up the second most important job in the Government for one that didn't amount to a hill of beans. I spent eight long years as Mr Roosevelt's spare tyre. *John Nance Garner*

Once there were two brothers; one ran away to sea, the other was elected Vice-President – and nothing was ever heard of them again.
Thomas Marshall

Against stupidity and vice-presidents the gods contend in vain. *Gregory Nunn*

The Vice-Presidency is sort of like the last cookie on the plate. Everybody insists he won't take it, but somebody always does.
Bill Vaughan

CONGRESS

The Capitol building is marble outside – garble inside.
Anon

Congress – a body of men who meet to repeal laws. *Ambrose Bierce*

Senate – a body of elderly gentlemen charged with high duties and misdemeanours.
Ambrose Bierce

Einstein's theory of relativity, as practised by Congressmen, simply means getting members of your family on the payroll.
James H. Boren

Congress would accomplish more with fewer 'blocs' and more tackle. *'Columbia Record'*

Draco wrote his laws in blood; the Senate writes its law in wind. *Tom Connally*

Wonder if it would be possible to slow down a phonograph to where it could play 'The Congressional Record'? *'Detroit News'*

POLITICS

The US Senate – an old scow which doesn't move very fast, but never sinks.
Everett Dirksen

On the House of Lords – We are fortunate to have inherited an institution which we certainly should never have had the intelligence to create. We might have been landed with something like the American Senate. *Lord Esher (1963)*

Some statesmen go to Congress and some go to hell. It is the same thing, after all.
Eugene Field

If the present Congress errs in too much talking, how can it be otherwise in a body to which the people send 150 lawyers.
Thomas Jefferson – 'Autobiography'

Office hours are twelve to one with an hour off for lunch. *George S. Kaufman*

The Senate is the last primitive society in the world. We still worship the elders of the tribe and honour the territorial imperative.
Eugene McCarthy

Congress is so strange. A man gets up to speak and says nothing. Nobody listens – and then everybody disagrees. *Boris Marshalov*

All I can say for the United States Senate is that it opens with prayer and closes with an investigation. *Will Rogers*

With Congress, every time they make a joke, it's a law, and every time they make a law, it's a joke. *Will Rogers*

It could probably be shown by facts and figures that there is no distinctly native American criminal class except Congress.
Mark Twain

THE PENTAGON

The Pentagon has five sides on every issue.
Anon Russian

THE WHITE HOUSE

The White House is the finest jail in the world. *Harry S. Truman (1949)*

POLITICAL PARTIES

Association of American States
They couldn't pour piss out of a shoe if the instructions were written on the heel.
Lyndon B. Johnson

Democratic Party
The Democratic Party is like a mule – without pride of ancestry or hope of posterity. *Edmund Burke*

The Democratic party is like a man riding backward in a carriage. It never sees a thing until it has gone by. *Benjamin Butler*

Any Democrat is mentally ill.
'Cagney & Lacey'

I never said all democrats were saloon-keepers; what I said was all saloon-keepers were Democrats. *Horace Greeley*

Its leaders are always troubadours of trouble; crooners of catastrophe. A Democratic President is doomed to proceed to his goals like a squid, squirting darkness all about him.
Clare Booth Luce

On the 1960 Party – A cigar-smoking, stale-aired, slack-jawed, butt-littered, foul, bleak, hard-working, bureaucratic death of gas and faces – lawyers, judges, ward heelers, mafiosos, Southern goons and grandees, grand old ladies, trade unionists and finks; full of pompous words and long pauses which lie like a leaden pain over fever.
Norman Mailer

The reason the Democrats are so virtuous is probably because money is the root of all evil. *'Philadelphia North American'*

They have made inflated claims about what they intend to do. But that's only to be expected, since they are the party of inflation.
Ronald Reagan (1988)

The leaders of the Democratic Party have gone so far left, they've left the country.
Ronald Reagan

I belong to no organised party – I am a Democrat. *Will Rogers*

The Democratic Party can always be relied on to make a damn fool of itself at the critical time. *Ben Tillman*

Ku Klux Klan
They wear white sheets and their hats have a point – which is more than can be said for their beliefs. *David Frost (1986)*

The Ku Klux Klan never dies. They just stop wearing sheets because sheets cost too much. *Thurgood Marshall*

The Ku Klux Klan has been the vulture of America for almost a century. It is one enemy that has engaged in continual warfare against America since the Civil War. It's all hatred. Its weapon is fear. The Klan runs like a bloody thread through the noose every subversive outfit was eager to wrap around America's neck. *Walter Winchell*

Pacifists
On Vietnam war protestors – Their signs said, 'make love not war!' It didn't seem to me as if they were capable of either. *Ronald Reagan*

Republican Party
A bureaucrat is a Democrat who holds some office that a Republican wants.
Allen W. Barkley

They've been pedalling eyewash about themselves and hogwash about the Democrats. What they need is a good mouthwash. *Lyndon B. Johnson*

It is an ancient political vehicle, held together by soft soap and hunger and with front-seat drivers and back-seat drivers contradicting each other in a bedlam of voices, shouting 'go right' and 'go left' at the same time.
Adlai Stevenson (1952)

The elephant has a thick skin, a head full of ivory, and as everyone who has seen a circus parade knows, proceeds best by grasping the tail of its predecessor. *Adlai Stevenson*

If the Republicans stop telling lies about us,

we will stop telling the truth about them.
Adlai Stevenson

I like Republicans, have grown up with them, worked with them and would trust them with anything in the world, except public office.
Adlai Stevenson

The Republican Party either corrupts its liberals or expels them. *Harry S. Truman*

The trouble with the Republican Party is that it hasn't had a new idea for thirty years.
Woodrow Wilson

POLITICAL FIGURES

A candidate running for Congress needs two assistants – one to dig up the facts and the other to bury them. *Anon*

You can't use tact with a congressman. A congressman is a hog. You must take a stick and hit him on the snout. *Henry Adams*

A great many of our troubles would have been averted if the Constitution had provided for a mental test for candidates for Congress.
'Columbia Record'

Some representatives in Congress are only fairly so. *'Charleston Gazette'*

Senators are public servants. You can tell they are servants by the length of time it takes them to do anything.
'Fountain Inn Tribune'

When I first came to Washington, I thought, what is I'il ole me doing with these ninety-nine great people? Now I ask myself, what am I doing here with these ninety-nine jerks?
S. I. Hayakawa

Why are congressmen called public servants? You never see servants that anxious to keep their jobs. *Robert Quillen*

Members of Congress never open their mouths without subtracting from the sum of human knowledge. *Thomas Reed*

Rome had Senators – now I know why it declined. *Will Rogers*

Fleas can be taught nearly anything that a congressman can. *Mark Twain*

Suppose you were an idiot, and suppose you were a member of Congress, but I repeat myself. *Mark Twain*

Some people come to Washington and grow with their jobs, but a lot of politicians come and all they do is swell up. *Woodrow Wilson*

REPRESENTATIVES

Anon
He has every attribute of a dog except loyalty. *Thomas P. Gore*

On a recently deceased politician – I did not attend his funeral; but I wrote a nice letter saying I approved of it. *Mark Twain*

Dean Acheson
I watch his smart-aleck manner and his British clothes and that New Dealism, everlasting New Dealism in everything he says and does, and I want to shout, 'Get out, get out. You stand for everything that has been wrong with the United States for years.' *Hugh Butler*

John Adams
He is distrustful, obstinate, excessively vain, and takes no counsel from anyone. *Thomas Jefferson*

It has been a political career of this man to begin with hypocrisy, proceed with arrogance, and to finish with contempt. *Tom Paine*

He can't dance, drink, game, flatter, promise, dress, swear with the gentlemen, and small talk and flirt with the ladies – in short, he has none of the essential arts or ornaments which make up a courtier – there are thousands who with a tenth part of his understanding, and without a spark of his honesty, would distance him infinitely in any court in England. *Jonathan Sewall*

John Q. Adams
When they talk about his old age and venerableness and nearness to the grave, he knows better. He is like one of those cardinals, who as quick as he is chosen Pope, throws away his crutches and his crookedness, and is straight as a boy. He is an old roué, who cannot live on slops, but must have sulphuric acid in his tea. *Ralph Waldo Emerson*

Of all the men, whom it was ever my lot to accost and to waste civilities upon, Adams was the most doggedly and systematically repulsive. With a vinegar aspect, cotton in his leathern ears, and hatred of England in his heart, he sat in the frivolous assemblies of Petersburg like a bull-dog among spaniels; and many were the times that I drew monosyllables and grim smiles from him and tried to mitigate his venom. *W. H. Lyttleton*

Sherman Adams
The blunt-spoken New Englander ran the White House as the 'abominable no-man'. *James Brooks*

Spiro Agnew
He was a beautiful, beautiful body, and we were selling sex. *Robert Goodman (1966)*

Chester A. Allen
First in ability on the list of second-rate men. *Anon*

A nonentity in side whiskers. *Woodrow Wilson*

Judah P. Benjamin
Mr Benjamin was a brilliant lawyer, but he knew as much about war as an Arab knows of the Sermon on the Mount. *Anon*

The Mephistopheles of the Southern Confederacy. *James G. Blaine*

Thomas H. Benton
A liar of magnitude. *John Quincy Adams*

The greatest of all humbugs, and could make more out of nothing than any other man in the world. He ought to have gone about his life with quack doctors, and written puffs for their medicines. *John C. Calhoun*

James G. Blaine
Blaine! Blaine! J. G. Blaine

Continental Liar from the State of Maine.
Anon campaign slogan

He wallowed in corruption like a rhinoceros
in an African pool. *E. L. Godkin*

No man in our annals has filled so large a
space and left it so empty. *Charles E. Russell*

William E. Borah
The Prince of blatherskites, Senator Borah,
whose big mouth and tiny mentality have
made his name a by-word of reproach
wherever decent Americans gather. *Anon*

He was always winding himself up, but never
struck twelve.
*John C. Vinson – 'William E. Borah and the
Outlawing of War'*

William J. Bryan
A money-grabbing, selfish, office-seeking,
favour-hunting, publicity-loving, marplot
from Nebraska. *Anon*

A half-baked glib little briefless jack-leg
lawyer . . . grasping with anxiety to collar that
$50,000 salary, promising the millennium to
everybody with a hole in his pants and
destruction to everybody with a clean shirt.
John Milton Hay

One could drive a prairie schooner through
any part of his argument and never scrape
against a fact. *David Houston*

The national tear duct. *H. L. Mencken*

What a disgusting, dishonest fakir Bryan is!
When I see so many Americans running after
him, I feel very much as I do when a really
lovely lady falls in love with a cad. *Elihu Root*

His mind was like a soup dish, wide and
shallow, it could hold a small amount of
nearly everything, but the slightest jarring
spilled the soup into somebody's lap.
Irving Stone – 'They Also Ran'

The Great Inevitable. *Woodrow Wilson*

James Buchanan
There is no such person running as James

Buchanan. He is dead of lockjaw. Nothing
remains but a platform and a bloated mass of
political putridity. *Thaddeus Stevens*

Aaron Burr
I never thought him an honest, frank-dealing
man, but considered him as a crooked gun or
other perverted machine, whose aim or shot
you could never be sure of.
Thomas Jefferson (1807)

He was always at market, if they wanted him.
Thomas Jefferson

George Bush
All hat and no cattle. *John Connally*

On his tennis style – Real men don't lob.
'Runner's World' (1988)

John C. Calhoun
A rigid, fanatic, ambitious, selfishly partisan
and sectional turncoat with too much genius
and too little common sense, who will either
die a traitor or a madman. *Henry Clay*

Jimmy Carter
He would cut the cards if he was playing
poker with his mother. *Anon*

A yellow-pad President. *Howard Baker*

Carter has done what no other President has
done: He has brought into the sharpest
contrast the hypocrisy of the US in respect to
human rights. *Marlon Brando*

Sometimes when I look at all my children, I
say to myself, 'Lillian, you should have
stayed a virgin'. *Lillian Carter*

Carter is chicken-fried McGovern.
Robert Dole

President Carter says that he doesn't 'panic
in a crisis', but that's not the problem. The
problem is that he panics without a crisis.
Clayton Fritchey

A Frankenstein's monster with a Southern
drawl, a more cultivated version of the old
Confederate at the school-house door.
Richard Hatcher

Carter is your typical smiling, brilliant, back-stabbing, bull-shitting Southern nut-cutter.
Lane Kirkland (1976)

Jimmy Carter as President is like Truman Capote marrying Dolly Parton. The job is too big for him. *Rich Little*

If you're in the peanut business, you learn to think small.
Eugene McCarthy

They say Carter is the first businessman ever to sit in the White House. But why did they have to send us a small businessman.
George Meany

He smiles like a Christian with four aces.
Bill Moyers

Jimmy Carter's running for WHAT?
Reg Murphy – 'Atlanta Constitution' (1974)

Jimmy Carter is just Plains folk.
Norm Nathan

Depression is when you are out of work. A recession is when your neighbour is out of work. A recovery is when Jimmy Carter is out of work. *Ronald Reagan*

Carter is the best President the Soviet Union ever had. *William Safire*

Jimmy Carter had the air of a man who had never taken any decisions in his life. They had always been taken for him.
Guy Simon (1978)

Salmon Chase
Chase is a good man, but his theology is unsound. He thinks he is the fourth person in the Trinity. *Anon Ohio Senator*

If he becomes President, all right, I hope we may never have a worse man.
Abraham Lincoln

Henry Clay
The standard of Henry Clay should consist of his armorial bearings, which ought to be a pistol, a pack of cards, and a brandy bottle.
Anon

He had an undigested system of ethics.
John Q. Adams

He prefers the specious to the solid, and the plausible to the true. *John C. Calhoun*

He was a man of splendid abilities, but utterly corrupt. Like rotten mackerel by moonlight, he shines and stinks.
John Randolph

No one knew better than the Cock of Kentucky which side his bread was buttered on: and he liked butter. A considerable portion of his public life was spent in trying to find butter for both sides of the slice.
Irving Stone – 'They Also Ran'

He said 'I would rather be right than be president.' This was the sourest grape since Aesop originated his fable. *Irving Stone – Ibid.*

He was a chameleon; he could turn any colour that might be useful to him. To read of his career one must have cork-screw eyes.
Irving Stone – Ibid.

Grover Cleveland
A man of force and stubbornness with no breadth of view, no training in our history and traditions and essentially coarse fibred and self-sufficient. *Henry Cabot Lodge*

His whole, huge carcasse seemed to be made of iron. There was no give in him, no bounce, no softness. He sailed through American history like a steel ship loaded with monoliths of granite. *Henry L. Mencken – 'American Mercury' (1933)*

His Accidency. *Theodore Roosevelt*

Bill Clinton
Slick Willie. *Anon*

The Prince of sleaze. *Jerry Brown (1992)*

I have never seen . . . so slippery, so disgusting a candidate.
Nat Hentoff – 'Village Voice' (1992)

Roscoe Conkling
Vain as a peacock, and a czar in arrogance.
Matthew P. Breen

A cold, selfish man, who had no right to live
except to prey upon his fellow man.
Clarence Darrow

Calvin Coolidge
He had the mentality of a small town
Rotarian. *Anon*

He is so silent that he is always worth
listening to. *Anon*

Calvin Coolidge's perpetual expression was
of smelling something burning on the stove.
Sherwin L. Cook

The greatest man who ever came out of
Plymouth Corner, Vermont.
Clarence Darrow

Simply a cheap and trashy fellow, deficient in
sense and almost devoid of any notion of
honour – in brief, a dreadful little cad.
H. L. Mencken (1924)

Democracy is that system of government
under which the people, having 35,717,342
native-born adult whites to choose from,
including thousands who are handsome and
many who are wise, pick out a Coolidge to be
head of the State. *H. L. Mencken (1926)*

Here, indeed, was his one really notable
talent. He slept more than any other
President, whether by day or by night. Nero
fiddled, but Coolidge snored. He had no
ideas and he was not a nuisance.
H. L. Mencken – 'American Mercury' (1933)

I do wish he did not look as if he had been
weaned on a pickle.
Alice Roosevelt-Longworth
[*attributed by Alice to another patient of her
family doctor.*]

On his death – How can they tell?
Dorothy Parker

Calvin Coolidge didn't say much, and when
he did he didn't say much. *Will Rogers*

This runty, aloof, little man, who quacks
through his nose when he speaks.
William Allen White

He was an economic fatalist with a God-
given inertia. He knew nothing and refused
to learn. *William Allen White*

The slit-mouthed Puritan. *Art Young*

Mario Cuomo
A mean son-of-a-bitch who acted like a
mafioso. *Bill Clinton*

Carl Curtis
He can't talk. He's unpossessing. And he's
generally a shit. *John F. Kennedy*

Jefferson Davis
He is as ambitious as Lucifer, cold as a snake,
and what he touches will not prosper.
Sam Houston

Daniel De Leon
De Leon would have been politically sound if
he had not been economically hollow.
William D. Haywood

Thomas E. Dewey
The boy Orator of the Platitude. *Anon*

He is the nastiest little man I've ever known.
He struts along sitting down.
Mrs Clarence Dykstra (1852)

Dewey, cool, cold, low-voiced, was like a
softly growling bull terrier to take on all
comers if he could get in one good bite.
Edwin C. Hill

A political streetwalker accosting men with
'come home with me, dear'. *Harold L. Ickes*

On announcing his Republican candidacy –
Dewey has thrown his diaper into the ring.
Harold L. Ickes

I know Governor Thomas E. Dewey, and Mr
Dewey is a fine man. Yes, Dewey is a fine
man. So is my Uncle Morris. My Uncle
Morris shouldn't be President; neither should
Dewey. *George Jessel*

He resembled the little man on the wedding cake. *Alice Roosevelt-Longworth*

On his second Presidential nomination – You can't make a soufflé rise twice.
Alice Roosevelt-Longworth (1948)

You really have to get to know Dewey to dislike him. *Robert A. Taft*

Everett Dirksen
The Wizard of Ooze. *John F. Kennedy*

Stephen A. Douglas
Douglas can never be President, Sir, No, Sir; Douglas never can be President. His legs are too short, Sir. His coat, like a cow's tail, hangs too near the ground, Sir.
Thomas Hart Benton

His argument is as thin as the homeopathic soup that was made by boiling the shadow of a pigeon that had been starved to death.
Abraham Lincoln

He appears to have been called 'The Little Giant' more because he was little than because he was a giant.
Irving Stone – 'They Also Ran'

John Foster Dulles
A diplomatic bird of prey smelling out from afar the corpses of dead bodies.
James Cameron (1967)

J.F.D., the woolliest type of useless pontificating American. Heaven help us!
Sir Alexander Cadogan – 'Diary' (1942)

Foster Dulles is the only case I know of a bull who carries a china shop with him.
Sir Winston Churchill

John Foster Dulles was a strong personality with views as narrow as a small-gauge railway. *Kim Philby*

The world's longest range misguided missile.
Walter Reuther

On his foreign policies – The power of positive brinking. *Adlai Stevenson*

Smooth is an inadequate word for Dulles.

His prevarications are so highly polished as to be aesthetically pleasurable.
I. F. Stone (1953)

Dwight D. Eisenhower
As an intellectual, he bestowed upon the games of golf and bridge all the enthusiasm and perseverance that he withheld from his books and ideas. *Emmet John Hughes*

Eisenhower is the only living unknown soldier. *Robert S. Kerr*
[*Groucho Marx added* – Even this is giving him all the best of it.]

Meeting him was not at all like an experience in the modern world. More like meeting George III at Brighton.
Harold Macmillan

Now I can abandon my earlier reserve and call him an idle, ignorant, ungenerous old fraud. *Kim Philby*

If I talk over people's heads, Ike must talk under their feet. *Adlai Stevenson*

The Republicans have a 'me too' candidate running on a 'yes but' platform, advised by a 'has-been' staff. *Adlai Stevenson*

The General has dedicated himself so many times, he must feel like the cornerstone of a public building. *Adlai Stevenson*

Here we have a top cardiac case whose chief interest is getting away from his job as often as possible for golf and bridge. *I. F. Stone*

The trouble with Eisenhower is he's just a coward. He hasn't got any backbone at all.
Harry S. Truman

Geraldine Ferraro
I can't say it but it rhymes with rich.
Barbara Bush (1984)
[*There followed an apology from Mrs Bush – claiming she had meant 'witch'*].

Millard Fillmore
At a time when we needed a strong man, what we got was a man who swayed with the slightest breeze. *Harry S. Truman*

A vain and handsome mediocrity.
Glyndon G. van Deusen

Gerald Ford
Gerald Ford was unknown throughout America. Now he's unknown throughout the world. *Anon*

He's alive but unconscious, just like Gerald Ford. *'Airplane' (1980)*

Nixon impeached himself. He gave us Ford as his revenge. *Bella Abzug*

He looks like the guy in the science fiction movie who is first to see 'The Creature'.
David Frye

In the Bob Hope Golf Classic, the participation of President Gerald Ford was more than enough to remind you that the nuclear button was at one stage at the disposal of a man who might have either pressed it by mistake or else pressed it deliberately in order to obtain room service.
Clive James (1980)

Gerry Ford is so dumb that he can't fart and chew gum at the same time.
Lyndon B. Johnson

Gerry Ford is a nice guy, but he played too much football with his helmet off.
Lyndon B. Johnson

I've never met him, but I used to spend time in Ohio, and they turn out Gerry Fords by the bale. *Alice Roosevelt-Longworth*

If Ford can get away with this list of issues and get elected on it, then I'm going to call the dictator of Uganda, Mr Amin, and tell him to start giving speeches on airport safety.
Walter Mondale

It troubles me that he played center on the football team. That means he can only consider options for the twenty yards in either direction and that he has spent a good deal of his life looking at the world down through his legs.
Martin Peretz – 'New Republic'

Gerald Ford is the first President of the United States to be elected by a majority of one – and nobody demanded a recount.
Laurence J. Peter

Mediocre is a word in Grand Rapids often used to describe him, as though that would be the best kind of official to have. *Peter Rand*

He looks and talks like he just fell off Edgar Bergen's lap. *David Steinberg (1975)*

Benjamin Franklin
A crafty and lecherous old hypocrite whose very statue seems to gloat on the wenches as they walk the States House yard.
William Cobbett

Benjamin Franklin, incarnation of the peddling, tuppenny Yankee. *Jefferson Davis*

Prudence is a wooden Juggernaut, before whom Benjamin Franklin walks with the portly air of a high priest. *Robert L. Stevenson*

He is our wise prophet of chicanery, the great buffoon, the face on the penny stamp.
William C. Williams – 'In the American Grain'

James Garfield
Every President who dies in office, whether from bacteria or bullets, is regarded as a martyr to the public weal, at least to some degree. James A. Garfield, whose troubled six months were marred by office mongering, was probably helped, as far as reputation was concerned, by his assassination.
Thomas A. Bailey

He rushes into a fight with the horns of a bull and the skin of a rabbit. *Jeremiah Black*

Garfield has shown that he is not possessed of the backbone of an angle-worm.
Ulysses S. Grant

John N. Garner
He is a labour-baiting, poker-playing, whiskey-drinking, evil old man. *John L. Lewis*

General James Gavin
General James Gavin has announced that he is ready to move towards the presidency. If he had some ham, he could make a ham

sandwich, if he had some bread.

William F. Buckley Jr –
'National Review' (1967)

Barry Goldwater

It was hard to listen to Goldwater and realise that a man could be half Jewish and yet sometimes appear twice as dense as the normal gentile. *I. F. Stone (1968)*

Ulysses Grant

The people are tired of a man who has not an idea above a horse or a cigar.

Joseph Brown (1871)

Early in 1869 there was a cry for 'no politicians' but the country did not mean 'no brains'. *William Claflin (1870)*

He does not march, nor quite walk, but pitches along as if the next step would bring him on his nose. *Richard H. Dana*

How is it that Grant, who was behind at Fort Henry, drunk at Donelson, surprised at Shiloh and driven back from Oxford, Miss., is still in command? *Murat Halstead (1863)*

He is a scientific Goth, resembling Alaric, destroying the country as he goes and delivering the people over to starvation. Nor does he bury his dead, but leaves them to rot on the battlefield. *John Tyler (1864)*

He combined great gifts with a great mediocrity. *Woodrow Wilson*

Horace Greeley

Poor Greeley, nincompoop without genius.
James Gordon Bennett Sr.

He was experimental, self-contradictory, explosive, irascible, and often downright wrongheaded. *William H. Hale*

Alexander Hamilton

The bastard brat of a Scottish pedlar.
John Adams

Warren G. Harding

Everybody's second choice. *Anon*

Few deaths are unmingled tragedies.

Harding's was not, he died in time.
Samuel Hopkins Adams

Harding was not a bad man. He was just a slob. *Alice Roosevelt-Longworth*

His speeches leave the impression of an army of pompous phrases moving over the landscape in search of an idea. Sometimes these meandering words would actually capture a struggling thought and bear it in triumphantly a prisoner in their midst until it died of servitude and overwork.

William McAdoo

He writes the worst English that I have ever encountered. It reminds me of a string of wet sponges; it reminds me of tattered washing on the line; it reminds me of stale bean soup, of college yells, of dogs barking through endless nights. It is so bad that a sort of grandeur creeps into it. It drags itself out of the dark abysm of pish and crawls insanely up the topmost pinnacle of the posh. It is rumble and bumble, It is flap and doodle. It is balder and dash.

H. L. Mencken –
'Baltimore Evening Sun' (1928)

A tin horn politician with the manner of a rural corn doctor and the mien of a ham actor. *H. L. Mencken (1920)*

If ever there was he-harlot, it was this same Warren G. Harding. *William Allen White*

He has a bungalow mind. *Woodrow Wilson*

W. Averell Harriman

Averell Harriman who can accomplish less in more time than anybody in America.

William F. Buckley Jr –
'On the Right' (1965)

Benjamin Harrison

He is a cold-blooded, narrow-minded, prejudiced, obstinate, timid old psalm-singing Indianapolis politician.

Theodore Roosevelt

He is as tickled with the Presidency as is a young woman with a new bonnet.

Martin van Buren

Gary Hart

Hart is Kennedy typed on the eighth carbon.
Lance Morrow (1987)

Q. What do Gary Hart and the Boston Celtics have in common?
A. If they had played at home, they would have won. *'Playboy' (1988)*

Gary Hart is just Jerry Brown without the fruit flies. *Robert Strauss*

Rutherford Hayes

His Fraudulency. *Anon newspaper headline*

He is a third rate nonentity, whose only recommendation is that he is obnoxious to no one. *Henry Adams*

Patrick Henry

All tongue, without either head or heart.
Thomas Jefferson

Herbert Hoover

Hoover isn't a stuffed shirt. But at times he can give the most convincing impersonation of a stuffed shirt you ever saw. *Anon*

If you put a rose in Hoover's hand it would melt. *Gutzon Borglum*

A private meeting with Hoover is like sitting in a bath of ink. *Henry Stimson*

Such a little man could not have made so big a depression. *Norman Thomas (1960)*

Harry Hopkins

Mr Hopkins is a bull-headed man whose high place in the New Deal was won by his ability to waste more money in quicker time on more absurd undertakings than any other mischievous wit in Washington could think of. *'Chicago Tribune'*

He was generally regarded as a sinister figure, a backstairs intriguer, an Iowan combination of Machiavelli, Svengali and Rasputin.
Robert E. Sherwood

Charles Evans Hughes

A businessman's candidate, hovering around the status quo like a sick kitten around a hot brink. *William Allen White (1916)*

Hubert H. Humphrey

He talks so fast that listening to him is like trying to read *Playboy* magazine with your wife turning the pages. *Barry Goldwater*

One Democratic automobile, the Hubert, designed as the plain people's car, known as the 'Folks Wagon', has been withdrawn from the race, which is a pity, for it had acceleration. From a standing start, it could roar up to 300 words a minute in five seconds. *Kenneth Keating*

Vice-president Humphrey has no function in any game his government plays, except to lead the cheers. *Murray Kempton (1966)*

A treacherous, gutless old ward-heeler who should be put in a bottle and sent out with the Japanese current.
Hunter S. Thompson – 'Fear and Loathing on the Campaign Trail'

Harold L. Ickes

He was no better than the common cold and he wanted to be President the worst way.
Harry S. Truman

He refused to flex with the times.
T. H. Watkins

Thomas Jefferson

Jeffersonian Democracy simply meant the possession of the federal government by the agrarian masses led by an aristocracy of slave-owning planters. *Charles A. Beard*

A sterile worshipper of the people.
John B. McCaster

The moonshine philosopher of Monticello.
Timothy Pickering

Andrew Johnson

An insolent drunken brute, in comparison with whom Caligula's horse was respectable.
'New York World' (1865)

His mind had one compartment for right and one for wrong but no middle chamber where the two could commingle. *Howard K. Beale*

If Andy Johnson was a snake, he would hide in the grass and bite the heels of rich men's children. *Isham G. Harris*

He reduced the Presidency to the level of a grog house. *John Sherman*

He was a self-made man, the embodiment of the American success story, though hardly one of its more attractive products. *Kenneth M. Stampp*

You will remember that in Egypt He sent frogs, locusts, murrain, lice, and finally demanded the first-born of everyone of the oppressors. Almost all of these have been taken from us. We have been oppressed with taxes and debts, and He has sent us worse than lice, and afflicted us with Andrew Johnson. *Thaddeus Stevens (1866)*

Hiram Johnson
Q. Why is Hiram Johnson still alive?
A. Because he is too mean to die! *Saying*

Hiram Johnson always despised the two things he never had – money and a sound mind. *Saying*

Lyndon B. Johnson
He did not suffer from a poor education, he suffered from the belief that he had a poor education. *George Ball*

After two weeks in office – The editors of *National Review* regretfully announce that their patience with President Lyndon B. Johnson is exhausted. *William F. Buckley Jr – 'National Review' (1963)*

He is a man of his most recent word. *William F. Buckley Jr – 'National Review' (1965)*

We have now achieved a President of the United States who cannot deliver a speech except in an army camp. *William F. Buckley Jr – 'On the Right' (1968)*

On his federal aid programme – It's political Daddyism and it's as old as demagogues and despotism. *Barry Goldwater (1964)*

We have many people that have thin skins, Lyndon Johnson is one. His skin is a millionth of an inch thick. *Barry Goldwater*

He fiddled while Rome burned and faddled while men died. *Barry Goldwater*

Hyperbole was to Lyndon Johnson what oxygen is to life. *Bill Moyers (1969)*

A damn independent boy; independent as a hog on ice. *Sam Rayburn*

Lyndon Johnson's strategy is too slick to talk about and so subtle that only a few fellow con men appreciate it. *I. F. Stone*

Robert Johnson
Like a Good American Robert Johnson lived for the moment and died for the past. *Greil Marcus – 'Mystery Train' (1977)*

Edward Kennedy
Every country should have at least one King Farouk. *Gore Vidal (1981)*

John F. Kennedy
Kennedy after all has lots of glamour – Gregory Peck with an atom bomb in his holster. *William F. Buckley Jr – 'National Review' (1963)*

His speaking style is pseudo-Roman: 'Ask' not what your country can do for you . . .' Why not say, 'Don't ask . . .'? 'Ask not . . .' is the style of a man playing the role of being President, not of a man being President. *Herb Gold – 'New York Post' (1962)*

The enviably attractive nephew who sings an Irish ballad for the company and then winsomely disappears before the table-clearing and dishwashing begin. *Lyndon B. Johnson*

There is a lot of he-coon ingrained in the hide of the new President. He strikes me as practically cold all the way, with a hard blue eye on Valhalla. *Robert Ruark – 'New York World Telegram and Sun' (1960)*

It is said the President is willing to laugh at himself. That is fine. But when is he going to extend that privilege to us? *Mort Sahl*

Robert Kennedy

Bobby Kennedy and Nelson Rockefeller are having a row, ostensibly over the plight of New York's mentally retarded, a loose definition of which would include everyone in New York who voted for Kennedy or Rockefeller. *William F. Buckley Jr – 'National Review Bulletin' (1966)*

Bobby, Bobby, everywhere. It drives a man to drink. *William F. Buckley Jr – 'On the Right' (1966)*

That was the Kennedy way – you bit off more than you could chew and then you chewed it. *Gerald Gardner*

The highest-ranking withdrawn adolescent since Alexander Hamilton in 1794. *Murray Kempton – 'Newsweek' (1968)*

Henry Kissinger

On his joint nomination, with Le Duc Tho, for the Nobel Peace Prize – Like nominating a whore as honorary chairman of the PTA. *Anon South Vietnamese Minister*

An eel icier than ice. *Oriana Fallaci*

When Kissinger can get the Nobel Peace Prize, what is there left for satire? *Tom Lehrer*

'*The White House Years*' – Dr Henry Kissinger has constructed a diplomacy for a Hobbesian world. When he exercised that diplomacy he helped create the kind of world that would justify it. *'New Republic' (1979)*

Henry Kissinger is the cunning architect of America's planned destruction. *Meldrim Thomson*

Ed Koch

I think he is an entertainer. I would prefer him to be a performer. *Carol Bellamy (1985)*

'*Mayor*' – It's the greatest love story since *Tristan and Isolde*, and Ed Koch plays both parts. *Daniel Wolf – 'The Daily Telegraph' (1984)*

Fiorello La Guardia

If it's LaGuardia or bust, I prefer bust. *Joseph M. Price*

Abraham Lincoln

His mind works in the right directions but seldom works clearly and cleanly. His bread is of unbolted flour, and much straw, too, mixes in the bran, and sometimes gravel stones. *Henry Ward Beecher*

This man's appearance, his pedigree, his coarse low jokes and anecdotes, his vulgar similes and his frivolity, are a disgrace to the seat he holds. *John Wilkes Booth*

'*The Gettysburg Address*' – We did not conceive it possible that even Mr Lincoln would produce a paper so slipshod, so loose-jointed, so puerile, not alone in literary construction, but in its ideals, its sentiments, its grasp. He has outdone himself. He has literally come out of the little end of his own horn. By the side of it, mediocrity is superb. *'The Chicago Times' (1863)*

An elegant roué and malignant self-seeker. *R. W. Emerson*

Filthy story-teller, Despot, Liar, Thief, Braggart, Buffoon, Usurper, Monster, Ignoramus, Old Scoundrel, Perjurer, Robber, Swindler, Tyrant, Field-Butcher, Land-Pirate. *'Harper's Weekly'*

God damn your god damned old hellfired god damned soul to hell god damn you and godamn your godamn family's god damned hellfired god damned soul to hell and god damnation god damn them and god damn your god damn friends to hell. *Pete Muggins (1860)*

He is a huckster in politics; a first-rate second-rate man. *Wendell Phillips (1862)*

He is a Barbarian, Scythian, Yahoo, a gorilla in respect of outward polish, but a most sensible, straightforward old codger. *George T. Strong*

John Lindsay

A modern Justine could, in New York City, wake up in the morning in a room she shares with her unemployed husband and two children, crowd into a subway in which she is hardly able to breathe, disembark at Grand

Central and take a crosstown bus which takes twenty minutes to go the ten blocks to her textile loft, work a full day and receive her paycheck from which a sizeable deduction is withdrawn in taxes and union fees, return via the same ordeal, prepare supper for her family and tune up the radio full blast to shield the children from gamy denunciations her next-door neighbour is hurling at her husband, walk a few blocks past hideous buildings to the neighbourhood park to breathe a little fresh air, and fall into a coughing fit as the sulphur dioxide excites her latent asthma, go home, and on the way, lose her handbag to a purse-snatcher, sit down to oversee her son's homework only to trip over the fact that he doesn't really know the alphabet even though he had his fourteenth birthday yesterday, which he spent in the company of a well-known pusher. She hauls off and smacks him, but he dodges and she bangs her head against the table. The ambulance is slow in coming and at the hospital there is no doctor in attendance. An intern finally materialises and sticks her with a shot of morphine, and she dozes off to sleep. And dreams of John Lindsay? *William F. Buckley Jr – 'The Unmaking of a Mayor' (1966)*

Henry Cabot Lodge

Lodge had a hard enough time keeping his temper without stopping to consult his conscience. *Thomas A. Bailey*

A degenerate son of Harvard. *A. Lawrence Lowell*

He was as cool as an undertaker at a hanging. *H. L. Mencken (1920)*

He considers himself so far superior to the ordinary run of people that the mere addition of another enemy to his long string means nothing to him one way or another. *'Saturday Evening Post' (1910)*

Huey Long

The trouble with Senator Long is that he is suffering from halitosis of the intellect. That's presuming Emperor Long has an intellect. *Harold Ickes*

The Prince of Piffle. *'New Orleans Daily'*

He was a liar, and he was nothing but a damn demagogue. It didn't surprise me when they shot him. *Harry S. Truman*

Eugene McCarthy

He is meticulously liberal – never ever has he erred in the direction of common sense, when the alternative was vote liberal. *William F. Buckley Jr – 'On the Right' (1967)*

Joseph McCarthy

The only major politician in the country who can be labelled 'liar' without fear of libel. *Joseph and Stewart Alsop (1953)*

Joe McCarthy bought communism in much the same way as other people purchase a new automobile. *Roy Cohn (1950)*

This Typhoid Mary of conformity. *Richard Rovere*

He was nothing but a damn coward. *Harry S. Truman*

William McKinley

Why, if a man were to call my dog McKinley, and the brute failed to resent to the death the damning insult, I'd drown it. *William Cowper Brann*

McKinley shows all the backbone of a chocolate eclair. *Theodore Roosevelt*

Lestor Maddox

Maddox has the face of a three month old infant who is mean and bald and wears eye-glasses. *Norman Mailer (1968)*

James Madison

Jemmy Madison – oh poor Jemmy, he is but a withered little applejohn. *Washington Irving*

I do not like his looks any better than I like his Administration. *Daniel Webster*

Walter Mondale

His [*presidential*] campaign kickoff was so dismal that it needed a plastic surgeon instead of a press agent to put a face on it. *Jane Mayer – 'Wall Street Journal' (1984)*

Karl Mundt
The Leaning Tower of Putty.   *Saying*

Edward Muskie
Ed Muskie talked like a farmer with terminal
cancer trying to borrow on next year's crop.
*Hunter S. Thompson – 'Fear and Loathing on
the Campaign Trail' (1972)*

Richard M. Nixon
Fatty ham fried in grease.   *Anon*

Dick Nixon – before he dicks you.
Bumper sticker (1973)

Where is Lee Harvey Oswald now that his
country needs him.   *Graffiti*

Dick is a four letter word.
Democratic campaign slogan

He told us he was going to take crime out of
the streets. He did. He took it into the damn
White House.   *Ralph Abernathy*

A Main Street Machiavelli.   *Patrick Anderson*

Nixon is a purposeless man, but I have great
faith in his cowardice.
Jimmy Breslin

Nixon is a man that had the morals of a
private detective.
William S. Burroughs (1980)

A naive, inept, maladjusted Throttlebottom.
Emmanuel Cellar

Other administrations have had a love-hate
relationship with the press. The Nixon
administration has a hate-hate relationship.
John Chancellor

I wouldn't trust Nixon from here to that
phone. *Barry Goldwater – 'Newsweek' (1986)*

Avoid all needle drugs – the only dope worth
shooting is Richard Nixon.
Abbie Hoffman (1971)

Sir Richard – the Chicken-hearted.
Hubert H. Humphrey

On a Nixon speech – I may not know much,

but I know chicken-shit from chicken salad.
Lyndon B. Johnson

Last Thursday Mr Nixon dismissed me as
'another Truman'. I regard this as a
compliment. I consider him another Dewey.
J. F. Kennedy

Certainly he is not of the generation that
regards honesty as the best policy. However,
he does regard it as a policy.
Walter Lippman (1980)

Richard Nixon was like a kamikaze pilot who
kept apologising for the attack.
May McGrory (1962)

As President Nixon says, Presidents can do
almost anything and President Nixon has
done many things that nobody would have
thought of doing.   *Golda Meir*

Our founders did not oust George III in
order for us to crown Richard I.
Ralph Nader (1975)

Would you buy a second-hand car from this
man?   *Mort Sahl*

Richard Nixon means never having to say
you're sorry.   *Wilfrid Sheed – 'GQ' (1984)*

He forever perplexes and annoys. Every time
you think he is about to show the
statesmanship for which his intelligence and
experience have equipped him, he throws a
spitball.   *Ronald Steel (1985)*

He is the kind of politician who would cut
down a redwood tree, then mount the stump
for a conservation speech.   *Adlai Stevenson*

Nixonland is a land of slander and scare, of
lay innuendo, of a poison pen and the
anonymous telephone call, and hustling,
pushing and shoving – the land of smash and
grab and anything to win.   *Adlai Stevenson*

For years I've regarded his very existence as
a monument to all the rancid genes and
broken chromosomes that corrupt the
possibilities of the American Dream; he was a
foul caricature of himself, a man with no

soul, no inner convictions, with the integrity of a hyena and the style of a poison toad.

Hunter S. Thompson –
'The Great Shark Hunt' (1979)

Nixon is a shifty-eyed, goddamn lying, son-of-a-bitch, and people knew it. He's one of the few in the history of the country to run for high office talking out of both sides of his mouth at the same time – and lying out of both sides. *Harry S. Truman (1975)*

Thomas Paine

What a poor ignorant, malicious, short-sighted, crapulous mass, is Thomas Paine's *Common Sense.* *John Adams (1819)*

A mouse nibbling at the wing of an archangel. *Robert Hall*

Franklin Pierce

Many persons have difficulty remembering what President Franklin Pierce is best remembered for, and he is therefore probably best forgotten. *Richard Armour*

A man who cannot be befriended; whose miserable administration admits but of one excuse, imbecility. Pierce was either the worst, or he was the weakest, of all our Presidents. *Ralph Waldo Emerson*

Whoever may be elected, we cannot get a poorer cuss than now disgraces the Presidential Chair. *B. B. French*

James K. Polk

A victim of the use of water as a beverage.
Sam Houston

A more ridiculous, contemptible and forlorn candidate, was never put forth by any party. Mr Polk is a sort of fourth rate or rather fortieth rate lawyer and small politician in Tennessee. *'New York Herald'*

Adam Clayton Powell Jr

The relationship between corruption and Adam Clayton Powell Jr would appear to be something like the relationship between typhoid and Typhoid Mary.

William F. Buckley Jr –
'National Review' (1960)

John Randolph of Roanoke

His face is livid, gaunt his white body, his breath is green with gall; his tongue drips with poison. *John Quincy Adams*

J. Danforth (Dan) Quayle

An empty suit that goes to funerals and plays golf. *H. Ross Perot (1992)*

Ronald Reagan

Q. What ever happened to Rosemary's Baby?
A. He's in the White House. *Graffiti*

Reagan's in the news again. He's at his ranch chopping wood – he's building the log cabin he was born in. *Johnny Carson*

Ronald Reagan couldn't be here tonight; he's posing for the cover of *Guns and Ammo.*
Johnny Carson

Reagan is slightly to the right of the Sheriff of Nottingham. *Johnny Carson*

You don't have to be smart to act – look at the outgoing President of the United States.
Cher – 'Playboy' (1988)

I'm glad that Reagan is President. Of course, I'm a professional comedian. *Will Durst*

I listen to Reagan and I want to throw up.
Henry Fonda (1981)

That youthful sparkle in his eye is caused by his contact lenses, which he keeps highly polished. *Sheila Graham – 'The Times' (1981)*

In the heat of a political lifetime, Reagan innocently squirrels away tidbits of misinformation and then, sometimes years later, casually drops them into his public discourse, like gumballs in a quiche.
Lucy Howard – 'Newsweek' (1985)

A true velvet fascist. *Shirley MacLaine*

I believe that Ronald Reagan can make this country what it once was – an arctic region covered with ice. *Steve Martin*

Q. What do you get if you cross James Dean with Ronald Reagan?

A. A rebel without a clue. *'Playboy' (1988)*

Q. How many Reagan cabinet ministers does it take to change a lightbulb?
A. None – they prefer to keep Ron in the dark! *'Playboy' (1988)*

Ronald Reagan is the first President to be accompanied by a Silly Statement Repair Team. *Mark Russell*

Reagan is proof that there is life after death.
Mort Sahl

Washington could not tell a lie; Nixon could not tell the truth; Reagan cannot tell the difference. *Mort Sahl*

A working man voting for Reagan is like a chicken voting for Colonel Sanders.
Paul Sarbanes

We've got the kind of President who thinks arms control means some kind of deodorant.
Pat Schroeder

A triumph of the embalmer's art. *Gore Vidal*

There's a lot to be said for being 'nouveau riche', and the Reagans mean to say it all.
Gore Vidal (1981)

On being appointed the first US Poet Laureate – I don't expect you'll hear me writing any poems to the greater glory of Ronald and Nancy Reagan. *Robert Penn Warren (1986)*

What's really worrying about Reagan is that he always seems to be waiting for someone to say 'Cut' and has no idea how they've decided the script should end.
Katherine Whitehorn – 'The Observer' (1983)

I think that Nancy does most of his talking; you'll notice that she never drinks water when Ronnie speaks. *Robin Williams (1982)*

Satire is alive and well and living in the White House. *Robin Williams (1985)*

Abraham Ribicoff
During the Democratic convention – F*** you, you Jew son of a bitch, you lousy mother

f***er go. *Richard J. Daley (1968)*

Nelson Rockefeller
Governor Rockefeller has long since developed the knack of transforming expedience into an act of transcendent principle. *William F. Buckley Jr – 'National Review' (1963)*

Franklin D. Roosevelt
The best newspaperman who has ever been President of the United States.
Heywood Broun

I'd rather be right than be Roosevelt.
Heywood Broun

A chameleon on plaid. *Herbert Hoover*

He would rather follow public opinion than lead it. *Harry Hopkins*

The man who started more creations than were ever begun since Genesis – and finished none. *Hugh Johnson (1937)*

I would not employ him, except for reasons of personal friendship, as a geek in a common carnival. *Murray Kempston*

Two-thirds mush and one-third Eleanor.
Alice Roosevelt-Longworth

If he became convinced tomorrow that coming out for cannibalism would get him the votes he sorely needs, he would begin fattening a missionary in the White House backyard come Wednesday. *H. L. Mencken*

He had every quality that morons esteem in their heroes. *H. L. Mencken*

If Roosevelt was as busy as Rabbit and as bouncy as Tigger, he was too often, I fear, as big a bluffer as Owl. *Clinton Rossiter*

Thomas Jefferson founded the Democratic Party; Franklin Roosevelt dumbfounded it.
Dewey Short

Theodore Roosevelt
One always thinks of him as a glorified bouncer engaged eternally in cleaning out

bar-rooms – and not too proud to gouge when the inspiration came to him, or to bite in the clinches. *H. L. Mencken*

If there's one thing for which I admire you, it's your original discovery of the Ten Commandments. *Thomas B. Reed*

My father always wanted to be the corpse at every funeral, the bride at every wedding and the baby at every christening.
Alice Roosevelt-Longworth

He hated all pretensions save his own pretensions. *H. L. Mencken*

His idea of getting hold of the right end of the stick is to snatch it from the hands of somebody who is using it effectively, and to hit him over the head with it. *G. B. Shaw*

Theodore Roosevelt thought with his hips.
Lincoln Steffin

Roosevelt bit me and I went mad.
William A. White

Richard Rush
Never was ability so much below mediocrity so well rewarded; no, not even when Caligula's horse was made a consul.
John Randolph

Charles Schurz
A political career consistent only in the frequency and agility of its changes.
James G. Blaine – 'Twenty Years of Congress'

An insatiate appetite for opposition.
Louis A. Coolidge

William Seward
A dirty abolitionist sneak. *Mary Todd Lincoln*

Alfred Smith
The plain fact is that Al, as a good New Yorker, is as provincial as a Kansas farmer. He is not only not interested in the great problems that heave and lather the country; he has never heard of them.
H. L Mencken (1927)

Edwin Stanton
The man's public character is a public

mistake. *Abraham Lincoln*

The most unmitigated scoundrel I ever knew, heard or read of; if Stanton had lived during Jesus' lifetime, Judas Iscariot would have remained a respected member of the fraternity of apostles. *George McLellan*

Alexander Stephens
I could swallow him whole and never know the difference. *Walter T. Colquitt*

Never have I seen so small a nubbin come out of so much husk. *Abraham Lincoln*

Adlai Stevenson
Unexceptional as a glass of decent Beaujolais.
'Newsweek' (1965)

Stevenson himself hasn't even backbone training, for he is a graduate of Dean Acheson's spineless school of diplomacy which cost the free world 600,000,000 former allies in the past seven years of Trumanism. *Richard M. Nixon (1952)*

The real trouble with Stevenson is that he's no better than a regular sissy.
Harry S. Truman

Adlai Stevenson was a man who could never make up his mind whether he had to go to the bathroom or not. *Harry S. Truman*

Charles Sumner
Sumner's mind had reached the calm of water which receives and reflects images without absorbing them; it contained nothing but itself. *Henry Adams*

A foul-mouthed poltroon, who when caned for cowardly vituperation falls to the floor in an inanimate lump of incarnate cowardice.
'Richmond Examiner' (1856)

The great orb of the State Department who rises periodically in his effulgence and sends his rays down the steep places here to cast a good many dollars into the sea.
Roscoe Conkling

A man of huge and distempered vanity.
William Gladstone

He works adjectives so hard that if they ever catch him alone, they will murder him.

E. L. Godkin

He was essentially a free-lance, an independent in politics, the first great Mugwump of Massachusetts.

Archibald H. Grimke

Robert A. Taft

He has a positive genius for being wrong. He is an authentic living representative of the old Bourbons of whom it was said that they 'learned nothing, forgot nothing'.

Marvin Harrison – 'Robert A. Taft: Our Illustrious Dunderhead'

The Dagwood Bumstead of American Politics. *'Time' (1940)*

William Taft

It's very difficult for me to understand how a man who is so good as Chief Justice could have been so bad as President. *Louis Brandeis*

The amiable, good-natured, subthyroid Taft had the misfortune to follow the crusading, club-brandishing, hyperthyroid Roosevelt, much as a dim star follows a blazing comet. The Nation felt let down.

Thomas A. Bailey – 'Presidential Greatness'

The Great Postponer. *William J. Bryan*

Zachary Taylor

Old Rough-and-Ready! *Nickname*

Indifferent specimen of the Lord of Creation. He is a short, thick-set man looking neither like the President of a great nation nor a military hero tho' he bears both honours.

Margaret Gardiner

A most simple-minded old man . . . He is a remarkable man in some respects; and it is remarkable that such a man should be President of the United States. *Horace Mann*

Quite ignorant for his rank, and quite bigoted in his ignorance. *Winfield Scott – 'Memoirs'*

Samuel Tilden

Mr Tilden is incapable of doing the simplest thing without a mask.

'New York Herald' (1880)

David C. Treen

He's so slow that he takes an hour and a half to watch *Sixty Minutes*.

Edwin W. Edwards (1983)

Harry S. Truman

The two-bit President of a five-star general.

Anon

Among President Truman's many weaknesses was his utter inability to discriminate between history and histrionics.

Anon

To err is Truman. *Republican slogan*

Even a Chinaman could beat Truman.

Republican slogan (1948)

Truman seemed to stand for nothing more spectacular than honesty in war contracting, which was like standing for virtue in Hollywood or adequate rainfall in the Middle West. *George E. Allen – 'Presidents Who Have Known Me'*

He is a man totally unfitted for the position. His principles are elastic, and he is careless with the truth. He has no special knowledge of any subject, and he is a malignant, scheming sort of an individual.

John L. Lewis (1948)

Mr Truman is not performing, and gives no evidence of his ability to perform, the function of Commander-in-Chief. At the very centre of the Truman Administration there is a vacuum of responsibility and authority. *Walter Lippman*

It defies all commonsense to send that roughneck ward politician back to the White House. *Robert A. Taft (1948)*

Harry Truman proves the old adage that any man can become President of the United States. *Norman Thomas*

John Tyler

The Executive Ass. *Anon*

There was nothing forceable or striking in his speech; no bright thoughts, no well-turned expressions; nothing that left an impression on the mind from its strength and beauty – nothing that marked a great man.

'Daily Pittsburgher' (1840)

Martin Van Buren

A servile dough-face . . . Madison had none of his obsequiousness, his sycophancy, his profound dissimulation and duplicity. In the last of these he much more resembles Jefferson though with very little of his genius. The most disgusting part of his character, his fawning servility, belonged neither to Jefferson nor to Madison.

John Quincy Adams

He is not of the race of the lion or tiger; he belongs to a lower order: the fox.

John C. Calhoun

He rowed to his object with muffled oars.

John Randolph

Gore Vidal

Mr Gore Vidal, the playwright and quipster who lost a Congressional race a few years ago but continues to seek out opportunities to advertise his ignorance of contemporary affairs.

William F. Buckley Jr – 'On the Right' (1964)

George Wallace

I don't think you'll have to worry that this mental midget, this hillbilly Hitler from Alabama, is anywhere near becoming the nominee of the Democratic Party.

Julian Bond

Henry Wallace

Much of what Mr Wallace calls his global thinking is, no matter how you slice it, still Globaloney.

Clare Booth Luce (1943)

A fellow who wanted to be a great man, but didn't know how to go about it.

Harry S. Truman

George Washington

That Washington was not a scholar is certain. That he is too illiterate, unlearned, unread for his station and reputation is equally beyond dispute.

John Adams (1782)

If ever a nation was debauched by a man, the American nation has been debauched by Washington. If ever a nation was deceived by a man, the American nation has been deceived by Washington.

Benjamin F. Bache – 'Aurora'

The man who is the source of all the misfortunes of our country.

William Duane

That dark designing sordid ambitious vain proud arrogant and vindictive knave.

Charles Lee

As to you, sir, treacherous in private friendship and a hypocrite in public life, the world will be puzzled to decide whether you are an apostate or an impostor, whether you have abandoned good principles, or whether you ever had any.

Thomas Paine (1796)

Daniel Webster

The gigantic intellect, the envious temper, the ravenous ambition, and the rotten heart of Daniel Webster.

John Quincy Adams

The word honour in the mouth of Mr Webster is like the word love in the mouth of a whore.

Ralph Waldo Emerson

Daniel Webster struck me much like a steam engine in trousers.

Sydney Smith

Gideon Welles

Retire, O Gideon, to an onion farm
Ply any trade that's innocent and slow
Do anything, where you can do no harm
Go anywhere you fancy – only go.

Anon

Woodrow Wilson

President Wilson indeed came to office with a noble message of hope, but unhappily in the sequel, hope proved to be his main equipment.

Lord Birkenhead

A sleepy man from a sleepy college [*Princeton*] in a sleepy little town.

Nicholas M. Butler

The spacious philanthropy which he exhaled upon Europe stopped quite sharply at the coasts of his own country.
Sir Winston Churchill

Mr Wilson bores me with his 'Fourteen Points'; why God Almighty has only ten.
Georges Clemenceau

Mr Wilson's mind, as has been the custom, will be closed all day Sunday.
George S. Kaufman

The air currents of the world never ventilated his mind.
Walter H. Page

A Byzantine logothete.
Theodore Roosevelt

He would not recognise a generous impulse if he met it on the street.
William H. Taft

Mr Wilson stands not only for the uncrossed 't' but the uncrossed 'I'.
'Wall Street Journal'

I am suspicious of a man who has a handshake like a ten-cent pickled mackerel in brown paper.
William A. White

OTHER

Samuel Gompers – *Union leader*
Sam was very short and chunky with a big head that was bald in patches, resembling a child with ringworm. He had small snapping eyes, a hard cruel mouth, wide with thin drooping lips, heavy jaws, a personality vain, conceited, petulant and vindictive.
William D. Haywood

Gompers says that strikes are a blessing to society. Must be one of those blessings in disguise.
'Nashville Southern Lumberman'

On his hair – Like a piece of worn-out buffalo robe which has lain in the garret and been chewed by the moths since 1890, and then been thrown out in the rain and laid in the gutter for a year or two, and then dragged by a puppy dog to cut his teeth on.
Mark Sullivan

Arthur Henderson – *Labour leader*
We will support Henderson as a rope

supports a man who is hanged.
V. I. Lenin

Jimmy Hoffa – *Union leader*
During his trial – If Jimmy Hoffa actually sat in Memphis for nine whole weeks without corrupting somebody, it would probably be for the first time since he was six.
William F. Buckley Jr –
'National Review' (1963)

Jimmy Hoffa's most valuable contribution to the American labour movement came at the moment he stopped breathing on July 30, 1975.
Dan E. Moldea (1978)

Walter Reuther – *Union leader*
It's hard to guess where Walter's ideas come from. If you have an idea that is worth anything, you might as well give it to him because if you don't, he'll steal it from you.
Anon

Mr Reuther may deplore General Motors' hold on the automobile industry, as rising on 60 per cent. He has never been heard to deplore his own control over the automobile industry, which rises on 100 per cent.
William F. Buckley Jr –
'On the Right' (1966)

You are like a nightingale. It closes its eyes when it sings and sees nothing and hears nobody except itself.
Nikita Khruschev

John W. Dean – *Counsel to President Nixon*
I think in all fairness to the man, you'd have to put him right up there with Judas Iscariot.
G. Gordon Liddy

J. Edgar Hoover – *Head of the FBI*
A mythical person first thought up by the *Reader's Digest*.
Art Buchwald

Harry Hopkins – *Adviser to F. D. Roosevelt*
A bull-headed man whose high place in the 'New Deal' was won by his ability to waste more money in quicker time on more absurd undertakings than any other mischievous twit in Washington could think of.
'Chicago Tribune'

He was generally regarded as a sinister figure,

a backstairs intriguer, an Iowan combination of Machiavelli, Svengali and Rasputin.
Robert E. Sherwood

George Meany – *Union leader*
A Cardinal Richelieu with a plumber's face.
Virgil Day (1976)

I don't think he'd know a trade unionist if he tripped over one. *Frank Fitzsimmons*

Joseph V. Reed –
United Nations' Under Secretary
He is a fourteen-carat nitwit. *Thomas Eagleton*

He isn't a diplomat, he's a dope. *Ed Koch*

Rosemary Woods –
Richard Nixon's Secretary
If Rosemary Woods had been Moses' secretary, there would only have been eight commandments. *Art Buchwald (1974)*

PRESIDENTIAL RELATIONS

Barbara Bush – *Wife of George Bush*
An extremely protective, secretive, old-style WASP who has been able project herself as an earth mother with no real proof.
Andrew Sullivan – 'New Republic'

Amy Carter – *Daughter of Jimmy Carter*
The former 'First Brat' has become a Yippie of yuppiedom.
Don Lessem – 'Boston Globe' (1987)

Billy Carter – *Brother of Jimmy Carter*
Jimmy Carter needs Billy like Van Gogh needs stereo. *Johnny Carson (1977)*

Hillary Clinton – *Wife of Bill Clinton*
The yuppie wife from hell. *Anon (1991)*

Jackie Kennedy (Onassis)
The one thing I do not want to be called is the First Lady. It sounds like a saddle horse.

Celebrities in general are chosen, like the Calendar of Saints, to meet certain needs: thus, Frank Sinatra is the patron celebrity of comebacks, Liza Minnelli of daughters, Jackie Onassis of curious marriages
Wilfrid Sheed (1975)

Tricia Nixon – *Daughter of Richard Nixon*
I didn't much like it when Mr Nixon and his wife started matching me up with their eldest daughter. Which one is she, Tricia, isn't that right? I found her artificial and plastic.
Prince Charles

Nancy Reagan – *Wife of Ronald Reagan*
The First Toothpick. *Julie Burchill*

Nancy Reagan has agreed to be the world's first artificial heart donor. *Andrea C. Michaels*

Eleanor Roosevelt –
Wife of Franklin D. Roosevelt
Following Mrs Roosevelt in search of irrationality was like following a burning fuse in search of an explosion, one never had to wait long. *William F. Buckley Jr –*
'Up From Liberalism' (1968)

Eleanor is a Trojan mare.
Alice Roosevelt-Longworth

No woman has ever so comforted the distressed – or so distressed the comfortable.
Clare Booth Luce

Alice Roosevelt-Longworth – *Daughter of Theodore Roosevelt*
Princess Malice. *Nickname*

THE REST OF THE WORLD

GENERAL

Foreign Aid is taxing poor people in rich countries for the benefit of rich people in poor countries. *Bernard Rosenberg*

POLITICAL BODIES

Communism
A communist is one who hath yearnings
For equal share of unequal earnings.
Ebenezer Elliott (1840)

The European Economic Community
The last time Britain went into Europe with any degree of success was on 6 June 1944.
'The Daily Express'

It is a most profligate, wasteful and useless

organization.   *Teddy Taylor*

I do not see the EEC as a great love affair. It
is more like nine middle-aged couples with
failing marriages meeting at a Brussels hotel
for a group grope.   *Kenneth Tynan (1975)*

European Community institutions have
produced European beets, butter, cheese,
wine, veal and even pigs. But they have not
produced Europeans.
                Louise Weiss – 'The Observer' (1980)

Geneva Convention
A set of rules that make it illegal to hit below
the toes.   *Leo Rosten*

North Atlantic Treaty Organisation (NATO)
I bear solemn witness to the fact that NATO
heads of state and of government meet only
to go through the tedious motions of reading
speeches, drafted by others, with the
principal activity of not rocking the boat.
                              Pierre Trudeau

The United Nations
Called the UN, because it is UNable to
UNderstand anything.   *Anon*

The Security Council can't really bite, but if
you're a small country they can gum you to
death.   *Anon Israeli diplomat*

A forum in which nations meet in order
handily to exchange insults, bribes,
intimidations, and cynicisms.
                       *William F. Buckley Jr –
                       'National Review' (1957)*

If the UN is a country unto itself, then the
commodity it exports most is words.
         Edna B. Fein – 'New York Times' (1985)

This organisation is created to prevent you
from going to hell. It isn't created to take you
to heaven.   *Henry Cabot Lodge Jr*

The UN cannot do anything, and never
could; it is not an animate entity or agent. It
is a place, a stage, a forum and a shrine . . . a
place to which powerful people can repair
when they are fearful about the course on

which their own rhetoric seems to be
propelling them.
         Conor Cruise O'Brien – 'New Republic' (1985)

The main thing that endears the UN to
member governments, and so enables it to
survive, is its proven capacity to fail, and to
be seen to fail.   *Conor Cruise O'Brien – Ibid.*

You can safely appeal to the UN in the
comfortable certainty that it will let you
down.   *Conor Cruise O'Brien – Ibid.*

On the third Tuesday of every September,
floodgates are opened in a tall building on the
East River in New York and a Niagara of
rhetoric gushes forth for three months.
            Anthony Parsons – 'The Times' (1979)

It is the very capital and new Jerusalem of
humbug.   *Enoch Powell – 'Listener' (1981)*

A declaration of love without the promise of
marriage.   *Alfred von Tirpitz*

The UN is a temple to Parkinson's Law –
where inefficiency and extravagance worship
at its shrines and hypocrisy at its altars.
                         R. J. Turnbull (1970)

The United Nations building is just another
World Tirade Centre.   *Frank Tyger*

New York would rather be the permanent
home of the World Series than capital of the
League of Nations.   *'Vancouver Province'*

COUNTRIES AND POLITICAL
FIGURES

AFRICA

Marcus Garvey –
Self-proclaimed 'President of Africa'
It's a pity the cannibals do not get hold of
this man.   *Anon (1924)*

Boastful, egotistic, tyrannical, intolerant,
cunning, shifty, smooth and suave,
avaricious; as adroit as a fencer in changing
front, as adept as a cuttlefish in beclouding
an issue he cannot meet, prolix to the nth
degree in devising new schemes to gain the

money of poor ignorant Negroes; gifted at self-advertisement, without shame in self laudation, promising ever, but never fulfilling, without regard for veracity, a lover of pomp and tawdry finery and garish display, a bully with his own folk but servile in the presence of the Man, a sheer opportunist and a demagogic charlatan.
Robert W. Gagnall (1923)

Cecil Rhodes – *Prime Minister of the Cape*
Too big to get through the gates of Hell.
Olive Schreiner

I admire him, I frankly confess it; and when his time comes I shall buy a piece of the rope for a keepsake. *Mark Twain*

ARGENTINA

Juan Peron – *President*
I have never met a man who was both intelligent and a Peronist. *Jorge Luis Borges*

AUSTRALIA

Australia is governed by a hierarchy of hicks.
H. B. Turner (1970)

Sir Henry Bolte – *Premier of Victoria*
I doubt even the Premier's ability to handle the petty cash box at a hot-dog stall at the local Sunday school picnic.
George Moss (1969)

Malcolm Fraser – *Prime Minister*
He does the work of two men – Laurel and Hardy. *Graffiti*

He could be described as a cutlery man – he was born with a silver spoon in his mouth and he uses it to stab his colleagues in the back. *Bob Hawke (1975)*

Sir William Lyne
The rogue elephant of Australian politics.
E. H. Collis (1948)

His politics were a chaos and his career contemptible. *Alfred Deakin (1944)*

Sir George Reid
A sophist-statesman, ever-grey,

Whose brow no cares corrode;
He loves the shady, crooked way,
And hates the plain, straight road.
Victor Daley (1963)

Billy Sneddon
Billy Sneddon couldn't go two rounds with a revolving door. *Vince Gair (1974)*

Wilson Tuckey
I heard his library burned down and that both books were destroyed – and one of them hadn't even been coloured in yet.
John Dawkins

CANADA

Canadian politics in British Columbia is an adventure, on the Prairies a cause, in Ontario a business, in Quebec a religion, in the Maritimes a disease. *Paul St Pierre*

John G. Diefenbaker – *Prime Minister*
I did not write S.O.B. on the Rostow document. I didn't think Diefenbaker was a son of a bitch, I thought he was a prick.
John F. Kennedy
[*Kennedy later defended his words* – I couldn't have called him an S.O.B. – I didn't know he was one at the time.]

Jean Lesage – *Premier of Quebec*
The only person I know who can strut sitting down. *John G. Diefenbaker*

Pierre Trudeau – *Prime Minister*
The greatest thing in political circles since Christine Keeler. *Anon (1969)*

In Pierre Elliott Trudeau, Canada has at last produced a political leader worthy of assassination. *Irving Layton* – '*The Whole Bloody Bird*' (1969)

CHINA

Mao Tse-tung –
Chairman of the People's Party
The greatest genocidal maniac in the history of the world, the same Mao Tse-tung who killed four times as many Chinese as Hitler killed Jews. *William F. Buckley Jr* –
'*On the Right*' (1964)

CUBA

Fidel Castro
When it comes to Castro – there's only one thing that keeps him from being a bare-faced liar. *Robert Orben*

As far as I am concerned, Castro is a four-dimensional SOB. An SOB no matter how you look at him. *Robert Orben*

EGYPT

Gamal Nasser – *President*
Nasser knew what he did not want, but not quite what he wanted. *Mohammad Heikal*

Anwar Sadat – *President*
Sadat and Begin remind me of the musical *Annie Get Your Gun* – anything you can do I can do better. *Yitzhak Rabin (1978)*

FRANCE

Political thought in France is either nostalgic or Utopian. *Raymond Aron (1957)*

A small acquaintance with history shows that all Governments are selfish and the French Government more selfish than most. *Viscount David Eccles (1962)*

The French will only be united under the threat of danger. How can anyone govern a nation that has 210 different kinds of cheese? *Charles de Gaulle (1951)*

Bertrand Barere – *Revolutionist*
'*Memoirs*' – A man who has never been within the tropics does not know what a thunderstorm means; a man who has never looked on Niagara has but a faint idea of a cataract; and he who has not read Barere's *Memoirs* may be said not to know what it is to lie. *Thomas Macaulay*

François R. de Chateaubriand
He is a miserable boaster without character, with a grovelling soul and an itch for wanting. *Napoleon Bonaparte (1818)*

He thinks himself deaf because he no longer hears himself talked of. *Charles Maurice de Talleyrand*

Charles de Gaulle – *President*
Of all the crosses I have to bear, the heaviest is the Cross of Lorraine. *Sir Winston Churchill*

He is like a female llama surprised in her bath. *Sir Winston Churchill*

De Gaulle thinks that he is both Joan of Arc and Clemenceau. *Franklin Roosevelt*

He is not a genius, just a political cosmonaut, continually in orbit. *Josef Strauss (1966)*

An artlessly sincere megalomaniac. *H. G. Wells (1943)*

Jean Marie Le Pen
Le Pen is a bastard and people who vote for him are bastards, too. *Bernard Tapie (1992)*

Comte de Mirabeau
He is capable of anything for money, even of a good action. *A. Comte de Rivarol*

Valéry Giscard D'Estaing – *President*
If an atom bomb fell on France, he would be there to congratulate himself that there had not been two. *Françoise Giroud*

Raymond Poincaré – *Prime Minister*
This devil of a man is the opposite of Briand: the latter knows nothing, and understands everything; the other knows everything, and understands nothing. *Georges Clemenceau*

Charles M. Talleyrand – *Prime Minister*
Sir, you are in love with yourself. And you don't have a rival on earth. *Napoleon Bonaparte*

You, Sir, are a stocking full of shit. *Napoleon Bonaparte*

GERMANY

Adolf Hitler
The greatest and worst 'seizer' of them all. *Anon*

This bloodthirsty guttersnipe launches his mechanized armies upon new fields of slaughter, pillage and devastation. *Sir Winston Churchill (1941)*

I always hate to compare Napoleon with Hitler, as it seems an insult to the great Emperor and warrior to connect him in any way with a squalid caucus boss and butcher.
Sir Winston Churchill

If Hitler invaded Hell I would make at least a favourable reference to the Devil in the House of Commons.
Sir Winston Churchill (1941)

Hitler is a queer fellow who will never become Chancellor; the best he can hope for is to head the Postal Department.
Field Marshal Paul von Hindenburg (1931)

A psychopath who somehow found his way from a padded cell to Potsdam.
Malcolm Muggeridge

That garrulous monk. *Benito Mussolini*

In politics, as in grammar, one should be able to tell the substantives from the adjectives. Hitler was substantive; Mussolini only an adjective. Hitler was a nuisance. Mussolini was bloody. Together a bloody nuisance.
Salvador de Madariaga y Rogo

A [*horse*] racing tipster who only reached Hitler's level of accuracy would not do well for his clients. *A. J. P. Taylor*

A combination of initiative, perfidy, and epilepsy. *Leon Trotsky*

INDIA

Mohandas (Mahatma) Gandhi
A seditious Middle Temple lawyer, posing as a fakir of a type well known in the East.
Sir Winston Churchill (1931)

Gandhi has been assassinated. In my humble opinion a bloody good thing but far too late.
Noël Coward – 'Diary' (1948)

Rajiv Gandhi
The so-called leader of the world's largest democracy struts like a bloated peacock on the international stage. *Terry Dicks*

IRELAND

Politics is the chloroform of the Irish people.
Oliver St John Gregory (1937)

Eamonn de Valera – *Prime Minister*
The Spanish onion in the Irish stew.
David Lloyd George

Mr De Valera is so slippery to deal with it is like trying to pick up quicksilver with a fork.
David Lloyd George

Conor Cruise O'Brien
Conor O'Brien is the kind of person who would sooner uphold the proposition that Nkrumah is divine, than that Christ was. O'Brien is an ideological swashbuckler, a nose-tweaker who doesn't know the bounds of taste, nor cares much for the hurt he inflicts. He is most likely not a Communist, although he does their work for them.
William F. Buckley Jr – 'On the Right' (1965)

Daniel O'Connell
A systematic liar and a beggarly cheat; a swindler and a poltroon. He has committed every crime that does not require courage.
Benjamin Disraeli

His fame blazed like a straw bonfire, and has left behind it scarce a shovelful of ashes. Never any public man had it in his power to do so much good for his country, nor was there ever one who accomplished so little.
J. A. Froude – 'Short Studies'

The only way to deal with such a man as O'Connell is to hang him and erect a statue to him under the gallows. *Sydney Smith*

Sir Boyle Richard
Every time he opens his mouth he puts his foot in it. *Anon (1770)*

ISRAEL
Put three Zionists in a room and they will form four political parties. *Levi Eshkol*

Menachem Begin – *Prime Minister*
He makes Arafat look like a Boy Scout.
Jesse Helms

He is like a man who steals your cow. You ask for it back and he demands a ransom.
Anwar Sadat

ITALY

It is not impossible to govern Italians. It is merely useless. *Benito Mussolini*

Political parties in Italy repeat themselves like broken gramophone records.
Professor Predarotti (1980)

Benito Mussolini – *'Il Duce'*
'The Cardinal's Mistress' – My dream-life is largely made up of scenes in which I say to him, 'Oh, Il Duce, yourself, you big stiff,' and thus leave him crushed to a pulp . . . Well do I know, from reading the newspapers, that those who attempt disagreement with the Dictator trifle with their health; so I shall remark, in a quiet way, that if *The Cardinal's Mistress* is a grande romanzo, I am Alexandre Dumas père et fils.
Constant Reader [Dorothy Parker] – 'New Yorker' (1928)

A Sawdust Caesar. *George Seldes (1932)*

JAPAN

The Japanese policy is to make hell while the sun shines. *Sir Winston Churchill*

LIBYA

We are not going to tolerate these attacks from states run by the strangest collections of misfits, loony tunes, and squalid criminals since the advent of the Third Reich.
Ronald Reagan

Colonel Muammar Gaddafi
Not only a barbarian, but flaky.
Ronald Reagan

Gaddafi is the lunatic of Libya – a dwarf who thought he was a giant. *Anwar Sadat (1976)*

MEXICO

Mexican metric system – Ten bandits make one revolution. Ten revolutions make one government. One government makes ten revolutions. *'Boston Transcript'*

In Mexico an air conditioner is called a politician because it makes a lot of noise but doesn't work very well.
Len Deighton – 'Mexico Set' (1985)

It seems to be the custom for Mexican Presidents to come in by the ballot and go out by the bullet. *'Nashville Lumberman'*

Mexico has had 59 revolutions in 63 years, and needs another. *'Philadelphia Press'*

In Mexico, the 'ex' of ex-President is an abbreviation of extinct.
'Richmond News-Leader'

Now that Mexico's new President has been sworn in, it's up to the family to go ahead with the funeral arrangements.
'Topeka Capitol'

Mexican politics is a form of ruler derby.
Frank Tyger

NEW ZEALAND

David Lange – *Prime Minister*
Lange is the only sixteen stone world leader that can be considered a lightweight.
Anon Australian MP

Robert 'Piggy' Muldoon – *Prime Minister*
The United States has Ronald Reagan, Johnny Cash, Bob Hope and Stevie Wonder. New Zealand has Robert Muldoon, no cash, no hope and no bloody wonder. *Graffiti*

New Zealanders are dumb. We are the only country that put a pig in a bee-hive [*The Parliament Building*]. *Graffiti*

NICARAGUA

Anastasio Somozo – *President*
He may be a son of a bitch, but he's our son of a bitch. *Franklin D. Roosevelt*

RUSSIA

I think the only advantage of their form of government is that it stops graffiti.
John Lindsay

The Soviet Union would remain a one-party nation even if an opposition party were permitted – because everyone would join that party. *Ronald Reagan (1982)*

The Kremlin is like a baby – it has an appetite one end and no sense of responsibility at the other. *Ronald Reagan*

Dealing with Russia is like handling a jackass. You can talk to him and talk to him, but watch out he don't kick you. *Alex Wiley*

Mikhail Gorbachev – *Premier*
This man has a nice smile, but he's got iron teeth. *Andrei Gromyko (1985)*

Nikita Kruschev – *Premier*
A pig-eyed bag of wind. *Frank L. Howley*

Nikolai Lenin – *Premier*
The Russians' worst misfortune was Lenin's birth; their next worse, his death.
Sir Winston Churchill

Lenin was an intriguer, a disorganiser and an exploiter of Russian backwardness.
Leon Trotsky

Molotov
I have never seen a human being who more perfectly represented the modern conception of a robot. *Sir Winston Churchill*

Joseph Stalin – *Premier*
Genghis Khan with a telephone. *Anon*

Leon Trotsky
His abilities seem to consist chiefly in vigorous abuse of the people who disagree with him – say ninety-nine out of every hundred in every country and political party in the world. *Lord Birkenhead*

SOUTH AFRICA

Nelson Mandela – *Leader of the ANC*
Sounds more like an avenging angel than a guardian angel. *Anthony Beaumont-Dark*

TURKEY

Kemal Ataturk – *President*
A man who, though he abhorred political assassination, was not above judicial murder.
Lord Kinross (1964)

Turan Gunes – *Foreign Minister*
He was a dark loquacious character who looked somewhat like Groucho Marx but without the humour. *James Callaghan*

UGANDA

Idi Amin Dada – *President*
The African violent. *Bruce B. Randall Jr*

His is a clown face . . . Satan's buffoon.
Tony Samstag – 'The Times' (1980)

The solitary conductor of an orchestra of devils. *Ian Smith*

LAW & ORDER

LAW

GENERAL

Perhaps there would be more respect for law if we could conjure up more respect for the law-makers. *Anon*

One would risk being disgusted if one saw politics, justice, and one's dinner in the making. *Anon*

Law school is the opposite of sex. Even when it's good it's lousy. *Anon*

Go to law for a sheep and lose your cow.
German proverb

Laws, like the spider's web, catch the fly and let the hawk go free. *Spanish proverb*

Law is the expression of the will of the strongest for the time being. *Brooks Adams*

Laws are like cobwebs, for if any trifling or powerless thing falls into them, they hold fast; but if a thing of any size falls into them, it breaks the mesh and escapes.
Anacharsis (600 BC)

Law is a bottomless pit. *John Arbuthnot*

Law is reason free from passion. *Aristotle*

The only laws that ever enforce themselves are of the kind that Isaac Newton discovered.
'Boston Herald'

The portion of the law that is unconstitutional is the teeth.
'Canton Dispatch'

There is no such thing as justice – in or out of court. *Clarence Darrow*

Law is a horrible business.
Clarence Darrow – 'New York Times' (1936)

The law is an ass. *Charles Dickens*

Arguing for capital punishment – Where would Christianity be if Jesus got eight to ten years with time off for good behaviour?
James H. Donovan

A malpractice suit is the law of the bungle.
John H. Dromey

If we were in Scotland, we could bring in 'Not Proven'. That's 'Not Guilty – but don't do it again'. *Winifred Duke*

Frequently the blindfold over the eyes of Justice looks suspiciously like greenbacks.
'Greenville Piedmont'

Justice delayed is democracy denied.
Robert F. Kennedy (1964)

If more of the law's delays were in the making of laws, and less of it in enforcing 'em, this would be a better world for everyone save lawmakers and lawyers.
'Louisville Courier-Journal'

Law is a sort of hocus-pocus science, that smiles in yer face while it picks yer pocket.
Charles Macklin (1759)

Injustice is relatively easy to bear: what stings is justice. *H. L. Mencken*

Ignorance of the law is no excuse; neither, unfortunately, is the ignorance of law-makers.
George J. Nathan – 'Buffalo Evening News'

Justice is blind, but seldom too blind to distinguish between the defendant who has a roll and the one who is dead broke.
'Moline Dispatch'

I believe that people would be alive today if there were a death penalty. *Nancy Reagan*

Man is an able creature, but he has made 32,647,389 laws and hasn't yet improved on the Ten Commandments.
'Richmond News-Leader'

For many persons, law appears to be black magic – an obscure domain that can be fathomed only by the professional initiated into mysteries. *Susan C. Ross*

Legislation is like a sausage – it's a mixture of pleasant and not so pleasant things.
Charles Royer

Laws are nets of such a texture, as the little creep through, the great break through, and the middle-sized alone are entangled.
William Shenstone

When I hear a man talk of unalterable law, I am convinced he is an unalterable fool.
Sydney Smith

Of course there's a different law for the rich and the poor; otherwise, who would go into business? *E. Ralph Stewart*

Laws are like cobwebs, which may catch

small flies, but let wasps and hornets break through. *Jonathan Swift*

After the rogues, what honest people dread most of all is a court of law. *A. Tournier*

The law and the stage – both are forms of exhibitionism. *Orson Welles*

LAWSUITS

Something nobody likes to have, but nobody likes to lose. *Anon*

A lawsuit is a fruit tree planted in a lawyer's garden. *Italian proverb*

A lawsuit is a machine which you go into as a pig and come out as a sausage.
Ambrose Bierce

The only successful lawsuit is one worn by a policeman. *Robert Frost*

A lawsuit is to ordinary life what war is to peacetime. *Jean Malcolm*

LAWYERS

You're an attorney. It's your duty to lie, conceal and distort everything, and slander everybody.
Jean Giraudoux – 'The Madwoman of Chaillot' (1945)

A town that cannot support one lawyer can always support two. *Lyndon B. Johnson*

Anon
The moment my learned opponent begins to talk, his mental processes cease. He is like a little steamboat which I once saw on the Saugamon River. The little steamer had a five-foot boiler and a seven-foot whistle, and every time it whistled the engine stopped – like my opponent's mind. *Abraham Lincoln*

He can compress the most words into the smallest ideas of any man I ever met.
Abraham Lincoln

Joseph H. Choate
All you need to get a speech out of Mr

Choate is to open his mouth, drop in a dinner and up comes a speech.
Chauncey Depew

Alan Dershowitz – *lawyer to Klaus Von Bulow, Mike Tyson and Leona Helmsley*
He really has the worst reputation in the profession of anybody I know who purports to have a reputation. *Michael Armstrong*

John Gill
Beneath this smooth stone by the bone of his bone
Sleeps Master John Gill;
By lies when alive
This attorney did thrive.
And now that he's dead he lies still. *Epitaph*

Gabriel Harvey
This dodipoule, this didopper. Why, thou arrant butter whore, thou cosqueane and scratop of scoldes, wilt thou never leave afflicting a dead Carcasse. A wispe, a wispe, jippe, rippe, you kitchin-staffe wranger.
Thomas Nashe

Thomas Puccio
A lawyer who usually operated with the delicacy of a Lexington Avenue express train.
Joyce Wadler (1985)

James St Clair – *Watergate lawyer*
The trouble with St Clair is that he is all case and no cause. *William S. Coffin*

Wendell L. Wilkie
Trying to give Wilkie advice is just as effective as giving castor oil to the Sphinx.
Anon

JUDGES

A judge is a lawyer who once knew a politician. *Anon*

A judge is a person in a very trying position.
Anon

A judge is a law student who marks his own paper. *Anon*

Judges are the weakest link in our system of justice, and they are also the most protected.

Alan M. Dershowitz (1978)
A lifetime diet of the law alone turns judges into dull, dry husks. *William Douglas*

Appellate Division judges – the whores who became madams. *Martin Erdmann (1971)*

Judges are apt to be naïve, simple-minded men. *Oliver Wendell Holmes (1913)*

A judge is a man who is not supposed to know anything about the facts of life until they have been presented in evidence and explained to him at least three times.
Lord Chief Justice Parker

Justice in moderate judges is only love of their elevated position.
François, Duc de la Rochefoucauld

Lord Brougham – *Lord Chancellor*
If the Lord Chancellor only knew a little law he would know something of everything.
Anon

As Lord Chancellor, he distinguished himself by belching from the woolsack.
Esme Wingfield-Stratford

Samuel Chase – *Associate Justice, US Supreme Court*
Cursed of thy father, scum of all that's base, Thy sight is odious, and thy name is . . .
'Philadelphia Aurora'

Earl Warren – *US Chief Justice*
Some people want to impeach Earl Warren. Hanging would be more deserved.
Colonel Mitchell Paige

JURIES

A jury consists of twelve persons chosen to decide who has the better lawyer.
Robert Frost

The real crime wave is the failure of juries to convict. *'Greenville Piedmont'*

A jury is a group of twelve men who, having lied to the judge about their hearing, health and business engagements, have failed to fool him. *H. L. Mencken*

A jury is composed of twelve men of average ignorance. *Herbert Spencer*

The jury system puts a ban upon intelligence and honesty, and a premium upon ignorance, stupidity and perjury. *Mark Twain (1872)*

COURTS OF LAW

A court is where a suit is pressed and a man can be taken to the cleaners. *Anon*

The plaintiff is a court fool. *Ambrose Pierce*

The court does not make a man contented. It prevents him being so anywhere else.
Jean de la Bruyere

The US Supreme Court
There is about as much danger of the establishment of religion in the USA as there is of the return of sanity to the Supreme Court. *William F. Buckley Jr – 'National Review' (1963)*

The Supreme Court is the greatest single threat to the [*American*] Constitution.
James Eastland

One of the best jobs in the world for a pregnant woman would be a position on the Supreme Court. The work is sedentary and the clothing is loose-fitting. *Patricia Schroeder*

LAW ENFORCEMENT

POLICE

If pigs could fly, Scotland Yard would be London's third airport. *Anon*

There is a sleeping cop in all of us. He must be killed. *French graffiti (1968)*

I have never seen a situation so dismal that a policeman couldn't make it worse.
Brendan Behan

A black pig, a white pig, a yellow pig, a pink pig – a dead pig is the best pig of all.
Eldridge Cleaver (1970)

However low a man sinks he never reaches

the level of the police.   *Quentin Crisp (1984)*

For the middle classes, the police protect property, give directions, and help old ladies. For the urban poor, the police are those who arrest you.   *Michael Harrington (1962)*

I'm not against the police; I'm afraid of them.
Alfred Hitchcock

Policemen are numbered – just in case they get lost.   *Spike Milligan*

OFFICERS OF THE LAW

Wyatt Earp – *lawman*
Wyatt's reputation and attainment, such as they were, may have been acclaimed by the Dodge City gang, but elsewhere he was merely another of the flotsam of the frontier.
E. Bartholomew

J. Edgar Hoover – *first Director of the FBI*
Whom you wouldn't trust as much as you would a rattlesnake with a silencer in the tail.
Dean Acheson (1960)

A mythical person first thought up by the *Reader's Digest*.   *Art Buchwald*

CRIMINALS

William H. Bonney (Billy the Kid)
A nondescript, adenoidal, weasel-eyed, narrow-chested, stoop-shouldered, repulsive-looking creature with all the outward appearance of a cretin.
Burton Roscoe – 'Belle Star' (1941)

Al Capone
He is Neapolitan by birth and Neanderthal by instinct.   *Fred D. Palsey – 'Al Capone: The Biography of a Self-Made Man'*

Jesse James
Jesse James shot children, but only in fact,

not in folklore.
John Greenway – 'The Inevitable Americans'

PRISON SYSTEM

GENERAL

'Stone walls do not a prison make' in this semantic age;
They make a 'correctional facility' that's nonetheless a cage.
Dal Devening

Prisons are the black flower of civilised society.   *Nathaniel Hawthorne*

Putting a homosexual in prison is like trying to cure obesity by incarceration in a candy shop.   *Martin Hoffman (1968)*

Prison is a Socialist's Paradise – where equality prevails, everything is supplied and competition is eliminated.   *Elbert Hubbard*

You can't hope for much in the way of prison reform until we get to sending a better class of folks there.
'San Francisco Chronicle'

While we have prisons, it matters little which of us occupy the cells.
G. B. Shaw – 'Man and Superman'

On being held, handcuffed, in the pouring rain at a train station – If this is the way Queen Victoria treats her convicts, she doesn't deserve to have any.   *Oscar Wilde*

PRISONS

Prisons are wall-to-wall walls.   *T. K. Ryan*

Alcatraz
Alcatraz, the federal prison with a name like the blare of a trombone, is a black molar in the jawbone of the nation's prison system.
Thomas E. Gaddis

EDUCATION

The reason they're called lessons is because they lessen from day to day. *Lewis Carroll*

How long did it take six men to build a wall if three of them took a week? I recall that we spent almost as much time on this problem as the men spent on the wall. *Gerald Durrell*

Public schools are the nurseries of all vice and immorality.
Henry Fielding – 'Joseph Andrews'

It is tiresome to hear education discussed, tiresome to educate, and tiresome to be educated. *Lord Melbourne*

Education, the great mumbo-jumbo and fraud of the age, purports to equip us to live and is prescribed as a universal remedy for everything from juvenile delinquency to premature senility. For the most part it only serves to enlarge stupidity, inflate conceit, enhance credulity and put those subjected to it at the mercy of brain-washers with printing presses, radio and TV at their disposal.
Malcolm Muggeridge – 'The Observer' (1966)

Superfluity of lecturing causes ischial bursitis. *Sir William Ostler*
[NB Ischial bursitis – numb bum.]

We are faced with the paradoxical fact that education has become one of the chief obstacles to intelligence and freedom of thought. *Bertrand Russell*

Pressing people to learn things they do not want to know is as unwholesome and disastrous as feeding them on sawdust.
G. B. Shaw

There is nothing on earth intended for innocent people so horrible as a school. To begin with, it is a prison. But it is in some respects more cruel than a prison. In a prison, for instance, you are not forced to read books written by the warders and the governor. *G. B. Shaw*

An English university is a sanctuary in which exploded systems and obsolete prejudices find shelter and protection after they have been hunted out of every corner of the world.
Adam Smith –
'Wealth of Nations'

In the first place, God made idiots; this was for practice; then he made school boards.
Mark Twain

TEACHERS

I have seen men trying to teach history who hardly knew whether the Armada was a town in Brazil or a winner of the Derby. *Balaam*

Academic and aristocratic people live in such an uncommon atmosphere that common sense can rarely reach them. *Samuel Butler*

A lecturer is a literary strumpet, subject for a greater than whore's fee to prostitute himself.
Oliver Wendell Holmes

The truth is that the average schoolmaster, on all the lower levels, is and always must be . . . next door to an idiot, for how can one imagine an intelligent man engaging in so puerile an avocation?
H. L. Mencken –
'New York Evening Mail' (1918)

Every schoolmaster after the age of 49 is inclined to flatulence, is apt to swallow frequently, and to puff.
Harold Nicolson – 'The Old School'

The schoolteacher is certainly underpaid as a childminder, but ludicrously overpaid as an educator. *John Osborne (1985)*

The vanity of teaching often tempteth a man to forget he is a blockhead.
George Savile – 'Maxims'

It is when the gods hate a man with uncommon abhorrence that they drive him

into the profession of a school-master.
Seneca

SEATS OF LEARNING

Colleges are like old age homes, except for the fact that more people die in colleges.
Bob Dylan

Anyone who has been to an English public school will always feel comparatively at home in prison. *Evelyn Waugh*

Gordonstoun
The beds are hard as iron, it's straw mattresses and bread and water. It's just like prison. *Prince Andrew*

Trinity College, Cambridge
Trinity is like a dead body in a high state of putrefaction. The only interest of it is in the worms that come out of it.
Lytton Strachey (1903)

University College, London
A humbug joint-stock subscription school for Cockney boys, without the power of granting degrees or affording honours or distinctions, got up in the bubble season.
John Bull (1827)

Winchester College
I went to Winchester in 1840 at twelve years old, able to work a quadratic equation well, and left it at eighteen, competent to perform the same task badly. *W. Tuckwell*

RELIGION

There are many preachers who do not hear themselves. *German proverb*

Man appoints and God disappoints.
*Miguel de Cervantes –
'Don Quixote' (1605)*

Go into one of the cool churches, and begin to count the words that might be spared, and in most places the entire sermon will go.
R. W. Emerson – 'Journals' (1832)

God? I have no need of that theory. *Laplace*

FAITHS

BLACK MUSLIM

A pseudo-religion for unbright neurotics who feel the need to hate all white people.
*William F. Buckley Jr –
'On the Right' (1965)*

CALVINIST

On April in Massachusetts – What a misnomer in our climate to call this season spring, very much like calling Calvinism religion.
*Lydia Maria Child –
'Daughters of the Puritans'*

CATHOLICISM

Catholicism is like Howard Johnson [*Hotels*], and what they have are these franchises and they give all these people different franchises in different countries but they have one government, and when you buy the Howard Johnson franchise you can apply it to the geography – whatever's cool for that area – and then you, you know, pay the bread to the main office. *Lenny Bruce*

I'm as ratty as hell with the Catholic Church, which I suppose might be a bit complex, except that I'm right and the stupid idiots are wrong. I can't bear the new Mass. I simply can't bear it. You've got guitars and ladies in the tabernacle. Just unbelievable stuff.
*Alice Thomas Ellis –
'The Sunday Telegraph' (1992)*

High Anglo-Catholic are beneath contempt – All intellectual and moral wrecks.

They love the frills but hold themselves
   exempt
From self-denial in the line of sex.
They call their horrid kids after saints
And educate them by such dubious means
They eagerly succumb to strange complaints
Or turn psychotic in their early teens.
James Fenton and John Fuller –
'New Review' (1976)

The Papacy is the ghost of the deceased
Roman Empire, sitting crowned upon the
grave thereof. *Thomas Hobbes*

Abhor that arrant Whore of Rome,
And all her blasphemies; And drink not of
her cursed cup,
Obey not her decrees.
'New England Primer' (1688)

On the English translation of the Mass – Its
language is as bare as a monk's cell, and as
uninviting.
Clifford Longley – 'The Times' (1984)

The mass is the greatest blaspheming of
God, and the highest idolatry upon earth, an
abomination the like which has never been in
Christendom since the time of the Apostles.
Martin Luther

The Catholic faith is confession on Saturday.
Absolution on Sunday. At it again on
Monday. *H. G. Wells*

CHRISTIANITY

A Christian is one who follows the teachings
of Christ in so far as they are not inconsistent
with a life of sin. *Ambrose Bierce*

A Christian is one who believes the New
Testament is a divinely inspired book
admirably suited to the spiritual needs of his
neighbour. *Ambrose Bierce*

Christian ethics are seldom found save in the
philosophy of some unbeliever.
Heywood Broun

Science has done more for the development
of western civilisation in one hundred years
than Christianity did in eighteen hundred
years. *John Burroughs*

The weak rely on Christ, the strong do not.
Richard Burton (1963)

The problem with born-again Christians is
that they are an even bigger pain the second
time around. *Herb Caen (1981)*

If Jesus were to come today, people would
not even crucify him. They would ask him to
dinner, and hear what he had to say, and
make fun of him. *Thomas Carlyle*

Christianity is the bastard progeny of
Judaism. It is the basest of all national
religions. *Celsus (c. 178)*

The Christian ideal has not been tried and
found wanting, it has been found difficult
and left untried. *G. K. Chesterton (1910)*

The Christian religion not only was at first
attended by miracles, but even at this day
cannot be believed by any reasonable person
without one. *David Hume – 'On Miracles'*

Organised Christianity has probably done
more to retard the ideals that were its
founders than any other agency in the world.
Richard le Gallienne

With soap, baptism is a good thing.
Richard G. Ingersoll

The white Christian church never raised to
the heights of Christ. It stayed within the
limits of culture. *Jesse Jackson (1977)*

Christianity will go. It will go. It will vanish
and shrink. We are more popular than Jesus
now. I don't know which will go first – rock
and roll or Christianity. Jesus was all right,
but his disciples were thick and ordinary.
John Lennon

My dislike of the Christian religion is based
on the natural revolt of the pagan against a
creed that has nothing to do with Mother
Earth, humanism and the gusto for life but
croaks of sin, death, punishment, fear, with a

very dull promissory note on Paradise.
Sir Lionel Lindsay

The act of worship, as carried on by Christians, seems to me to be debasing rather than ennobling. It involves grovelling before a Being who, if He really exists, deserves to be denounced instead of respected.
H. L. Mencken

I call Christianity the one great curse, the one enormous and innermost perversion, the one great instinct of revenge for which no means are too venomous, too underhand, too underground and too petty – I call it the one immortal blemish of mankind.
Friedrich Nietzsche – 'The Antichrist'

As with the Christian religion, the worst advertisement for Socialism is its adherents.
George Orwell (1937)

The study of theology, as it stands in Christian churches, is the study of nothing; it is founded on nothing; it rests on nothing; it proceeds by no authorities; it has no data; it can demonstrate nothing and it admits of no conclusion.
Thomas Paine (1794)

The greatest service that could be rendered the Christian peoples would be to convert them to Christianity.
'Palatka News'

Christianity might be a good thing if anyone ever tried it.
G. B. Shaw

The Jews generally give value. They make you pay; but they deliver the goods. In my experience the men who want something for nothing are invariably Christians.
G. B. Shaw – 'Saint Joan' (1923)

If I had been the Virgin Mary, I'd have said, 'No!'
Stevie Smith

Too many of today's Christians want Christ without the cross.
J. K. Stern

I think there is an immense shortage of Christian charity among so-called Christians.
Harry S. Truman

The strange fate of Christianity in its modern dress is precisely that it has reduced man to the futility of idly gossiping about God.
Gabriel Vahanian – 'The Death of God' (1962)

Christianity must be divine, since it has lasted 1,700 years despite the fact that it is so full of villainy and nonsense.
Voltaire

A great deal of what passes for current Christianity consists in denouncing other people's vices and faults.
Henry Williams

A Christian is a man who feels repentance on a Sunday for what he did on a Saturday and is going to do on Monday.
Thomas R. Ybarra

Scratch the Christian and you will find the pagan – spoiled.
Israel Zangwill

CHURCH OF ENGLAND

One of the sacraments of the Church of England, the confirmation, tends to be like a spiritual sheep-dip.
H. L. Mencken

ISLAM

Unlike Christianity, which preached a peace that it never achieved, Islam unashamedly came with a sword.
Steven Runciman

JESUIT

I do not like the reappearance of the Jesuits. If ever there was a body of men who merited damnation on earth and in Hell it is this society of Loyola's.
John Adams (1816)

Their philosophic undertakings are much like his who spent his time darting cummin seeds through the eye of a needle.
Joseph Glanville (1661)

Bland as a Jesuit, sober as a hymn.
William E. Henley

METHODISM

Methodism is spiritual influenza.
George Crabbe (1810)

MORMONISM

Mormons invented themselves just as other

religious and ethnic groups invented themselves. But Mormons did so in such a singularly impressive way that we will probably always remain baffled as to how exactly it happened.

Laurence Moore – 'New York Times' (1985)

ORTHODOX

An ox wearing the popular religious yoke.

Ambrose Bierce

PRESBYTERIANISM

Not a religion for gentlemen.   *King Charles II*

PROTESTANTISM

The chief contribution of Protestantism to human thought is its massive proof that God is a bore.   *H. L. Mencken (1956)*

Hemiplegic paralysis of Christianity – and of reason.   *Friedrich Nietzsche (1888)*

PURITANISM

A Puritan is a person who pours righteous indignation into the wrong things.

G. K. Chesterton

Puritanism is the haunting fear that someone, somewhere, may be happy.   *H. L. Mencken*

QUAKERISM

The sedate, sober, silent, serious, sad-coloured sect.   *Thomas Hood –*
'The Doves and the Crows'

Quakers are under the strong delusion of Satan.   *Increase Mather – 'Remarkable*
Providences' (1684)

UNITARIANISM

Unitarianism is, in effect, the worst kind of atheism joined to the worst of one kind of Calvinism, like two asses tied tail to tail.

Samuel T. Coleridge (1832)

UNBELIEVERS

An atheist is one point beyond the devil.

Anon

A heathen is a benighted creature who has the folly to worship something he can see and can feel.   *Ambrose Bierce*

An atheist is a man with no visible means of support.   *John Buchan*

Thank God, I am still an atheist.

Luis Buñuel (1969)

A dead atheist is someone who's all dressed up with no place to go.

James Duffecy – 'New York Times' (1964)

Atheists have an excellent longevity record because we have no place to go after we die, so we take good care of ourselves and our world while we are here.

Madalyn Murray O'Hair

I'm an atheist and I thank God for it.

G. B. Shaw

To all things clergic
I am allergic.   *Alexander Woollcott*

I once wanted to become an atheist, but I gave it up – they have no holidays.

Henny Youngman

MISCELLANEOUS

ARCHBISHOPS

An archbishop is a Christian ecclesiastic of a rank superior to that attained by Christ.

H. L. Mencken

THE BIBLE

The Bible may be the truth, but it is not the whole truth and nothing but the truth.

Samuel Butler

The Bible should be taught so early and so thoroughly that it sinks straight to the bottom of the mind where everything that comes along can settle on it.   *Northrop Frye*

Had The Bible been in clear straightforward language, had the ambiguities and contradictions been edited out, and had the language been constantly modernised to accord with contemporary taste it would almost certainly have been a work of lesser influence. *J. K. Galbraith*

The inspiration of The Bible depends upon the ignorance of the gentleman who reads it. *Robert G. Ingersoll*

The Bible is nothing but a succession of civil rights struggles by the Jewish people against their oppressors. *Jesse Jackson*

The New English Bible – Even the end of the world is described as if it were only an exceptionally hot afternoon. *Peter Mallen (1985)*

Say what you will about the Ten Commandments, you will always come back to the pleasant fact that there are only ten of them. *H. L. Mencken*

The Old Testament is responsible for more atheism, agnosticism, disbelief – call it what you will – than any book ever written; it has emptied more churches than all the counter-attractions of cinema, motor bicycle and golf course. *A. A. Milne*

One had better put on gloves before reading the New Testament. The presence of so much filth makes it very advisable. *Friedrich Nietzsche – 'The Antichrist' (1888)*

It is a history of wickedness that has served to corrupt and brutalise mankind. *Thomas Paine – 'The Age of Reason' (1794)*

'Genesis' – Take away from 'Genesis' the belief that Moses was the author, on which only the strange belief that it is the word of God has stood, and there remains nothing of 'Genesis' but an anonymous book of stories, fables, and traditoary or invented absurdities, or of down-right lies. *Thomas Paine – 'The Age of Reason' (1794)*

It isn't the style of The Bible that makes it unpopular with moderns, but the fact that it cramps their style. *'Pasadena Evening Post'*

So far as I can remember, there is not one word in the Gospels in praise of intelligence. *Bertrand Russell*

The Bible is literature, not dogma. *George Santayana*

There can be no doubt that The Bible became a stumbling block in the path of progress, scientific, social and even moral. It was quoted against Copernicus as it was against Darwin. *Preserved Smith*

The total absence of humour from the Bible is one of the most singular things in literature. *Alfred North Whitehead*

I read the Book of Job last night – I don't think God comes well out of it. *Virginia Woolf*

BISHOPS

It is no accident that the symbol of a bishop is a crook, and the sign of an archbishop is a double-cross. *Dom Gregory Dix*

THE KORAN

A wearisome, confused jumble, crude, incondite; endless iterations, long-windedness, entanglement, most crude, incondite – insupportable stupidity, in short! Nothing, but a sense of duty could carry any European through the Koran. *Thomas Carlyle (1840)*

NUNS

A convent is a place of retirement for women who wish for leisure to meditate upon the vice of idleness. *Ambrose Bierce*

Life in a convent is the supreme egotism, resulting in supreme self-denial. *Victor Hugo – 'Les Misérables'*

PILGRIM FATHERS

The pious ones of Plymouth, who, reaching the Rock, first fell upon their own knees and then upon the aborigines. *William Evarts – 'Louisville Courier-Journal' (1913)*

PRIESTS

Hell is paved with priests' skulls.
St John Chrysostom (390 AD)

Priests are no more necessary to religion than politicians to patriotism.
John H. Holmes (1933)

In all ages, hypocrites, called priests, have put crowns upon the heads of thieves, called kings. *Robert G. Ingersoll*

Visiting museums bastardises the personality, just as hobnobbing with priests makes you lose your faith. *Maurice Vlaminck*

SAINTS

A saint is a dead sinner revised and edited.
Ambrose Bierce

The history of saints is mainly the history of insane people. *Benito Mussolini (1904)*

Saints should be judged guilty until they are proved innocent. *George Orwell (1950)*

THE SALVATION ARMY

On dropping $50 into their tambourine – Don't bother to thank me. I know what a perfectly ghastly season it's been for you Spanish Dancers. *Tallulah Bankhead*

MEN AND WOMEN OF GOD

Anonymous liberal bishop
He'd believe anything provided it's not in the Holy Scripture.
Douglas Feaver – Bishop of Peterborough

Francis Atterbury – *Bishop of Rochester*
A mind inexhaustibly rich in all the resources of controversy, and familiar with all the artifices which make falsehood look like truth and ignorance like knowledge.
Thomas Macaulay

Henry Ward Beecher – *preacher*
Mankind fell in Adam, and has been falling ever since, but never touched bottom until it got to Henry Ward Beecher. *Thomas Appleton*

On why he did not attend church to hear

Beecher preach – Why, Beecher, the fact is, I have conscientious scruples against going to places of amusement on Sunday.
Park Benjamin

He came out for the right side of every question – always a little too late.
Sinclair Lewis

In Boston the human race is divided into 'the good, the bad and the Beechers'.
W. M. Taylor

A dunghill covered with flowers.
Henry Watterson

Dean of Canterbury
He is a clown in gaiters. *Lord Hailsham*

William Channing – *clergyman*
Not so much a conscientious intellect as an intellectual conscience.
Rev. Ephraim Peabody (1852)

Mary Morse Baker Eddy – *founder of the Church of Christ Scientist*
To be a moral thief, an unblushing liar, a supreme dictator, and a cruel, self-satisfied monster, and attain, in the minds of millions, the status of a deity, is not only remarkable but a dismal reflection on the human race. She had much in common with Hitler, only no moustache. *Noël Coward – 'Diary' (1962)*

A brass god with clay legs.
Mark Twain (1907)

What she has really 'discovered' are ways and means of perverting and prostituting the science of healing to her own ecclesiastical aggrandisement, and to the moral and physical depravity of her dupes.
Josephine Woodbury (1899)

Jonathan Edwards – *theologian*
He believed in the worst God, preached the worst sermons, and had the worst religion of any human being who ever lived on this continent. *M. M. Richter (1920)*

Bishop of Exeter
I have to believe in the Apostolic Succession. There is no other way of explaining the

descent of the Bishop of Exeter from Judas Iscariot. *Sydney Smith*

Jerry Falwell – *TV evangelist*
Every good Christian ought to kick Falwell right in the ass. *Barry Goldwater*

Louis Farrakhan – *National Church of Islam*
He is a charismatic figure and a superb speaker. So was Adolf Hitler. And, like Hitler, Farrakhan is a hatemonger. When he preaches, truth is abandoned.
Ed Koch

Dr John Fell – *Bishop of Oxford*
I do not love thee, Doctor Fell,
The reason why I cannot tell,
But this one thing I know full well:
I do not love thee, Doctor Fell.
Thomas Brown

Margaret Fuller – *social reformer*
No person has appeared among us whose conversation and morals have done more to corrupt the minds and hearts of our Boston community. For religion she substitutes art; for the Divinity she would give us merely the Beautiful. *Orestes Brownson*

She was a great humbug; of course, with much talent, and much moral ideality, or else she could not have been so great a humbug. But she had stuck herself full of borrowed qualities, which she chose to provide herself with, but which had no root in her.
Nathaniel Hawthorne

To whom Venus gave everything except Beauty, and Pallus everything except Wisdom.
Oscar Wilde

Billy Graham – *evangelist*
Dr Graham has, with great self-discipline, turned himself into the thinking man's Easter Bunny.
Garry Wills – *'New York Times' (1979)*

Anne Hutchinson – *religious reformer*
A dangerous instrument of the Devil raised up by Satan amongst us.
Rev. John Wilson (1683)

A woman not fit for our society.
John Winthrop (1683)

William Inge – *Dean of St Paul's*
A poet laureate of adolescent sexuality and middle-age longing.
William A. Henry III – *'Time' (1983)*

Pope John Paul II
If the Italians knew about his taste in wines, they never would have agreed to have him as Pope. *Anon*

Martin Luther King
If we are henceforward to treat Martin Luther King as a saint, which is in some respects okay by me, I do believe he should try very hard to act like a saint.
William F. Buckley Jr – *'On the Right' (1964)*

Martin Luther King is the most notorious liar in the country. *J. Edgar Hoover*

He got the peace prize, we got the problem. I don't want the white man giving me medals. If I'm following a general, and he's leading me into battle, and the enemy tends to give him rewards, or awards, I get suspicious of him. Especially if he gets a peace award before the war is over. *Malcolm X*

John Knox – *religious reformer*
There was more of Jesus in St Theresa's little finger than in John Knox's whole body.
Matthew Arnold

C. Gordon Lang – *Archbishop of Canterbury*
Old Lang Swine. *Anon (1936)*

William Laud – *Archbishop of Canterbury*
The Stye of all pestilential filth that hath infested the state and government of this commonwealth. *Sir Harbottle Grimston*

He was by nature rash, irritable, quick to feel for his own dignity, slow to sympathise with the sufferings of others, and prone to the error, common in superstitious men, of mistaking his own peevish and malignant moods for emotions of pious zeal.
Thomas Macaulay – *'History of England'*

Malcolm X
Maestro of the manifesto, it is doubtful that

Malcolm X ever flexed any part of his body in service of the black community except his jawbone. X may have changed his name, but was Little all his life.

Julie Burchill – 'The Disappearing Black'

He spoke like a poor man and walked like a king. *Dick Gregory*

Father Lawrence Lucas – *Roman Catholic leader*
He is a theological maverick in clerical garb. He has given new meaning to the word vile.

Ed Koch

Martin Luther
Luther was the foulest of monsters.

Pope Gregory XV

If we wish to find a scapegoat on whose shoulders we may lay the miseries which Germany has brought upon the world, I am more and more convinced that the worst evil genius of that country is not Hitler or Bismarck or Frederick the Great, but Martin Luther. *William R. Inge*

John McLaughlin
Father John McLaughlin is merely an apprentice bricklayer with a forked tongue for a trowel and hot air for mortar.

'Newsweek'

Aimee Semple McPherson
The Barnum of religion. *Anon*

She is a frank and simple fraud, somewhat like Texas Guinan, but more comical and not quite so cheap.

Morrow Mayo – 'New Republic' (1929)

Mrs McPherson has the nerve of a brass monkey and the philosophy of the Midway – 'Never give a sucker an even break' is grounded in her. *Morrow Mayo – Ibid.*

'In the Service of the King' – It is the story of her life, and it is called *In the Service of the King*, which title is perhaps a bit dangerously suggestive of a romantic novel. It may be that this autobiography is set down in sincerity, frankness, and simple effort. It may be, too,

that the Statue of Liberty is situated in Lake Ontario. *Constant Reader [Dorothy Parker] – 'New Yorker' (1928)*

'In the Service of the King' – On the occasions she drifts into longer and broader sentences, she writes as many other three-named authoresses have written before. Her manner takes on the thick bloom of rich red plush. The sun becomes 'That round orb of day' (as opposed, I expect, to those square orbs you see about so much lately). . . . *In the Service of the King* has caused an upset in my long-established valuations. With the publication of this, her book, Aimee Semple McPherson has replaced Elsie Dinsmore as my favourite character in fiction.

Dorothy Parker – Ibid.

Paul Moore – *Bishop of New York*
He is more a Pontius Pilate than a humble worker at the feet of the poor. *Ed Koch*

Moses
Moses with his law is most terrible; there never was any equal to him in perplexing, affrighting, tyrannizing, threatening, preaching, and thundering.

Martin Luther (1569)

Cardinal John Newman – *theologian*
Poor Newman! He was a great hater!

Cardinal Manning

Bishop of Oxford
I do not hate him nearly as much as I fear I ought to. *Thomas Carlyle*

Norman Vincent Peale
I find St Paul appealing and Peale appalling.

Adlai Stevenson

Joseph Priestley – *theologian*
He is one of the most voluminous writers of any age or country, and probably he is of all voluminous writers the one who has the fewest readers. *Henry, Lord Brougham*

His works tend to unsettle everything and yet settled nothing. *Samuel Johnson*

Cardinal Ratzinger
The Norman Tebbitt of the Holy See . . . the

Vatican Rottweiler.
Kate Saunders and Peter Stanford –
'Catholics and Sex' (1992)

Oral Roberts – *TV evangelist*
He has no intention of living in the ghetto of
heaven or even its suburbs.
Jan Dargatz – 'Boston Globe' (1987)

Dr David Runcie –
Archbishop of Canterbury
His contribution to Christianity could be
written in longhand on a pinhead and still
leave room for the Lord's Prayer.
Terry Dicks

Rev. Al Sharpton
Kick him out and get rid of him. He is
absolute poison. *Geoffrey Dickens*

Sydney Smith
A more profligate parson I never met.
King George IV

Thomas à Becket
Becket was a noisy egotist and hypocrite.
Thomas Carlyle –
'Past and Present'

Will no one free me of this turbulent priest?
Attributed to King Henry II

A bearer of the iniquity of the clergy.
Henry VIII (1538)

A minister of iniquity. *John of Salisbury*

Frederick Temple –
Archbishop of Canterbury
A beast, but a just beast. *Anon*

George Whitefield – *leader of the Calvinistic*
Methodist Church
I heard him once, and it was as low,
confused, puerile, conceited, ill-natured,
enthusiastic a performance as I ever heard.
Jonathan Mayhew (1740)

John Whitgift –
Archbishop of Canterbury
Of all the Bishops that ever were in that place
[*Canterbury*] none ever did so much hurt
unto the Church of God, as he hath done,
since his coming. No Bishop had ever such
an aspiring and ambitious mind as he: no,
not Stephen Gardiner of Winchester. None
so tyrannous as he: no, not Bonner.
Martin Marprelate

Rabbi Stephen Wise
A man of vast and varied misinformation.
William Gaynor

John Wycliffe – *religious reformer*
He was a great dissembler, a man of little
conscience, and what he did as to religion,
was more out of vaine glory, and to obtaine
unto him a name, than out of honestie.
Dr John Fell

THE WORLD

NATIONALITIES

GENERAL

Abroad is unutterably bloody and foreigners
are fiends. *Nancy Mitford*

THE AMERICANS

A Texan virgin is a girl who can run faster
than her brother. *Anon*

Texans are living proof that Indians screwed
buffaloes. *Graffiti*

The Americans of the South – to this day the
most blood simple meatheads on this earth,
outstripping even the Catholic Irish.
Julie Burchill – 'The Disappearing Black'

Californians have got this thing about open
space. They have lots of it – mostly between
their ears. *Peter Cook*

Their demeanour is invariably morose, sullen, clownish and repulsive. I should think there is not on the face of the earth a people so entirely destitute of humour, vivacity, or the capacity of enjoyment.
Charles Dickens – 'Martin Chuzzlewit'

The American has no language. He has dialect, slang, provincialism, accent, and so forth. *Rudyard Kipling*

The 100 per cent American is 99 per cent idiot. *G. B. Shaw*

The people of America are just not born with culture. *Phil Spector*

We are the lavishest and showiest and most luxury-loving people on the earth; and at our masthead we fly one true and honest symbol, the gaudiest flag the world has ever seen.
Mark Twain – 'Diplomatic Pay and Clothes' (1899)

AUSTRALIANS

In many ways the Australian resembles an anaesthetized guinea-pig or a pithed frog: the body works, so to speak, but the mind doesn't.
A. J. Marshall – 'Australia Limited' (1942)

THE BRITISH

The British race are generally the most spiteful, contrived, deceitful bunch of hypocrites to ever hit the planet.
Johnny Rotten

THE DUTCH

What a po-faced lot these Dutch are.
Prince Philip

THE ENGLISH

An Englishman will burn his bed to catch a flea. *Turkish proverb*

The English have no exalted sentiments. They can all be bought. *Napoleon Bonaparte*

Silence can be defined as conversation with an Englishman. *Heinrich Heine*

We are overspent, overborrowed, overgoverned, overtaxed, overmanned, underpoliced, underdefended, and rather badly undereducated.
Sir Keith Joseph (1979)

The Englishman has all the qualities of a poker except its occasional warmth.
Daniel O'Connell

The English are the most obtuse and barbarous people in the world.
Henri-Marie Stendhal

I dunno, maybe it's that tally-ho lads attitude. You know, there'll always be an England, all that Empire crap they dish out. But I never could cop Poms. *Jeff Thomson (1987)*

One has often wondered whether upon the whole earth there is anything so unintelligent, so unable to perceive how the world is really going, as an ordinary young Englishman of our upper classes.
Evelyn Waugh – 'Decline and Fall'

EUROPEANS

I don't think Europeans make better films – they can't even keep their johns clean.
Peter Fonda (1970)

THE FRENCH

The Almighty in His infinite wisdom did not see fit to create a Frenchman in the image of Englishmen. *Winston Churchill (1942)*

There has always been something fishy about the French.
Noël Coward – 'Conversation Piece'

The French complain about everything and always. *Napoleon Bonaparte (1804)*

There has always been something Vichy about the French.
Ivor Novello – 'Ambrosia and Small Beer'

France has neither winter nor summer nor morals. *Mark Twain – 'Notebooks' (1935)*

THE GERMANS

Everything ponderous, viscous, and solemnly clumsy, all long-winded and boring types of style are developed in profuse variety among Germans. *Friedrich Nietzsche (1886)*

The great virtues of the German people have created more evils than idleness ever did vices. *Paul Valéry (1924)*

THE IRISH

The Irish are a very popular race – with themselves. *Brendan Behan*

An Anglo-Irishman is a Protestant with a horse. *Brendan Behan – 'The Hostage'*

THE ITALIANS

The agglomeration which was called and which still calls itself the Holy Roman Empire was neither holy, nor Roman, nor an empire. *Voltaire*

THE SCOTTISH

I have been trying all my life to like Scotchmen, and am obliged to desist from the experiment in despair. *Charles Lamb*

THE WELSH

Show a Welshman 1001 exits, one of which is marked 'Self-Destruction' and he'll go right through that one.
Joseph L. Mankiewicz (1963)

There are still parts of Wales where the only concession to gaiety is a striped shroud.
Gwyn Thomas – 'Punch' (1958)

An impotent people, sick with inbreeding, Worrying the carcase of an old song.
R. S. Thomas – 'Welsh Landscape'

The Welsh are the only nation in the world that has produced no graphic or plastic art, no architecture, no drama. They just sing. Sing and blow down wind instruments of plated silver.
Evelyn Waugh – 'Decline and Fall'

COUNTRIES AND PLACES

EARTH

I have recently been all round the world and have formed a very poor opinion of it.
Sir Thomas Beecham (1946)

That cold accretion called the world, so terrible in the mass, is so unformidable, even pitiable, in its units. *Thomas Hardy (1891)*

The world just doesn't work. It's an idea whose time is gone. *Joseph Heller (1974)*

Maybe this world is another planet's hell.
Aldous Huxley

The world is a stage, but the play is badly cast. *Oscar Wilde*

ARGENTINA

A shadow state gripped by psychoses because the world has passed it by.
John Gunther – 'Inside South America' (1967)

ASWAN, EGYPT

I hate two towns: Edmonton and Aswan.
John Cleese

AUSTRALIA

Australia is a big blank map, and the whole people is constantly sitting over it like a committee, trying to work out the best way to fill it in. *Charles E. W. Bean*

If you're honest you go to America to earn a fortune; if you're a criminal you have to go further – to Australia. *Brendan Behan*

You don't say 'Cheers' when you drink a cup of tea in the bush, you say, 'Christ, the flies!'
Prince Charles

A Portaloo in the Pacific. *'Daily Star' (1992)*

To live in Australia permanently is rather like going to a party and dancing all night with one's mother.
Barry Humphries (1976)

A sort of glorified French Riviera.
Viscount Northcliffe – 'My Journey
Round the World' (1921)

When I look at the map and see what an ugly
country Australia is, I feel that I want to go
there and see if it cannot be changed into a
more beautiful form.
Oscar Wilde – 'Lady Windermere's Fan'

AUSTRIA

Austria is Switzerland speaking pure German
and with history added.
J. E. Morpugo – 'The Road to Athens'

BLACKPOOL

It may be famous for fresh air and fun, but
apart from the tower and the funfair, it is
endowed by nature with a sea which is rough
and cold and somewhat redolent of human
effluent. *Lord Hailsham*

BUDLEIGH SALTERTON

Nobody but a monumental bore would have
thought of having a honeymoon at Budleigh
Salterton.
Noël Coward

CAMBRIDGE

Oxford is on the whole more attractive than
Cambridge to the ordinary visitor, and the
traveller is recommended to visit Cambridge
first, or to omit it altogether if he cannot visit
both. *Karl Baedeker*

What distinguishes Cambridge from Oxford,
broadly speaking, is that nobody who has
been to Cambridge feels impelled to write
about it. *A. A. Milne*

This is the city of perspiring dreams.
Frederic Raphael –
'The Glittering Prizes'

CANADA

If the mental illness of the United States is
megalomania, that of Canada is paranoid
schizophrenia. *Margaret Atwood*

Perhaps the most striking thing about
Canada is that it is not part of the United
States. *J. Bartlet Brebner*

A country so square that even the female
impersonators are women. *Richard Brenner*

A collection of ten provinces with strong
governments loosely connected by fear.
Dave Broadfoot

You have to know a man awfully well in
Canada to know his surname. *John Buchan*

The beaver is a good national symbol for
Canada. He's so busy chewing he can't see
what's going on. *Howard Cable*

I don't even know what street Canada is on.
Al Capone

I am rather inclined to believe that this is the
land God gave to Cain. *Jacques Cartier*

Canada could have enjoyed: English
government, French culture, and American
know-how.
Instead it ended up with: English know-how,
French government, and American culture.
John R. Colombo – 'Oh Canada' (1965)

Canada is a society, rather than a nation.
Kildare Dobbs

Canada has never been a melting pot; more
like a tossed salad. *Arnold Edinborough*

Canada has a climate nine months' winter
and three months late in the fall. *Evan Esar*

For some reason, a glaze passes over people's
faces when you say 'Canada'.
Sondra Gottlieb (1982)

Canada is the boring second fiddle in the
American symphony. *Andrei Gromyko (1953)*

Canada's national bird is the grouse.
Stuart Keate

Canada reminds me of vichysoisse – it's cold,
half French and difficult to stir.
Stuart Keate

THE WORLD

The most parochial nationette on earth.
Wyndham Lewis

The trouble with this whole country is that it's divided up into little puddles with big fish in each one of them. *Hugh MacLennan*

Canada is the only country in the world that knows how to live without an identity.
Marshall McLuhan

Very little is known of the Canadian country since it's rarely visited by anyone but the Queen and illiterate sports fishermen.
P. J. O'Rourke – 'National Lampoon' (1976)

Canada is only useful to provide me with furs. *Madame de Pompadour*

A few acres of snow. *Voltaire*

CATFORD

Christ! I must be bored. I just thought of Catford. *Spike Milligan*

DUBLIN

What's Dublin? Can you play it?
Louis Armstrong

ENGLAND

On a fine day the English climate is like looking up a chimney; on a foul day, like looking down one. *Anon*

England is a prison for men, a paradise for women, a purgatory for servants, a hell for horses. *Thomas Fuller (1642)*

It is good to have one foot in England; it is still better, or at least as good, to have the other out of it. *Henry James*

Pass a law to give every single whingeing bloody Pommie his fare home to England. Back to the smoke and the sun shining ten days a year and shit in the streets. Yer can have it. *Thomas Keneally*

The paradise of little men, and the purgatory of great ones. *Cardinal John Newman*

England is the most class-ridden country under the sun. It is a land of snobbery and privilege, ruled largely by the old and silly.
George Orwell – 'The Lion and the Unicorn' (1941)

England is a horrible place with horrible people, horrible food, horrible climate, horrible class system, horrible cities and horrible countryside.
Stephen Pile – 'Sunday Times'

England is a Jew-owned deer park, with tea rooms. *Ezra Pound*

A soggy little island huffing and puffing to keep up with Western Europe.
John Updike (1969)

I did a picture in England one winter and it was so cold I almost got married.
Shelley Winters

EUROPE

Goddamn the continent of Europe. It is merely of antiquarian interest. Rome is only a few years behind Tyre and Babylon. Already the Italians have the souls of blackamoors. France makes me sick. I think it's a shame that England and America didn't let Germany conquer Europe.
F. Scott Fitzgerald (1921)

FRANCE

A long despotism tempered by epigrams.
Thomas Carlyle

The largest country in Europe, a great boon for drunks who need room to fall.
Alan Coren – 'The Sanity Inspector' (1974)

France is a dog-hole, and it no more merits the tread of man's foot.
William Shakespeare – 'All's Well that Ends Well'

The only country where the money falls apart and you can't tear the toilet paper.
Billy Wilder

GERMANY

The diseased world's bathhouse.
Mark Twain – 'Autobiography' (1906)

GIBRALTAR

It is suggestive of a 'gob' of mud on the end of a shingle.
Mark Twain – 'The Innocents Abroad' (1869)

GRENADA

Grenada immemorially has been as funny a word in Trinidad as Wigan in England.
V. S. Naipaul – 'The Middle Passage' (1962)

INDIA

India is a geographical term. It is no more a united nation than the Equator.
Sir Winston Churchill

A despotism of office boxes tempered by an occasional loss of keys.   *Lord Lytton*

'Sub-' is no idle prefix in its application to this continent.
P. J. O'Rourke – 'National Lampoon' (1976)

IRELAND

The old sow that eats her farrow.
James Joyce

Italy, at least, has two things to balance its miserable poverty and mismanagement: a lively intellectual movement and a good climate. Ireland is Italy without these two.
James Joyce (1906)

The trouble with Ireland is that it's a country full of genius, but with absolutely no talent.
Hugh Leonard

Scientists say that of all the colours green is the most quieting to the nerves. But Ireland has never affected England that way.
'New York American'

ISRAEL

Hitler's revenge on the world.   *Anon*

In Israel, in order to be a realist you must believe in miracles.   *David Ben-Gurion*

ITALY

A country that has made an art of being vanquished.   *Anon*

A poor country full of rich people.
Richard Gardner

LIMA, PERU

Lima is a gigantic dustbin into which has been tipped all the rubbish from North America and industrial Europe.
Paul Foot – 'Socialist Worker' (1983)

The saddest place on earth.
Herman Melville – 'Moby Dick'

LONDON

Nobody is healthy in London, nobody can be.   *Jane Austen*

A modern Babylon.   *Benjamin Disraeli*

LOS ANGELES

I f***ing hate LA! People talk of LA as the Mecca of enlightened thinking. I get out there and it's a f***ing hole.
Alec Baldwin (1990)

Los Angeles should be wiped off the face of the earth.   *David Bowie*

Los Angeles is like one of those machines that treat flour. When the wheat goes in, it's full of interesting ingredients – but it goes through this machine and what you get out at the end is perfect white crap.   *Brian Eno*

Awful . . . like Liverpool with palm trees.
Johnny Rotten (1987)

LUXEMBOURG

On a clear day you can't see Luxembourg at all. This is because a tree is in the way.
Alan Coren –
'The Sanity Inspector' (1974)

THE WORLD

MELBOURNE

While filming 'On the Beach' – Melbourne is the perfect place for a film about the end of the world.   *Ava Gardner (1958)*

MEXICO

Mexico should adopt the cactus as its national flower.   *'Grand Rapids Herald'*

A country where men despise sex, and live for it.   *D. H. Lawrence*

THE MIDDLE EAST

The Middle East is where oil is thicker than water.   *James Holland*

MOZAMBIQUE

Shangri La with a bull whip, behind the door.
John Gunther – 'Inside Africa' (1955)

NEW SOUTH WALES

I'd rather be a noxious weed in Queensland than a rose in New South Wales.
'Galloping Jack' Parsons

NEW YORK

The only real advantage of New York is that all its inhabitants ascend to heaven right after their deaths, having served their full term in hell right on Manhattan Island.
'Barnard Bulletin' (1967)

The Yappian Way.   *O. Henry (1908)*

It's like living on top of a rotting corpse.
John Hiatt (1982)

The faces in New York remind me of people who played a game and lost.
Murray Kempton – 'Is This All?' (1963)

In the heart of New York financial district there is an animal hospital. *News item:* We didn't know New York's financial district had a heart.   *'Little Rock Arkansas Gazette'*

The list of 'don'ts' issued by New York's police commissioner as a means of avoiding being robbed might have been condensed into one, 'Don't go to New York!'
'Pittsburgh Gazette Times'

After a fierce hurricane struck New York City, local officials estimated that the storm did $10,000,000 worth of improvements.
'Playboy' (1988)

In New York City, the common bats fly only at twilight. Brickbats fly at all hours.
George D. Prentice – 'Prenticeana' (1860)

Speaking of New York as a traveller I have two faults to find with it. In the first place there is nothing to see; and in the second place there is no mode of getting about to see anything.   *Anthony Trollope*

Skyscraper National Park.
Kurt Vonnegut – 'Slapstick'

Prison towers and posters for whisky.
Frank Lloyd Wright – 'New York Times' (1955)

NEW ZEALAND

A country of thirty thousand million sheep – three million of whom think they're human.
Barry Humphries

Terrible tragedy in the South Seas. Three million people trapped alive!
Tom Scott – 'The Listener' (1979)

NIAGARA FALLS

A vast unnecessary amount of water going the wrong way and then falling over unnecessary rocks.   *Oscar Wilde*

NORTHERN EUROPE

I do not find Northern Europe an ideal zone for human habitation. It is a fine place for industrial productivity, but its climate breeds puritans and the terrible dictates of the Protestant Work Ethic. The Romans were right to pull out when they did.
Kenneth Tynan – 'The Sound of Two Hands Clapping' (1975)

OXFORD

Home of lost causes, and forsaken beliefs, and unpopular names, and impossible loyalties.   *Matthew Arnold*

PAKISTAN

After returning from a cricket tour – Pakistan is the sort of place every man should send his mother-in-law to, for a month, all expenses paid.   *Ian Botham (1984)*

PARIS

To err is human, to loaf Parisian.
                    Victor Hugo – 'Les Misérables' (1862)

PERSIA (IRAN)

Persia consists of two parts: a desert with salt, and a desert without salt.   *Persian saying*

ROME

Rome is just a city like anywhere else. A vastly overrated city, I'd say. It trades on belief just as Stratford trades on Shakespeare.
                    Anthony Burgess – 'Mr Enderby'

RUSSIA

Russia scares me – the people on the buses are so serious they look like they're going to the electric chair.   *Muhammad Ali (1978)*

A riddle wrapped in a mystery inside an enigma.   *Sir Winston Churchill*

A collapse, not a revolution.
                    D. H. Lawrence

Probably the most boring country in the history of nations.   *Norman Mailer (1968)*

Russia is a country that buries its troubles. Your criticism is your epitaph. You simply say your say, and then you're through.
                    Will Rogers

Russia is the only country of the world you can be homesick for while you're still in it.
                    John Updike

SCOTLAND

A land of meanness, sophistry and mist.
                    Lord Byron (1815)

That garret of the earth – that knuckle-end of England – that land of Calvin, oat-cakes and sulphur.   *Sydney Smith*

Had Cain been a Scot, God would have
    changed his doom;
Not forced him to wander, but confined him
    home.   *Sydney Smith*

SHREWSBURY

If I had the chance of sweeping the streets of Broadway or being Mayor of Shrewsbury, I think I would sweep the streets of Broadway. It would be more fun.   *Brendan Behan*

THE DEEP SOUTH   .

For all its size and all its wealth and all the 'progress' it babbles of, it is almost as sterile, artistically, intellectually, culturally, as the Sahara Desert.   *H. L. Mencken*

SPAIN

A country that has sold its soul for cement and petrol and can only be saved by a series of earthquakes.   *Cyril Connolly*

Spain imports tourists and exports chambermaids.   *Carlos Fuentes*

ST KILDA BEACH, MELBOURNE

It's been like swimming in undiluted sewage.
                    Prince Charles

SWITZERLAND

It is a curst, selfish, swinish country of brutes placed in the most romantic region of the world.   *Lord Byron*

A country where very few things begin, but many things end.   *F. Scott Fitzgerald*

A nation of money-grabbing clockmakers.
                    Nick Lowe (1978)

The Swiss managed to build a lovely country around their hotels.

George Mikes – 'Down with Everybody' (1951)

I look on Switzerland as an inferior sort of Scotland.

Sydney Smith

The only interesting thing that can happen in a Swiss bedroom is suffocation by feather mattress.

Dalton Trumbo

Switzerland is simply a large, humpy, solid rock, with a thin skin of grass stretched over it.

Mark Twain

We in England whimsically see William Tell as the crashing bore whose apple-splitting bolt transformed a whole nation of carefree mountain folk into a precision-crazy confederation of modern designer dullards.

Alexander Waugh – 'Mail On Sunday' (1992)

SYDNEY

There are very few suburbs that I want to live in, and none that I want to die in.

James Edmond

Why didn't they call it Bert?

Robert Morley

TORQUAY

When I think of Torquay it saddens me. There is no culture there at all. It's a musical desert.

Charles Ernesco (1980)

USA

In America, an hour is forty minutes.

German saying

The best poor man's country in the world.

William Allen

In America you watch TV and think it's totally unreal – then you step outside and it's just the same.

Joan Armatrading

What a pity when Christopher Columbus discovered America that he ever mentioned it.

Margot Asquith

America is the country where you buy a lifetime's supply of aspirin for one dollar and use it in a week.

John Barrymore

It's the land of permanent waves and impermanent wives.

Brendan Behan

Only Americans think America is important; no one else.

Brendan Behan

America is the best half-educated country in the world.

Nicholas M. Butler

A land of the most persistent idealism and the blandest cynicism.

Alistair Cooke – 'America'

America is where you can become a blueblood simply by having more greenbacks.

Bill Copeland

This is the only country in the world where businessmen get together over 20-dollar steaks to discuss hard times.

Honey Greer

This will never be a civilised country until we spend more money for books than we do on chewing gum.

Elbert Hubbard

America is a mistake, a giant mistake.

Sigmund Freud

You don't die in the United States, you underachieve.

Jerzy Kosinski

Thanks to the Interstate Highway System, it is now possible to travel from coast to coast without seeing anything.

Charles Kuralt

When you are actually in America, America hurts.

D. H. Lawrence

The trouble with America is that there are far too many wide open spaces surrounded by teeth.

Charles Luckman

A land of boys who refuse to grow up.

Salvador de Madariaga

America is God's own country. He's the only one who can afford to live there.

Benno Moisewitsch

Our national flower is the concrete cloverleaf.

Lewis Mumford

A country that has leapt from barbarism to decadence without touching civilisation.

John O'Hara

America is a country that doesn't know where it is going but is determined to set a speed record getting there.

Laurence J. Peter

America is gangsterism for the private profit of the few. *Vanessa Redgrave*

Nobody really believes in the American city. We have lived so long with old, wornout, ugly places that we have become anaesthetised to their condition.

James Rouse

America is the child society par excellence, and possibly the only one ever politically arrived at. It is the society of all rights and no obligations, the society of deliberate wreckage and waste, the only society that ever raised gangsterism to the status of myth and murder to the status of tragedy or politics.

Karl Shapiro – 'To Abolish Children'

The reason American cities are prosperous is that there is no place to sit down.

Alfred Talley

America is a large friendly dog in a small room. Every time it wags its tail, it knocks over a chair. *Arnold Toynbee*

It was wonderful to find America, but it would have been more wonderful to miss it.

Mark Twain

America is somewhat like Palestine before Christ appeared – a country full of minor prophets. *Peter Ustinov – 'Illustrated London News' (1968)*

In America, through pressure of conformity, there is freedom of choice, but nothing to choose from. *Peter Ustinov – 'Time & Tide'*

One long expectoration. *Oscar Wilde*

It is absurd to say there are neither ruins nor curiosities in America when they have their mothers and their manners. *Oscar Wilde*

Of course America had often been discovered before Columbus, but it had always been hushed up. *Oscar Wilde*

I doubt if there is anything in the world uglier than a Midwestern city.

Frank Lloyd Wright (1954)

VANCOUVER

A terrible hole. *Brendan Behan*

WALES

The land of my fathers? My father can have it. *Dylan Thomas*

Wales. That slagheap! *'The Vikings'*

We can trace nearly all the disasters of English history to the influence of Wales.

Evelyn Waugh – 'Decline and Fall' (1928)

WASHINGTON DC

The District of Columbia is a territory hounded on all sides by the USA.

Irving D. Tressler – 'Reader's Digest' (1949)

The loss of the physical city of Washington would be a benefit not only to government, but to aesthetics. *Philip Wylie (1942)*

ZANZIBAR

It might be called Stinkibar rather than Zanzibar.

David Livingstone – 'Journal' (1866)

SPORT

GENERAL

When it comes to sports I am not particularly interested. Generally speaking, I look upon them as dangerous and tiring activities performed by people with whom I share nothing except the right to trial by jury.
Fran Lebowitz – 'Metropolitan Life' (1978)

The ball is man's most disastrous invention, not excluding the wheel. *Robert Morley (1965)*

AMERICAN FOOTBALL

The game of football is played all over the world. In some countries, such a game may be called a soccer match. In others, a revolution. However, there are several differences between a football game and a revolution. For one thing, a football game usually lasts longer and the participants wear uniforms. Also, there are usually more casualties in a football game. The object of the game is to move a ball past the other team's goal line. This counts as six points. No points are given for lacerations, contusions, or abrasions, but then no points are deducted, either. Kicking is very important in football. In fact, some of the more enthusiastic players even kick the ball, occasionally. *Alfred Hitchcock*

ARCHERY

Poetry is an absolutely dead art – like taking up archery. *Sacheverell Sitwell (1976)*

AUSTRALIAN RULES FOOTBALL

Without giving offence to anyone, I may remark that it is a game which commends itself to semi-barbarous races.
Edward Kinglake – 'The Australians at Home' (1891)

Australian Rules football might best be described as a game devised for padded cells, played in the open air. *James Murray*

BASEBALL

New York Yankees
When I was a little boy, I wanted to be a baseball player and join the circus. With the Yankees I've accomplished both.
Graig Nettles

BOXING

Boxing is the only racket where you're almost guaranteed to end up as a bum.
Rocky Graziano

George Foreman
Some people say George is fit as a fiddle, but I think he looks more like a cello.
Lou Duva (1990)

CRICKET

Geoff Boycott
To offer Geoff Boycott a new contract is akin to awarding Arthur Scargill the Queen's Award for Industry.
Letter to 'The Yorkshire Post' (1984)

FOOTBALL

Justin Fashanu
He's been a born-again Christian and a follower of Hare Krishna. Now he is gay. I don't believe him. We'll talk again when he comes back to earth. *John Fashanu*

Paul Gascoigne
He has the brain-power of an iron filing.
Marcus Berkman – 'Punch' (1992)

Gary Lineker
The Queen Mother of football.
James Christopher – 'Time Out'

Ian Rush
His hooter's so big he should have 'Long Vehicle' stencilled on the back of his head.
Danny Baker – 'Radio 5' (1992)

GOLF

A golf-course is nothing but a pool-room
moved outdoors.   *'Going My Way'*

If you want to take long walks, take long
walks. If you want to hit things with sticks,
hit things with sticks. But there's no excuse
for combining the two and putting the results
on TV. Golf is not so much a sport as an
insult to lawns.   *'National Lampoon' (1979)*

Golf is a game where white men can dress up
as black pimps and get away with it.
                  Robin Williams (1986)

Golf is the Great Mystery.
   P. G. Wodehouse – 'The Heart of Gold' (1926)

ICE HOCKEY

On the Los Angeles Kings' low home crowds –
There are eight hundred thousand Canadians
living in the Los Angeles area, and I've
discovered why they left Canada. They hate
hockey.   *Jack Kent Cooke*

ICE-SKATING

Ice-skating – with its meticulously
preordinated choreography, fanciful dress
and movements that consist of wandering
around in apparently pointless, ever-
decreasing circles – is closer to Trooping the
Colour than to a sport.
           Julie Burchill – 'Only a Game'

Jan Hoffman
During the 1980 Winter Olympics – Hoffman
knocked off the triples with the awesome
precision of a fighter pilot swatting flies. He
made the same artistic impression as a fringe
theatre company producing a minor play by
Brecht in the back room of a pub.
                     Clive James

THE OLYMPICS

The US Olympics Committee singled out the
'Gay' Olympics with a lawsuit prohibiting the
use of the word 'Olympics'. They didn't sue
the Armenian Olympics, the Black Olympics,
the Chinese Olympics. They only sued the
Gay Olympics. I know that the USOC claims
that it was a question of trademark law, not
homophobia. But let me tell you this: Anyone
who believes that must think that Rosa Park's
struggle to sit where she wanted on a
Montgomery bus was really about transit
policy.   *Art Agnos (1988)*

The Olympics create no enduring benefit for
the world, they simply represent a gigantic
organised playground.   *Dr H. Campbell*

Murphy's Law and Parkinson's Law have
both contributed to an Olympics Law which
says that the bigger a thing becomes, the
more problems it attracts and the sooner it
hastens its own demise.
        Norman Harris – 'The Observer' (1984)

California shared the L.A. Olympics with the
athletes of the world, I suppose, but first and
foremost it shared them with ABC TV.
                  Frank Keating –
               'The Guardian' (1984)

RUGBY

*During the 'Dolphin Hooks Penis Round Man's
Leg' indecent sexual acts court case –* Men do
not greet one another like this – except
perhaps at rugby club dinners.
      Alan Cooper's defence counsel (1991)

'Most Misleading Campaign of 1991' –
England's Rugby World Cup squad, who
promoted a scheme called 'Run with the
Ball'. Not, unfortunately, among themselves.
                  'Time Out' (1991)

Rugby football is a game I can't claim
absolutely to understand in all its niceties, if
you know what I mean. I can follow the
broad, general principles, of course. I mean
to say, I know that the main scheme is to
work the ball down the field somehow and
deposit it over the line at the other end and
that, in order to squalch this programme,
each side is allowed to put a certain amount
of assault and battery and do things to its
fellow-man which would normally attract, in
fourteen days without the option, coupled
with some strong remarks from the Bench.
   P. G. Wodehouse – 'Very Good, Jeeves' (1930)

SKIING

There are two main forms of this sport: Alpine skiing and Nordic skiing. Alpine involves a mountain and a $5,000 to $10,000 investment, plus $300,000 for the condo in Aspen and however much you spend on drugs. It is a sport only a handful of people ever master, and those who do, do so at the expense of other skills like talking and writing their own name. *'National Lampoon' (1979)*

The sport of skiing consists of wearing three thousand dollars' worth of clothes and equipment and driving two thousand miles in the snow in order to stand around at a bar and get drunk.
P. J. O'Rourke – 'Modern Manners' (1983)

TENNIS

At Wimbledon, the ladies are simply the candles on the cake. *John Newcombe*

John McEnroe
McEnroe claims John Lloyd is more popular than him because Lloyd married Chris Evert. McEnroe wouldn't be popular if he was married to Marie Osmond. *Anon (1979)*

Hooliganism incarnate, a walking, talking, screaming, squawking metaphor for What's Wrong With Young People Today.
Julie Burchill

Ilie Nastase
Nastase is a Hamlet who wants to play a clown, but he is no good at it; his gags are bad, his timing is terrible and he never knows how he's going over the top – which last drawback is the kiss of death for a comic.
Clive James – 'The Observer' (1975)

WRESTLING

If it's all-in, why do they wrestle? *Mae West*

SPORTS MEDIA

GENERAL

One can recognize minority sports by the bland, uncritical way they're reported.
George Allan (1985)

On his drug habit – How did I get hooked? Well, it's something like a journalist having a drink after work. *Tyrrell Biggs (1988)*

To get a job you've either got to be pretty or be a big star or both. Heck, any guy who can string two sentences together and look good at the same time can be a sportscaster.
Jim Bouton

I'd like to strike oil and buy all the newspapers and radio and TV stations in the country and fire all the jerks in the sports department. *George Brett*

On British sports journalists – They ring me up from London, smooth-talk you for half an hour, hang up and then slag you off as if you were some mad rapist. *Joe Bugner*

The press are gin-swilling, beer-swilling slobs. *Joe Bugner*

Sports writing only survives because of the guys who don't cheer. *Jimmy Cannon*

It's those buggers on the sports pages I hate the most. *Brian Clough*

Sports-writers are probably the only individuals in our universe who actually have less constructive jobs than I do. I don't do nothing but hit people. And they don't do nothing but talk about what I do.
Randall 'Tex' Cobb

Sport is one of the great factors in the lives of tens of thousands of Britishers, and yet there are supercilious gentlemen who speak and write of sport as though it were just the merest side issue. *Eugene Corri (1915)*

Sports announcers are as colourless as a glass of gin. Most of them are like a bunch of barbers cutting each other's hair. They emulate each other and fawn over each other on the air. The same dull, successful ones show up everywhere. The broken-down old ball-players are the worst, but almost all are equally appalling. *Bill Curry*

Sports writing is a job into which men drift, since no properly constituted parent would agree to his son starting a career in that way. Having tried something else which bores them they take to this thing which is lightly esteemed by the outside world but which satisfies in them some possibly childish but certainly romantic feeling.   *Bernard Darwin*

Writing about sport is worth nothing without gusto.   *Bernard Darwin*

Plainly no way has yet been found to stop long-jump commentaries sounding like naughty stories after lights-out in the dorm – Ooooh! It's enormous. It was so long!
    Russell Davies – 'The Sunday Times'

Journalism and batting are not so different – a few good strokes are often better remembered than all the padding in between.
    Ted Dexter (1974)
[*Michael Parkinson had his view on Dexter –* Ted Dexter is to journalism what Danny La Rue is to Rugby League.]

I do not consider any writer on boxing fully equipped for his job unless he can advise a trainer on how to prepare his man for the championship.   *B. J. Evans – 'How to Become a Sporting Journalist'*

On female sports reporters being allowed access to the men's changing room – It doesn't make any difference to me. They don't ask any dumber questions than the guys do.
    Jim Fregosi

Sports pages of the popular press are still woefully old-fashioned. Numerous talented sports journalists on popular papers in Fleet Street might as well check in their perceptions, their originality, and their seriousness at the front desks for all the use they'll be allowed to make of them.
    Brian Glanville (1977)

Much that passes for literature in the lauded realm of cricket now often seems whimsical or over-written.
    Brian Glanville – 'The Sunday Times'

There isn't anything on earth as depressing as an old sportswriter.   *Ring Lardner*

Well-meaning people often ask sports-writers, even middle-aged sports-writers, what they are going to do when they grow up.   *Robert Lipsyte*

The popular assumption that professional boxers do not have brains comes from sportswriters, but then sportswriters' brains are themselves damaged by the obligation to be clever every day. And the quantities of booze necessary to lubricate such racing of the mental gears ends up giving sportswriters the equivalent of a good many punches to the head.   *Norman Mailer*

The capacity of sporting journalists to wax lyrical in face of the exceptional is matched only by the speed with which they run out of adjectives in doing so.
    Derek Malcolm – 'The Guardian'

Because football is so badly reported a great number of spectators are ignorant about the game. One solution might be to cut down on the free drink in the press box.
    Patrick Marnham (1979)

The coverage of the America's Cup is unbelievable. Never have the media done so much for so few.   *Herman L. Masin (1980)*

On the Argentinian sporting press – Not only do they know nothing about football, but if you were to shut them up in a room by themselves, they couldn't even write a letter to mother.   *Cesar Menotti (1982)*

By and large baseball writers and baseball managers get along like man and wife. They respect each other, but not much.
    Jim Murray – 'Los Angeles Times'

The 'Superstars' programme – talented sportsmen being asked to jump through hoops when somebody blows a whistle. I think that cheapens sport. People say it makes sportsmen look human. I think it makes them look foolish.   *Steve Ovett*

On the special 'hares' he uses in greyhound training – I use sportswriters and when we get a broken-down dog, we give him a typewriter.   *Ralph Ryan*

I don't have anything against media people. I just don't want my daughters going to school with them. *Bo Schembechler*

We're beginning to understand the TV sportscaster. For example, when one of his favourite teams loses – that's an upset. *Edward Stevenson*

Speech at a sportswriters' dinner – I'm here to propose a toast to sportswriters and it's up to you if you stand up. *Fred Trueman*

After surgery – It was a brain transplant. I got a sportswriter's brain, so I could be sure I had one that hadn't been used. *Norm van Brocklin (1980)*

If baseball was half as complicated as some of these writers make out it is, a lot of us boys from the farm would never have been able to make a living at it. *'Bucky' Walters*

To hell with sportswriters, you can buy any of them with a steak. *George Weiss*

SPORTS JOURNALISTS AND COMMENTATORS

David Coleman
Anything that matters so much to David Coleman, you realise doesn't matter so much at all! *Clive James – 'The Observer'*

The difference between commentating and Colemantating is that a commentator says things you would like to remember and a Colemantator says things you would like to forget. *Clive James – 'The Observer' (1979)*

Howard Cosell
Howard Cosell is the kind of guy who'd rearrange the furniture in Helen Keller's house. *Anon*

Howard looks like the lone survivor of an Indian massacre who got scalped and put somebody else's hair on. *Anon*

If Howard Cosell was a sport, he'd be the roller derby. *Jimmy Cannon*

In the next issue of *Cosmopolitan*, Howard Cosell will be the centrefold with his vital organ covered – his mouth. *Burt Reynolds*

The Russians have a weapon that can wipe out two hundred eighty thousand Americans. That puts them exactly ten years behind Howard Cosell. *Red Smith*

Joe Garagiola
He is considered something of a humorist and, like Mark Twain, is from Missouri. The resemblance is purely residential. *Jim Brosnan*

Murray Walker
Under James Hunt's exemplary tutelage Murray has quietened down considerably lately, so that you can almost hear the cars. *Clive James – 'The Observer'*

Murray sounds like a blindfolded man riding a unicycle on the rim of the pit of doom. *Clive James – 'The Observer'*

Eddie Waring
Eddie Waring has done as much for Rugby League as Cyril Smith would do for hang-gliding. *Reg Bowden*

Dick Young
A juvenile delinquent who grew up to become a senior cynic. *Joe Trimble*

FOOD AND DRINK

TYPES

AIRLINE MEALS

Anything that's white is sweet
Anything that's brown is meat
Anything that's grey don't eat.
Hermione Gingold

ALCOHOL

The point about white Burgundies is that I
hate them myself . . . so closely resembling a
blend of cold chalk soup and alum cordial
with an additive or two to bring it to the
colour of children's pee.
Kingsley Amis – 'The Green Man'

Alcohol may pick you up a little bit, but it
sure lets you down in a hurry.
Betty Ford (1979)

After being served drinks at Buckingham Palace
– We had typical British gin and tonics –
lukewarm and flat. *Tamara Fraser*

Wine turns a man inside outwards.
Thomas Fuller

The wine is full of gases,
  Which are to me offensive;
  It pleases all you asses
Because it is so expensive.
A. P. Herbert

'Bucks Fizz' – The orange improves the
champagne. The champagne definitely
improves the orange. *Prince Philip*

The Germans are exceedingly fond of Rhine
wines; they are put up in tall, slender bottles,
and are considered a pleasant beverage. One
tells them from vinegar by the label.
Mark Twain – 'A Tramp Abroad'

BEVERAGES

English coffee tastes like water that has been
squeezed out of a wet sleeve.
Fred Allen – 'Treadmill to Oblivion'

If I had known there was no Latin word for
tea, I would have let the vulgar stuff alone.
Hilaire Belloc

It is the duty of all papas and mamas to
forbid their children to drink coffee, unless
they wish to have little dried-up machines,
stunted and old at the age of twenty.
Jean-Anthelme Brillat-Savarin

I view the tea-drinking as a destroyer of
health, an enfeebler of the frame, an
engenderer of effinancy and laziness, a
debaucher of youth and a maker of misery
for old age.
William Cobbett – 'The Vice of Tea-Drinking'

The tea is always excellent in England, but
nowhere do they drink worse coffee.
B. Faujas de Sainte-Fond –
'Voyage en Angleterre' (1797)

Coffee, as drunk in England, debilitates the
stomach, and produces a slight nausea . . . it
is usually made from bad Coffee, served out
tepid and muddy, and drowned in a deluge
of water.
William Kitchiner, M.D. – 'The Cook's Oracle'

Hotel tea – You have to mix together a plastic
envelope containing too much sugar, a small
plastic pot of something which is not milk
but has curdled anyway, and a thin brown
packet seemingly containing the ashes of a
cremated mole. *Frank Muir*

An English tea-party – You are offered a piece
of bread and butter that feels like a damp
handkerchief and sometimes, when
cucumber is added to it, like a wet one.
Sir Compton Mackenzie

Why do they always put mud into coffee on
board steamers? Why does the tea generally
taste of boiled roots? *William M. Thackeray*

FOOD & DRINK

BREAD

A waffle is merely a pancake with a non-stick tread.
Anon

A garlic sandwich is two pieces of bread travelling in bad company.
Denison Flamingo

You can travel 50,000 miles in America without once tasting a piece of good bread.
Henry Miller – 'The Staff of Life'

The bread I eat in London is a deleterious paste, mixed up with chalk, alum, and bone-ashes; insipid to the taste, and destructive to the constitution.
Tobias Smollett

CEREAL

I wouldn't eat 'Shredded Wheat'. I don't like sawdust with milk all over it.
Ian Botham (1990)

Oatmeal is good for to make a fair and well-coloured maid to look like a cake of tallow.
John Gerard – 'Herball'

CHOCOLATE

On the unrelated 'Time Out' chocolate bar –
Interestingly, the new bar is described as being in 'a two-fingered format', which pretty much sums up our attitude to the launch.
'Time Out' (1992)

DAIRY PRODUCTS

The milk, in London, should not pass unanalysed, the produce of faded cabbage-leaves and sour draff, lowered with hot water, frothed with bruised snails, carried through the streets in open pails, exposed to foul rinsings discharged from doors and windows, spittle, snot, and tobacco-quids from foot-passengers, over-flowings from mud-carts, spatterings from coach-wheels, dirt and trash chucked into it by roguish boys for a joke's sake, the spewings of infants, who have slabbered in tin-measure, which is thrown back in that condition among the milk, for the benefit of the next customer; and, finally, the vermin that drops from the rags of the nasty drab that vends this precious mixture, under the respectable denomination of milk-maid.
Tobias Smollett

DELICATESSEN

A delicatessen is a shop selling the worst parts of animals more expensively than the nice parts.
Mike Barfield – 'The Oldie' (1992)

DIETS

Not for me the heresies of healthy eating favoured by Edwina Currie, or the hypochondriacal fears of cholesterol.
Lord Hailsham

GOURMET COOKING

A gourmet is just a glutton with brains.
Phillip Haberman – 'Vogue' (1961)

The appeal of nouvelle cuisine is that the sauces are all based on condensed milk, thus allowing sophisticates to eat babyfood without revealing their true, insecure colours.
Julie Burchill

MEAT

Who'd want to eat a hamburger? I'm not gonna get into the bullshit to find out what the bull ate.
Captain Beefheart

What a shocking fraud the turkey is. In life preposterous, insulting – the foolish noise they make to scare you away! In death – unpalatable. The turkey has practically no taste except a dry fibrous flavour reminiscent of a mixture of warmed-up plaster of Paris and horsehair. The texture is like wet sawdust and the whole vast feathered swindle has the piquancy of a boiled mattress.
'Cassandra' [William Connor] –
'The Daily Mirror' (1953)

His last words – Doctor, do you think it could have been the sausage?
Paul Claudel – French composer (1955)

I shrink instinctively from one who professes to like minced veal.
Charles Lamb

Wood-pigeons check and blunt the manly powers: let him not eat this bird who wishes to be amorous. *Martial*

PASTA

Macaroni – An Italian food made in the form of a slender, hollow tube. It consists of two parts – the tubing and the hole, the latter being the part that digests. *Ambrose Bierce*

REGIONAL FOOD

There is nothing so vile or repugnant to nature; but you may plead prescription for it, in the customs of some other nation or other. A Parisian likes mortified flesh. A native of Legiboli will not taste his fish till it is quite putrefied. *Tobias Smollet*

For, famed as the French always are for ragouts,
No creature can tell what they put in their stews,
Whether bull-frogs, old gloves, or old wigs, or old shoes. *R. H. Barham*

The Portuguese have the stomachs of ostriches to digest the loads of greasy victuals with which they cram themselves. Their vegetables, their rice, their poultry are all stewed in the essence of ham, and so strongly seasoned with pepper and spices that a spoonful of pease or a quarter of onion is sufficient to set one's mouth in a flame. *William Beckford*

SEA FOOD

Squid, an animated ink-bag of perverse leanings, which swims backwards because all other creatures go forwards and whose indiarubber flesh might be useful for deluding hunger on desert islands, since, like American gum, you can chew it for months, but never get it down. *Norman Douglas – 'Siren Land'*

'Turbot, sir,' said the waiter, placing before me two fishbones, two eyeballs, and a bit of black mackintosh. *Thomas E. Welby – 'The Dinner Knell'*

SOUP

Bouillabaisse is only good because it is cooked by the French, who, if they cared to try, could produce an excellent and nutritious substitute out of cigar stumps and empty matchboxes. *Norman Douglas – 'Siren Land'*

The leek soup tasted like rusty water which had somehow leaked through the ceiling on to the plates. *Frank Muir*

SUGAR

The worst drug of today is not smack or pot – it's refined sugar. *George Hamilton (1980)*

SWEETS AND DESSERTS

I consider plum pudding to be one of the most barbarous institutions of the British. It is a childish, silly, savage superstition; it must have been a savage inspiration, looking at it all round. *Henry Lawson (1907)*

TINNED FOOD

We may find in the long run that tinned food is a deadlier weapon than the machine-gun. *George Orwell – 'The Road to Wigan Pier'*

ARTICHOKES

Artichokes heat the genitals. *French saying*

Jerusalem Artichokes – They are meat more fit for swine, than men. *John Gerard – 'Herball'*

BEANS

On eating beans – My bowels shall sound like an harp. *The Bible – Isaiah*

Abstain from beans. *Pythagoras*

CABBAGE

Boiled cabbage à l'Anglaise is something compared with which steamed coarse newsprint bought from bankrupt Finnish salvage dealers and heated over oil stoves is an exquisite delicacy. Boiled British cabbage is something lower than ex-Army blankets stolen by dispossessed Goanese doss-housekeepers who used them to cover busted-down hen-houses in the slum district of Karachi, found them useless, threw them in anger into the Indus, where they were recovered by convicted beachcombers with grappling irons, who cut them into strips with shears and stewed them in sheep-dip before they were sold to dying beggars. Boiled cabbage!

'Cassandra' [William Connor] –
'Daily Mirror' (1950)

CUCUMBER

Raw cucumber makes the churchyard prosperous. *English proverb*

HERBS AND SEASONING

Thyme causes a man to make water.
Andrew Boorde

Garlic makes a man wink, drink and stink.
Thomas Nashe (1594)

LETTUCE

Lettuce does extinct sexual acts.
Andrew Boorde

It is said that the effect of eating too much lettuce is 'soporific'.
Beatrix Potter – 'The Tale of
the Flopsy Bunnies'

ONIONS

Onions do promote a man to sexual acts, and to somnolence. *Andrew Boorde*

POTATOES

If you have formed the habit of checking on every new diet that comes along, you will find that, mercifully, they all blur together, leaving you with only one definite piece of information – french fried potatoes are out.
Jean Kerr – 'Please Don't
Eat the Daisies' (1957)

RHUBARB

Rhubarb – Vegetable essence of stomach

ache. *Ambrose Bierce*

VEGETARIANS

You are what you eat and who wants to be a lettuce? *Peter Burns (1984)*

I have known many meat-eaters to be far more non-violent than vegetarians.
Mohandas Gandhi (1948)

EATING PLACES

COCKTAIL PARTIES

A gathering where you spear olives and stab friends. *Anon*

A party where two and two make bore.
Anon

A bad cocktail party is a fête worse than death. *Anon*

Where they serve whisky on the knocks.
Anon

A gathering held to enable forty people to talk about themselves at the same time. The man who remains after the liquor is gone is the host. *Fred Allen*

A device either for getting rid of social obligations hurriedly en masse, or for making overtures towards more serious social relationships, as in the etiquette of whoring.
Brooks Atkinson – 'Once Around the Sun'

A cocktail party waiter is a boretender.
Bess Beavers

A cocktail party hostess is a din mother.
Raymond J. Cvikota

A hundred standing people smiling and talking to one another, nodding like gooney birds. *William Cole (1972)*

Some folks like cocktail parties,
Where small talk is the rule –
Small talk is fine,
But friends of mine
Make talk that's minuscule. *Dick Emmons*

If the population explosion continues, the world will be like one big cocktail party – too many people and not enough food.
Tom Fallon

The cocktail party is easily the worst invention since castor oil. *Elsa Maxwell*

A cocktail party is what you call it when you invite everyone you know to come over to your house at six p.m., put cigarettes out on your rug, and leave at seven to go somewhere more interesting for dinner without inviting you. Cocktail parties are very much on their way out among rug-owning, hungry, snubbed people.
P. J. O'Rourke – 'Modern Manners' (1983)

I misremember who first was cruel enough to nurture the cocktail party into life. But perhaps it would be not too much to say, in fact it would be not enough to say, that it is not worth the trouble.
Dorothy Parker – 'Esquire' (1964)

A device for paying off obligations to people you don't want to invite for dinner.
Charles M. Smith – 'Instant Status' (1972)

There must be some good in the cocktail party to account for its immense vogue among otherwise sane people. *Evelyn Waugh*

A place where you talk with a person you don't know about a subject you have no interest in.
Lin Yutang – 'With Love and Irony'

Canapés are sandwiches cut into twenty-four pieces. *Anon*

Appetizers are those little bits you eat until you lose your appetite. *Anon*

DINNER PARTIES

A buffet dinner is a function where the guests outnumber the chairs. *Anon*

At Dr Hunter's – In the centre was a bad thin soup, poisoned with celery; at the top a dish of threaded skate, bedevilled with carrots and turnips – this is supposed in York to be both a Phoenix and a chef d'oeuvre; at bottom, roast beef, so-so; at side, ill-boiled beetroot, stewed with a greasy sauce, without vinegar; potatoes, veal cutlets, cold and not well-dressed; anchovy toast and tartlets. Second course: two partridges, ill-trussed and worse stuffed; at bottom, an old hare, newly killed and poorly stuffed; at side, celery and some other trash; in short, a very poor performance on the whole.
Alexander Gibson Hunter (1805)

RESTAURANTS

Anonymous
The food here is so tasteless you could eat a meal of it and belch and it wouldn't remind you of anything. *Redd Foxx*

Bar Carvery, New York
It may not be possible to get rare roast beef but if you're willing to settle for well done, ask them to hold the sweetened library paste that passes for gravy.
Marian Burros – 'New York Times' (1984)

Chatfield's, New York
Dining at Chatfield's is like kissing your kid sister – it's just not worth the effort.
'W' Magazine

Cleveland
The only difference between Cleveland and the *Titanic* is the *Titanic* had better restaurants. *Barney Nagler*

Hungry Horse, London
At the Hungry Horse the cooking is a Spanish or Italian or Malaysian idea of English home-cooking – which is at least preferable to the English idea of English home-cooking. *John Meades – 'The Times'*

Le Cirque, New York
If it is true that oversalting means the cook is in love, at least one cook at Le Cirque must be head over heels. *Mimi Sheraton (1977)*

London
London restaurants – All that changing of plates and flapping of napkins while you wait forty minutes for your food.

Hugh Casson (1985)

Palm Restaurant, New York
Their steaks are often good, but the lobsters
– with claws the size of Arnold
Schwarzenegger's forearms – are as glazed
and tough as most of their customers.

Malcolm Forbes (1980)

Pig Heaven, New York
The moist, flavourful meat is concealed
under a thick slab of crisp fat that would
make a cardiologist blanch.

Bryan Miller (1984)

WAITERS/WAITRESSES

A waiter is an employee who thinks money
grows on trays.

Anon

New York waiters, probably the surliest in
the western world, are better images of their
city than that journalistic favourite – the taxi
driver.

Alan Brien

The waitress intoned the specialities of the
day – 'Chicken Cordon Bleu, Sole
Amandine, Veal Marsala.' She might have
been a train conductor in a foreign country,
calling out the strange names of the stations.

Ilma Wolitzer – 'Hearts' (1980)

MILITARY

Lord Haig
He's brilliant – to the top of his boots.

David Lloyd George

Lord Kitchener
One of the revolving lighthouses which
radiate momentary gleams of revealing light
and then suddenly relapse into complete
darkness. There are no intermediate stages.

David Lloyd George

Field-Marshal Montgomery
In defeat, indomitable; in victory,
insufferable; in NATO, thank God, invisible.

Sir Winston Churchill

General Plastiras
Plaster-Ass! Plaster-Ass! I hope he hasn't got
feet of clay, as well.

Sir Winston Churchill (1945)

ROYALTY

Julius Caesar
A man of great common sense and good
taste – meaning thereby a man without
originality or moral courage. *G. B. Shaw*

King Edward VII
You cannot imagine what a Satan he is.

Kaiser Wilhelm II

King Edward VIII
He had hidden shallows. *Clive James*

Queen Elizabeth II
A piece of cardboard that they drag round on
a trolley. *Johnny Rotten (1977)*

King George I
In private life he would have been called an
honest blockhead. *Lady Mary Montagu*

King Henry VIII
He was a male chauvinist wanker.

Captain Sensible (1987)

Capt. Mark Phillips
Foggy – dense and wet.
Diana, Princess of Wales

Prince Philip
The working girl's Adam Faith. *Bud Flanagan*

I'm prepared to take advice on leisure from
Prince Philip. He's a world expert on leisure.
He's been practising for most of his adult life.
Neil Kinnock (1981)

Diana, Princess of Wales
Diana: 1. Roman goddess of hunting.
2. British goddess of shopping and film
premières. *Mike Barfield – 'The Oldie' (1992)*

Kaiser Wilhelm II
He can be fascinating, and win hearts
wherever he goes – and doesn't stay.

Count Paul Waldersee

Sarah, Duchess of York
After that breathtakingly bad taste visit to the
Florida Everglades Club, which refuses entry
to those of the Red Sea pedestrian persuasion
. . . and . . . given the Hebraic warnings
against contact with things porcine, it might
be wise for all remotely Jewish people to
avoid the Duchess altogether.
Julie Burchill –
'The Mail on Sunday' (1992)

Fergie is to motherhood what her husband
Andrew is to nuclear physics.
Vernon Coleman –
'The Sun'

She's not a real princess, she's a slap-them-
on-the-bottom princess. *Earl Spencer*

Princess Margaret

She's a dumb broad. *Sue Mengers*

OTHERS

Francis Crick – *scientist*
Already for thirty-five years he had not
stopped talking and almost nothing of
fundamental value had emerged.
James Dewey Watson –
'The Double Helix'

Sir Michael Edwardes –
chairman of British Leyland
Looks like a victim of forceps delivery.
Auberon Waugh – 'Private Eye'

Albert Einstein
As a rational scientist, Einstein is a fair
violinist. Einstein is already dead and buried
alongside Andersen, Grimm and the Mad
Hatter. *George F. Gilette (1929)*

Havelock Ellis – *psychologist*
He had the air of a false prophet, like Santa
Claus at Selfridges. *Graham Greene*

Mr Ellis has a tendency to dwell on

excrement. *'London Mercury'*

Sir Alexander Fleming
Had he not been an untidy man and apt to
leave his cultures exposed on the laboratory
table, the spore of hyssop mould, the
penicillin notatum, might never have floated
in from Praed Street and settled on his dish
of *staphylococci*.
André Maurois

Milton Friedman – *economic adviser to*
Israel
Any country that can stand Milton Friedman
as an adviser has nothing to fear from a few
million Arabs. *John K. Galbraith (1979)*

Yuri Gagarin
After a 'state' visit to London – It would have
been twice as bad if they had sent the dog.
Harold Macmillan

Leona Helmsley

The Queen of Mean. *Anon*

Friedrich Nietzsche
He belongs, body and soul, to the flock of
mangy sheep. *Max Nordau – 'Degeneration'*

Tiny Rowlands
The unacceptable face of capitalism.
Edward Heath

Mark Thatcher
He is rather brash, rude, brutish in the way
he behaves . . . but if you knew the bloke you
wouldn't find him the remotest bit
interesting. *Sir Tim Bell*

Donald Trump
He likes to make a big deal about the deals he
makes. I agree with the man who said, 'I
wouldn't believe him even if his tongue were
notarized.' For the most part he strikes me as
a miserable person. *Ed Koch*

George Villiers – *Duke of Buckingham*
The Lord of useless thousands.
Alexander Pope

AWARDS

GENERAL

I don't deserve this award, but then, I have
arthritis, and I didn't deserve that either.
Jack Benny

I can't say I believe in prizes. I was a whizz in
the three-legged race – that's something you
can win. *Katharine Hepburn (1969)*

I'm not out to win prizes – that's for horses.
Werner Herzog (1984)

Awards are merely the badges of mediocrity.
Charles Ives

Awards are like haemorrhoids; in the end
every asshole gets one. *Frederic Raphael*

Nothing reveals more about the insecurity of
many people than the avalanche of awards
that sprouts on television like a fungus. Why
is there a show biz obsession with self-
congratulation? Other trades don't do it.
Glue makers consider prizes tacky. Butchers
do not loin-ise each other. Awards would rub
furriers the wrong way. And we all remember
the candidate for Best Waiter, who said, 'If
elected, I will not serve.' But in show biz,
there is no end to it. Emmys, Grammys,
Tonys. Do bakers give out Crummies?

Hardly any awards are as silly as Emmys,
which aside from having the most grotesque
statuette, have the most categories. So let's
put an end to it all. Let's invoke the statuette
of limitations.
Gene Shalit –
'Man About Everything'

ADVERTISING

On the abundance of ad awards – It goes back
to all of us wanting to be in Hollywood.
We're dying to win an Oscar.
Jerry Della
Femina (1987)

On the 'Clio' award – It's like having a
designer dress compared with one from
Woolworth's. Which one is more impressive
when you go to the debutante ball?
Bill Evans (1987)

You're never too bad to win.
Tom McElligott (1987)

Hollywood has its Oscars. Television has its
Emmys. Broadway has its Tonys. And
advertising has its Clios. And its Andys,
Addys, Effies, and Obies. And 117 other
assorted awards. And those are just the big
ones.

LITERATURE

Joan Lippman (1987)

GENERAL

Prizes are for the birds. They fill the head of one author with vanity and 30 others with misery. *Louis Auchinloss*

On receiving an award for 'Armies in the Night' – Awards are a measurement of the degree to which an Establishment meets the talent which it hindered and helped.
Norman Mailer (1969)

BOOKER PRIZE

After acting as a judge – To be a judge you don't have to know about books, you have to be skilled at picking shrapnel out of your head. *Joanna Lumley*

PULITZER PRIZE

The Pulitzer Prize in fiction takes dead aim at mediocrity and almost never misses.
William H. Gass

On being told that he had won the Pulitzer Prize – Give it to a waiter. It is a tip. I don't accept tips. *Charles Ives*

THE NOBEL PRIZE

You only have to survive in England and all is forgiven you . . . if you can eat a boiled egg at ninety in England they think you deserve the Nobel Prize. *Alan Bennett (1984)*

I don't believe in awards of any kind. I don't believe in the Nobel Peace Prize.
Marlon Brando – 'Playboy' (1979)

The Nobel Committee is, to begin with, a semi-mysterious group of intellectuals and bureaucrats who appear to be influenced alternately by sentimentalism (the award to Cordell Hull), pseudo-cosmopolitanism (Halldor Laxness of Iceland), literary proletarianism (Italy's Quasimodo), and out-and-out left-pacifism (Linus Pauling). Any redblooded Westerner should think twice before accepting a Nobel award, precisely because to do so is to lend the recipient's prestige not merely to the idiosyncratic criteria the Committee uses, but to its political relativism. *William F. Buckley Jr – 'National Review' (1964)*

An orotundity, which I define as 'Nobelitis' – a pomposity in which one is treated as representative of more than oneself by someone conscious of representing more than himself. *William Faulkner (1985)*

I can forgive Alfred Nobel for having invented dynamite, but only a fiend in human form could have invented the Nobel Prize. *G. B. Shaw*

Literature

On winning – The Nobel is a ticket to one's own funeral. No one has ever done anything after he got it. *T. S. Eliot (1948)*

On reviewers – It wasn't until the Nobel Prize [*1983*] that they really thawed out. They couldn't understand my books, but they could understand $30,000. *William Faulkner*

On winning – One of the things which makes me happier today is that I will never be a Nobel Prize candidate again.
Gabriel G. Marquez (1982)

On refusing the award – In view of the meaning given to this honour in the community to which I belong, I should abstain from the undeserved prize that has been awarded to me. *Boris Pasternak (1958)*

On refusing the award – A writer who takes political, social or literary positions must act only with the means that are his. These means are written words.
Jean-Paul Sartre (1964)

On refusing the award – The money is a lifebelt thrown to a swimmer who has already reached the shore in safety. *G. B. Shaw (1925)*

The Nobel Prize for Literature, judged by a committee of humourless Swedes, might as well be awarded on the tombola principle.
Auberon Waugh

THE OSCARS

The Oscar ceremony is a place where everybody lets off esteem. *Anon*

On his absence from the Oscar ceremony – I am not interested in an inanimate statue of a little bald man, I like something with long, blonde curls. *Woody Allen (1978)*

This Oscar thing is a sort of popularity contest. When it's your turn – you win it. *Woody Allen*

If Hollywood keeps gearing movie after movie to teenagers, next year's Oscar will develop acne. *Mel Brooks*

Nothing would disgust me more, morally, than receiving an Oscar. *Luis Buñuel*

On the Oscar ceremony – We are drawn to our TV sets each April the way we are drawn to the scene of an accident. *Vincent Canby*

On the ceremony – Two hours of sparkling entertainment spread over a four-hour show. *Johnny Carson (1979)*

The honours Hollywood has for the writer are as dubious as tissue-paper cuff-links. *Ben Hecht – 'Charlie' (1957)*

It's a game show. *Kevin Kline*

It's a big publicity contest. Oh, voting is legitimate, but there's the sentimentality. One year when I was a candidate, when Elizabeth Taylor got a hole in her throat, I cancelled my plane. *Shirley MacLaine*

The statuette is a perfect symbol of the picture business – a powerful athletic body clutching a gleaming sword, with half his head, the part that holds his brains, completely sliced off. *Fred Marion*

Gandhi was everything the voting members of the Academy would like to be: moral, tall, and thin. *Joe Morgenstern – 'Los Angeles Herald-Examiner' (1983)*

On refusing the 1970 Best Actor award for 'Patton' – The contest is made more important than the achievement. *George C. Scott*
(Scott also refused a nomination in 1961 for Best Supporting Actor in *The Hustler*.)

It's just a meat parade in front of an international television audience. *George C. Scott (1971)*

TELEVISION

Getting an award from TV is like getting kissed by someone with bad breath. *Mason Williams*

HONOURS

On being asked if he would accept an award in the honours list – Being Bernard Shaw is sufficient honour for any man. . . . Anyway, if I want to satirise the Establishment and all of its rituals, I must be free to do so. *G. B. Shaw*

M.B.E. (Member of the British Empire)
Lots of people who complained about the Beatles receiving the M.B.E. received theirs for heroism in the war – for killing people. We received ours for entertaining people. I'd say we deserve ours more. *John Lennon*

Order of the Garter
After losing the 1945 general election – I could not accept the Order of the Garter from my sovereign, when I have received the Order of the Boot from the people. *Sir Winston Churchill*

RETORTS

LITERARY

Lady Elizabeth Dryden
Lord, Mr Dryden, how can you always be poring over those musty books? I wish I were a book, and then I should have more of your company.
John Dryden
Pray, my dear, if you do become a book let it be an almanack, for then I shall be able to change you every year.

Lewis Morris
On being overlooked for the Poet Laureateship –
It is a conspiracy of silence against me – a conspiracy of silence. What should I do?
Oscar Wilde
Join it!

DRAMATIC

Sam Wood
While directing the Marx Brothers' 'A Day at the Races' (1937) – You can't make an actor out of clay.
Groucho Marx
Nor a director out of Wood!

James Agate
My dear Lillian, I have long wanted to tell you that in my opinion you are the second-best actress in London.
Lillian Braithwaite
Thank you so much, I shall cherish that, coming from the second-best dramatic critic.

Mrs Patrick Campbell
Always remember, Mr Froham, that I am an artist.
Charles Froham – *producer of 'Pygmalion'*
Your secret is safe with me!

Anon
I passed by your house yesterday, Oscar.
Oscar Wilde
Thank you very much.

POLITICS

Heckler
You want to put a tax on my food!
Lord Birkenhead
No, sir, I don't believe there is any proposal to put a tax on thistles.

Neville Chamberlain
Eamon De Valera . . . like trying to pick up mercury with a fork.
Eamon De Valera
On hearing the above – Why doesn't he try using a spoon?

Wilfred Paling
You, sir, are a dirty dog!
Sir Winston Churchill
If you aren't careful, I'll show you what a dirty dog does to a Paling.

Anonymous lady
I've made a bet with a friend that I can get you to say at least three words this evening. What do you say about that?
Calvin Coolidge
You lose!

Lady: There are two things I don't like about you, Mr Churchill – your politics and your moustache.
Churchill: My dear madam, pray do not disturb yourself. You are not likely to come into contact with either.

Harold Wilson
Yorkshiremen are not born; they are forged.
Nye Bevin
Forged, were you? I always thought there was something counterfeit about you.

Harold Wilson
On Lord Home's election as Tory leader (1963) – After half a century of democratic advance, the whole process has ground to a halt with a 14th Earl.
Alec Douglas-Home

As far as the 14th Earl is concerned, I suppose Mr Wilson, when you come to think of it, is the 14th Mr Wilson.

Edwina Currie
During the 'fluoridation' debate in the House –
Fluoridation has been nothing but good. Anything is a poison if we take enough of it. Were we to spreadeagle my honourable friend on the floor of the House and pour absolutely pure water into him, it would kill him in hours.
Nicholas Fairbairn
All the poison that my honourable friend suggested I would happily take, rather than be spreadeagled on the floor of the house by her.

Eva Peron
During a visit to Italy – Admiral, your people are calling me a whore!
Anonymous Admiral
Quite so. I have not been on a ship for fifteen years and people still call me 'Admiral'.

Anonymous French MEP
Why is it the Irish always fight for money while the French only fight for honour?
Anonymous Irish MEP
Because each is fighting for what he doesn't have.

LAW

Judge Willis
Mr Smith, have you ever heard of a saying by Bacon that 'youth and discretion are ill-wed companions'?
Lord Birkenhead (F. E. Smith)
Yes, your honour. Has your honour ever heard of a saying by Bacon that 'a much-talking judge is like an ill-tuned cymbal'?
Judge Willis
You are extremely offensive, young man.
Lord Birkenhead
As a matter of fact, we both are; the only difference between us is that I am trying to be and you can't help it.

RELIGION

Horatio Bottomley
On learning that Lord Birkenhead had been
made Lord Chancellor – I shouldn't be surprised to hear that you've also been made Archbishop of Canterbury.
Lord Birkenhead
If I had, I would ask you to accompany me at my installation.
Horatio Bottomley
That's very noble of you.
Lord Birkenhead
Not really, I would have need of a crook.

John Wilmot (Earl of Rochester)
Doctor, I am yours to my shoe tie.
Isaac Barrow – *theologian*
My lord, I am yours to the ground.
Wilmot
Doctor, I am yours to the centre of the earth.
Barrow
My lord, I am yours to the Antipodes.
Wilmot
Doctor, I am yours to the lowest pit of hell.
Barrow
And there, my lord, I leave you!

Cardinal Vaughan
Now, Dr Adler, when may I have the pleasure of helping you to some ham?
Chief Rabbi Hermann Adler
At your eminence's wedding!

SCIENCE

Lalanda – *astronomer*
Sitting between the outspoken Madame de Staël and the beautiful Madame Recamier – How happy I am to find myself between wit and beauty.
Madame de Staël
And without possessing either.

Albert Einstein
After playing the violin with great flourish –
How well did I play?
Gregor Piatigorsky – *cellist*
You played 'relatively' well.

Margaret Fuller
At a transcendentalist meeting – I accept the universe.
Thomas Carlyle
By God, she'd better!

INDEX OF PEOPLE AND PERIODICAL PUBLICATIONS

INDEX OF PEOPLE AND PERIODICAL PUBLICATIONS

GENERAL SUBJECT INDEX